Dla Ju

z najlepszymi życzeniami,

Piotr Sadowski

Dublin, 10 maja 1999

MW01250625

The Knight
on His Quest

The Knight on His Quest

Symbolic Patterns of Transition in
Sir Gawain and the Green Knight

Piotr Sadowski

DELAWARE

Newark: University of Delaware Press
London: Associated University Presses

Associated University Presses
440 Forsgate Drive
Cranbury, NJ 08512

Associated University Presses
16 Barter Street
London WC1A 2AH, England

Associated University Presses
P.O. Box 338, Port Credit
Mississauga, Ontario
Canada L5G 4L8

The paper used in this publication meets the requirements
of the American National Standard for Permanence of Paper
for Printed Library Materials Z39.48-1984.

Library of Congress Cataloging-in-Publication Data

Sadowski, Piotr, 1957–
    The knight on his quest : symbolic patterns of transition in Sir Gawain and the Green Knight / Piotr Sadowski.
        p.   cm.
    Includes bibliographical references and index.
    ISBN 0-87413-580-X (alk. paper)
    1. Gawain and the Grene Knight.   2. Gawain (Legendary character)—Romances—History and criticism.   3. Arthurian romances—History and criticism.   4. Knights and knighthood in literature.
5. Symbolism in literature.   6. Chivalry in literature.   7. Quests in literature.   8. Transition (Rhetoric)   9. Rhetoric, Medieval.
I. Title.
PR2065.G31S23   1996
821′.1—dc20
                                                                96-74
                                                                CIP

PRINTED IN THE UNITED STATES OF AMERICA

To Andrzej Wierciński

Contents

List of Tables

List of Figures

Preface

The Knight on His Quest offers an integrated interpretative analysis of the major thematic aspects of the English fourteenth-century romance *Sir Gawain and the Green Knight* (British Museum MS. Cotton Nero A. x). The word *integrated* implies a certain comprehensiveness of approach, and indeed my chief aim is to look at the contents of the narrative in their entirety and to take full advantage of the poem's exceptional and widely praised harmony of structure and general design. Within that design I intend to focus my analytical discussion on the poem's presentation of the main protagonist and his adventures, seen first of all as a metaphor for human life as a spiritual quest, and in a more historical sense as an expression and critique of certain ideals, values, and anxieties that characterized the late medieval institutions of the court, chivalry, and the Church.

The poem's concept of the chivalric quest involving a series of liminal situations and transitions seems to express a human pursuit towards resolving certain typical and crucial moral, psychological, and metaphysical problems as defined by the medieval worldview. The process in question is basically that of a struggle to overcome some perennial weaknesses and limitations of the human condition, as well as certain unsurmountable paradoxes of human life that reinforce these limitations. The detailed examination of the poem's structure, both in its overall temporal aspect and with regard to the internal arrangement of the parts of the narrative, will serve to bring out possible textual implications for the above issues. The successive chapters will then offer close interpretative analyses of particular motifs, themes, and symbols, which I consider important in view of the underlying quest-based structure of *Sir Gawain*.

Since the advent of new literary theories in the last two decades or so, I think it is no longer possible to preface a work in literary criticism without stating one's interpretative methods and theoretical framework. It is not my intention, however, to address here the intriguing problems from a vast and often confusing field of modern literary theory, although at the same time it has to be said that the questions of theory and methodology are by no means irrelevant in the present study. The interpretative framework used here has been rather eclectically built from what I think is most valuable and useful in the theoretical approaches to early literature developed to date, and although the purity of method may suffer as a result, no single theory or "ism" is here called upon as the governing credo. Chapter 1 will serve as the Introduction proper to spell out some of the methodological problems encountered in medieval literary studies. It will also develop a line of critical analysis of early texts adopted throughout this book, which basically makes liberal use of the available critical contributions whatever their ideological standpoint, leaving aside for another occasion the polemics with the theories and methods with which one may feel less inclined to concur.[1] The main focus for me remains the literary text itself, created by an author who communicates his view of the world through his poem; it is accordingly this view, seen against the backdrop of medieval literature and culture, that I am trying to analyze and interpret, rather than what other critics, representing particular interpretative approaches, have seen in the text. I will of course give due attention to the vast literature of the subject and the various contributions that have been made over the decades, but again I will quote the authorities in a rather unpolemical way, seeing each critical contribution as some approximation to what I see as the original authorial intention behind the literary text that constitutes its meaning.

The methodological and theoretical option proposed in this book is systems theory, its major tenets accordingly presented and explained in chapter 1. The term *theory* may be slightly misleading here, because the systemic approach consists less of some philosophical or ideological assumptions applied to a literary text as an interpretative paradigm than of certain formal procedures, in themselves uncontaminated by ideological preconceptions, that are used to analyze and sort out the manifold elements constituting a literary text into meaningful patterns. Systems theory as formulated in chapter 1 contains no specific ideology that will seek to validate itself through a literary text; in this sense it is, as I said, more of a method with a set of formal procedures than a theory. Its primary aim is not self-justification but to help discover and sort out into logical, structured patterns whatever ideas and meanings are provoked by the text itself in the course of a critical, interpretative interaction between it and the reader.

Accordingly, the interpretative procedure employed in this book will basically be that of close reading and then of amplification; that is, a selected element of the narrative (a character and its attributes, an image, a discriptive passage, or an element of structure) will be first analyzed in its immediate textual context and then in relation to other relevant systems of reference existing outside the poem. The external evidence will include first of all the medieval literary tradition with which—it can be assumed—the author of *Sir Gawain* was familiar: contemporary romance literature, allegory, the scriptural tradition and so on. On the other hand, in the study of the meaning and function of particular aspects of the poem I will also avail of textual evidence, thematically related or otherwise relevant, which cannot be claimed to have been known by the *Gawain*-poet, but which nonetheless deserves attention as an amplification of what the poem directly suggests. In practise this means that a particular idea, image, or plot element from *Sir Gawain* will be complemented by similar or analogous elements from texts not necessarily linked with *Sir Gawan* in a historical way. These texts will include, for example, Continental Arthurian romances, allegorical and religious writings, mystical, philosophical, and hermetic texts, popular devotional manuals and lyrics, which despite surface variation in form and genre represent an essentially homogenous and unified picture of the world, of the kind spoken of some time ago by C. S. Lewis.[2] In a word, the search will be for the content and meaning rather than for possible historical and textual connections.

This book has evolved over the years as a result of multiple close readings and analyses, often in a classroom context, of this intriguing and in many respects exceptional romance, coupled naturally with the reading of the vast critical output that has accumulated around *Sir Gawain* over the decades. Once a medievalist's favorite, *Sir Gawain and the Green Knight* seems to be enjoying visibly less critical attention in recent years, although it remains one of the most attractive Middle English poems, chiefly due to its beautiful story and despite its rather daunting language. The reader acquainted with the poem and its basic critical literature will surely recognize many of the problems raised in this book, as most of them have already been addressed by other critics on more than one occasion. However, despite the great amount of critical material on *Sir Gawain* some of the poem's specific problems still needed—in my opinion—to be examined afresh and reappraised, and indeed were it not for the sense of some dissatisfaction with the interpretations of *Sir Gawain* published to date this book would never have been written. The successive chapters will therefore address some of the old *Gawain* issues but will examine them in what I hope is fresh light, with each chapter offering an original contribution to the interpretation of otherwise known problems.

Accordingly, chapter 2 will analyze the overall narrative structure of the poem from the point of view of its dominating quest theme. Sir Gawain's annual cycle of adventures appears to be related to other temporal frameworks, such as the mythico-historical time, the astronomical and liturgical years, and the allegorical span of individual life, that are mutually inclusive and supportive, lending the poem a sense of structural multi-dimensionality, greatly enhancing its literary and intellectual sophistication. The discovered patterns and regularities in the temporal structure of the narrative will be presented "systemically" by means of tables and diagrams to offer additional support to the poem's widely praised inner consistency and balance.

Chapter 3 will in turn address a perennial question of the Green Knight's color and its possible intended significance(s). I will interpret the figure's most conspicuous external characteristic both in the light of the physical properties of the green color, and in view of the numerous significant references to greenness found in a different sources. The symbolic potential of the green color will emerge as polyvalent and complex, by no means linked only to the popular and rather obvious associations of greenness with life in general. The actual use of the green in traditional sources suggests a whole network of ideas related to the universal and ambivalent symbolism of life-death-rebirth. The complex and paradoxical nature of the color and its wearer in *Sir Gawain* will find support in evidence extending from the pagan Irish tradition to medieval mystical writings and Renaissance alchemy, and the discovered meaning(s) of greenness will then be related to other green objects and references to green found in the poem.

The notoriously enigmatic and elusive nature of the pentangle displayed on Gawain's shield will be dealt with in chapter 4. The five-pointed star in *Sir Gawain* has so far been viewed mostly either as a magical sign or as a symbol of moral perfection, but I contend that the figure can also serve as a mnemonic device containing a medieval synthesis of the microcosmic man. The five pentads, that is, the elements grouped in fives, attributed in the text to the five points of the pentangle will be seen here as a system of interrelated symbolic elements functioning as a unified entity, internally bound through the geometry of the pentangle. I shall also argue that the principle that determines the interrelatedness of the pentads and ensures their holistic, all-embracing nature, is the rule of the Golden Section (*sectio aurea*), a universal law of integration and harmonious unity in diversity, found both in the natural world and in numerous works of art. In moral philosophy the concept of the Golden Section with its Golden Mean seems also to be related to the Aristotelian notion of the mean virtue of temperance, whose positive as well as negative examples are shown in the poem in the behavior of Sir Gawain in his dealings with the other characters.

The rule of the Golden Mean epitomized in the pentangle is further applied to the sphere of human conduct in chapter 5, devoted to the famous Fitt III of *Sir Gawain* with its unique parallelism between the action of hunting and sexual temptation. The threefold nature of Gawain's test will be related to other tripartite ideological systems, notably the three Platonic souls, which are further linked with the Christian concept of the three stages of sin and the traditional tripartite social structure. In my view the three souls: the concupiscible, the irascible, and the rational, spoken of by Plato and other philosophers, determine both the number of days of Gawain's temptation and the comprehensive nature of the knight's moral and psychological testing.

Finally, chapter 6 will explore the more neglected aspect of the narrative, the motif known as the Beheading Game, which I will interpret in terms of Gawain's rite of passage into maturity through the liminal experience of quasi-death. A discussion of the decapitation motif in early Irish heroic saga and Arthurian romances will substantiate the claim for placing the ritual beheading in the context of initiation rites into chivalric orders. It will be argued in this context that the widespread ritual gesture of dubbing the knight at the admission ceremony (the patting on the head or shoulder with the flat of the sword) is a reflection of the symbolic beheading, understood as a "death" for the former personality and identity, and the emergence of a "new man" in the Pauline sense. The origin and significance of the dubbing ceremony will also be discussed in relation to the religious idea and ritual of the circumcision, suggested in the poem by the "nick on the neck" inflicted on Gawain by the Green Knight's axe.

The main object of the interpretative analysis of *Sir Gawain* offered in this book springs less from an ambition to present an entirely new reading of a well-known poem, but rather from an intention to reconstruct some aspects of the cultural background relevant to the narrative, together with the possible thoughts, emotions, and other responses that the poem may have evoked in its original audience, the kind of *Weltanschauung* that the *Gawain*-poet assumed in his readers. I find this "reconstructionist" approach more intriguing and intellectually rewarding than the alternative attempts of reading into a fourteenth-century text certain philosophical and ideological preconceptions of the late twentieth century. Nor do I think that a reconstruction of the original sensibility and the worldview that shaped the creation and reception of works such as *Sir Gawain* distances these works from the modern reader. Quite to the contrary: an underlying idea of the present study is that beneath the surface of a still readable, attractive, and fairly uncomplicated story of chivalric adventure there lie certain crucial questions and paradoxes regarding man and his existential and metaphysical condition that were just as valid in the Middle Ages as they seem to be today.

Acknowledgments

After years of purely aesthetic fascination with *Sir Gawain* as simply a beautiful story, I began my work on the poem in earnest during my memorable stay in Wolfson College, Oxford as a British Council research student in the year 1987/88. I had been working as a lecturer in English literature at Warsaw University at the time, and if not for the library work that I did while at Oxford my personal pursuit of the *Gawain* cause would still today be far behind the planned schedule. I would also like on this occasion to express my thanks to Professor Douglas Gray from Lady Margaret Hall, University of Oxford, then my academic supervisor and tutor, whose professionalism and erudition helped me find my way amid the sea of primary and secondary sources of Middle English studies.

The book was then created piecemeal over several years, and today I see that any delay has done it good by giving me time to draft, rethink, and revise the successive chapters into what I myself can accept as a final product, although still far from being fully satisfactory. During the years of its preparation especially stimulating in developing my ideas about the various aspects of the poem have been my classes on *Sir Gawain*, taught first at Warsaw University, and in more recent years in Trinity College, Dublin. I need not convince any academic teacher how revealing students' comments and contributions often are, and how helpful and fruitful interacting with a text in a classroom context can be. My debt to my students, from Warsaw and Dublin alike, for the stimulating freshness and intelligence of their response to *Sir Gawain* over the years, is hereby duly acknowledged.

In the course of the composition of this book a number of Middle English scholars have kindly read and commented on the individual chapters. My thanks are especially due to Professor John V. Scattergood and Doctor Gerald Morgan from Trinity College, Dublin, as well as to Professor Joerg O. Fichte from the University of Tübingen, who found time in their tight schedules to read and generously comment on the drafts of some of the chapters of this book. My knowledge of medieval literature owes a lot to the expertise and competence of these scholars, although at the same time I stress that the final shape of this book, as well as the ideas and opinions expressed in it, are a result of my own research and deliberation, for which I alone take responsibility. I would also like on this occassion to thank Professor Seán Ó Coileáin from University College Cork for his assistance with Old Irish texts, and Doctor Tim Jackson from Trinity College Dublin for his advice regarding the German texts used in the present book.

This book is dedicated to Andrzej Wiercinski, professor of anthropology at the University of Warsaw, with whom I have been associated first as a student in my undergraduate years in Warsaw in the late 1970s, and later as a colleague and friend. Wherever my book owes something to Andrzej's ideas in a direct way, this fact is duly acknowledged in a relevant footnote, but these are few. Indirectly, however, my view of early literature and the picture of the world presented by it have been to a large degree inspired by the intellectual climate created by Andrzej, which for many years shaped my perception and comprehension of various aspects of human culture. That life is a quest with a meaning is one of the things I came to realize through my acquaintance with Andrzej. My debt to his wide-ranging scientific interests, his philosophy of science, his penetrating mind, and his academic charisma is enormous, and I can only hope that he will accept my book as a modest token of gratitude for his personal inspiration and influence.

* * *

Permission to reproduce material has been granted by the following:

Oxford University Press: *Sir Gawain and the Green Knight*, edited by J. R. R. Tolkien and E. V. Gordon, second edition revised by Norman Davis (1967).
The Council of the Early English Text Society: *The Middle English Physiologus*, edited by H. Wirtjes (1991); *The Poems of John Audeley*, edited by E. K. Whiting (1931); *Stanzaic Life of Christ*, edited by F. A. Foster (1926); *Lydgate and Burgh's Secrees of Old Philiosoffres*, edited by R. Steele (1894); *Le Morte Arthur*, edited by J. O. Bruce (1903).
Houghton Mifflin Company: *The Riverside Chaucer*, edited by Larry D. Benson (1987).

University of Pennsylvania Press: *The Continuations of the Old French Perceval of Chrétien de Troyes: The First Continuation,* edited by W. Roach (1949).

University of Chicago Press: *Le Haut Livre du Graal: Perlesvaus,* edited by Nitze & Jenkins (1932-37)·

Scottish Academic Press, Ltd.: *Two Old French Gauvain Romances,* edited by R. C. Johnston and D. D. R. Owen (1972).

E. J. Brill: Jan van Ruusbroec, *The Seven Enclosures,* in *Opera Omnia* (1981).

Penguin Books, Ltd.: Plato, *Timaeus* (1965).

Editions RODOPI: Heinrich von dem Türlin, *Diu Crône* (1966).

Thames and Hudson Ltd.: Robert Lawlor, *Sacred Geometry: Philosophy and Practice*, 1982, illustration on page 59; Joscelyn Godwin, *Robert Fludd: Hermetic Philosopher and Surveyor of Two Worlds*, 1979, illustration on page 69.

Chatto & Windus. The Hogarth Press: *Pearl,* edited by Sir Isreal Gollancz, 1936.

The Knight
on His Quest

1

Problems with Methodology

The sheer volume and methodological diversity of the *Gawain* scholarship is truly impressive, and rarely does one find a single literary text (and relatively short at that) that would attract so much critical interest and attention. Ever since the poem was brought to the public view by Sir Frederic Madden's edition of 1839,[1] scholars' devotion to *Sir Gawain* can only compare with that to Chaucer's poems, and indeed both do not cease to inspire new approaches and critical evaluations, revealing at the same time what Ian Robinson called "the great power of surviving academic treatment."[2] But the proliferation of different critical theories and approaches to literature, especially in the last generation, though in itself very exciting and stimulating, ultimately appears to be something of a mixed blessing. On the one hand one is pleased if somewhat bewildered by the sheer number and variety of new methods, always ready to offer a different perspective to suit different scholarly needs and tastes. On the other hand, however, after testing the available theoretical options and checking their results one often does not seem to grow any wiser, but instead more confused and even frustrated. The question inadvertently if somewhat naively arises why a single literary work, with a given number of internally related elements, and with what looks like a uniform, coherent, and finite system of authorial intentions underlying its meaning, can yield so many and often so different interpretations, depending on the critical method employed. This frustration and confusion seems to grow as one reads one interpretative essay after another, all addressing the same text and its semantic potential, with the results reflecting usually the critics' rather than the authors' intentions, as well as intellectual and literary predilections. The practical impossibility of arriving at some definitive and adequate reading of a literary work well explains the appeal of those theories that relativize the very notion of meaning and negate it as a positive and constructive value: since on theoretical grounds there is no such thing as unequivocal and objective meaning, perhaps

25

a negative procedure of "deconstructing" a text by mainly pointing out its semantic ambiguities and contradictions is epistemologically more justified. Whatever the adopted approach, problems with the meaning of any given literary work remain and will probably never be solved to everybody's satisfaction.

A study of *Sir Gawain* offered in this book also follows a particular theoretical approach to the literary reality presented by the poem, one that is likewise far from providing any final interpretative formula, which simply does not exist. Before more is said about the proposed theoretical framework later in this chapter, let me venture a brief critical sketch of the methodological and theoretical landscape of *Sir Gawain* developed to date. The purpose of this overview would be twofold: to outline and evaluate the existing major interpretative trends and to cast a methodological background against which to situate the approach to *Sir Gawain* offered here. Needless to say, any comprehensive and systematic critical examination of the various interpretative schools of *Sir Gawain* is beyond the scope of this chapter, and indeed of the entire book, which is more analytical than theoretical in character although it does seek to locate its view of the poem within a more or less clearly defined formal framework. What follows, therefore, is of necessity a very rough classification of the approaches to *Sir Gawain* that have emerged over the last century, together with their various pros and cons.

Schools and Approaches

In the early history of the *Gawain* criticism one notices a tendency to split the harmonious coexistence of the various constituent elements of the poem by distinguishing between "form" and "matter": between the problems of language, prosody and style on the one hand, and of the story, plot, sources, and meaning on the other hand. This duality of approach to early texts is manifest in two main critical trends: one involving formal analyses (manuscript status, language, meter, and so forth), and the other devoted to interpretative studies of the poem's sources and thematic content. Without intending to discuss the existing enormous literature on the subject,[3] nor even its most valuable specimens, in what follows I offer a chronological critical review of the general trends in the *Gawain* scholarship. Far from being in any way exhaustive or definitive, the proposed survey is designed to help locate the reading of *Sir Gawain* offered here in some kind of methodological perspective.

Accordingly, unless an alternative classification is offered, it is possible to give the following taxonomy of critical and theoretical approaches to *Sir Gawain,* as far as they can be identified in the vast literature of the subject:

1. the ethnological-genetic school;
2. the literary critical school;
3. the theological school;
4. the psychological school;
5. the literary historical school.

Below I give brief characteristics and a critical evaluation of the distinguished approaches.

1. The early research on *Sir Gawain* was marked by a strong predilection for detailed analysis of the poem's literary, folk, and mythological sources, with a view to establishing their proper evolutionary sequence, mutual affiliations, and, finally, their impact on the *Gawain* plot. This genetic approach was first of all concerned with establishing a possibly exhaustive body of associated texts and analogues to show the occurrence and dissemination of selected plot elements, themes, and motifs, and with locating them, whenever possible, on a chronological scale. The main strength of the genetic research lies, naturally enough, in its chief objective: to collect the existing "sources and analogues" of *Sir Gawain* from a vast area of folk tale, heroic saga, romance and myth, with the eye less perhaps for the meaning of the text itself than for its origin, or rather for that kind of "meaning" that is determined by the poem's sources. For Jessie L. Weston, for example, the chief concern was "to discover what were the original features of the story, and who was its earliest hero."[4] The methodological weakness of the ethnological approach thus formulated lies basically in ignoring the poem's intrinsic artistic value and specific literary meanings, or sometimes even the way the sources are handled in the poem—considerations that lie beyond mere source-hunting. For scholars such as Jessie L. Weston, George L. Kittredge, Alice Buchanan, Roger S. Loomis, and Laura H. Loomis[5] discussions of *Sir Gawain* relied for the most part on attaching ethnological labels to types of plot, motifs, and characters, and finding their analogues in traditional material. Regardless of the actual degree of relevance of this material for the poem composed in a different literary and cultural milieu, the main effort of the genetic scholars seems to have gone into establishing connections between, for example, Sir Gawain and the Old Irish "solar deity," or between

Sir Bertilac *alias* the Green Knight and the pagan "thunder deity" or the popular figure of Jack-in-the-Green. In plot analyses motif-labels such as "the Beheading Game," "the Exchange of Winnings Theme," and "the Temptation Theme," supported by parallels from traditional material, were explained away by the indication of their sheer occurrences in thematically related narratives.[6] Although in itself valuable, the search for ethnocultural antecedents often simply meant the reduction of the poem's complex literary texture to the level of general structural resemblances to the hypothetical sources. This was, of course, easy to criticize, as exemplified by C. S. Lewis:

> If the medieval poet knew the Celtic story at all (which I need not deny), it has been to him merely a starting point from which he went on to invent something radically new, indeed incommensurable. That new invention, not its trivial and external similarity to some earlier thing, is the proper object of literary criticism.[7]

Despite the limited scope of its interest, the undisputable merits of the genetic school lie in providing the next generations of critics with an exhaustive body of edited source material, without which any historical or comparative studies of *Sir Gawain* would not be possible today. But objections such as those raised by C. S. Lewis led inevitably to the recognition and appreciation of the intrinsic values of the text itself, regardless of the initial input of traditional material. This brings us to what I earlier called the literary critical approach.

2. In the context of the presented taxonomy of the *Gawain* scholarship, by literary criticism I mean here an approach that focuses on the interpretation of the poem in its own right, on the evaluation of its intrinsic, aesthetic and poetic qualities, as well as on placing the poem within the immediate literary context of its age. Logically enough, this trend in literary analysis must have arisen as a reaction to the one-sidedness and reductionism of the ethnological-genetic school with its emphasis on external evidence. By contrast, the literary critical approach analyzes the internal features of the work, its literary qualities such as the originality of treatment of the received material, questions of form, style, diction, and narrative techniques, often viewed against the background of literary conventions directly pertaining to the text in question. In short, if the genetic school sought common elements between the historically or thematically related texts, literary criticism stresses the differences, both in form and content, between the texts under scrutiny. Even the early critics of *Sir Gawain*, although preoccupied primarily either with the

sources or textual and linguistic analyses, could not fail to acknowledge the overwhelming effect produced by the poetic form and the internal structural balance of the poem. Sir Israel Gollancz, for example, observed in 1928 that "any didactic purpose on the part of the poet is lost sight of under the spell of the story, which is told in the revived alliterative verse."[8] Among the scholars of later generations the exclusively genetic approach to *Sir Gawain* was ardently criticized, as for example by Charles Moorman, who wrote that the traditional approach merely "insisted that the poem is only a repository of myth patterns" and that it centered solely on "elucidating Gawain's relationship to the British Jack-in-the-Green, the Celtic sun god, and the omnipresent vegetation god."[9] A literary critic making recourse to mythology should, according to Moorman:

> be able to show how the poet uses myth and, in doing so, to concentrate not on the identity of the myth, but on its function, not on its closeness to the known pattern, but on the changes which the poet effects in that pattern, not on origin, but on use.[10]

The uniqueness and originality of treatment of the received, traditional story material in romance is also what interested such scholars as Larry D. Benson,[11] Eugene Vinaver,[12] or more recently Joerg O. Fichte.[13] For Benson a romance writer is both a "clerk," in the sense of presenting what was regarded as "authentic history" drawn on traditional, respected sources, and a "maker," in the sense of originality and artistic creativity.[14] Likewise for Vinaver the medieval romance is formed by the constant tension between conte, the traditional story, and conjointure, the art of arranging and connecting the known story patterns into new literary forms.[15] Fichte in turn analyzes the impact of Arthurian pre-text on *Sir Gawain* and the way in which the author of the poem handles and manipulates the various romance traditions while playing with the audience's literary expectations. Literary criticism thus understood aims at combining both the external and the internal aspects of the poem to paint a fuller literary picture. For example, Edward Wilson in his study of the *Gawain*-poet writes the following:

> The proper procedure in criticism is to look first at the work itself, and then turn to the whole background, so far as this may be recovered, in order to find what givens, if any, the author has merely adopted, and what he himself has altered and contributed.[16]

The need to study both the text and its background in all their complexity is obvious enough, but sometimes the literary criticism in its "purer" form may dangerously drift its attention onto the text alone, with the exclusion of what constituted this text's original input and background. This type of limitation of complex literary reality to its chosen aspect resembles the reductionist view of the genetic scholars, but in reverse. A poem may, for example, be taken out of its historical and literary context to be analyzed in artificial isolation, purely for its supposedly independent literary value. In intention, such an "unbiased" approach is meant to examine as objectively as possible and without preconceptions the poem's intrinsic values and their aesthetic effect on the reader. For example, W. A. Davenport consistently abandons the philological and antiquarian approach to the poems from the Cotton Nero A.x. MS in favor of one centering on the poems' emotional appeal and the readers' spontaneous reaction to them. He writes: "more critics are concerned to relate the four anonymous works to a historical, cultural or moral context than to try to define the effects they have on the reader and the way the reader responds to them."[17] Apparently leaving aside the issue of the influence of the cultural norms upon the reader's, as well as the critic's, perception of a literary work, Davenport advocates an "unbiased" approach, "with no more preconceptions than those which are unavoidable with poetry written six hundred years ago."[18] Stripped of its context and background, the poem may then be praised for its "mystery, trickery and jesting" or for "a curious mixture of affects, considerable ambiguity, and a sense of interwined and subtle richness of detail," as well as for the "intricacy of intention" and "a pleasurable variety of incidents and scenes."[19] The question of whether pure and unbiased literary criticism exists at all, and whether it is possible to look first at the work itself without a priori assumptions of what one is looking for in analysis is again a theoretical and philosophical issue, one that seems to go beyond literary criticism proper into the general area of epistemology and philosophy of science. It is also a matter of contention whether the *how* of a literary work can be isolated from the *what*, and which is the more important.

In the literary critical approach in its purest form, however, both the question of content as inherited from the poem's sources and its meaning within the poem seem to recede into the background, and what comes into the focus of critical attention are questions of style, diction, prosody, narrative and descriptive techniques, language, characterization, and so on; in short, all that can be distilled from a close reading of the text as it stands, with little or no contextualization. Despite this methodological restriction, literary criticism of this type has yielded some excellent results within their defined fields; for example, with regard to style and metre of *Sir Gawain* the most noteworthy and comprehensive study remains the one by Marie Borroff;[20] with regard to style and other literary and poetic qualities, a study of the *Gawain*-poet by Anthony C. Spearing;[21]and with regard to the content and its immediate literary meaning, a work by John A. Burrow,[22] to cite only the most outstanding contributions.

The main strength of the literary critical approach lies in just this meticulous and thorough analysis of the poem's internal structure and composition of its narrative, stylistic, and formal elements—all that constitutes the uniqueness of the poem as a work of art. On the other hand, the main methodological weakness or limitation of purely literary analysis lies often in ignoring, or simply excluding from consideration, questions of contextual meaning and function of the poem within a larger frame of literary, cultural, or religious reference. However convenient it may sometimes be for a critic to isolate a poem from its environment, no literary work, objectively speaking, exists in a cultural vacuum, and none, least of all in the Middle Ages, seems to have been composed for aesthetic reasons alone. Unless one reduces, again for convenience, the complexity of a literary phenomenon to a "text," there does not seem to be anything like a literary work as such, able to "speak for itself." Literature at any stage appears to be both a product of the author's unique talent and artistic intention and a result of the use of the received literary conventions, of the intellectual or cultural climate of its age, from which the author's artistic design naturally derives, and with which the author's artistic personality is very subtly interlinked. The notion of an unbiased and unprejudiced criticism is therefore dubious on theoretical grounds, because any critical analysis, even one deliberately ignoring the poem's context, involves of necessity at least the a priori imposition on the scrutinized work of the critic's own, subjective, literary and intellectual attitudes. To remove the original context for the sake of theoretical clarity and to isolate the text for what is regarded as its pure literary value may sometimes lead to highly subjective and impressionistic evaluations when it emerges, for example, that "there is nothing problematic in *Gawain,*" whose only value lies in "brilliant polychromatic rendition of scenes of rich banquets, of venery, of the wild terrain of northern Wales," and the whole poem is nothing but a "high comedy" and "an entertainment."[23]

3. By the theological school I mean an approach, well represented in the history of the *Gawain* scholarship, that concentrates neither on the sources and analogues of the poem, nor on its intrinsic literary value, but on religious concepts, doctrines, and ideas reflected in the

poem's content. It is of course banality to say that medieval literature was produced in a world dominated intellectually by the Church, its dogmas, liturgy, beliefs, practices, and general religious sensibility, to the extent that it is virtually impossible to find a medieval literary work that would not, at least indirectly, refer to some religious idea. Although *Sir Gawain* is not an ecclesiastical or devotional poem (as a romance it catered to the lay courtly audiences whose values and lifestyle it reflects), but it is not a secular work, either, and is both overtly and allegorically imbued with such crucial Christian concepts as temptation, carnal sin, free will, confession, penance, and resurrection. Indeed, the two dimensions of the reality depicted in *Sir Gawain*, as well as the tension between the worldy, the secular, and the absolute and the divine, greatly enhance the intellectual attractiveness of the poem, already a high achievement by purely literary standards.

The balance between the divine and the secular in *Sir Gawain,* however, seems to depend on the reader's preconceptions about these two realms, and attitudes in favor of both are reflected in the corresponding rift among the *Gawain* critics with regard to the poem's religious dimension. Some readers see the poem and its author as generally sympathetic towards secular reality, while others perceive human actions and institutions implicitly condemned in the poem from the point of view of absolute and divine reality and its standards. The theological approach to *Sir Gawain* has produced some excellent results in unraveling many hidden layers of allegorical and spiritual meaning by referring various elements of the narrative to the vast body of ecclesiastical writings existing outside the text in medieval religious tradition.[24] The indisputable merits of this approach lie in placing the poem in the context of medieval religious life, devotion, and theological debate, without which any serious interpretation of the text is left in a cultural vacuum. On the other hand, it is all too often possible to overemphasize the ecclesiastical dimension of what is, after all, a story of romantic adventure and to treat the narrative merely as a didactic piece illustrating in a literary form some particular Christian doctrine or belief. Needless to say, problems of style, form, and the human and secular aspects are then played down or viewed merely as part of the world's *vanitas* to be condemned in the light of the absolute, divine values that the poem at least implicitly is said to uphold. Again, the decision regarding the balance between the secular and the religious in *Sir Gawain* often derives from the critics' rather than the authors' preconceptions. The fact remains, however, that for all its unquestionable allegorical and spiritual layers of meaning, the poem is not primarily a devotional or theological tract, but represents a basically secular and worldly genre of chivalric romance, although pervaded to the highest degree by serious moral and spiritual concerns.

4. The adherents of what I propose to call the psychological school of interpretation are interested neither in the direct sources of the poem, nor in its literary qualities, nor even in the religious ideas reflected in the content of the narrative. Instead, their primary interest lies in the operation of certain psychic forces, processes, and motivations, either conscious or unconscious, individual or collective, that are perceived to be implicitly present in various elements of the narrative. This offshoot of literary studies is usually a direct descendant of an originally Freudian and/or Jungian school of psychoanalysis, to which its interpretative apparatus is indebted. Seen from the Freudian perspective some literary themes or motifs are generally regarded as artistic expressions or sublimations of either the author's or the protagonist's (or both) emotional and instinctive drives, as well as their unresolved subconscious problems and anxieties. The actions of literary characters are then seen as indicative of resolving and overcoming these inner problems and conflicts, which are more often than not of a sexual nature.

On the other hand, a Jungian approach perceives certain literary forms, particularly those bordering on mythology or fairy tale, as symptomatic of archetypal urges within the depths of the largely unconscious psyche. C. G. Jung's archetypes are described in his works as certain inborn mental dispositions, "primordial images" or psychic residua of numberless human experiences of the same type, inherited by individuals from their ancestors in the structure of their brains. These inherited images and associated mental reactions may refer to such universal experiences as maternity, paternity, confrontation with the opposite sex, with evil, liminal encounters with death, and so on. According to Jungian depth psychology, due to the inborn and normally unconscious nature of archetypes certain poems or works of art are able to spontaneously stir specific emotional and cognitive reactions in their recipients by giving expression to these unconscious and very powerful mental forces, shared by all members of the human species.[25] In this way the psychological approach shifts the focus of analytical attention both from the literary work proper and from its historical context, and concentrates on the author's and the reader's un- or half-realized intentions, urges, and emotions, expressed symbolically in the actions and motivations of literary protagonists. When historical literary conventions are examined in this light, the medieval allegory, for example, appears to be "a manifestation of a particular type of mental experience," a "crisis of the spirit," while actions of the protagonists of an allegorical narrative are seen as a means of achieving "a balance of rational and intuitive elements"—that is, a much-desired though vaguely defined "psychic integration." Allegory, romance, and other visionary narratives are accordingly viewed as exteriorization and intellectualization of these inner spiritual processes that had also been expressed in ancient myth and ritual.[26]

The first to apply the psychoanalytical apparatus of Sigmund Freud, C. G. Jung, and comparative religion to some elements of the *Gawain* narrative was Heinrich Zimmer,[27] who interpreted the main plot elements of the poem in a wide, crosscultural context of myths and fairy tales in which the main incidents revolve around the archetypal theme of death and rebirth. For example, Gawain's threefold temptation in the bedroom scenes was compared by Zimmer to an incident from the life of Buddha: "just as Gawain was tempted thrice by a woman, so was the Buddha by the three daughters of Mara," and "the correspondences between these temptations of Gautama . . . and those of Sir Gawain are obvious."[28] In such ahistorical interpretations, relying for the most part on free crosscultural comparisons, the solutions to particular problems raised by a literary work is often provided by little more than sticking psychoanalytical and ethnological labels on certain elements of the narrative in an unceasing pursuit of analogous themes and motifs all over the world. Such a procedure implies of course the critic's belief in psychoanalysis and the idea of psychic universals, regarded accordingly as useful tools in uncovering the hidden intentions and motivations behind a literary work. In this way the analysis of what is intersubjective, universal, and timeless in the poem can sometimes revealingly complement a perhaps more mundane but definitely less elusive and vague study of what is particular, individual, specific, and historic in a literary work.[29] For example, Christopher Wrigley in his combined historical/psychoanalytical approach to *Sir Gawain* recognized "that a traditional story operates on several levels, some of them below the normal level of conscious awareness."[30] Similarly to C. G. Jung, Wrigley states that "such stories derive . . . from universal, or almost universal, structures of the human mind in its relationship to the family, to society and to ever-present problems of life and death." In relation to *Sir Gawain* the critic said that its story "cannot be explained within the accepted boundries of naturalistic and literalistic analysis."[31]

Ideally, of course, a combined and more comprehensive approach seems always methodologically sounder than a one-sided one, but analyses of *Sir Gawain* that would link psychology with historical and literary considerations are disappointingly rare. "One who seeks to utilize the archetypal approach of depth psychology must use it in conjunction with the "historical" aspect of the individual work of literature," wrote S. Manning in connection with *Sir Gawain*.[32] This would involve, for example, relating the possible motivations of Sir Gawain's and other protagonists' actions as described in the poem to the medieval predilection for the supernatural and the irrational, as well as to certain mental habits and modes of behavior characteristic of such institutions as the Church, the court, and chivalry.[33] Adherents of depth psychology are nonetheless often tempted to isolate the text from its historical context and the specific problems it addresses and apply the archetypal method exclusively, especially to romance, built as it is on a mythlike, "heroic" narrative pattern, and often filled with non-naturalisms, elements of fantasy and magic, supernatural stylization, fairy-tale atmosphere, and, not infrequently, dreamlike logic. The same can be said for dream allegory and other types of visionary narratives, so characteristic of medieval literature.

The main strength of the psychological school of literary analysis lies therefore in providing the conceptual tools with which to examine and interpret the hidden intentions and certain standard psychic processes underlying the content of a literary work. In my view, particularly valuable in this context is the theory of archetypes by Jung, which can account for structural similarity of traditional narratives such as heroic myths, fairy tales, and romances, as well as for the frequent and independent occurrence of similar, sometimes strikingly identical plots, themes, motifs, symbols, and types of characters in culturally different times and places. If the factor of the universality of the human mind and certain psychic processes is taken into account in literary analysis, no constant and often obsessive recourse to source hunting seems necessary, and no instances of borrowing or diffusion need to be called forth to account for every similarity between the texts. In other words, the psychological approach, when sensibly handled, can provide reasons for what is timeless and universal in a literary work, treated either as a conscious or semiconscious expression of certain typical and panhuman psychic and emotional reactions of both its author(s) and readers.

Problems may occur, however, when a literary work and its author are treated like a psychiatric case, and when the characters' behavior is described exclusively as symptomatic of "repression" or "sublimation" of certain instinctual urges, notably the famous libido. The critic's work relies then for the most part on attaching psychoanalytical and anthropological labels to elements of the plot, whereby in *Sir Gawain,* for example, Sir Bertilac emerges as a father figure or a "shadow;" Queen Guinever as the maternal archetype; the beheading motif as a castration symbol; and Gawain's encounter with the Green Knight as a puberty initiation rite, and so on.[34] In certain extreme cases psychoanalysis can offer a vehicle for the critic's own predilection for certain details of human anatomy when, for example, the topographical setting of the Green Chapel becomes "readily identifiable with the features of the feminine genitalia," with a ravine (2162) as the vulva, a steep bank on either side (2165) as the labia, and the mound above (2172) as the *mons Veneris* overgrown with grass, that is, pubic hair. This imagery too has been accounted for by the "unconscious process" at work.[35] For all its numerous and undeniable analogies with fairy tales, folk stories, and even spontaneous dreams, it is, I think, sane to say that *Sir Gawain* remains first of all a product of a self-conscious, poetically and intellectually sophisticated mind, rather than a free play of its author's drives and uncontrolled sexual associations. Without denying the existence of certain standard psychic processes that can derive from the postulated unity of human nature, one should perhaps be more inclined to ascribe literary works such as *Sir Gawain* to their authors' conscious artistic intentions, rather than to their unrealized, suppressed sexual drives.

5. Last but not least there remain the followers of what I rather broadly call here historical criticism, involving critics who interpret *Sir Gawain*, like Hans Schnyder for example, "by viewing it against the background of its own time and within the context of its genuine cultural climate."[36] In other words, neither the establishing of the immediate sources of the poem nor the literary values for their own sake nor solely the ecclesiological dimension of the poem nor even the unconscious creative processes involved are of primary interest for historical critics; their attempt is "to investigate the cultural and religious currents of past times as closely as possible in order to arrive at some sort of mental re-establishment of those patterns."[37] Closest to historical criticism thus understood is, as it appears, the theological school of interpretation, except that in addition to purely religious contents the historical critics are reconstructing other realms of thought, intellectual trends, and cultural processes that may have had some impact on the form and content of the literary work in question. As Donald R. Howard also observed: "to uncover the essential concern of a literary work is to reconstruct the thought of its age and especially to relive, through a creative act of the historical imagination, the feelings which it would have evoked."[38] A historical critic is therefore concerned both with the author's conscious

intellectual and artistic design and with the audience's possible responses (intellectual, aesthetic, and emotional) to the literary work. For example, Patricia M. Kean in her book on *Pearl* speaks precisely of the need to reconstruct "the kind of background of feelings and associations which the original audience must have had."[39] D. W. Robertson, Jr., likewise defines historical criticism as "that kind of literary analysis which seeks to reconstruct the intellectual attitudes and the cultural ideas of a period in order to reach a fuller understanding of its literature."[40] This kind of criticism rests on the assumption that the recognizable center of gravity of a literary work lies outside the text itself, in the sphere of ideas born both in the author's mind as a reflection of his historical-cultural milieu, and in the thoughts and associations evoked in the minds of its audience. This assumption is exactly what is questioned by literary critics, for whom a literary work should speak for itself, and no prior recourse to external sources or inspirations to elucidate its meaning is necessary.[41] It is true that unless historical analysis also takes into consideration the aesthetic and intrinsic values of a literary work, there is a danger of ignoring the poem's uniqueness as a work of art and of treating it merely as a literary vehicle for particular cultural contents. On the other hand, the main strength of historical criticism, provided it is applied thoroughly and consistently, lies in its complexity of approach, which does not concentrate on a selected aspect of a literary work at the expense of other literary dimensions, but regards the work itself, the authorial intentions, and the audience's responses, all immersed in a clearly defined cultural environment, as simultaneous and equally important frames of reference.

Systems Theory

The critical approach adopted in this study of *Sir Gawain* appears closest to what I defined above as historical criticism, combined with some elements of literary analysis. The full theoretical perspective, however, needs now to be worked out in greater detail. The approach used here is called systemic; that is, one that follows the basic premises of the general systems theory, first formulated in 1950s by Vienna biologist Ludwig von Bertalanffy,[42] and later reworked into a general scientific paradigm by a Polish cyberneticist Marian Mazur.[43] Systems theory in its formal language is akin to structuralism but has not in itself been applied yet to literary studies; its use as a tool in literary analysis is still a matter of possible future.[44] The present study is—to my knowledge—the first attempt to treat a literary work as a "system" according to the main assumptions of systems theory and to employ some of the theory's formal procedures to sort things out in the text under scrutiny.

The fundamental tenet of systems theory is that it treats reality as an organized whole, consisting of a hierarchy of systems, understood here as sets of interrelated elements. Any set of identifiable elements of reality can form a system whose holistic structure is determined by the nature of relations existing between its elements. The idea is nothing new in itself and refers back to the philosophical notion of holism, which says that the whole is greater than the sum of its parts, and that a system as a whole may have properties above those of its parts and their organization. A literary work understood as a system is likewise a set of interrelated elements such as letters, sounds, words, phrases, formulae, sentences, verse forms, parts of text, images, characters, elements of plot, and so on. The structure of a literary work is then defined by the way in which these different elements are interrelated on the levels of language, style, poetic form, descriptive and narrative techniques, content, and plot. A system, moreover, can contain within itself other systems, referred to as subsystems. This means, for example, that a subplot or an episode can be regarded as a subsystem of a larger plot, or that any element of the narrative; for example, a clearly differentiated descriptive passage or a motif can be treated as a separate system with its own interrelated elements determining its structure.

In general systems theory any system can interact with another system and by interaction is basically meant an exchange of physical states involving information, energy, and matter. In the literary context what is most important in interactions between systems is the exchange of information; that is, physical states that determine both the number and character of the involved elements and interactions among these elements. Interaction in turn is a two-way process involving both the stimulus (S), and the reaction (R): a stimulus (S) is an interaction at the input of the system, whereas a reaction (R) is an interaction at the output of the system, as presented in figure 1.

In systems theory not only a literary work but also the author can also be regarded as a system, as can the reader. The interaction between the author and the literary work treated as two systems describes the creative process of literary composition, when the author engages in the process of arranging the selected literary elements according to the designed types of internal relations. On the other hand the interaction between the reader and the literary work describes the creative process of literary interpretation, when the reader reproduces in his intellect and imagination both the elements of the literary work, their character, and the types of existing inter-relations.

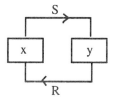

Fig. 1. Interaction Between Systems Involving Stimulus (S) and Reaction (R).

Let us now, still theoretically, look closer at the character of the input and output interactions of any system. It usually happens that different systems, due to their individual characteristics, will react differently to different stimuli. It is therefore useful, and indeed nec-essary, to introduce another factor, namely the system's ability to receive and transform the stimuli, called here reactivity (r), measured as a ratio of the reaction of the system (R) to the received stimulus (S).

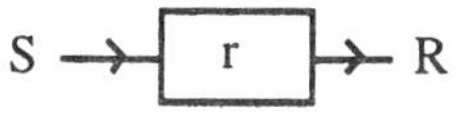

$$S \rightarrow \boxed{r} \rightarrow R \qquad\qquad r = R/S$$

Fig. 2. Reactivity of the System.

A simple transformation of the above formula gives us the following:

$$R = r \times S$$

Fig. 3. Reaction of the System.

which is a formula for the reaction of the system. It tells us some-thing very important: namely that the reaction of the system has always two causes, of which one comes from within the system (its reactivity—r), while the other comes from outside the system (the provided stimulus—S). The consequences of this simple theorem for the literary context are far-reaching. It means for example that a literary work understood as a product of the author's creativity (reaction—R) is neither exclusively a result of the author's talent or genius (reactivity—r), nor solely a result of the random amassment of all sorts of literary sources and material (stimulus—S). In other words, neither the literary talent alone nor the talentless accumulation of literary sources is likely to produce a literary work, because, as is seen in the formula, reaction of a system is a product, not the simple sum, of the system's reactivity and the received stimulus. This means that there can be no literary work (R=0) if at least one of the factors equals zero, and, consequently, a systemic approach to literature must simultaneously take into account both the received literary material and the individual way with which it is handled in a literary work.

If the above general formula is to be referred back to the theoretical approaches to *Sir Gawain* described earlier in this chapter, it can clearly be seen that what I called the ethnological-genetic school of interpretation concentrated for the most part on the "stimulus" side of a literary work; that is, on the sources, analogues, affiliated texts, motifs, and plots that formed the input of the poem conceived as a system. The presented systemic formula clearly shows the theoretical limitations of such a one-sided approach; a study of the material existing beyond the analyzed text does not in itself address the problem of literary composition and says little about the particular text under scrutiny. On the other hand, literary criticism in its pure form analyzes only the internal interrelations between the elements of a literary work understood as system (its reactivity-r), excluding from analysis the nature and meaning of these elements in the context outside the text. As we see, both approaches, if used exclusively, reduce the holistic nature of a literary process to one of its constituent aspects at the expense of the others.

Equally important as the problem of the inseparable connection between the origin of the elements constituting a literary work and their unique arrangment within the work is the nature of the author-text-reader relationship. Before I address this crucial problem in the light of systems theory, the following definitions seem necessary:

—by *author* I mean here a system creating another system ("text"), by combining and arranging the various literary elements into a unified and meaningful whole;

—by *text* I mean a system of linguistic signs (in literature) arranged in a way designed by the author; and

—by *reader* I mean a system interacting with the text and engaging in an intellectual process of arriving at the method in which the elements organizing the text have been meaningfully arranged.

The author-text-reader relationship is inextricably linked with another crucial problem of literary analysis, namely the meaning of the text. In contemporary literary theory and akin branches of linguistics much ink has been used on deciding, or ultimately failing to decide, what constitutes the "meaning," and where it is: is it in the text, in the author's mind, in the reader's mind, in all of these at once, or somewhere still beyond all that? Semiotics is a complex and often highly formalized discipline, and a traditional philological procedure that takes for granted that the meaning of the text is in the text itself (where else?) can no longer be accepted by a critic conscious of his or her theory and methods. The complexity of the problem, however, far exceeds the scope of this very preliminary theoretical presentation, but some working definition of *meaning* in line with the proposed systemic approach to literature seems necessary in the context of our considerations.

Accordingly, in a literary work treated as an organized system of linguistic signs the meaning of these signs is determined by the cognitive associations evoked by those signs both in the mind of the author and in the minds of the readers. The associations can be of intellectual, aesthetic, or emotional character. In the creative process of literary composition (understood here as an interaction between the author and the text), the original authorial associations become attached in the author's mind to the selected literary signs and elements, chosen and arranged in such a way so as to reflect those associations. These may have to do with the author's artistic intention(s) deriving from a particular view of the world, or with whatever motivated the author to create a literary work in the first place.

On the other hand, the process of reading and interpreting a literary work would then consist in reattaching to the elements of a literary work (in the reader's mind in turn) of the associations that are thought to have originally given rise to the literary work under scrutiny. This of course presupposes some common background between the author and the reader (overlap of associations), at least on purely linguistic level; that is, both the author and the reader must first of all share a common language. Ideally, a full reading of the text would imply total overlap of imaginative associations and literary competence between the author and the reader, but this is of course physically impossible (one can also argue, of course, that the reconstruction of the original authorial intentions is not necessarily the main object of literary criticism). What is possible, however, and what should indeed constitute at least one of the main objects of literary criticism, is to engage in a process of arriving as closely as possible at the original authorial associations underlying the literary work, which determine its meaning. With the notion of *meaning* thus rather generally defined, the literary process as a whole (comprising both composition and interpretation) would then rely on encoding by the author of the various ideas, thoughts and emotions into a system of linguistic signs constituting a literary work, and on allowing the reader to work on his associations in an attempt to decode the meaning of the text. The meaning of a literary work thus understood is therefore never in the text; it exists beyond the text in the minds of its author and readers, but is stirred and provoked by the text.

The three differentiated systems fundamental to the literary process—author, text, and reader, together with their mutual interactions—can be presented in a block diagram (figure 4). The diagram is very simple and lucid and can be easily grasped as one integrated whole, which is the essence of the systemic approach:

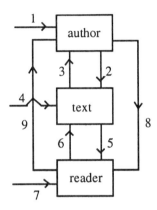

Fig. 4.   The Block Diagram of the Literary Process

The three blocks represent the systems themselves, as defined earlier, whereas the arrows show the directions of interactions both between the systems and between the systems and the environment (also understood as a system). As we can see, the number of possible types of interactions involved between the coupled systems of author, text, reader and the environment is nine, a finite number: that is, no other types of interactions within the literary process thus formulated come into play. Very briefly, the indicated interactions involve the following kinds of literary problems:

1. The influence of the environment upon the author (author's education and social background, his knowledge of existing literary sources and conventions, possible biographical influence,);

2. The influence of the author upon the text (literary process itself involving the artistic design, choice of literary resources, author's handling of these resources, and so on; in sum, all conscious intellectual and artistic work put by the author into the creation of a text);

3. The influence of the text upon the author (a reverse side of the creative process, whereby the author engages in a feedback interaction with the text, revising and correcting it during the process of composition);

4. The influence of the environment upon the text (problems of preservation of the text, particularly important in medieval studies, dissemination, availability, and so forth);

5. The influence of the text upon the reader (stimulation of the reader's response, associations and literary competence, the process of reading and interpretation, for example);

6. The influence of the reader upon the text (such as glossing, correcting, revising, editing, engaging in critical analysis, writing another text in response);

7. The influence of the environment upon the reader (reader's education, accessibility of the text, knowledge of literary conventions and interpretative procedures, and so on);

8. The influence of the author upon the reader (without the mediacy of the text, when both the author and the reader either know each other pesonally or share a similar cultural background);

9. The influence of the reader upon the author (usually in the form of reader's expectations that the author takes into account while creating the text, or else the reader's reaction to an already created text).

The main methodological advantage of the block diagram is its holistic character: it describes all possible types of interactions existing between the author, text, and reader. In other words, any particular literary study or analysis must take into account problems from within the given range, unless of course an alternative model is proposed. The diagram also treats the author-text-reader relationship as an organized whole consisting of a given number of systems and interactions occurring among them. This means that a full and comprehensive description of a given literary phenomenon has to consider all the systems and interactions involved. In practice, however, any particular literary study naturally concentrates on a selected problem or aspect of a literary process (a selected system or type of interaction), in which case the limitations of the assumed perspective become clear when compared with the totality of the literary process as presented in the diagram. When the methodological boundaries are clearly drawn, a particular aspect of the literary process in question can thus be referred to a larger whole of which it is a part (that is, an element of a system), so that the clarity of the general picture and its constituent parts can be maintained. According to the diagram, the complexity of the literary process cannot on theoretical grounds be reduced to any of its constituent systems or interactions, although of course to achieve such a full treatment in actual critical practise is an unattainable ideal. In nearly all cases, like in this study, conscious choices have to be made by the critic as to what systems and kinds of interactions constitute the object of investigation and what is left out of analysis as a result.

Accordingly, from among the aspects of the literary process described above, those relevant to this study are interactions numbered as 1, 2, 5, 7, and 9. These include the author's ideological background and its reflection in the artistic design of the poem (1, 2), the possible responses evoked by the poem in its medieval audience on the intellectual, moral, emotional, and aesthetic levels (5), the type of the audience and its literary expectations presupposed by the author (7), and the influence of these expectations upon the artistic design and meaning of the poem (9). Compared with the theoretical schools and approaches to *Sir Gawain* as outlined earlier, such a perspective will appear closest to historical criticism with elements of literary criticism and source study, the latter determining both the character of literary material used in the poem and the audience's literary competence and expectations, built as they were on various sorts of pre-text. Since the literary work understood as a system is not a simple sum of its constituent elements but an integrated set of interacting literary components, I will place much emphasis on some of the intrinsic literary qualities of the poem itself, particularly of its narrative structure looked upon from a holistic point of view. In fact, I will make use of whatever appears helpful in each of the described theoretical frameworks, because a systemic approach relies in its essence on complexity and versatility of approach.

The Background of *Sir Gawain*

Sir Gawain and the Green Knight is placed historically within a network of multifarious literary and cultural elements, and in terms of sources and inspirations it represents a unique blend of the most important medieval traditions: the ideology and practices of the court and the Church, and elements of popular custom and tradition. Due to its genre, the romance of *Sir Gawain* is most strongly embedded first of all in the feudal and chivalric world of the medieval court, whose system of values and patterns of thought and social behavior it reflects. These in turn are inseparably intertwined with religious notions and rituals: a historical link that connected chivalry with religion ever since the merger of military patterns with the Christian faith came into effect in the time of the First Crusade in the late eleventh century. The idea of *militia christi* and of knighthood conceived as a defense of Christianity and an embodiment of the Christian ideal then took its shape, becoming firmly established in European consciousness for many centuries to come. For this reason it is impossible to discuss the content of a late-medieval romance such as *Sir Gawain,* or the ideal of perfection it addresses, without combining the chivalric military code and ritual with the Christian teaching and practise. Nor is it conceivable to discuss fully the ethical ideal propagated by a story of chivalric adventure without incorporating into it the religious idea of the *imitatio christi,* with all its consequences for the type of plot, character, and literary symbolism employed in poems such as *Sir Gawain*. The whole point of *Sir Gawain*'s immersion in the medieval religious milieu is obvious enough, but it is nonetheless worth reiterating, maybe because the poem is not primarily a devotional piece.

A study of the ideological background (both religious and secular) that can be presupposed for the author of *Sir Gawain* and his audience must take into account different systems of cultural reference used as possible inspirations for the various literary elements that are combined in the poem into an artistically unified whole. The main medieval cultural domains, together with their chief modes of literary and ritual expression, that can be considered relevant in this connection are summed up in table 1. The table includes, as seems logical in the light of what we know about the medieval romance, the domains of the Church, the court, and the popular tradition. Both the court and the ecclesiastical institutions had in the Middle Ages their own modes of literary and ritual expression for the purpose of dissemination and sustenance of their respective ideologies and worldviews. But despite the clear separation of the two institutions, it is often misleading to think exclusively in terms of the Church-court dichotomy or to divide medieval literature accordingly into its religious and secular components. It is true that in a predominantly religious medieval environment one deals with strictly ecclesiastical sources such as homilies, sermons, hagiography, and devotional or mystical writings, but it is also true that much of secular or courtly literature such as romances, love poems, and allegories are all with varying degrees pervaded by religious thought and symbolism, and every theme, no matter how mundane, always has a spiritual and moral dimension to it. One needs only to think of Langland's transcendental perspective of his social satire in *Piers Plowman*, of Chaucer's realistic though still very allegorical general design of *The Canterbury Tales*, or of the profoundly religious and spiritual dimension of chivalric adventures and courtly life as described in *Sir Gawain*. As a result of the penetration of religious thinking into otherwise secular domains, it is possible to apply the same hermeneutic procedures, such as those developed by Augustinian semiotics for example, to the interpretation of both strictly religious and quasi-religious sources. Saint Augustine's well-known method of elucidating and interpreting the Scripture, expounded in the *De doctrina christiana* (2:1-4, 6, 8-10), laid down the foundations for textual exegesis not only of the Bible, but of any symbolic type of narratives, the romance or poetic allegory included.[45] One perceives it almost as a natural habit of medieval writers, including those working in the courtly milieu, to think and compose their works using such hermeneutic terms as *signum*, the immediate *sensus literalis*, and then of *sententia* containing the metaphysical truth,[46] and to apply Saint Augustine's allegorical, tropological, and anagogical senses to texts other than the Scripture.[47]

Table 1

The Medieval Church, the Court, and Popular Tradition with the Corresponding Modes of Literary and Ritual Expression

Church	Court	Popular Tradition
Modes of Literary Expression		
- Scripture - Patristic sources - Hagiography - Theological tracts - Penitential writings - Mystical texts - Religious lyrics - Moral allegory - Religious drama - Philosophical writings (such as Scholasticism and Neoplatonism)	- Heroic epic - Romance - Love allegory and lyrics - Historical chronicles - Manuals on chivalry and courtesy	- Ballads - Folk epic tales - Fabliaux
Modes of Ritual Expression		
- Liturgy - Devotional practices	- Courtly decorum - Chivalric code	- Folk customs - Seasonal rituals

The Augustinian rules of allegorical exegesis and the constant search for deeper, spiritual truths in various kinds of texts seem to reflect a characteristic mental and philosophical disposition whereby one tends to use visible, tangible signs or images to express often complex, multitiered structures of intangible concepts, ideas, and emotions—in other words, to attach abstract entities to concrete physical forms in literature or pictorial arts, for example. In terms of historical expression this allegorizing tendency of the medieval mind was a direct heir of the Neoplatonic philosophy of late antiquity, very influential in the later Middle Ages, which operated on the assumption that "this visible world is but a picture of the invisible, wherein, as in a portrait, things are not truly but in equivocal shapes, as they counterfeit some real substance in that invisible fabric," to use the words of C. S. Lewis.[48] Philosophers such as Calcidius, Macrobius, Boethius, Plotinus, and others, the twelfth-century School of Chartres with William of Conches, Thierry of Chatres, and Alan of Lille, and the unstopped reception of some works by Plato and the Hermetic writings throughout the Middle Ages all created an intellectual climate in which symbol and allegory were conceived as keys to the understanding of the world treated as a code hiding divine mysteries.[49] The symbolic language of the Platonic philosophers, their allegories, personifications, images and dream visions for many centuries inspired the poetic repertoire of medieval writers and artists, shaping the spiritual climate and sensibility of whole epochs practically until the dawn of the Enlightenment.[50]

Although the medieval chivalric romance, particularly in its developed, more refined classical form, as in Chrétien de Troyes, did share many features with the explicitly allegorical and symbolic types of writing, its origin was of course different. The roots of the romance go neither directly to Greek philosophy nor to Christian teaching but to the pagan epic tradition of the Celto-Germanic world, where stories of heroic adventure had for centuries reflected and glorified martial virtues and qualities, typical for the patriarchal, warlike, largely tribal societies of much of northwest pre-Christian Europe. The pagan heroic epic did not evolve, however, into the medieval romance until its full merger with the Christian patterns and ideals of courtly love in mid-twelfth-century France, when the atmosphere of religious and missionary zeal of the Second Crusade and the tradition of Provençal love poetry blended with the heroic spirit of the traditional *chanson de geste* to create the romance—by far the most popular literary genre of many centuries to come and an antecedent of the modern novel. Under this twofold influence of the crusading idea of knighthood as *militia christi* and of the subtle and civilizing notion of courtly love the Christian heroes of *chanson de geste* underwent an ideological shift from "communal exercise of endurance to a view of life as individual seeking and journeying,"[51] now understood as an inward quest for spiritual goals, much in the spirit of the ascetic monastic orders founded then, such as the Cistercians or the Knights Templar. Most of the early classical romances of the *matière de Bretagne*, notably those by Chrétien or Robert de Boron, and especially those from the Grail cycle, bear clear witness to the heightened religious and mystical sensitivity in their presentation of knights pursuing otherwordly and spiritual goals.

The motif of the inner quest emerged then as the main regulating structural pattern of romance, an organizing principle of plot and action, while the Christian spiritual ideal and the quasi-religion of romantic love determined both the character of the quest and its ultimate goal.[52] The great themes of romantic love, feudal loyalty, and the Christian perfection, either in accord or in conflict with one another, came to characterize the content and determine the meaning of medieval romance in its most developed form. With the appearance of romance as *the* type of epic narrative of the Middle Ages, the way of telling a story of military adventure changed as well. The often anonymous and collective process of poetic narration in the traditional epic and folk tale in the works of such authors as Chrétien gives way to a highly individualized, learned, and fully conscious creative endeavor, in which the amorphous *matière* of traditional stories is given a new form according to certain fixed rules. Eugene Vinaver sees here a direct influence of medieval grammar and rhetoric upon the narrative techniques consciously employed by learned romance writers.[53] Especially important in the context of this study of *Sir Gawain* is the indebtedness of the romance to the tradition of biblical exegesis and allegory, whereby a romance story, its characters, and their behavior acquire a *sensus spiritualis* and convey meanings lying far deeper and beyond the immediate naturalness or realism of description.[54] Hans Schnyder sees in the romance "the continuous presence of allegory," springing from "a vast cosmic vision that whatever existed in the universe already possessed a symbolic function."[55]

Like allegory proper or other visionary narratives, the romance begins then to exhibit lack of realism in the modern sense; the universe and its manifestations are treated as *signa* of the invisible and the divine, and even the tiniest "realistic" detail in the poem can stir manifold associations with the moral, spiritual, or doctrinal contents, as was often no doubt intended by its author.[56] This means that medieval hermeneutics with its conceptual tools for textual analysis and interpretation could apply not only to the Scripture and the works overtly religious, but also to poems classified in modern times as secular, like the romance for example. However traditional the source material, we know that the romance writers were often educated clerics operating within both the ecclesiastical and courtly environments who cleverly turned a familiar story of adventure into *signa* or *pictura*, pregnant with some hidden *sententia* or *sensus spiritualis.*[57]

In my interpretation of the *Gawain* romance offered in the following chapters I will treat the text accordingly as a system of manifold signs able to stimulate imaginative and intellectual associations with ideas existing beyond the poem itself, in its author's and the readers' minds—ideas that are important in light of the medieval view of man, his self-perception and his position in society and in the larger, divine scheme of things. In the reconstruction of some of the imaginative associations constituting the poem's meaning I will make use of whatever systems of cultural reference that appear relevant, notably those indicated in table 1. In doing so I will use any methodological perspective from among those outlined in the earlier section of this chapter that will help adequately contextualize the selected elements of the poem. The appearance of eclecticism and heterogeneity of approach that may result seems a minor deficiency, because my aim is not the purity of methodological approach or a validation of a theory, but rather the exciting intellectual adventure of engaging in a mental interaction with the *Gawain*-poet through his text. Besides, the systemic approach *is* eclectic in the sense that it offers a complex, holistic view of literary reality, proceeding from general problems to particular and specific ones, always seen against the complex background of the whole. Despite this general of description, however, the formalized language of systems theory, its use of simple mathematical formulae, tables, and diagrams, creates a possibility of employing quite exact and intersubjective procedures able to sort out the selected elements of the literary work and analyze their contents and interrelations with a good deal of precision.

2

The Temporal Structure of *Sir Gawain*

A holistic approach to the literary reality of *Sir Gawain* postulated in the preceding chapter should require that the following analysis of the poem begin with an overall view of its structure and content conceived as a whole. Accordingly, my present objective is to examine the narrative framework of *Sir Gawain*—that is, the way the main elements of the poem are interrelated and referred to the whole—and to deduce possible meaning(s) from the identified general structure. The reconstructed narrative skeleton of the romance will then be fleshed out in later chapters with more analytical and textual considerations of particular literary problems raised by the poem.

The Quest Theme

The following discussion aims chiefly at examining and interpreting the temporal significance of the narrative, in particular, the poet's use of different time scales in the framework of the story. My main postulate here is that there coexist in the structure of *Sir Gawain* a number of embedded time scales, mainly of cyclic nature and often parallel to one another, whose implications are of vital importance for the overall meaning of the story. As has already been amply illustrated by critics,[1] the constituent elements of the poem—scenes, episodes, certain descriptive passages, selected images and symbols—are all characterized by a very fine and intricate structural balance and symmetry, and indeed very few medieval literary works can compare with *Sir Gawain* as far as consistency and harmony of the internal composition are concerned. In the following pages, however, I am concerned first of all with the framework of the poem seen from the temporal perspective, and, consequently, with the possible interpretative implications of the use of time in *Sir Gawain*.

The story of *Sir Gawain* is too well known to require even a brief summary, but it is useful to recall that the content of the poem reveals a pattern, typical for the chivalric romance as well as for the heroic epic as its historical prototype, which shapes the story's action according to a general regulating narrative principle, that for want of a better term can be called the quest.[2] The quest is to be understood as a sequence of events and adventures involving the main protagonist(s), leading towards some goal or solution. The sequential nature of the quest implies a linear, goal-oriented, and purposeful movement in time from one important event or stage of action to another, usually framed within a fictitious life span of some exemplary individual. Epic narratives, whatever their type or cultural origin, are naturally about heroes—that is, individuals who have risen above the ordinary human level and have undergone tests and trials in the course of which they managed to attain fully human, or suprahuman, dimensions. In general terms this holds true for the martial heroes of Celto-Germanic pagan heroic epic or of classical heroic myths, for martyrs of Christian saints' lives, as well as for heroes of popular ballads or knights of the chivalric romance. In each type of epic narrative the protagonists' characters and actions tend to exemplify their culture's propagated virtues and qualities, socially accepted attitudes and patterns of personality, that are set up as a model and ideal for members of the community to be attained in the course of social upbringing or moral and religious instruction. Despite occasional flaws and shortcomings that are part of human nature, the heroes' personalities are generally fashioned to be exemplary and "ideal," and so are their fictitious lives and doings, illustrating the propagated values and moral standards of their culture. It can, I think, be accepted as an axiom that in a traditional, premodern worldview each individual life was as a rule perceived as goal-oriented and purposeful. Despite the fact that the precise nature of this goal or purpose could vary in time and place, in all premodern cultures the ultimate aim of human life was always perceived and defined from a religious perspective, usually as a kind of postmortem spiritual reward, described as most precious and valuable, in the Christian context referred to as "salvation" or "redemption," granted to those who adhered faithfully to the culture's governing values and ideals. To a greater or smaller degree all traditional narratives (including chivalric romance) are about individuals struggling to rise above the common level by overcoming their personal and historical limitations and shortcomings to achieve the defined highly spiritual goals. The process is usually depicted as long and painful, involving strenuous and dangerous tests and trials, fashioned in epic stories as a series of adventures forming a hero's quest—a structural pattern universally used as a dominant formal device organizing the plot in such narratives.

The quest therefore describes a sequence of related events usually framed within a fictitious, imaginary life span of the protagonist, or at least within a crucial part of his life, with particular emphasis on moments of transition. Such idealized biographies of the heroic type provide personal examples of individuals who have overcome, or are struggling to overcome, the limitations of their human condition through the experience of existential, often ritualized *rites de passage*, as a result of which they achieve "la modification radicale du status religieux et social," as Mircea Eliade noted concerning the socioreligious problem of initiation.[3] In traditional societies the whole of human life is treated as a kind of rite of passage from one stage to another, from one social role or position to another, until death completes the cycle of life, conceived in itself as a passage to another, otherworldy existence. This "radical modification" of one's socioreligious and existential status mentioned by Eliade often assumes the form of a drastic or even catastrophic change or crisis in life, best compared to, and indeed often symbolically identified with the "death" of an individual for his former life and existence, followed by a subsequent "rebirth" as a "new man," readapted to the society with different parameters of personality. As a rule all traditional epic narratives that describe the lives and exploits of exemplary individuals in pursuit of spiritual goals center in their stories on the theme of death and rebirth, expressing thereby their protagonists' radical transition from one psychological, metaphysical, and social state to another.

If we accept that the story of *Sir Gawain* follows in its overall design the quest-based type of epic narrative (which appears to be the case even at first reading of the poem), there consequently follow certain important implications for the poem's interpretation.

First and most generally, the story of Sir Gawain as a particular literary manifestation of the standard epic heroic biography symbolically describes human life conceived as a pursuit of higher spiritual values, attained through a series of tests and trials of physical, psychological, and moral nature.

Second, in the medieval context the adventures of Sir Gawain can be viewed as an allegory of human life based on the doctrine of *imitatio christi*—that is, a normative conviction propagated by the Church whereby every Christian should follow and imitate in his or her life the spiritual example of Christ as described in the Gospel and the Christian Tradition.

Third, in a more historical sense the story of Sir Gawain is both a literary expression and a critique of the chivalric ideal of its age, in all probability composed during the Arthurian revival in England in the initial stages of the Hundred Years' War under the reign of King Edward III (1327-77). By "chivalric ideal" I mean a system of values, patterns of personality, and modes of social behavior and rituals combining feudal militarism with the Christian ethos that was characteristic of the aristocratic knightly elite of late medieval Europe.[4]

Fourth, the quest theme in *Sir Gawain*, represented simultaneously as an allegory of human life in general and of the life of a perfect Christian knight in particular, is embedded within the temporal scheme of the Church's liturgical calendar with its feast days and related rituals and customs, and harmonized with the natural cycle of the seasons of the astronomical year as well as with the popular beliefs and folk customs associated with them. The main time scale of the poem is that of the solar year: from midwinter celebrations in Camelot to New Year's Day at the Green Chapel and back in Camelot a year later. This circular movement of Gawain's adventure, both in space and time, naturally suggests the idea of cyclicity, completeness, and universality, with the full round of the year easily homologized with great historical or mythological cycles, as well as with the complete age of a society or of an individual life.

In short, the dynamic, quest-based structure of *Sir Gawain* can generate simultaneous and interrelated time scales that refer to cosmological, mythological, historical, seasonal, christological, social, and individual layers of meaning. We shall now see how this complex general design works on particular levels of the narrative.

Principle of Cyclicity

It did not escape the critics' notice[5] that the poem is embraced by a significant reference to the mythico-history of Britain, with its well-known story of the peopling of the country by Brutus and the descendants of the refugees from Troy.[6] The opening line of the poem, "Siþen þe sege and þe assaut watz sesed at Troye" is followed by a compressed account of the exploits of Aeneas and "his highe kynde" (5), of Romulus and other legendary Roman figures, of Brutus, Aeneas's great grandson, the eponymous founder of Britain, and finally of Arthur (26). All this mythico-historical material is repeated in an even briefer form at the end of the last stanza of the poem (before the wheel), but in a reversed order:

þus in Arthurus day þis aunter bitiddee,
þe Brutus bokez þerof beres wyttenesse;
Syþen Brutus, þe bolde burne, boȝed hider fyrst,
After þe segge and þe asaute watz sesed at Troye,

(2522-25)

Such a formal enveloping device,[7] by all indications consciously employed, introduces a principle of cyclicity to the events described in the poem, because by returning to the point of departure at the end of the story the poet suggests that the beginning of an historical cycle is analogous to its end. Moreover, the device implies that every end is followed by a new beginning, because the fall of Troy that gave rise to the British race had in itself marked the end of an older civilization. Likewise the mention of Romulus (8-10) and other great-city founders (11-12) must evoke associations not only with the grandeur of Roman civilization but also with its equally spectacular decline and fall. Therefore, behind the opening and the closing references to Troy, Rome, and later Arthur's Camelot, one clearly suspects a moral and providential warning about the inevitable fall of famous people and places, chiefly due to the working of Providence itself, but also as a result of the people's moral trespasses and sins such as pride or treachery. The story of the fall of Troy, immensely popular in the Middle Ages mainly due to the reception of the *Historia Destructionis Troiae* by Guido delle Colonna (1287),[8] was commonly viewed as a spectacular example of the unfolding of God's universal plan. The same must have held true for the history of the Roman Empire; especially telling in this respect is the mention in the opening stanza of *Sir Gawain* of the "gret bobbaunce"(9) with which Romulus first built the Eternal City. The word *bobbaunce* (OFr) is glossed by the *Middle English Dictionary (MED)*[9] as "ostentatious or boastful behavior," "vain display, worldly vanity," "pride, arrogance, insolence," and as such clearly carries an implicit moral meaning of the fall of a nation through its pride.[10] The message inherent in the cyclic conception of history is therefore a double one: that of rise and fall, beginning and end, and hence the opening stanza of *Sir Gawain* moves logically from the destruction of Troy (1-2) to the reestablishment of the Trojan race throughout Europe (5-12), and finally to the foundation of Britain by Brutus (13-14).[11] The paradigm of cyclicity and oscillation between the ups and downs, glory and decline, in the history of famous nations is thus firmly established at the very outset of the poem, with specific consequences for the story itself.

The emphasized cyclic regularity in the growth of nations (Troy, Rome, Britain), applies also to famous individuals, as evidenced by the indicated succession of Aeneas, Brutus, Arthur, and finally Gawain. The prototype of Arthur's and Gawain's duality of character, as revealed in the poem, is Aeneas, ambiguously referred to in the early lines of text as "þe tulk (*man*) þat þe trammes (*machinations*) of tresoun þer wroȝt," who was "tried for his tricherie, þe trewest on erthe" (3-4). These lines have occasioned some debate as to who is meant by the *tulk* tried for his treason,[12] but in the light of the structural regularities under discussion here I would be inclined to accept the view that no other figure than Aeneas himself is meant. The grand epic sweep and the evocation of the glorious descent of Arthur's reign with which the poem begins should not preclude an allusion to a more embarrassing episode from Aeneas's legendary life, popularized by Guido della Colonna. The story has it that the illustrious Trojan hero was sentenced to permanent banishment by the Greeks, with whom he had collaborated at the downfall of Troy, for his deceit in concealing from them Polyxena, through whom Achilles had lost his life.[13] The infamous episode, which formed a stain on Aeneas's otherwise noble character, was probably intended by the author of *Sir Gawain* as a prefiguration and a parallel of both Arthur's imperfections and, to a greater extent, of Sir Gawain's fault as described later in the poem. Besides, despite their blemishes both Aeneas and Gawain still remained the illustrious heroes of their nations, both eventually fell short of the heroic ideal o f absolute perfection and of demands of honor for fear of their lives, and both used personal strength to purge themselves of disgrace through trial and self-knowledge.[14]

In this way the pattern of rising and falling with regard to nations, and of the fluctuation between fame and shame, success and failure in relation to individuals, set in a framework of cyclic, mythico-historical time with its recurring beginnings and ends, departures and returns, is introduced at the outset of the Gawain story as a principle organizing and regulating the poem's structure on a number of levels. The larger, mythico-historical cycle referring to Troy, Rome, and Britain—that is, the truthful *historia*[15]—is embracing a smaller cycle of Gawain's story, a fictitious *fabula* set in Arthur's Camelot and the kingdom of Logres, covering a calendar rotation of one year and, allegorically, the span of an individual life.

The pivotal episodes of *Sir Gawain*—that is, the two parts of the Beheading Game—are placed on consecutive New Year's Days: the decisive moments of the year that mark the end of one annual cycle and the beginning of a new one.[16] The two gruesome encounters with the Green Knight, moreover, are in both cases preceded by contrasting descriptions of joyful celebrations of Christmas, first at Camelot (37-71), and then at Hautdesert a year later (1648-85, 1952-59), providing the middle of the poem with a symmetrical framework. In symbolic and ritual terms the New Year marks a transition from one life or mode of existence to another, a "death" for the previous life followed by a spiritual "renewal." The catastrophic and liminal nature of the Beheading Game for both parties involved, so dramatically described in the embracing Fitts I and IV of the poem, strongly supports the meaning of the New Year's Day as a moment of vital change and transition, in general as well as in the individual sense.

Yearly Revolution and Human Life

By the way of analogy, the placing of the Beheading Game at the beginning of the year can be linked with the notion of an "absolute beginning" of life, suggested first by the opening reference to Troy and the implied beginning of a new mythico-historical cycle. The resurrectional character of the entire Christmas season, and of the New Year in particular, is clearly borne out by the liturgy of the Church, and despite the obvious concentration on Christ's Resurrection in Easter celebrations, the Feast of the Nativity likewise centers on the spiritual rebirth of humanity[17] and on the hope of redemption through the birth of the Savior.[18] New Year's Day also has a special place in the liturgy as the Feast of the Circumcision (1 January), conceived by medieval theologians as the Old Testament prefiguration of the New Testament baptism, both being clearly associated with the idea of the death to flesh and sin, and the rebirth to spiritual life (Deut.10:6; 30:6; Col.2:11-15).

On the other hand, the time intervening between the two pivotal moments of the New Year, filled in *Sir Gawain* with events and episodes constituting the knight's quest and coinciding with other important liturgical feasts, can be perceived as an allegorical life span of an individual, whose phases are exemplified by the order and nature of Gawain's adventures. The symbolic homology between the seasons of the year and the ages of human life is a medieval commonplace, to the extent that no description of nature or season found in medieval literature seems ever to have functioned without some reference to human life or to the state of the soul in connection with a particular age of life. Despite a good deal of original detail in each description, in essentials the medieval poets seem to have followed a well-established rhetorical tradition of *descriptio temporis* or *descriptio naturae,*[19] which always served a functional and didactic purpose of placing the human life within the larger natural, cosmic, and moral perspective. Nature served as a mirror of the human mind, and the sequence of the seasons described in poetry or represented in calendar vignettes was meant to signify a progression of the human soul through life from cradle to tomb and the Last Judgment. The *Gawain*-poet fully observes this tradition, and the key passage describing the progression of the seasons between the joyous Christmas and the sorrowful Feast of All Saints, the day of Gawain's departure from Camelot, is the one at the start of Fitt II. The combined *descriptio temporis et naturae* depicts a continuous flux of good and bad days and seasons, a constant oscillation between life's rises and falls, growths and declines, according to the mutable nature of time:

> A ȝere ȝernes ful ȝerne, and ȝeldez neuer lyke,
> þe forme to þe fynisment foldez ful selden.
> Forþi þis ȝol ouerȝede, and þe ȝere after,
> And vche sesoun serlepes sued after oþer:
> After Crystenmasse com þe crabbed lentoun,
> þat fraystez flesch wyth þe fysche and fode more symple;
> Bot þenne þe weder of þe worlde wyth wynter hit þrepez,
> Colde clengez adoun, cloudez vplyften,
> Schyre schedez þe rayn in schowrez ful warme,
> Fallez vpon fayre flat, flowrez þere schewen,
> Boþe groundez and þe greuez grene ar her wedez,
> Bryddez busken to bylde, and bremlych syngen
> For solace of þe softe somer þat sues þerafter

(498-510)

After the dramatic happenings of New Year's Day described at length in Fitt I, there follows a very condensed passage (two stanzas only) covering the rest of the calendar year, which inexorably "ȝernes (*runs*) ful ȝerne (*swiftly*), and ȝeldez neuer lyke (*never returns the same*)" (498). The times alternate between the joyous "Crystenmasse" and the unconvivial ("crabbed") Lent, between cold winter and warm spring and "softe somer." The idea of the cyclicity of natural life is continued in the second stanza with the description of summer and autumn, in which the central image is that of a life cycle of the seed (517), which turns into a plant ("wort") in the summer's sun and the moistening ("donkande") dew, to full ripeness in harvest time (518-522). The passage closes with the coming of new winter and with a *sententia* containing a nostalgic realization of the brevity of life, leading inevitably towards its end, "as is the way of the world":

> And þus 3irnez *(runs)* þe 3ere in 3isterdayez mony,
> And wynter wyndez *(returns)* a3ayn, as þe worlde askez
>
> (529-30)

In a similar way William Langland uses the formula "at one yeres ende" to mean "at the end of life."[20] Nor are the unequivocal ascriptions of the order of the seasons to the traditional four ages of human life lacking in medieval literature, as exemplified by the fourteenth-century *Stanzaic Life of Christ*::

> March is likenet, is no3t to layn,
> to childehede wel, as reden we.
> Somer to 3outh liknet is,
> that gro3yng time is cald expres,
> harnest to monnes eld, i-wys,
> in whiche is kyndle soburnes,
> Winter to elde wihthouten wer
> is likenet to wel and skilfully,
> wen mon is passit sixty 3er,
> in four our life thus diuise I.[21]

Similarly, John Lydgate in his *Secrees of Old Philiosoffres*, a free rendition of the famous *Secretum Secretorum*, upholds the popular view of the fourfold division of the human life allegorized with the seasons, starting—naturally—with the beginning of life in spring:[22]

> Thus four tymes makith us a merour cleer
> Off mannys lyff and a ful pleyn ymage.
> Ver and iuventus togedir have sogeer;
> Estas folwith, longyng to saddere age;
> To us autumque bryngeth his massage
> Off senectus; wynter last of alle,
> How dethys orlogge doth on us calle.[23]

It is only natural that winter as the season marked by the suspension of life processes should symbolically be the time when the "death's clock" ("dethys orlogge") calls on man, just as March and the beginning of spring at vernal equinox should coincide with the first age of the human life. The idea is no doubt implicit in Chaucer's famous opening of *The Canterbury Tales*, when we hear of "the droghte of

March" penetrated "to the roote" by April's life-giving "shoures" (1-2), or openly expressed in *The Nun's Priest's Tale*, when Chaucer analogizes the beginning of the year in spring with the creation of man:

> Whan that the month in which the world bigan,
> That highte Marche, whan God first maked man. . . .[24]

But the four seasons of the annual cycle are only one frame of reference for the fourfold division of the human life, for the concept can be based on other quaternary systems as well. For example, Dante in *Il Convivio*[25] talks at length abouth man's adolescence, maturity, old age, and senility, drawing mainly on Plato and other philosophers, and Bede in *De Temporum Ratione*[26] (ca. 725) expounds a scheme whereby the four ages of man are interlinked both with the seasons and with the four qualities: hot, cold, dry, and moist. Accordingly, human life is fourfold, governed in turn by each of the four humors in the body and harmonized with a macrocosmic order of the seasons and the elements. Bede's system can be summarized in the following comprehensive set of tetrads:[27]

Table 2

Bede's Tetradic System of Qualities, Ages, Humors, Seasons, and Elements

Qualities	Age	Humor	Season	Element
moist and hot	childhood	blood	spring	air
hot and dry	youth	red choler	summer	fire
dry and cold	maturity	black choler	autumn	earth
cold and moist	old age	phlegm	winter	water

The number four first of all directly relates to "earthly" and "temporal" man, composed as he is of the four elements, governed by the four humors, inhabiting the four quarters of the globe, and living within a temporal cycle of the solar year, easily divided into four equal parts by the two solstices and two equinoxes. The division has its moral and religious dimension as well, for which the Scripture provides ample evidence. Due to its association with worldliness and temporality, the number four and its multiples, forty and four hundred, are frequent numerical symbols referring to life in this world as a time of penance, suffering, privation, and purification, followed—as is suggested—by a resurrection into the state of heavenly bliss. For example, it took forty days for the Flood to purge the world of all sin and impurity (Gen. 7:17),[28] and for forty years the Jews wandered through the desert in search of the Promised Land (Deut. 2:7). Similarly, Christ spent forty days in the Wilderness fasting and resisting Satan's temptation (Mark 1:13), the episode reflected in the Church's calendar in the forty days of Lent preceding the Savior's Resurrection. In similar fashion Moses had spent forty days fasting and praying on Mount Sinai before the reception of the Law (Exod. 24:18). The penitential significance of the number four is also found, to use a literary example, in Langland, where Piers Plowman explains that he was sowing, planting, and laboring hard on his half-acre for penance's sake "al this fourty wynter."[29] The well-grounded concept also explains why Jacobus de Voragine at the beginning of his *Legenda Aurea* divides human life on earth into four periods, describing the consecutive phases in terms of the earthly pilgrimage towards resurrection and unity with God.[30]

The Poem's Four Fitts

I now want to relate the above discussion of the overall temporal framework of *Sir Gawain* and of the universal tetradic conception of human life to the poem's content, especially to its widely acknowledged internal division into four Fitts, marked by large ornate capitals at lines 1, 491, 1126, and 1998 in the manuscript.[31] A brief glance at this textual division, however, reveals immediately that the four Fitts do not automatically match the four seasons and the associated ages of life but rather serve simply to split the text into four parts of more or less equal length, distinguished by the place of action more than by anything else (Fitt I—Camelot; Fitt II—journey from Camelot to Hautdesert; Fitt III—the hunting and bedroom scenes at Hautdesert; Fitt IV—the Green Chapel). In terms of time as well the Fitts only generally follow the succession of the annual seasons, with the action very significantly concentrated on the time around Christmas in Fitts I, III, and IV, and on the period between All Saints' Day and Christmas Eve in Fitt II. Apparently these moments of the year were for some reason more important for the *Gawain*-poet than the much longer calendar time between 1 January and 1 November, significantly contracted to only two descriptive stanzas in the opening of Fitt II.

Given these modifications it still holds true, as Donald R. Howard put it, that "the specific events in Sir Gawain's life are presented in some measure as metaphors of the life of man, and specific spans of

Table 3

Time Scales in the Narrative Framework of *Sir Gawain*

	The Story	Seasons of the Year	Liturgical Feasts	Ages of Man	Phases of Life
Fitt I	Christmas celebrations at Camelot ↓ 1st Part of the Beheading Game	Midwinter ↓ New Year's Day (1 Jan.)	The Nativity (25 Dec.) ↓ The Circumcision (1 Jan.)	Adolescence	Birth ↓ Infancy
Fitt II	Sojourn at Camelot ↓ Journey through North Wales ↓ Christmas at Hautdesert	Winter ↓ Spring ↓ Summer ↓ Autumn ↓ Midwinter	Lent ↓ Michaelmas ↓ All Saints' ↓ Christmas ↓ St. John's	Adolescence (cont.)	Childhood ↓ Youth ↓ Maturity ↓ Old Age
Fitt III	Three Days of Hunting and Temptation	Midwinter (cont.) ↓ Last Day of the Year	St. Thomas' Day (29 Dec.) ↓ New Year's Eve	Early Maturity	Old Age (cont.)
Fitt IV	Departure for the Green Chapel ↓ 2nd Part of Beheading Game ↓ Return to Camelot	New Year's Day	The Circumcision	Maturity	Death ↓ Rebirth

time as metaphors of the entire temporal world."[32] In order to extend this idea, as well as to sum up and systemically integrate my earlier discussion on the temporal framework of *Sir Gawain*, all the differentiated textual, spatial, and temporal frames of reference suggested by the poem have been combined in table 3. The table shows the correspondences existing simultaneously between the fourfold textual division of the poem, Sir Gawain's adventures, the seasons of the year, the liturgical calendar, the traditional ages of man as illustrated in the poem, and the objective phases of human life stretched from birth to death. It my opinion any comprehensive discussion of the content of the successive Fitts should take into account all of the existing systems of reference, regarded as a multidimensional spatiotemporal conceptual background of the narrative.

Accordingly, the successive parts of the romance as presented in the table refer to the following simultaneous layers of meaning:

Fitt I. The Christmas festivity at Camelot extends from the time around midwinter—that is, the astronomical beginning of the solar year—to its octave on New Year's Day proper, the start of the calendar year. By way of analogy this point in time denotes an "absolute beginning" of life, additionally reinforced by the initial reference to Troy and the implied beginning of a new mythico-historical cycle.[33] It is only understandable that the crucial character of this moment be highlighted in the story by placing the highly dramatic and consequential first part of the Beheading Game at the turning point of the cosmic, historical, and yearly cycles. In terms of the liturgy as well the resurrectional character of the season is clearly emphasized by the Feast of the Nativity (25 December), celebrating as it does the spiritual regeneration of humanity and a hope of future redemption, and by the following Feast of the Circumcision (1 January), a prefiguration of Christ's redemptive passion. The reader will also notice that throughout the entire story the poet carefully alludes to the feast days on which significant events occur, and if these dates may appear merely ornamental to us today, both the poet and his audience would have recognized that Gawain's adventures coincided at each stage with the relevant religious feasts, together with their moral and spiritual significances. The themes and lessons of the liturgical year would no doubt have provided a moral and religious comment on the ongoing events in the poem by reminding the reader of "the duties of the Christian warrior in the battle of life."[34]

The beginnings of the calendar, mythico-historical, and liturgical cycles are interrelated in Fitt I with the traditional ages of human life, here understood first of all in a collective sense. Sir Gawain does not fully emerge as an individual hero until later in the scene, when, because of his exceptional courage and sense of honor, he alone among the knights of the Round Table accepts the deal with the Green Knight. Prior to Sir Gawain's intervention Arthur's court is described as "þis fayre folk in her first age" (54), and there seems to be little doubt that the phrase "first age"[35] signifies here a "spring-time" of life, the *adolescentia*—that is, an age following the child-hood but before full maturity. Childhood itself is not, naturally enough, literally involved in Camelot, although significant metaphor-ical allusions to it are made on a number of occasions: the author describes Arthur as "sumquat childgered" (86), and a moment later the Green Knight contemptuously calls the assembled knights "berdlez chylder (*children*)" (280). Not that these epithets are entire-ly undeserved: both Arthur's loss of temper, his boyish rashness to seize the Green Knight's axe, and the court's ineptness to handle the crisis caused by the intruder seem to justify fully this characteri-zation.[36] Moreover, things are generally "new" and "young" at Camelot: for example, the "Nw ȝer watz ȝep (*fresh*) þat hit watz nwe cummen" (60), Christmas comes "onewe" (65), King Arthur is in his "joyfness" (*youth*) (86) and of "ȝonge blod" (89), in his vigor and mirth compared to the New Year itself ("Ful ȝep in þat Nw ȝere", 105). All in all, the carefree merrymaking and jollity of the Christmas season at Camelot in Fitt I fully accord with the character of the "springtime" of humanity, "hapnest vnder heuen" (56) in its first age.

On the individual level both the Nativity and the New Year—as the very names of the feasts suggest—signify new birth, both biological and, as in the case of Sir Gawain, spiritual. What moves the knight to accept the beheading challenge in the first place is the maturing recognition of his social role as a member of the Round Table—his conscious realization of the moral duties and responsibilities as a knight and as the king's nephew. Psychologically, the acceptance of the Beheading Game is in effect tantamount for Gawain to the real-ization of the inevitability of his death to occur a year hence, since the given conditions of the game are such that unless a miracle happens no chance of survival for a mortal man is at all possible. And despite Arthur's attempts to laughingly dismiss the game as yet one more "Cristmasse craft" (471), specially arranged for courtly enter-tainment, the author closes Fitt I with a stern reminder to Sir Gawain of the perilous nature of the adventure he has just undertaken ("For woþe *[danger]* þat þou ne wonde *[neglect]* / þis auenture for to frayn," 488-89).

Fitt II. The second part of the poem opens with a brief but highly significant and memorable *descriptio* of the passing of the seasons from early spring until Michaelmas ("Meȝelmas mone," 532), and the following All Hallows ("Al-hal-day," 536), when the action is resumed. The pattern of the flow of the natural seasons, with its fluctuation between good and bad times, growths and declines of life until "wynter wyndez aȝayn, as þe worlde askez" (530), is a reiteration of the principle of cyclicity of life oscillating between "blysse and blunder" (18) on which the temporal structure of the entire poem is built. The passing reference to Michaelmas (29 September) is particularly important in the context of Gawain's story, as the feast coincides astronomically with the autumn equinox, which together with the other solsticial feasts of the Annunciation (25 March), St John's Day (24 June), and the Nativity (25 December), belong to the "quarter days." One of the practical significances of these feasts in the Middle Ages was that financial accounts were settled and rents were paid on these days, especially on Michaelmas, which marked the end of the fiscal year and the deadline for reconciling all debts and dues.[37] The mention of Michaelmas in the poem (532) is thus a reminder for Sir Gawain of his "wynter wage" (533)—that is, his pledge with the Green Knight that will have to be fulfilled after an "anious uyage" (535). Nor is the character of the saint without relevance to the heroic nature of Gawain's adventure; the Archangel Michael, one of the patron saints of chivalry, was traditionally famed for having overcome Satan, pictured as the dragon in the Revelation (12:7-9), and Sir Gawain too has to fight with "wormez" *(dragons)* (720) in the wilderness of North Wales.

The resumption of the story on All Saints' Day (1 November), another important feast in the Church's calendar[38] and one which celebrates the dead, sets a sorrowful and funereal atmosphere at the outset of Gawain's journey in search of the Green Chapel. Despite "much reuel and ryche of þe Rounde Table" (538) on that day for Sir Gawain's sake ("for þe frekez sake," 537), the mood is woeful ("þere watz much derue doel *[grievous lament]* driuen in þe sale / þat so worthe as Wawan schulde wende on þat ernde," 558-59), simply because Gawain is not expected to return alive from his perilous journey: "to dryȝe *(endure)* a delful dynt *(grievous blow)*, and dele no more wyth bronde *(sword)*" (560-61). Sir Gawain's departure from Camelot and his solitary journey through North Wales cover the month of November and the period of Advent (starting 24 November), both times of the year laden with allegorical meaning. The period between the autumn equinox and the winter solstice is the "darkest" time in the year (the days being the shortest), and for purely practical reasons traveling in November was regarded in the Middle Ages as uncomfortable and dangerous.[39] For Christians Advent is also a time of penance, moral purification, and spiritual preparation for the coming of Christ.[40] In the life of the Savior the four weeks preceding the Nativity correspond to the last phase of his gestation in Mary's womb as a preparation for his "death" for heaven, followed by his birth as a mortal man. On the traditional scale of the ages of life Advent and early winter coincide with old age, in its traditional characterization marked by a growing awareness of approaching death and filled with penitential thoughts. It is therefore in perfect accord with the seasonal and liturgical symbolisms that Sir Gawain's solitary journey through "þe Norþe Walez" (697) and "þe wyldrenesse of Wyrale" (701) be full of discomforts, privations, hardships, and dangers. The wintry journey is a traditional occasion for penance in medieval literature, just as it is also a journey "inward," a pilgrimage of the soul into the region of death located geographically in the north,[41] a descent into an underworld in the Danteian sense,[42] suggestive of spiritual combats with the temptations of the flesh.

The knight's journey through the wintry landcape devoid of life reaches its nadir on Christmas Eve, which marks the "lowest" point in the astronomical year, the day before the sun again begins to wax at midwinter. The thought of the Nativity of Christ ("þat syre, þat on þat self ny3t / Of a burde *[maid]* watz borne oure baret *[sorrow]* to quelle," 751-52), triggers both a complete reversal of mood in Gawain (from sorrow to pious hope, 751-63) and a sudden transformation of the bleak scenery into a splendid and somewhat otherworldly Castle of Hautdesert, where the troubled knight spends the holy time of Christmas. After the seasonal celebrations at Camelot at the beginning of the poem, the story has now come full circle, with the first phase of temptations of more physical and heroic nature prior to the arrival at Hautdesert now giving way to the more subtle and therefore more dangerous moral and psychological tests in the short period between Christmas and the New Year. For Gawain it is a time of increasing realization of his impending doom and a period of spiritual transition from the carefree adolescence of Arthur and Camelot that he left behind, to the age of maturity, sobriety, modest calm, and self-awareness, epitomized by Sir Bertilac and his household.

Fitt III. After a very compressed account of the seasons intervening between the New Year's Day and All Saints' Day, followed by a slightly less compact but still comparatively short description of Gawain's solitary peregrinations through North Wales, crowned by the knight's festive sojourn at Hautdesert at Christmas, Fitt III slows down the tempo of action even more to encompass a period of only three days following Christmas, that is, from Saint Thomas' Day (29 December) to New Year's Eve (31 December). In liturgical terms this part of the year directly follows the Nativity, symbolic of the spiritual *renovatio* of humanity, and covers the early infancy of Jesus, filled as it is in the Gospel with dangers and persecutions of the newborn.[43] In the playful and carefree Christmas atmosphere at Hautdesert Sir Gawain is maneuvered into entering a seemingly innocent game with the host, whereby each of them will return to the other their winnings from the day's hunt for three consecutive days covered by Fitt III. The liturgical period of the infancy and vulnerability of the baby Christ serves here as a background for Gawain's childlike innocence as well as his ignorance of the threats to his soul involved both in the game itself and in its connection with the sexual temptation in the bedroom scenes and with the beheading game.

The last days of the year also correspond to the last phase of human life, the "second childhood" of old age, with its maturing realization of approaching death and the necessity of penance and soul-cleansing. The anxiety about the impending doom at the Green Chapel compels Gawain to breach the covenant with Sir Bertilac by concealing from him the life-saving magic girdle, even though it is not until the very end of the poem that the full moral significance and consequence of this act are revealed to Sir Gawain. Throughout the story the knight remains ignorant of the true nature of his trials and temptations, but their outcome will nonetheless appear vital for his moral evaluation and, consequently, for his survival.

Fitt IV. New Year's Day has been defined earlier as an allegorical passage between two complete cycles of life, as a critical transition from one mode of existence to another, best expressed by means of imagery evoking "death-and-rebirth" symbolism. The resurrectional nature of events described in Fitt IV of *Sir Gawain* is prefigured by the opening lines, which depict the coming of day after dark night, as is bidden by God:

> Now ne3ez þe Nw 3ere, and þe ny3t passez,
> þe day dryuez to þe derk, as Dry3tyn biddez;

(1998-99)

The story has again come full circle after the "Nw 3er . . . nwe cummen" (60) the year before, and the following short description of the hardships of new winter once more reminds us of the insecurity of old age and the irrevocability of death:

> Bot wylde wederez of þe worlde wakned þeroute,
> Clowdes kesten kenly þe colde to þe erþe,
> Wyth ny3e (*ham*) innoghe of þe norþe, þe naked to tene;
> þe snawe snitered ful snart (*bitterly*), þat snayped þe wylde;
> þe werbelande wynde wapped fro þe hy3e,
> And drof vche dale ful of dryftes ful grete.

(2000-2005)

Again Sir Gawain has to leave the comfort and shelter of the castle and face his destiny on the day of his judgment ("God wyl me suffer / To dele on Nw 3erez day þe dome of my wyrdes," 1967-68). The ultimate trial assumes the form of an elaborate beheading ritual amid the infernal surroundings of the Green Chapel. As in the previous year, the Feast of the Circumcision provides an ecclesiological, resurrectional context for Gawain's symbolic "death" under the Green Knight's axe, with the "nick on the neck" analogous to the occasion when Christ shed his blood for the first time. The ritual is followed by a full confession of Gawain's sins, and a kind of "last judgment" at the hands of the now benevolent Green Knight, who points out the nature of both Gawain's guilt and his virtue and assesses his character accordingly. The received insight into the true nature of his being has a cleansing and regenerative effect on Gawain, who experiences his spiritual "rebirth" in an almost Paulian sense:

> þou art confessed so clene, beknowen of þy mysses,
> And hatz þe penaunce apert of þe poynt of myn egge,
> I halde þe polysed of þat ply3t, and pured as clene
> As þou hadez neuer forfeted syþen þou watz fyrst borne.

(2391-94)

The subsequent return and reintegration with the chivalric society of the Round Table completes the cycle of Gawain's adventures, but the question of Camelot's reception and assimilation of Gawain's newly acquired spiritual maturity remains open: the confusion and ambiguity about the nature and meaning of the green girdle, now adopted by the Round Table as a badge of honor, may point to the misunderstanding of the spiritual message of Gawain's adventure by the chivalric community. Either unable or unwilling to accept the complex moral truth signified by the girdle, Camelot seems to remain as immature as before, and Gawain's adventure turns out to be an individual and incommunicable experience, affecting no one but himself.

The Spiral of Life

So far I have been analyzing the cyclical development of action in *Sir Gawain* within the large mutually inclusive and interrelated cycles of Britain's mythico-history, the seasonal and calendar time, the liturgical year, and the phases of the human life. The poem's plot itself also follows a circular motion both in space and time by beginning and ending at Camelot on New Year's Day, according to the poem's overall regulating structural principle of cyclicity. However, at closer scrutiny the story, complete in its roundness as it is, appears to consist of a number of smaller circular units of varying size when measured by calendar time, and the same pattern of repeated oscillation between the life's ups and downs that governs the structure of the poem as a whole seems also valid for its constituent parts. The principle of oscillation that characterizes the structure of the successive episodes of the Gawain story requires—theoretically speaking— both a pair of opposing elements and an alternating movement between these opposites. Before the whole idea is tested against textual evidence, let us, purely theoretically, call these opposing elements "Culture" and "Nature" and define them in respect to *Sir Gawain* in the following way:

Culture. This realm comprises a system of values and modes of behavior characteristic of the courtly and chivalric milieu; the world of aristocratic refinement of manners and the knightly ethos that combines the Christian ideal with feudal military activity, represented in *Sir Gawain* by King Arthur's Camelot and Sir Bertilac's Castle of Hautdesert;

Nature. By contrast, nature embraces forces and phenomena that originate and operate in the realm beyond culture as opposed to it: for example, magic as opposed to institutionalized and official religion; wilderness as contrasted with human habitations; chaos as different from social and divine order; the supernatural versus the natural; the alien versus the familiar; the unconscious and its forces as opposed to the waking, conscious mind; or the body and its powers as set against the mind and soul. In short, nature complements culture as shadow complements light to form the whole of reality, and in *Sir Gawain* this other, complementary side of things is represented topographically by the wilderness of North Wales, and the bleak surroundings of the Green Chapel.

Throughout the entire story the strain of action constantly shifts between these two realms in a series of repeated descending and ascending movements, as Sir Gawain's adventures and chivalric tests unfold—a feature that ensures a kind of dynamic balance between culture and nature in the poem. The periodic interplay between these realms, placed within the dimension of linear time that characterizes a simple flow of the story in *Sir Gawain*, can be shown in a following schema:

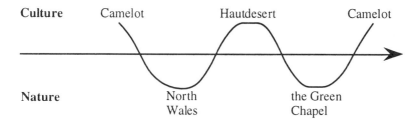

Fig. 5. The Sinuous Development of the Story in *Sir Gawain*.

From this perspective Sir Gawain appears, albeit unknowingly, as a mediator between the domains of culture and nature, acting on behalf of culture (Camelot), just as the Green Knight alias Sir Bertilac emerges at the end of poem as a go-between (and a conscious one) between the two realms, at first acting on behalf of nature as the Green Knight. As the story unfolds Sir Gawain's alternating movement between culture and nature relies on periodical exposures to the forces of the unknown and subsequent reintegrations with civilization; the process suggests a tendency within the poem towards ultimate unification of the two domains and the correspondiong reconciliation of the opposites of the human condition. For example, the parallelism of action and the interconnections between the hunting and bedroom scenes in Fitt III, representing nature and culture respectively; the final merger of the Green Knight with Sir Bertilac at the Green Chapel; and the partial assimilation of Gawain's adventure by Camelot in their adoption of the green girdle, may all be seen as structural indications of the intended synthesis of culture and nature in *Sir Gawain*, or at least of a tendency in that direction. I will analyze this idea more closely in later chapters, but here let me note what appears to be a general principle responsible for the internal equilibrium of the poem's structure: namely, that Sir Gawain's yearly sequence of adventures reflects, as the above sinuous diagram shows, the oscillation between the opposing realms of culture and nature, possibly leading towards some sort of unity of the two.

It could be observed here that the opposition and periodic interplay between culture and nature have of course a universal character in human culture and are especially present in the type of experiences involved in the traditional rites of passage, where the conflict between these two spheres of existence asserts the essential paradox of human life. The duality of the human condition consists in that as nature dictates the fundamental components of man's existence: birth, reproduction, and death, so culture determines the ways in which man manipulates and modifies these biological imperatives.[44] The universal human phenomenon of the rites of passage, understood as a decisive transition between two qualitatively different existential phases of life, embodies this paradox of human existence, suspended between the borders of nature and culture. In actual terms, the passage between the two realms is ensured by ceremonies and rituals that occur at specific times and places, and this general anthropological observation holds true for the story of Sir Gawain, which likewise signals the dominance of the nature/culture dichotomy and recounts, structurally, "the title hero's rite of passage into warriordom within the context of the nature:culture conflict."[45]

Simple and clear as is the above schema of the opposition between culture and nature in the Gawain story, in its general form it fails, however, to take account of the following important features of the poem's structure:

1. First and foremost I have already observed that both spatially and temporally Sir Gawain's wanderings describe a circle, and not merely a sinuous line;

2. Moreover, the periods of the consecutive windings in the shifts between culture and nature differ in length as the story progresses, the principle being that of fairly regularly decreasing time-intervals between the successive episodes;

3. Despite its circularity the story's end is *not* the same as its beginning because Sir Gawain's perception of himself and Camelot is different at the end of his adventure. The knight's tests bring about the hightening of his moral sensitivity both in relation to himself and towards chivalry and its duties, an understanding that sets Gawain at odds with the view of chivalry still evinced by the rest of the knights of the Round Table.

Considering the above important aspects of the poem's temporal structure, let us modify the earlier presented sinuous schema by introducing a more lucid and effective way of describing the internal dynamic structure of *Sir Gawain,* one that takes into account both the dimensions of place and time, the varying lengths of the successive episodes, and Gawain's point of arrival as distinct from his point of departure. What is needed is a formula that combines both the linear and the circular movements into a formally integrated whole; mathematically, a schema that meets these requirements is a spiral.

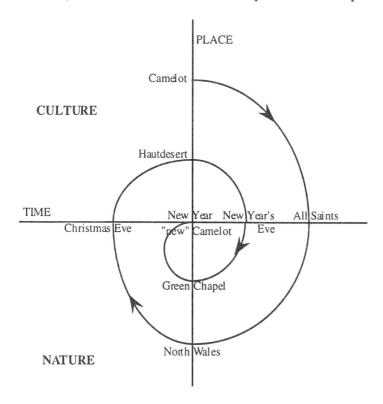

Fig. 6.   The Spiral Time-Flow of Action in *Sir   Gawain.*

Accordingly, a revised and more adequate representation of the dynamic temporal structure of *Sir Gawain* is shown in the spiral diagram (fig. 6). The diagram illustrates the winding flow of the story with its consecutive episodes alternating between culture and nature, as the curve of continuous time goes around in a series of descending and ascending movements describing a spiral. The intersections of the curve with the horizontal axis of Time mark the crucial moments of the calendar year at which Gawain's transitions between the realms of culture and nature occur. On the other hand, the intersections of the spiral with the vertical axis of Place indicate locations where these transitions take place. Consequently, the upper part of the diagram contains locations of episodes occurring in the realm of culture (Camelot, Hautdesert), while the lower part of the diagram describes loci belonging to what has been defined as nature (the Wilderness of North Wales, the Green Chapel). The constant interplay between the two domains as Sir Gawain's adventures unfold is visualized in the repeated cyclic movements of descent towards nature (the right-hand side of the diagram), and of the following ascent towards culture (the left-hand side of the diagram).

As is the nature of the mathematical spiral, the curve is divided into a number of ever-shortening arcs, which correspond here to the decreasing time intervals between the consecutive episodes of the story. Neither a simple circle nor a sinusoid produce such an effect. It is enough to look at the calendar of events happening in the poem to see that what governs their duration is the operative rule of the progressively diminishing time intervals. Let us only consider the following data:

—the duration of Gawain's sojourn at Camelot from 1 January to 1 November is 308 calendar days (the period covered by the description of the progress of the seasons at the beginning of Fitt II);

—the length of Gawain's wintry journey from 2 November to 24 December is 54 days (the rest of Fitt II);

—Gawain's subsequent Christmas sojourn at the Castle of Hautdesert from 25 to 31 December, split between Christmas celebrations proper (end of Fitt II) and the following three days of hunting and temptation (Fitt III), lasted 7 days;

—and the final showdown at the Green Chapel (Fitt IV) occurred on one day (1 January), much in the same fashion as the initial dramatic encounter with the Green Knight at Camelot (Fitt I).

This simple calculation of the calendar duration of the successive episodes in *Sir Gawain* gives us the following series of numbers: 308, 54, 7, 1, which diminish at similar ratios:

$$308 \div 54 = 5.7 \qquad 54 \div 7 = 7.7 \qquad 7 \div 1 = 7$$

The obtained quotients are of course unequal, but they are comparable, and remain within the same order of magnitude, circling around the average of 6.8. Equal figures in each ratio are by no means necessary, because what matters in the time structure of *Sir Gawain* is not mathematical precision for its own sake (after all, we are dealing with a work of literature and not with a physical mechanism) but the reader's *perception* of the time flow organizing the events in the story according to the principle of progressively diminishing intervals.

Besides taking account of this important feature of the story's temporal structure, the spiral diagram reveals an even more important characteristic: namely, the earlier signaled distinction between Gawain's point of departure and his ultimate point of arrival. From the perspective of the knight's spiritual journey from ignorance and complacency, through humility and penance, to renewed spiritual integrity and maturity,[46] the beginning of the adventure is of course not the same for Gawain as its end. This seems to be true despite the conclusion of the story at the same Camelot of King Arthur, the place that seems to remain both unchanged during the course of Gawain's adventure and unaffected by it at the end. First Sir Gawain leaves Camelot, the symbol of chivalric civilization with its noble values and ideals, a kind of medieval aristocratic paradise, then undergoes his tests, gains self-knowledge as a result, and finally returns to Camelot a different man, perfected through his fall and humiliation, probably only now worthy of being a Christian knight, a position he represented only nominally prior to his adventure. The "old" Camelot, with its rash and "childgered" Arthur and convivial but complacent knights of the Round Table, is left behind by Sir Gawain as inferior to what might have been a "new" Camelot, filled with people like Gawain and representing chivalry that is spiritually and morally renewed and more mature. But the blithe and lighthearted reaction of both Arthur and the court to the account of Gawain's adventure shows their complete misunderstanding of the spiritual meaning of the quest, and in adopting the green girdle, the sign of Gawain's sin and disgrace, as their badge of honor, the knights turn the significance of Gawain's message topsy-turvy, shutting their eyes to any possibility of moral and spiritual improvement. In doing so they also forestall any possible constructive criticism of their own behavior and avoid the whole issue by turning Gawain's ordeal into a joke ("Laȝen loude þerat," 2514), misinterpreting it as a proof that no one, not even the "gode Gawan" (109), the best of them, is capable of perfection. In this way King Arthur's "old" Camelot and Sir Gawain's would-be "new" Camelot fall apart, since the newly acquired spiritual maturity of the latter no longer matches the ordinary moral standards and expectations of the former. Instead of properly confessing their faults, as Gawain did, and proceeding on the penitential path of redemption, the knights at Camelot fall back upon their former ways and "run backwards," failing to absorb Gawain's lesson. The spiral diagram shows this incongruity very clearly: the postulated Camelot of spiritually regenerated chivalry exemplified by Sir Gawain, a kind of "New Jerusalem" of knightly civilization, is situated at the very center of the diagram, at the zero point existing beyond time, space, and history, denoting a state that is as desirable and ideal, as it is probably unattainable and therefore unreal.

Sir Gawain's individual sense of the radical change in his own character and, consequently, in the character of chivalry he represents, introduces us to a larger problem of psychological subjectivity in the perception of events described in the poem. The varying intensity with which different episodes can be perceived by the reader is borne out by various features, among them the textual space allotted to the episodes. The spiral in figure 6 as it stands describes the objective flow of calendar time, the duration of episodes measured in natural, or "divine" time, determined by the passage of the seasons, the movements of heavenly bodies, and finally by God's Providence. But the subjective, psychological time, measured by individually perceived intensity rather than factual duration, is different, and depends on mental and emotional states attached to particular moments or periods. One of the indicators of the psychological intensity of certain times in the poem is textual space; that is, simply, the number of lines (or stanzas) allotted by the author to given episodes. It is not difficult to see that this variable is subject to considerable changes in the poem, by no means following proportionately the amount of objective, calendar time covered by the episodes. The questions justifiably arise then: is there any regularity in the expression of subjective time in the poem, and what are (if any) the relationships between the two kinds of time, the psychological and the objective?

To check this, let us simply compare the number of calendar days from the consecutive episodes of *Sir Gawain* with the number of lines of text describing these episodes. What emerges is the numerical arrangement shown in table 4. As can be seen, far from being congruent with the flow of calendar time the subjective perception of the intensity of certain moments and periods appears inversely proportional to their actual duration, or at least depends on other factors than "objective" time. For example, the most critical scenes of the story, the two parts of the Beheading Game, each happen on one day only, and at the same time each is covered by an entire Fitt of approximately five hundred lines of textual space. On the other hand, the famous description of the round of the seasons occupying about four-fifths of the whole calendar year is economically packed in two stanzas covering thirty seven lines only, showing that the period of expectation and relatively carefree "putting off" of the fatal tryst passes quickly. In addition, another important day in Sir Gawain's spiritual calendar, the feast of All Saints', the day of the knight's elaborate leave-taking, dressing up (with the famous pentangle passage), and bidding farewell to the familiar and

Table 4

Calendar and Psychological Time in *Sir Gawain*

Calendar Time (measured in days)		Psychological Time (measured in lines of text)	
New Year's Day at Camelot	1	453	ll. 37-490
January—1 November	308	37	ll. 498-535
All Saints' Day at Camelot	1	150	ll. 536-686
2 November—24 December (Gawain's journey)	54	71	ll. 691-762
Christmas at Hautdesert	4	362	ll. 763-1125
Hunting/Temptation	3	871	ll. 1126-997
New Year's Day at the Green Chapel	1	527	ll. 1998-2525

secure world, is again extended to as many as 150 lines, proportionately to its significance as a caesura separating two distinct periods of Gawain's quest. The psychological time is again diluted when almost two months of Gawain's peregrinations through the wilderness are compressed in as few as seventy one lines, indicating the rapidity of the time passing amid rather conventional heroic actions and adventures.[47] Perceived time gradually intensifies yet again during the last week of the year, directly preceding the final encounter at the Green Chapel, when the four days of Gawain's Christmas sojourn at Hautdesert are covered by 362 lines, and the three crucial days of the knight's temptation in Fitt III are decribed in as many as 871 lines. The rapidly growing textual space as the time intervals between the later episodes get shorter and shorter builds up tremendous psychic tension, with the torturous crawl of perceived time drawing inexorably towards the main event. The final "execution" too, at first thought by Gawain to last as little as it takes to deal "on *(one)* strok" (2252), turns out to be an elaborate ritual of almost annoying duration described in seventy eight lines (2252-330) to intensify the extremity of the knight's ordeal.

If the amount of textual space and authorial attention to certain elements of the story is indicative of their importance, as appears to be the case, then the handling of psychological time in *Sir Gawain* should teach its audience the following things:

A. The first most important event in the human life is one's birth (which is understandable enough), described allegorically in Fitt I as Sir Gawain's "birth" into manhood and his realization of the mortality of the human condition, as he entered the consequential bargain with the Green Knight;

B. At the other end another important moment in life is one's death (again fairly obvious), understood, however, not as a momentary event terminating one's life, but as a process of extreme mental and physical suffering and anguish;

C. What is maybe even more important than death itself is a period of mature life directly preceding death, filled with moral and psychological tests, seen as a preparation to face the ultimate destiny with conscious self-determination;

D. All the rest—that is, the period between birth and maturity, no matter how long it would last in terms of actual duration—is a relatively insignificant time of the gestation of consciousness in preparation for the acceptance of death as part of the human game, as well as for death itself.

What finally emerges from this overall view of the temporal structure of *Sir Gawain* are basically two kinds of time scales used in the framework of the narrative: one referring to objective, or divine, time, physically manifest as the flow of calendar days, determined by the revolution of the heavenly sphere; and the other of subjective, psychological nature, whose pace depends on individually perceived density and intensity of the moment. The objective temporal dimension of the poem is expressed in the numbers of days allotted to particular events, while the subjective time scale is reflected in terms of textual space as a measure of importance attached to these events by the author. With these two time scales in mind, one can visualize the former as the earlier-presented centripetal spiral of the simple flow of the story (fig. 6), illustrating the progressively shortening time intervals between the described episodes, and the latter as an opposite, centrifugal spiral, expanding outwards along the ever-increasing arcs that reflect the rising intensity of the psychological time. It is the complementary coexistence of these two kinds of time that determines the nature of the overall temporal structure of *Sir Gawain* and adds greatly to the formal and intellectual sophistication of this exceptional narrative.

These two main dimensions of time, the objective and the subjective, are ingeniously combined by the poet into what is perceived by the reader as a harmonious artistic whole of a well-structured poem. Of course, the spiral as a mathematical formula is only an approximation of the general tendency and perceived regularity in the passage of time in *Sir Gawain,* and it is not by any means an exact quantitative representation of the temporal reality exhibited in the poem. *Sir Gawain* remains first of all a work of art, a creation of a poet of the highest caliber that in the end resists formalisms such as the devised spiral chiefly because as a literary work the poem appeals more to the reader's imagination and emotions than to his or her rational faculty. But the discovered structural patterns are there all the same and are perceived by the reader, often in a semiconscious way, as a sense of exceptional harmony, balance, and truth, emanating from the text as the reader allows him- or herself to be absorbed in Sir Gawain's spiritual adventure and moral dilemma. The knight's quest along the line of symbolic events and places brings to the reader's mind those moments of life that are crucial and decisive from the point of view of the absolute, divine reality and its demands. The periodic recurrence of analogous places and situations in life, involving fairly typical and universal moral tests and equally typical human behavior and response, also reminds the reader of the repetitiveness and circularity of life on individual, social, historical, natural, and cosmic levels. The main protagonist of *Sir Gawain* is first of all a paragon of medieval chivalry and its historically determined values, but he is also an archetype of a human being, an Everyman, whose life is synchronized and regulated by the larger rhythms of culture, the natural seasons, and the sacred calendar of religion, against which he projects his individual though fairly typical human dilemma. All these manifold systems of reference are fused together and unified in *Sir Gawain* with exceptional and superb artistic mastery, giving us a rare example of a poetic synthesis of certain vital concepts regarding man and his place in the world.

3

The Greenness of the Green Knight

The problem raised in the title of this chapter belongs to those obvious and self-imposing critical issues that arise for anyone who has even once read *Sir Gawain*, as indeed are most of the problems that constitute the subject matter of this book. The Green Knight's color and its meaning first became an issue for the early scholars of *Sir Gawain*,[1] and the matter is now considered more or less resolved, at least in its essentials. The sharply decreasing frequency with which the problem of greenness in *Sir Gawain* has been addressed in the last two decades or so might suggest that the file has been closed, and there seems to be a silent consensus among the more recent critics that there is little or nothing to add to the existing interpretations.[2] These generally view the Green Knight's major external characteristic either as a reflection of old Celtic fairy lore or as a popular feature of the devil or both, or else as an incarnation of God, none of these (it is assumed) bearing substantially upon the meaning of the poem composed in a late medieval courtly milieu. Far from regarding green as "just" a fairy color[3] or linking it solely with medieval popular notions about the devil's occasional appearance, thus dismissing the problem as marginal and more concerned with the cultural antecedents of the Green Knight's figure than with the actual role he plays in the poem, in this reappraisal I seek to move considerations on color in *Sir Gawain* into the center of the poem's gravity by showing that the color imagery in a very important way complements and underpins the poem's meaning(s), established by other literary features, such as the overall structure of the narrative.

The following discussion rests of course on the assumption that references to colors in a literary text "mean" something: that is, that they have a semantic and not only a decorative value. This premise is especially valid in the case of traditional narratives such as *Sir Gawain*, employing as they do mythological, fantastic elements of undoubted if often obscure symbolic significance. Color symbolism in general tends to be rather elusive and ambiguous; that is, the imaginative associations stirred by particular color attributes can often be contradictory (or should we say complementary), as is usually the case with traditional symbols. However, no holistic view of *Sir Gawain* can overlook this important aspect of the narrative, and even the absence of a definite, clear-cut meaning of the employed color imagery does not in itself invalidate its positive semantic value. One is once more reminded of the necessity to think of traditional symbols in inclusive, rather than exclusive terms, and to analyze the elusive artistic reality in all its complexity.

þe grene gome

The context of the appearance of the Green Knight in the story is too well known to require reiteration. The figure looms large at the beginning of the poem, threatening the astounded knights gathered for the Christmas feast with its sudden, unexpected arrival, imposing stature, and—not least—with its unusual color, for the knight is "oueral enker-grene" (150), that is, "bright green." The disclosure of this most conspicuous and important characteristic is, however, postponed by the poet until the end of the first stanza describing the appearance of the Christmas visitor: first we learn that he is "an aghlich mayster" (136)—that is, a "terrible" knight, one of the largest on earth in size (137), indeed, "half etayn (*giant*) in erde" (140), due to "his lyndes and his lymes so longe and so grete" (139). But he is not a monster: his parts are well proportioned and his looks are handsome ("myriest," 142; "alle his fetures . . . ful clene," 145-46), the fact suggesting that he partook—despite his color—to some degree of the human nature, and of the elegant and gracious kind at that.[4]

The description of the Green Knight is superbly handled by the poet in that the figure's most visible and astonishing feature, his greenness, comes as something of a shock to the reader in the last line of the first stanza devoted to him, after what looks like a picture of an ordinary and "natural" man, if of somewhat exaggerated proportions. The following three long stanzas (151-231) are probably unrivaled in medieval literature as far as meticulousness, attention to detail, and precision of description are concerned. This impressive *descriptio personae* gives us the minutiae of the Green Knight's clothes and gear, item by item (151-74), then his horse and trappings, in like fashion (175-98), and finally "a holyn bobbe" and a fearsome axe that he was holding in his hands, the latter again described in a very detailed way (202-23), to complete the picture. However, the feature that links the Green Knight's whole attire, his accoutrements and the horse's trappings is, of course, their green color, and this is accordingly given due prominence in the description, to the extent that the reader is not allowed to lose sight of the visitor's uncanny hue even for the space of one line. The word *grene* or its equivalents[5] are mentioned about twenty-five times in the passage, in addition to at least three general statements repeatedly making it clear that the Christmas visitor in Camelot was green *all over*, his hair included (180-81).[6] The color applies likewise to the Green Knight's horse ("A grene hors gret and þikke," 175), and— very importantly—to the two objects that the man was holding in his hands: a holly bough, "þat is grattest in grene when greuez ar bare" (207), and an axe, "hoge and vnmete *(monstrous)"* (208), with a blade of "grene stele and of golde hewen" (211), and with a handle "al bigrauen with grene in gracios werkes" (216).

This imposing *descriptio personae* is not monochrome, however, for the clothes and trappings of the Green Knight have golden finish, and that is another semantically important fact worth bearing in mind. The man's spurs were "of bry3t golde" (159), the birds and butterflies embroidered on the silk covering the knight's body had ornamentation "of grene, þe golde ay inmyddes" (167). The horse's mane and forelock also were plaited with "fildore" (189)—that is, *fil d'or,* a golden thread, so that golden and green strands were twisted together: "ay a herle *(strand)* of þe *[green]* here, an oþer of golde" (190). In addition to that the horse had "mony bellez ful bry3t of brende golde" (195) ringing about him as he moved, and the fearsome axe was likewise made of "grene stele and of golde" (211). The word *golde* or its equivalents are mentioned nine times in the passage,[7] against twenty-five or so references to green, which establishes a color combination in just this proportion (predominance of green with a marked admixture of gold) that is of paramount importance for the symbolic role and function played by the Green Knight in the Gawain story, as well as for Sir Gawain himself and the character of his adventure.

Green Color and Its Perception

The adduced textual evidence from *Sir Gawain* (and it is only a part of it) with regard to the color green is too overwhelming in its effect to be dismissed as a mere descriptive ornament or simply as an authorial attempt to "impress" the reader through an unusual and uncanny association of a human figure with a "nonhuman" color. Not that this first impression is unimportant, because it is significant, but as a literary side effect rather than the author's primary intention. And what the author may have intended in this descriptive tour de force can be deduced from the reaction to the Green Knight's appearance on the part of the audience at Camelot; this highly dramatic scene suggests much about the direction in which one should seek the possible significances of the color green and its bearer.

The knights of romance tradition (King Arthur included) are generally accustomed to confronting and fighting all sorts of giants and monsters, often of fantastic, supernatural character, to say nothing of ordinary human foes, as this is simply a prerequisite of the genre. The *Gawain*-poet himself does not fail to mention later in the poem the "wormez" (dragons), "wolues," "wodwos" (satyrs), "bullez and berez, and borez oþerquyle," as well as "etaynez" (giants) (720-23), that Sir Gawain has to cope with on his solitary journey through North Wales. The passing and cursory manner with which the poet lists these monstrous creatures clearly suggests their conventional character as stock-in-trade elements of a story of chivalric adventure. From the point of view of the romance knights' usual fighting habits there is therefore nothing extraordinary in the Green Knight's big stature and bold behavior, nor in his formidable axe, and it is consequently not these expected aspects of his appearance that come as a real shock to the knights of the Round Table gathered for the Christmas feast. What virtually stupefies and paralyzes them is first of all the visitor's dazzling greenness,[8] and the text is quite unambiguous about this powerful effect of the figure in green on the audience. The knights were staring "on lenþe" at the stranger, trying to figure out

> quat hit mene myʒt
> þat a haþel and a horse myʒt such a hwe lach,
> As growe grene as þe gres and grener hit semed,
> þen grene aumayl on golde glowande bryʒter.

(233-36)

As true knights of romance, many marvels had they seen, "bot such neuer are *(before)"* (239), and it is strange to note that a basically human creature, save his green color glistening with gold here and there, should be a greater "selly" (wonder) than, say, dragons or other monsters. Apparently on account of the visitor's greenness alone did "þe folk þere" classify him as "fantoum and fayryʒe" (240), that is, an apparition from the fairy world, and a supernatural being.[9] And it is the sudden realization that they are dealing with an otherwordly creature that casts the knights in a kind of stupor, very effectively rendered in the text by an accumulation of *s*-sounding words running for as many as three alliterative lines, creating an overwhelming sense of stony silence and sleepy passivity at the sight of the knight in green:

> And al stounded at his steuen and stonstil seten
> In a swoghe sylence þurȝ þe sale riche;
> As al were slypped vpon slepe so slaked hor lotez
> in hyȝe.

(242-45)

But how is this hypnotic and stupefying effect made by the green creature on Arthur's court actually to be accounted for? Does it have to do with the color itself or with its combination with the human figure? To address these questions it seems necessary first of all to discuss the physical nature of greenness and its perception as an objective basis against which to assess the particular use of the color in a literary text. In my opinion no analysis of what colors symbolically "mean" in art or literature can proceed without first specifying their physical characteristics because these determine or at least largely modify the color perception and the nature of possible imaginative associations stirred by the colors in the observer.

To begin, in the spectrum of white light dispersed by a prism green occupies an interesting middle wavelength position and is situated between blue and yellow—a fact easily observable in a rainbow or crystal and recorded, for example, by Aristotle in his *Meteorologia* (3: 2-4). As a midband of the spectrum, green carries the greatest amount of energy contained in sunlight, and for this reason it is rejected by chlorophyll, the green pigment in vegetable cells that traps the energy of sunlight for photosynthesis, because it is too powerful and therefore dangerous to living vegetable tissues. Paradoxically then, it is because plants do *not* assimilate the green band of the spectrum that the vegetable world reveals itself to our eyes as green. The color is thus objectively pernicious to the processes of plant life, although subjectively, in terms of color perception, it is *the* color of natural life and vegetation. It is impossible (unless one is color-blind) to miss an easily observable fact that green, particularly bright, fresh green, is a dominant hue of the natural environment, chiefly of grass, foliage, and vegetation. On the other hand, deep, dark, and "moist" green is a color of natural water reservoirs, such as lakes, rivers, or seas and—not infrequently—of putrefying organic remains, this time both vegetable and animal.

Apart from decomposing plants or flesh, a pale, livid, sickly, or dead human body—especially the face—may occasionally reveal a greenish hue, a fact usually evoking negative emotions such as disgust or irrational fear. This reaction occurs not only because greenish complexion indicates disease or death: it is because green as the color of vegetation is by its very nature alien to the animal and human kingdoms, since chlorophyll is absent in animal cells. And it is this biological fact, together with certain perceptual and partly unconscious expectations connected with it, that to some extent explain the effect of utter surprise and wonder on the part of Arthur's court on the sudden appearance of the knight in green. It was not so much the man's stupendous size or the threatening weapon in his hand (both very much expected in the world of romance) that caused this irrational and inexplicable fear in the assembled knights; it was above all the instinctive and incomprehensible realization that greenness, the color of the vegetable world, is here for some strange and unknown reason attributed as a generically alien feature to an otherwise "human" personage. This is why the visitor is promptly labeled as "fantoum and fayry3e," a strange, nonhuman being despite his looks, an otherwordly creature, and as such arousing feelings of instinctive, irrational terror like the "Martians" or "green people from outer space" of modern science fiction literature and film—creatures that belong to a different order of things and are almost always hostile and death-bearing to humans.[10]

For the medieval audience, therefore, the immediate effect and significance of the color green may have been as follows: in respect of the external natural environment the color would have been perceptually and therefore subjectively associated both with vegetation—that is, with natural processes of life—and to a smaller degree with the inevitable processes of decay and decomposition following the death of an organism, vegetable and animal alike. The natural phenomena denoted by greenness would generally have been associated with the elements of water and earth: the former both as a life-supporting and dissolving element and the latter as a domain in which the vegetable, animal, and human organisms are "born," and where they ultimately "return" after their death, figuratively speaking. The possible symbolic connotations of the color emerge therefore as ambiguous, by no means limited, as may superficially seem, to the generally positive associations with life and growth. The greenness can thus encompass the totality of life processes occurring in nature, viewed as a never-ending cycle of birth-growth-death-decay-rebirth associated with the elemental forces of water and earth.

This eternal cycle of life is naturally synchronized with the annual rhythm of the seasons, which again incorporates the smaller life-cycles of plants, animals, and people with their societies, and ensures—despite the death of individual organisms—the generic continuity of life. This is another way of saying that the color green may in certain contexts denote such ideas as resurrection after death or immortality, in addition to the basic complex of meaning associated with natural life, nature at large, the element of earth, and further, figuratively: corporeality, flesh, sin, death, and so on.

Unsurprisingly, these common perceptions associated with greenness are borne out by linguistic evidence, as for example in the semantic field of the Middle English word *grene,* used so many times in *Sir Gawain.* The *MED* lists accordingly the following classes of meaning for this word (as an adjective), given below in order of frequency of occurrence (together with the number of listed occurrences in medieval sources):

1. leafy, grassy, covered with green grass;	30
2. of plants: alive, vigorous, also fig.;	23
3. of skin or complexion: pale, colorless, livid;	15
4. of fruit and vegetables: unripe, immature, sour;	13
5. of wound or pain: recent, unhealed, bitter;	13
6. of a plant or wood: freshly cut;	12
7. of persons: young, immature, inexperienced, rash;	10
8. of persons: suggestive of envy and ill feeling;	3

The existing semantic scatter of the word *grene* well illustrates both the inherent ambiguity of greenness and the sphere of phenomena it denotes. Categories 1, 2, 4, and 7 cover the *positive* aspect of greenness, associated with life, growth, and vigor, occupying seventy six listed occurrences of the word—64 percent of the total. On the other hand, the remaining categories 3, 5, 6, and 8 cover the *negative* aspects of greenness, connected with sickness, death, wounds, pain, and ill feeling and include forty three occurrences (36 percent), roughly half the number of textual loci illustrating the positive meaning of *grene.* This simple survey confirms first of all the semantic ambivalence of greenness, by no means suggesting a one-sided connection with the processes of life and growth, and also that the positive aspect of greenness, although counterbalanced by the negative associations with the lack of life and so on, nonetheless clearly prevails in the overall semantic field covered by the word *grene.*

Now how does this semantic ambivalence of greenness apply to the Green Knight? The weird and unexpected attribution of green to an otherwise human figure, a circumstance already pointed out, determines the character's "unnatural" aura, in addition to the equally uncanny, miraculous, and supernatural capability of surviving decapitation later in the scene (430-36). But in the Christian world, where life is conceived as a battleground between the principles of good and evil and the spiritual powers standing behind them, the supernatural can either be of heavenly, divine nature, or else of infernal, devilish provenance. Justifiably then the question arises as to where the visitor in green from *Sir Gawain* originally comes from, and how is greenness to be reconciled with his domain. My working hypothesis, to be tested against further textual evidence from *Sir Gawain* as well as from other sources, is that the Green Knight embodies comprehensively features of *all* worlds, including heaven and the underworld, natural and human, himself transcending and unifying these spheres into a complex image that comprises the totality of existential experience. Due to the all-encompassing nature of greenness it can be postulated that the Green Knight is neither solely a "fairy" nor the "devil" nor a "courtly figure"[11] nor even "Christ"[12]; he is a personified synthesis of all these, uniting in himself the negative, fiendish elements associated with the underworld; death and decay; the elements of nature and the cyclicity of life processes; human, worldy affairs through his involvement in courtly and chivalric civilization; and finally the divine, heavenly forces that act upon the lower regions ensuring the continuity of life through the possibility of rebirth. There is ample evidence both within *Sir Gawain* and in other medieval sources to support this unified and holistic picture of the Green Knight, and in almost each of the distinguished aspects of the figure greenness plays an important symbolic role.

The Branch of Holly

The equivocality of the Green Knight and his color is reinforced by the significance of the two objects ascribed to him in the text: a branch of holly and an axe. The man himself refers to the holly bough as a sign of peace: "ȝe may be seker bi þis braunch þat I bere here / þat I passe as in pes, and no plyȝt seche" (265-66). However, his arrogant behavior, the challenge of the Beheading Game, and the potentially fatal consequences of it for the participants all seem to suggest a different meaning of this "sign of peace." The textual context in which holly appears also evokes rather unpleasant, if not altogether sinister associations; the reference is preceded by a neg-

ative description of the Green Knight's armor and weapons, or
rather their absence:

> Wheþer hade he *no* helme *ne* hawbergh *nauþer,*
> *Ne no* pysan *ne no* plate þat pented to armes,
> *Ne no* schafte *ne no* schelde to schwue *ne* to smyte . . .
>
> (202-205, italics added)

The amassment of negatives is directly followed by a juxtaposing
conjunctive *bot,* which introduces "a holyn bobbe, / þat is grattest in
grene when greuez ar bare" (206-7). This suggests that although the
Green Knight is factually unarmed as far as the usual chivalric
weapons are concerned (he left them at home, 268-70), he has
nonetheless a holly bough in his one hand (apparently some kind of
weapon), to say nothing of the formidable axe in the other. It is
interesting to note here that in the pre-Christian context holly was
usually associated with violent death; for example, the references to
the plant in early Irish heroic sagas well illustrate the rather grim
connotations of holly.[13] In modern Welsh folklore we also find a
superstition that holly brought into a house meant death in the family
in the following year.[14] These unequivocally sinister traditional connotations were, however, mitigated in the course of time by Christianity, which readily incorporated the plant into the sphere of its
symbols, mainly by linking it with the figure of the Savior. The association was facilitated by the analogy between holly's prickly
leaves and Christ's crown of thorns,[15] between its white flowers and
red berries and the Redeemer's innocence, purity, and blood of the
Passion, respectively, and—not least—between the plant's visible
evergreenness and Christ's resurrection and immortality. Holly is a
"holy" plant *par excellence,* as such epitomizing the essence of the
christological experience understood as a voluntary or undeserved
self-sacrifice to suffering and death, followed by a resurrection.[16]
The "holyn bobbe" held in the Green Knight's hand on the New
Year's Day, still part of the Christmas festival,[17] assumes therefore a
symbolic value of a crucifix, reminding the convivial company of the
Round Table of the true significance of Christmas, which is that of
the Nativity of the Son of God, who is to offer himself in self-
sacrifice for the remission of human sins.
     In fact a similar offering is demanded, albeit on a smaller scale,
from an unfortunate participant in the Beheading Game proposed by
the visitor in green: the conditions of this basically unfair duel are
such that unless a miracle happens no ordinary mortal is able to
fulfill them without forfeiting his life, as only a supernatural figure

like the Green Knight can survive decapitation and walk off unconcerned, his head in his hand (457-59). To accept the challenge voluntarily, as Gawain does, amounts therefore to nothing less than offering oneself in an act of self-sacrifice, all in order to "save" the honor and the glory—the very *raison d'être*—of the Round Table. Through the extreme demands of the beheading challenge the cream of the world's chivalry are thus reminded of their true spiritual mission as *miles Christi,* by a messenger sent in all probability from heaven above, or on heaven's behalf, to interfere with the course of human events at Christmas. Whatever the mixed feelings about the Green Knight's uncanny appearance he does look "superior" to Arthur and his knights: he is imposingly big (137-39), but handsome and noble in his looks (142, 144-46), he is majestic, awe-inspiring, and frightening (199-202), but civilized and ultimately benevolent. Even his greenness is "enker-grene" (150)—that is, "bright green"— and his whole appearance is radiant and resplendant ("he loked as layt so ly3t," 199), features that may readily suggest traditional associations both with the light of God's wisdom and with lightning as a sign of God's wrath.[18] Nor is the pairing of the Green Knight's colors, green and gold, incompatible with these "heavenly" characteristics. Green, for all its associations with the earth and vegetation, is also, particularly in the Christian context, a color of heaven and things divine (see the section on the *nobilissima viriditas* below). Gold too, the color of the sun, is traditionally and unequivocally linked with the Christian heaven and divine glory; it is the color of the inner city of the New Jerusalem in the Revelation (21:18) or of the *sanctum sanctorum* in Solomon's temple (1 Kings 6:20-22), to cite only two biblical examples. Nor are these clear associations of gold with the idea of Christian perfection lacking in *Sir Gawain.* The best example is of course the famous pentangle "depaynt of pure golde hwez" (620) and attributed to Sir Gawain himself, whose character is accordingly described "as golde pured" (633).[19]

It is therefore not surprising that the strange visitor, all in green except for an admixture of gold, should evoke at Camelot rather fearful associations, possibly with a divine being admonishing God's children to follow Christ's "thorny path" symbolized by holly, an exhortation involving inevitably submission to God's will, self-sacrifice, and ultimately death—something that Arthur's court seems to have forgotten amid Christmas festivity and merriments. What the Green Knight is thus proposing in the form of a crude and barbaric beheading combat is a veiled invitation to a basically Christian ordeal, to an individual "way of the Passion" of voluntary self-sacrifice, as the christological content of the holly branch seems to suggest. The message is addressed to the Round Table in general, but in fact to Sir Gawain—Arthur's nephew and the best of knights—in particular. The exclusive character of the spiritual experience denoted by holly is confirmed by Malory in his *Tale of King Arthur*: Sir Bagdemagus, a knight aspiring to the membership of the Round Table

> rode forth, and there by the way he founde a braunche of holy herbe that was the signe of the Sancgreall, and no knyght founde no suche tokyns but he were a good lyver and a man of prouesse.[20]

"Sancgreall" is, of course, the Holy Blood of Christ (*sang real*), with which holly is symbolically linked through its red berries. It was due to its affinity with Christ that the plant was universally praised in the Middle Ages, as in the late-fourteenth-century romance *Ywain and Gawain,* where it is called "þe fayrest thorne þat ever groued sen God wes born,"[21] or in the lyrics composed in honor of this evergreen plant dedicated to Christ.[22]

We can, I think, assume with a fair degree of probability that the christological meaning of holly was well known both to the author of *Sir Gawain* and his audience, and that the understanding of the plant's meaning would accordingly have gone further than the acknowledgment of the simple fact that it is "grattest in grene when greuez ar bar" (207). The statement itself points also to another important aspect of the holly's meaning, namely its evergreen nature, the fact all the more significant in the poem as the Green Knight, all in bright, fresh green, makes his entry into King Arthur's hall at midwinter, when the natural verdure of plant life is dead. Could it be ventured, therefore, that the supernatural visitor, green all over in the middle of winter, derives his color and through it his whole existence and superhuman powers from the evergreen nature of the holly bough he is holding in his hand, a source of continuous life granted it through partaking of the divinity of Christ? And that by holding the holly bough for all to see the Green Knight is making the Christmas message clear to everyone: one has to follow Christ in order to die and be reborn,[23] a message of hope that counterbalances and mitigates the rather unfair and "hopeless" conditions of the Beheading Game symbolized by the cruel battle-axe held in the Green Knight's other hand. Even the axe itself, for all its fearsomeness, shares the same color characteristics and their allegorical significances as its bearer: the blade is "of grene stele and of golde hewen" (211), and the handle is "al bigrauen with grene" (216), the fact again suggesting a double message of violent death at the hands of the divine judge,[24] but also of hope of redemption. The two objects are thus complementary in character, epitomizing the twofold nature of experience personified by the Green Knight: the holly branch recalls the theme of Christ's Nativity and Passion, the plant's evergreenness represents the never-ending cycle and continuity of life, whereas the deadly weapon in the other hand conjures up grim images of a sudden, violent, and sacrificial death—after all a necessary condition in order to be reborn. The complementary opposition between life and death, symbolized by these two objects, is then synthesized in the green, ambiguous, and all-encompassing nature of their bearer, himself a personification of the totality of life experience—natural, human, and divine—an existential truth all of a sudden brought to the awareness of the unexpecting banqueters at Camelot, theretofore comfortably sheltered in the familiar and friendly environment of the court.

Green in Early Irish Tradition

But the confused reaction at Camelot, which was chiefly that of astonishment and fear ("all stouned . . . seten," 242, and "for doute *[fear]*," 246), must also have sprung from other, maybe even more immediate and instinctive associations with a figure in green than the christological theme of Passion and Redemption, only indirectly implied by the holly cluster and the shining nature of the visitor's color. As the text itself confirms, first to manifest itself to the people's consciousness was the "fairy" aspect of the figure, well grounded in popular beliefs going back to pre-Christian Celtic tradition, when green was a color linked chiefly with the earth and the underworld, as well as with its supernatural and not always friendly inhabitants. Early Irish literature and folklore abound with descriptions of supernatural beings, more often than not dressed in green,[25] who come to visit astounded mortals on certain ritual occasions and very often invite them to their otherwordly abodes. These are usually situated underground, with entrances found in the so-called *síde,* the "fairy mounds," identified with prehistoric burial places covered by a grassy knoll, often to be found in the countryside of the British Isles. A fairly typical example of a supernatural being dressed in green coming to fetch a mortal comes from the beginning of the famous Old Irish epic *Táin Bó Cúailnge.* In it we read how Queen Medb of Connaught sent a warrior named Fraech mac Idaid to fight with Cú Chulainn, the chief hero of Ulster. The two warriors wrestled naked in the river until Fraech was submerged and drowned:

> His people carried his body to the encampment . . . the whole encampment
> mourned for Fraech. They saw a band of women dressed in green tunics
> (uanib) bending over the corpse of Fraech. They carried him off into the fairy
> mound which was called Síd Fraich afterwards.[26]

The green exterior of these mounds matches the color of their fairy
inhabitants and that of the netherworld itself, which in the Celtic tradition is consistently green, too. Nor is it hard to see why. Just as
all plants are rooted in the earth, from which they draw their
nourishing sap, so it is possible to imagine life-bestowing spirits,
green in color or dressed in green, inhabiting the lower regions from
which, it may be believed, greenness as the essence of natural life
ultimately derives. And if the verdure of plant life can thus be said to
originate under the earth, so consequently it is to the netherworld
where it periodically descends at the end of each season, when
foliage loses its verdant color by turning yellow and red and then
disappears altogether from the face of the earth in winter—that is,
symbolically dies. "Death is greener than grass," says an answer to
an old riddle,[27] as if illustrating the notion of green as the color of
life "buried" in the earth in winter, before it is revived in spring. An
eleventh-century Irish *Tripartite Life of Patrick*, in a section on
eucharistic colors expressly states the idea of a periodical burial of
life in the earth, symbolized in liturgy by the priest's green vestment:

> This is what the green (uaine) denotes, when the priest looks at it: that his
> heart and mind be filled with great *faintness* and exceeding *sorrow*: for what is
> understood by it is his *burial* at the end of life *under mould of earth*; for *green
> is the original colour of every earth,* and therefore the colour of the priestly
> robe of offering is likened unto green.[28] (Italics added)

The Irish word for "green," *uaine,* used in the above source has very
revealing connotations,[29] not without analogy with the earlier indicated semantic ambivalence of the Middle English word *grene.* First
of all, *uaine* refers to green and verdant fields, hills, and rivers. In
descriptions of people the word can be used interchangeably with
glas, another word meaning "green," and can denote the color of
armor or clothes, for example *brat uaine*, "cloak of green," but
also—interestingly—fresh, unhealed wounds. *Uaine* can have even
more sinister associations, as in the phrase *dath na h-uaine,* "the
color green," which is glossed in an early Irish dictionary as "the
colour of green, death colour."[30]
  To develop the linguistic digression from the Irish language even

further let us examine the semantic range of yet another related word, *uraide* or *urda,* to see whether the earlier postulated twofold significance of greenness will hold also in this case. *Urda* means "fresh, green" with regard to fields, hills, earth, and vegetation; the verb *uraigid* means "to grow green," *urugud* is an act of growing green, freshening and renewing, *urde* means "earthly" (probably related to "earth," "die Erde"). In short, we have here all the positive senses of greenness associated with fresh and blossoming earth. On the other hand, the negative side of greenness linked with death and decay is represented by the following series: *ur,* meaning "fresh, new, green," but also "flesh, fatness," and "evil, an evil thing"; the same word spelled *uír* denotes "mould, earth, clay, soil," figuratively "the grave," and also "to kill" (in the sense of "bringing to the grave"), as well as "the material of the human body," "a human being." The cognate word *urulad* stands for "charnel house," and *uruscail* denotes "carcass."[31] In this way both in the color perception and the linguistic and literary use greenness reveals its complex, multifaceted meaning, ranging from fresh life through decay to death.

In pagan and Christian contexts alike the idea of the "burial" is unequivocally linked with a possibility of rebirth and resurrection—a hope enhanced by repeated observations of the transitoriness, death, and renewal of life in nature, exemplified also in the seasonal nature of the fieldwork. A universal image of the seed sown—that is, "buried"—in autumn that dies in the earth in winter to yield new life in spring, naturally lends itself as a metaphor of the death of the body and the possible resurrection of the soul, as the evangelical simile clearly illustrates: "Except a corn of wheat fall into the ground and die, it abideth alone: but if it die, it bringeth forth much fruit" (John 12:24).[32] The image occurs also in a fourteenth-century English lyric known as "A Winter Song" (MS. Harley 2253), in which the grain is buried or planted ("graueþ") green or unripe ("grene") in winter, soon to wither and die ("faleweþ") in the earth, giving a melancholy soul an occasion to contemplate the transitoriness of things and the hope of rebirth:

> al þat gre<i>n me graueþ grene
> nou hit faleweþ al by-dene—
> ihesu, help þat hit be sene
> ant shild us from helle,
> for y not whider y shal ne hou longe her duelle.

(11-15)[33]

The green color in winter has therefore a combined meaning of death, burial, and the future resurrection—the last made possible by the first, as the Gospel of John makes manifest. It is probably this Christian idea, in combination with the related pagan fairy lore, that is suggested to Gawain first by the mention and later by the actual appearance and function of the gravelike "grene chapel." As the Green Knight himself reveals through the mouth of his severed head at Camelot, his abode is allegedly known by many (454), although evidently by no one in Arthur's court, least of all by Sir Gawain, who openly expresses his ignorance of the Green Knight's identity and whereabouts (398-403). As Gawain finds out for himself a year later, the bleak "grene chapel" is a "bal3 ber3" (2172), a round barrow at the bottom of a wild valley, "ouergrowen with gresse in glodes (*patches*) aywhere" (2181), in somewhat infernal surroundings of a stream that "blubred (*bubbled*) þerinne as hit boyled hade" (2174), with the chapel itself, in which "my3t aboute mydny3t þe dele (*devil*) his matynnes telle" (2187-88). These "otherwordly" features of the Green Knight's uncouth dwelling, although unknown, or maybe forgotten, by the audience at Camelot, are nonetheless clearly foreshadowed by the visitor's greenness, instantly linked by the court with the traditional "fayry3e"—a layer of popular beliefs in magic and supernatural, malicious beings inhabiting the interior of the earth and commonly associated with death. It is by stimulating the deeper, more irrational and pagan layers of the psyche that the Green Knight manages to stupefy the civilized audience at Arthur's court, first by his greenness and all the ambivalent feelings it evokes, and later by his miraculous feat of surviving the beheading blow—another act of archaic and "barbaric" magic.

The Mystics and the *Nobilissima Viriditas*

The originally pagan connotations of greenness with the underworld and its fairy inhabitants seem to have lingered on in the popular imagination well into the high Middle Ages, as evidenced by their partial transformation into the Christian concept of the eternal enemy of God and man—the devil. This is another aspect of the Green Knight's complex persona,[34] by no means absent in *Sir Gawain,* and associated mainly with his role as a tempter, shapeshifter, and hunter—aspects of the figure strongly linked to his color as well. The possibility that the Green Knight may be the devil eventually dawns on Gawain as he approaches the weird and otherworldly whereabouts of the "chapel of meschaunce" (2195), whose

as-yet unseen inhabitant is suspected to be "þe fende" (2193), prac-
ticing his "deuocion on þe deuelez wyse" (2192) in that "corsedest
kyrk" (2196). The Green Knight's bleak abode apart, if not Gawain
himself, then at least the audience of the poem would have probably
known that like his pagan fairy prototype, the devil of medieval
Europe often wore a coat of green. But unlike in the Celtic tradition,
this feature of the devil was due not so much to the color of his
subterranean abode as to his role as a hunter of human souls; just as
medieval huntsmen were dressed in green to appear harmless to their
prey, so was the devil pursuing human souls in green guise. The
European folklore knows of the figure of a "green man," a
challenger to games and contests and a tempter, wearing a green
cloak of a huntsman: the German *Jägersmann, ein grüner Jäger*, or
ein grüner Mann.[35] The literary *locus classicus* of this aspect of the
devil's function and appearance is provided by Chaucer's *Friar's
Tale*, in which the Evil One is dressed in green, like a yeoman or
forester:

> And happed that he [the summoner] sough bifore hym ryde
> A gay yeoman, under a forest syde,
> A bow he bar, and arwes bright and kene;
> He hadde upon a courtepy of grene,
> An hat upon his heed with frenges blake.[36]

The yeoman is described in the *General Prologue* to *The Canterbury
Tales* as "clad in cote and hood of grene" (103), for he is a skilled
forester and huntsman ("Of wodecraft wel koude he al the usage,"
110), a feature that links him with the hunting lore employed in Fitt
III of *Sir Gawain,* where the expertise in "wodcraftez" (1605) was
likewise required. In *The Parlement of the Thre Ages* the poacher
who sets out on a morning hunt for deer is covered with leaves to
appear invisible to his prey. When he mercilessly kills a splendid
stag with his crossbow (52-53), and later breaks up its body (81-
82), one is reminded both of the grim death awaiting his prey in
hiding and coming suddenly and unexpectedly, and also of the
subsequent decomposition of the body.[37] An anonymous author of a
twelfth-century Latin *Bestiary* calls the devil the hunter of mankind
chasing man with temptations,[38] which corresponds precisely to the
character and meaning of the twofold action of hunting and sexual
temptation of Gawain in Fitt III.

The fairy and devilish allusions apart, the complexity of responses
provoked by the Green Knight allows simultaneously for the presence of the negative or evil significances just mentioned as well as

for the positive ones, associated earlier in this chapter with the shining nature of greenness, the christological meaning of holly, and with the unequivocally divine connotations of the golden elements in the Green Knight's attire. Notwithstanding the apparent loss of clarity and straightforwardness of interpretation,[39] one must accept this complex and elusive character of the figure, whose various facets should be considered in a complementary way, despite the contradictory and paradoxical nature of some of the Green Knight's features. And just as the very nature of the green color, as confirmed also by linguistic evidence, is ambiguous and at least twofold, so must be the meaning of the Green Knight suggested in the poem, additionally reinforced by other traits and attributes.

Consequently, one finds in the Christian thought a wide range of references to greenness in the contexts suggestive of the highest religious values and symbols. Interestingly, the popular association of greenness with the devil or underworld did not preclude a no less frequent connection of the color with such concepts as heaven, Divine Glory, the Holy Ghost, or Christ himself. The color of fresh vegetation was naturally related by medieval religious poets to the Garden of Eden or heaven itself, thus suggesting that greenness understood as the essence and source of life, though impermanent and periodical on earth, is eternal in heaven, where it ultimately belongs. The idea is expressed, for example, in the works of a twelfth-century German woman-mystic Hildegard von Bingen, whose one brief Latin song bears a telling title *Nobilissima viriditas,* "The Noblest Greenness":

> O nobilissima viriditas
> que radicas in sole
> et que in candida
> serenitate luces in rota
> quam nulla terrena
> excellentia comprehendit—
> tu circumdata es
> amplexibus divinorum
> ministeriorum.
> Tu rubes ut aurora
> et ardes ut solis flamma!

(You noblest greenness, with your roots in the sun, sparkling in white serenity in a wheel, that no earthly eminence comprehends—you are enfolded in the embraces of divine solicitudes. You glow like dawn and burn like the sun's flame!)[40]

Hildegard's mystical vision clearly places *viriditas* in heaven, near God, who embraces it with his care ("divinorum ministeriorum") and makes it shine ("luces") on earth like the sun, its excellence unmatched by anything terrestrial ("nulla terena excellentia comprehendit"). The glowing nature of heavenly greenness is additionally reinforced by comparisons with the break of day ("aurora") and the sun's flames ("solis flamma"), and the mystical ardor that informs the entire lyric unambiguously makes greenness here on earth but a terrestrial reflection of the celestial light and glory. One immediately recalls the Green Knight's "enker-grene" and his looking "as layt so ly3t," bright and resplendent (see note 8). The Christian use of greenness represents an interesting inversion of the pagan symbolism here: the color of subterranean dark abodes and their fairy inhabitants of popular belief becomes a characteristic of heaven above, from where the *nobilissima viriditas*, the divine life-giving green essence, beneficently pours down on earth in a nourishing stream. For Hildegard green is a celestial color *par excellence*: elsewhere she says that Christian saints are "the greenness of God's fingers" ("viriditas digiti dei"), the Virgin Mary is "the greenest branch," which when it flowers in Christ makes "all things appear in full greenness" ("in viridate plena"). The final chorale of Hildegard's religious play *Ordo Virtutum* opens with the following: "In the beginning, all creation was full of greenness; flowers blossomed in the midst of it; later, greenness sank away."[41] The color of eternal life is here logically associated with the paradisal state from before the Fall, just as it may also denote future heavenly bliss and fulfillment of the saved after death—the concept probably suggested in a thirteenth-century lyric, in which the crucified God has a green face:

> His bodi þat wes feir & gent
> & his neb sue scene
> Wes bi-spit & al to-rent,
> His rude wes worþen grene.[42]

Since salvation is ultimately granted by God's grace, it should be no wonder that this attribute of the Almighty is also associated with greenness and its renovative powers. In the thirteenth-century *Pélerinage de la vie humaine* by a Cistercian Guillame de Deguileville, a personification of God's grace ("Grace Dieu") is a lady dressed in green and gold, very much like the Green Knight at his first appearance at Camelot. The Middle English translation[43] reads:

> She hadde on a rochet beten with gold, and was gert with a grene tissue þat was, as me thouhte, al along arayed with charbuncles.
>
> (120-22)

Grace Dieu speaks of herself:

> I am gouernouvesse of alle thinge, and of alle harmes I am leche: I make þe blynde see, and give strengthe to þe feeble; I reise þo þat ben falle;
>
> (172-74)

and she is also the people's guide into the Heavenly Jerusalem ("into þe dwellinge of Jerusalem þou shalt not entre withoute me," 185-86), thus establishing a symbolic connection between green and gold and such Christian concepts as resurrection, salvation, and eternal life. Consequently, one finds greenness denoting divine bliss and glory in the Heavenly City itself, shining forth with the color of green precious stones; in the Revelation the Holy Jerusalem, the city of the saved, had

> the glory of God: and her light was like unto a stone most precious, even like a jasper stone, clear as crystal.
>
> (21:11)

Jasper is a green stone, in medieval lapidaries and devotional lyrics often used to signify the "greenness of faith," as in the late eleventh-century Latin song *Cives celestis patrie*: "Iaspis coloris viridi profert virorem fidei" ("the green jasper represents green faith").[44] Similarly, a Middle English lapidary says of jasper:

> þat stone þat is cleped feith . . . & he þat grene Iaspe beholdeth ayeins day, of þe feith of Ihesu Xrist he shulde haue mynde.[45]

This is why the base of the Holy City is made of jasper, the green stone of faith, as we read in *Pearl*:

> Jasper hy3t þe fyrste gemme,
> þat I on þe fyrste basse con wale;
> He glente grene in þe lowest hemme.[46]

The wall surrounding the Heavenly Jerusalem "was of jasper: and the city was pure gold, like unto clear glass" (Rev. 21:18), thus reinforcing the allegorical meaning that the foundation and the encircling wall of the city of the saved should be made of strong faith.

The *Pearl*-poet, by all accounts also the author of *Sir Gawain*, repeats after the biblical authority:

> þe wal abof þe bantels brent
> Of jasporye as glas þat glysnande schon—
> I knew hit by his denysement
> In þe Apocalyppeȝ, þe apostel John.

(1017-20)

It is interesting to recall in this context that the Green Knight's rich attire too was adorned with precious stones, whose color and the implied allegorical meaning could in all probability be similar to that found in the above-adduced sources. The man's "vesture uerayly watz clene verdure, / Boþe þe barres of his belt and oþer blyþe stones" (161-62), and his saddle bow and shirts "euer glemered and glent al of grene stones" (172), to say nothing of his green horse, "dubbed wyth ful dere stonez" (193).

The "grene stones" glistening on the Green Knight's accoutrements may have been either jaspers, whose soteriological significance has already been demonstrated, or else emeralds, also green stones rich in symbolic meaning. Emeralds were likewise used in the structure of the Heavenly Jerusalem (Rev. 21:19), as the author of *Pearl* promptly confirms: "þe emerade þe furþe se grene of scale" (1005). And both jasper and emerald are conspicuously present in the vision of the throne of God as described in the Apocalypse:

> And he that sat [on the throne] was to look upon like a jasper and a sardine stone: and there was a rainbow round about the throne, in sight like unto an emerald.

(4:3)

The two green stones seem thus well established in medieval tradition as emblems of "heavenly greenness," suggesting divine glory and spiritual bliss of the saved. This religious symbolism entered other types of visionary narratives, such as Chaucer's *Parliament of Fowls* for example, in which the heavenly and divine connotations of both greenness and the emerald stone lend additional sacred aura to the vision of the Garden of Love:

> For overal where that I myne eyen caste
> Were trees clad with leves that ay shal laste,
> Ech in his kynde, of colour fresh and greene
> As emerande, that joye was to seene.[47]

I began this brief review of medieval sources illustrating the "celestial" aspect of greenness with Hildegard's mystical vision of *nobilissima viriditas* rooted in heaven, and let me now end this section with a passage from the works of another spiritual writer, the late-thirteenth-century Flemish mystic Jan van Ruusbroec. His rich and complex description of the Heavenly Kingdom is a real visionary tour de force, in which the imagery of the green stones, jasper and emerald, and of the color green in three different shades play a central role. In the context of the foregoing discussion I cannot resist quoting this exceptional account in full:

> The brightness [of the heavenly light] is threefold, and in this brightness appears a green colour, with which the brightness is sensible. With it, God has filled and illuminated the highest heaven [where Christ, angels, and saints reign eternally]. In the brightness of heaven and in the brightness of the glorious bodies [of the saved], the green colour is manifest, which is like the stone we call jasper. We shall see the greenness with our bodily eyes, that is, all the outward good works that were ever done or ever shall be done, unto the end of the world, in whatsoever manner it might be. . . . See, this is the lovely green colour which shall enrich the glorious bodies, to a greater or lesser degree, everyone according to his efforts, merits, and dignity. The second brightness if eternal life is spiritual . . . and in this brightness a green hue displays itself like that of a stone they call smaragdus, that is, a green emerald beautiful and green and lovely to intelligent eyes beyond anything one might recall. By this, we understand enrichment, fruit, and all differentiation of virtue. This is the most beautiful and the loveliest hue of the kingdom of heaven. . . . Thus each saint is like the emerald, bright and green, beautiful, gracious and glorious, according to his own nobility and merits. This is why God has manifested the glory of the kingdom of heaven to the saints in the green colour of the precious emerald. The third heavenly brightness is divine, and is nothing other than the eternal wisdom and brightness which is God himself. . . . In the divine brightness a green hue appears which is incomparable, for it is so gracious and glorious that all vision is lost in gazing at it and is blinded and loses all its judgment. [This is therefore] a heavenly light with threefold brightness and greenness, the first sensible, the second spiritual, the third divine. . . . And everyone who loves stands before God's presence with his book [of merits], bright, green, lovely and glorious. . . . And the glory of God is measureless and so bottomless that one cannot completely see through it. Thus it resembles the smaragdus which also cannot be seen through.[48]

Thus in addition to the Green Knight's "unnatural" color evoking grim associations with the underworld, and in addition to the holly branch and the axe reminiscent of self-sacrifice and death, the sparks of green light coming from the stones adorning the Green Knight's attire can surely be linked with such important Christian notions as faith, divine grace, the resurrection of the soul, and the bliss of heaven. The full spiritual message of the Green Knight's visit to Camelot at Christmastime is gradually emerging with all its importance and complexity, firmly establishing itself against the background of religious, magical, and mystical ideas of manifold and often subtle character, most certainly shared by the learned author of *Pearl* and *Sir Gawain*, and partly at least by his audience.

Alchemical Greenness

Before I refer these wide-ranging analogies from the realm of color symbolism back to the immediate literary context of *Sir Gawain,* the reader is requested to bear with yet another digression. The "blyþe," "grene," and "dere stones" of the Green Knight's accoutrements can also lead us in a direction not much different from that chosen by the medieval mystics with their notions of the *nobilissima viriditas* and of the jasper or emerald as reflections of God's glory in heaven. Green stones and greenness as such, often in close connection with gold, play also an important role in medieval and Renaissance alchemy, which like mysticism was exploring divine mysteries contained in nature, but with the use of a more esoteric, technical, if sometimes obscure language of natural philosophy and magic.[49] In the alchemical tradition the green stone is connected first of all with the legendary ancient *Tabula smaragdina*, on which the essence of alchemical work is said to have been inscribed by Hermes Trismegistos, the mythical father of Hermetic philosophy. As in medieval mysticism, green in alchemy is linked with such high and exhalted values and ideas as resurrection, God's grace, paradise, the Holy Ghost, divine wisdom, and perfection. For medieval and Renaissance alchemists greenness achieved the meaning of life and redemption itself and was often referred to in the texts as the *benedicta viriditas,* "the blessed greenness." "O blessed greenness, which generates all things!" exclaims the author of the *Rosarium philosophorum* (Basel 1593, 2: 220)[50] and Johann Daniel Mylius, an early-seventeenth-century German Hermeticist thus refers to *benedicta viriditas* in his treatise *Philosophia reformata* (Frankfurt a.M., 1622, 11):

> Did not the Spirit of the Lord, which is a fiery love, give to the waters when it was borne over them a certain fiery vigour, since nothing can be generated without heat? God breathed into created things a certain germination or

greenness [*viriditas*], by which all things should multiply. . . . They called all things green, for to be green means to grow. Therefore this virtue of generation and the preservation of things might be called the Soul of the World (*Anima Mundi*).[51]

Due to its close relation to natural growth, both in alchemy and in the Christian thought in general, greenness has a procreative and fertilizing quality, and for this reason the color was often attributed to the Holy Ghost as the universal creative principle. Meister Eckhart says in his *Sermons* that the Holy Ghost is a force due to which God "grows green and blossoms" ("blühend und grünend") in the human heart.[52] Another German mystic, Johannes Tauler, likewise speaks of the soul's "greening" and "yielding of spiritual fruit" thanks to God's grace,[53] and a German alchemical tract called *Cherubinischer Wandersmann* (1: 190) in a similar way equates God with the life-supporting green substance pervading the natural world:

> God is my sap: the leaves and buds I show,
> They are His Holy Ghost, by whom I grow.[54]

The green emerald, compared by Ruusbroec to the measureless and bottomless glory of God, was similarly exhalted by alchemists and was often related to gold, an everlasting, incorruptible substance, the goal of the alchemical *opus*. For example, Apollonios, a natural philosopher of the second century b.c., compares emerald to gold in his treatise *On Primal Causes*:

> [Emerald] is the root of all precious stones, as gold is the chief of the smeltable bodies. The fire does not affect it, neither does the iron file it.[55]

Other alchemical texts also confirm the symbolic connection between green and gold as closely related elements of the *opus*. Arnoldus de Villanova writes in his *Speculum alchimiae* (printed in the *Theatrum chemicum*, Strasburg, 1613, 4: 605):

> Therefore Aristotle says in his book: our gold, [but] not the common gold, because the green which is in this substance signifies its total perfection, since by *our magistery that green is quickly turned into truest gold.*[56] (Italics added)

The above passage seems to convey a somewhat paradoxical idea that it is the green contained in gold that gives the latter its "perfection," and that the alchemist's art is to transform that green into the "truest gold." Strange though this concept may appear, it is independently confirmed by the *Rosarium philosophorum*, which provides more details about the process involved and in addition makes an interesting but not altogether surprising distinction between two types of alchemical greenness: the "positive" one, referred to above as the *benedicta viriditas,* and the "negative" one called *verdigris*, a greenish substance that forms on copper or bronze, in alchemy identified with the metal's "sickness" or "decay." The *Rosarium* has this to say about this double nature of alchemical greenness:

> Thou hast inquired concerning the greenness [*viriditas*], deeming the bronze to be a leprous body [i.e. rust] on account of the greenness it hath upon it. Therefore I say unto thee that whatever is perfect in the bronze is that greenness [here: *verdigris*] only, because *that greenness is straightaway changed by our magistery into our most true gold.*[57] (Italics added)

The alchemical greenness is therefore related to gold in two ways: first as *viriditas*—the heavenly, incorruptible, and pure substance, equivalent to gold as the aim of the *opus*; and second as *verdigris*—the earthly, sickly and impure "stain" or "rust" on unrefined metal, only to be transformed into "true gold." Either as an analogy or opposition or both, green in alchemy complements gold as shadow complements light or night, day. The "dark side" of greenness, *verdigris*, the metal's rust or "sickness," completes the perfect and heavenly gold to achieve wholeness and unity inconceivable without the synthesis of the earthly with the divine. What is more, the alchemical texts make it clear (obscure as they usually are) that it is exclusively through greenness that the final goal of the *opus* is reached, and wisdom and perfection of the alchemical art are achieved.[58] Or to translate the process into theological language: it is only through the purging of moral "rust" or "leprosy"—that is, sin— that perfection, symbolized by gold, is at all possible. Interestingly, the Greek Orthodox Church used an alchemical term, *aerugo peccati,* "rust of sin," to describe this human metaphysical condition: the "rust" can only be rubbed off and filed away through penance and mortification of body and soul, until the original splendor of the metal—that is, man's soul created in God's image and likeness— will break through again.[59] When applied to this process of moral purging the twofold greenness could thus represent humanity's innate sinfulness and imperfection resulting from the Fall, in alchemy rendered by *verdigris*, in itself the basis and the necessary condition for the preparation of the "perfect" man, whose spiritual and moral excellence is equal to the philosophical gold or the *benedicta viriditas*. The "shadowy" aspect of alchemical greenness appears anal-

ogous to the associations discussed earlier of the green color with
putrefaction, decay, death, burial, and the underworld. The sinful
man must "die" for the pure man to be "reborn," an idea fairly
consistent with the overall New Testament doctrine of man's relation
to God (Cf. John 3:3-8). In this way the mystical and alchemical
green and gold complement one another, denoting the totality and
oneness of human metaphysical condition by reconciling the earthly
with the heavenly in man.[60] And if gold represents divine perfection
as an a priori existing, ideal but static condition to be ultimately
achieved, then greenness with its double nature reflects the dynamic
aspect of the process, involving the transmutation of the sinful body
and soul through purging into a spiritual state from before the Fall,
symbolized by the "blessed" or "noblest" greenness of the mystics
and the alchemists.

The Greenness and Sir Gawain

Whether this complex of ideas was intended to be provoked by the
Green Knight's green attire with its specks of gold is an open
question. The answer would of course depend on the degree to
which the *Gawain*-poet shared in the mystical and hermetic writings
available to him. Unfortunately, unless his poem contains an
unequivocal reference or borrowing from an identifiable source, any
speculation about possible symbolic implications of some motifs
remains just that: speculative and conjectural. On the other hand, it
would be hard to accept that references to colors and their particular
combinations in the poem are a mere play of the author's fancy, let
alone chance, with so much external evidence to support the deliberate, doctrinal, or symbolic use of color imagery in medieval
tradition. Whatever the ultimate source and specific significance of
green and gold in relation to the Green Knight, in view of the above
material it seems impossible to reduce the figure to a single meaning,
because the complexity of the employed color characteristics
preclude simple attributions of the Green Knight, often made by
critics, either to the evil realm of death and the underworld or to
nature at large or alone to heaven or else equally exclusively to the
more sophisticated and civilized part of humanity. One is rather
inclined to think that the inherent ambivalence and paradoxical nature
of the Green Knight were fairly compatible with the sensibility of the
original medieval audience, whose dialectical minds should have
been well prepared to accept and comprehend metaphysical
contradictions, antitheses, and paradoxes of reality. And on account

of the ambivalence of his colors and other attributes, the Green Knight would probably have been perceived as a "complete" figure, partaking simultaneously of fiendish, natural, and divine realms, as such epitomizing man's crucial metaphysical anxieties in relation to life, death, and the hereafter. And he was not merely a philosophical "concept" allegorized in the poem into a figure in green; he was a living and inescapable reality, as the best of knights of the Round Table was to find out for himself.

Indeed, the confrontation between Sir Gawain and his challenger in green constitutes the main structural element of the story, regulating and subordinating other subplots of the narrative into a coherent and well-knit whole of exceptional internal order and consistency. The particular nature of the relationship between the two main protagonists of *Sir Gawain* is a very complex issue, and in this chapter my considerations will be confined to that aspect of their relationship which is borne out by the employed color symbolism.

The complementary character of green and gold seems thus well established in tradition, and the underlying idea of putting the two colors together was—as I have shown—that of the synthesis of the earthly, natural, and the divine in man.[61] With this in mind it is interesting to observe that just as green is initially the Green Knight's dominant color, so is gold for Sir Gawain. During the preparations for his departure from Camelot on All Saints' Day, a gilded armor ("þe gyld gere þat glent," 569) was given the knight to put on, with knee-pieces connected by "knotez of golde" (577), "gold sporez" (587), and all the loops and buckles glistening with gold ("þe lest lachet oþer loupe lemed of golde," 591). Like the Green Knight's matching horse, so Gawain's was "gurde with a sadel þat glemed ful gayly with mony golde frenges" (597-98), with the bridle "with bry3t golde bounden" (600), and "al watz rayled on red ryche golde naylez, / þat al glytered and glent as glem of the sunne" (603-4). The famous pentangle on Gawain's shield, itself a symbol of perfection and truth (625-35), was "depaynt of pure golde hwez" (620, 663), and the knight's character and moral standard were likewise "as golde pured, / Voyded of vche vylany" (633-34), meaning perfect and pure like the refined gold of the alchemists. Later at Hautdesert Gawain's splendid canopied bed had curtains of "clene sylk with cler golde hemmez" (854) and "red golde ryngez" (857), to match the excellency of this best of knights.

But there is clear irony in such a conspicuous attribution of gold and all the absolute values represented by it to Gawain, in that the knight, for all the unquestionable nobility of his character, has not yet fully lived up to these values, as the forthcoming trials at

Hautdesert and the Green Chapel sadly prove. Both the golden armor and the pentangle as symbols of chivalric perfection are worn by Gawain, either out of pride or simply ignorance, almost ostentatiously and apparently without their wearer's realizing that the objective absolute values need yet to be internalized, or—if this is not fully possible—that the failure to live by these ideals should be duly acknowledged. In the Christian world absolute perfection, symbolized here by gold, is basically unattainable to man, and the only possibility of getting close to it is by exploring one's fallen nature and by admitting one's innate sinfulness, or by becoming aware of one's weaknesses and vulnerability—a simple truth often most difficult to realize and accept, as Gawain's own predicament proved for him. Or to use the language of colors employed by alchemists: to obtain gold it is first necessary to assimilate and transform greenness and everything it symbolically denotes—the body and its frailty, proneness to sin, mortality, and so on. The Green Knight's arrival at Camelot gives Gawain (and the Round Table at large) the first opportunity to confront his latent "green" nature and to test and validate his claim to perfection, expressed in Gawain's "golden" external appearance. By accepting the challenge to the Beheading Game Gawain eventually comes to reconcile himself with the thought that he will have to face death, although the full gravity and inescapability of this fact do not begin to dawn on him until the day before the meeting with the Green Knight at the Green Chapel, when Gawain takes the green girdle as a secret magic weapon to protect himself in what must have seemed to him an unfair duel. A year before in Camelot it is Gawain who deals a deadly blow to his opponent in green, thus initiating his personal confrontation with death and mortality, using—significantly—the green axe provided by the challenger. What is more, according to the rules then laid down by the Green Knight, the volunteer is entitled to retain the axe as his own ("I schal gif hym of my gyft þis giserne *[battle-axe]* ryche," 288), apparently as a keepsake and a reminder—through its color and frightening appearance—of the "deadly" seriousness of the adventure thus undertaken. However, after the Green Knight left the hall, his severed head in his hand, the whole matter is blithely laughed off by the court (463-64), the fearsome green axe is hung as a trophy "abof þe dece" (478), where "all men for meruayl my3t on hit loke" (479), and the merry and carefree feast is again resumed (481-86). Only the author's comment closing Fitt I makes the reader aware of the perilousness and inescapability of the second half of the Beheading Game for Gawain:

Now þenk wel, Sir Gawan,
For woþe *(danger)* þat þou ne wonde *(fear)*
þis auenture for to frayn
þat þou hatz tan on honde *(undertaken)*.

(487-90)

Later at Hautdesert, at the crucial moment of his temptation Gawain cowardly and treacherously retains the magic girdle provided by the lady, in the understandable hope of saving himself from peril at the Green Chapel ("My3t he haf slypped to be unslayn, þe sle3t *[stratagem]* were noble," 1858). The girdle, a visible sign of Gawain's fear of death, is characteristically fashioned "with grene sylke and with golde schaped" (1832), and when Gawain puts it on himself[62] before his final ride to the Green Chapel, it is now the only green element ("þe gordel of þe grene sylke," 2035) on his otherwise gilded shining armor.   Nor is the armor itself, as the outward representation of the chivalric profession, left unaffected by Gawain's breach of covenant with Sir Bertilac (failure to return the lace, as was agreed): before the knight leaves the castle on the New Year's morning his gear has been "piked *(polished)* ful clene" and "rokked *(rubbed)* of þe roust," so that it now looks as "fresch as vpon fyrst" (2017-19)—that is, before contracting the sin. But although the "rust of sin" was temporarily removed from the knight's armor, the gold and the perfection it symbolizes (to say nothing of the pentangle) become nonetheless tarnished with a green stain of the unfortunate girdle—a shameful sign of the knight's breach of chivalric conduct, springing from cowardly, though so very human, fear for his life, or more precisely the natural instinct of self-preservation. Adopted in the vain hope as an instrument of defense, the green girdle turns out to be a symbol of Gawain's weakness and vulnerability and a clear reminder of the truth about man's fallen nature.[63] As a sign of human sinfulness the green girdle resembles the *verdigris* of alchemy, the metal's "sickness" or "leprosy," that has to be rubbed off through penitential purging in fire. In the course of adventure that aroused Gawain's natural fear for life the knight resolved to attach the green lace *onto* his gilded armor, as if externalizing and bringing up to the surface of consciousness his hitherto hidden and unrealized frailty. The full realization of this fact, however, did not reach Gawain's consciousness until his treachery was exposed by the Green Knight after the mock execution at the Green Chapel. Although physically alive, save for a little nick on the neck, Gawain still has to go through an agonizing and humiliating process of reconciling himself to the acceptance of the limitations of his character, as if his consciousness has now caught up with his changed apparel—the gold of his armor now stained by a green lace. The sudden and traumatic realization of his flawed nature makes Gawain momentarily lose his temper, as he blushes with shame (2370-72) and then flings the girdle angrily at the Green Knight (2377), in the first instinctive and still childish refusal to accept the truth about his character. A moment later, however, he composes himself to face reality and launches a tirade of self-accusation involving "cowarddyse and couetyse" (2374), "trecherye and vntrawþe" (2383) and sincerely confesses his fallen state ("Now am I fawty and falce," 2382). Afterwards Gawain accepts the girdle for the second time in the poem, but this time to wear it as a token and remembrance of his adventure and of the newly discovered truth about himself as a human being.

But unlike at Hautdesert, Gawain is now aware of the full meaning of the green lace, which has nothing to do with its supposed magical power, still less with its material value (2430-32), but is basically that of "surfet" (2433), or of the flesche crabbed" (2435), and of the body's susceptibility to take stains of filth ("to entyse teches of fylþe," 2436). The emerging moral significance of the green girdle is therefore in keeping with the meaning of the alchemical *verdigris,* as well as with all the ambivalent values denoted by the green color in general. In this light, Sir Gawain's subsequent decision to wear the green badge of disgrace on the outside of his armor is a clear sign that the revealed sinful aspect of his nature has now been assimilated by his conscious personality. Logically enough, the green girdle, which now forms a permanent part of Gawain's apparel, is derived from the Green Knight himself; more precisely, from his gown. In this way the continuity of greenness throughout the poem is maintained: "For hit is my wede *(garment)* þat þou werez, þat ilke wouen girdel" (2358), and "hit is grene as my goune" (2396). The greenness with which the Green Knight so astounded Camelot at the beginning of the poem has now become integrated with Gawain's personality, making it fuller and more mature. Just as traces of gold on the Green Knight's attire signified an admixture of divinity and perfection, so the green spot on Sir Gawain's otherwise purely golden armor now indicates his true nature: essentially good but with an admixture of weakness and sinfulness; that is, perfect as far as limited human perfection is possible. The green lace as a stain on the golden armor thus modifies the somewhat unrealistic demands of the chivalric ideal symbolized by the pentangle and complements it with a more human dimension that makes this ideal at all attainable in this world. And the two main protagonists of the moral drama presented in the poem, Sir Gawain and the Green Knight, emerge at the end in complementary opposition and symmetry to one another, both characterized by the two colors green and gold, but in reversed proportions.[64]

However, the claim that the green girdle stands solely for human weakness and sinfulness would be inconsistent with my earlier statements both about the dual nature of greenness and about the relation of green to gold. The girdle itself is, characteristically, "golde-hemmed" (2395); that is, it has a golden finish, similar to the axe and the Green Knight himself. The alchemical *verdigris* too, for all its connection with impurity and decay, was at the same time the basis for the attainment of the noble goal of the *opus*: that greenness which was "changed by our magistery into most true gold." Nor was Sir Gawain's adventure an utter failure and complete moral fiasco either, as the now benevolent Green Knight admits at the Green Chapel:

> I halde þe polysed of þat ply3t, and pured as clene
> As þou hadez neuer forfeted syþen þou watz fyrst borne,
>
> (2393-94)

The word *pured* was once before used of Sir Gawain in the description of his dressing-up to depart from Camelot, when his moral standard was defined "as golde pured" (633). But it clearly transpires that only now is the knight worthy of the gold he wears on himself, when in the course of his adventure he has "rubbed off" from his conscience the rust of sin through mortification and penance. And just as the green girdle was "with golde schaped"— that is, invested with a potential of purification and perfection—so Gawain's wearing it has also the double significance of both shame and glory. The latter, positive meaning of the girdle is precisely the one adopted one-sidedly by the knights of the Round Table after Gawain's return, when they all decide to wear similar green laces "for sake of þat segge" (2518), as tokens of honor. However, theirs is not the full knowledge of the girdle's double meaning, as they did not share nor even seem to comprehend the kind of spiritual experience that gave Gawain the right to wear the lace. The symbol of sin and fall becomes paradoxically a sign of honor and fame, except that the myopic knights at Camelot refuse to see the girdle in all its complexity, thus misinterpreting for themselves the spiritual import of Gawain's adventure. As at the Green Knight's visit the

year before, the whole matter is again cheerfully and laughingly
dismissed ("alle þe court als laȝen loude þerat," 2513-14), and Sir
Gawain's newly acquired spiritual maturity remains essentially an
individual, incommunicable experience. His alone is a profit gained
from the confrontation with the other dimension of reality signified
by greenness: with the fear of death, with mortality, and death itself,
which once transcended opens the way to that aspect of greenness
that the alchemists equaled with gold and referred to as the *benedicta
viriditas*, and that the mystics saw as a reflection of heavenly bliss
and divine glory.[65] Having accepted the two sides of his character
Gawain has become a whole individual, since it is rust that gives a
coin its true value.

4

Sir Gawain's Pentangle: The *Imago Hominis* and the Virtue of Temperance

The pentangle passage in *Sir Gawain* is notoriously puzzling and elusive, despite what on the surface looks like a coherent piece of allegorical *explicatio,* aimed at bringing home to an otherwise perplexed reader the doctrinal, moral, and spiritual truths of the geometrical figure displayed on Gawain's shield.[1] Textually the passage comes as a crowning of a long description of Gawain's magnificent dress and armor (566-618), which the knight puts on himself before his departure from Camelot to keep his tryst at the Green Chapel. His accoutrements include 'þe gyld gere þat glent þeralofte" (569), "a crafty capados (*hood),* closed aloft" (572) and lined with costly fur, all the individual pieces of armor covering his entire body (574-85), the "gold sporez" (587) and "a bront (*sword)* ful sure" (588)—all shining and glittering with gold (591). Gawain's famous steed Gringolet is likewise in splendid golden array, with a saddle "þat glemed ful gayly with mony golde frenges" (598), with the bridle, the crupper, and the rich cloth covering the body that "al glytered and glent as glem of the sunne" (604), and all the embroideries and ornamental stitches of the trappings of finest quality and craftsmanship (608-14).

This minute *descriptio personae*, a technique familiar in the repertoire of the alliterative poets with their use of traditional heroic diction and narrative *topoi,*[2] is followed by a passage on the pentangle (619-65), that is less descriptive but more speculative, and almost the same length as the two stanzas covering the formal arming of the ideal Christian knight. The textual space allotted to the pentangle undoubtedly testifies to the special significance attached to this symbol by the author, as does the placing of the device as a climax of the arming-of-the-hero passage, in itself important in an epic narrative of a heroic type. The author himself is clearly aware of the unusual character of the sign on Gawain's shield as well as of its importance for his hero, for he deliberately halts the action, already suspended by the preceding description ("I am in tent yow to telle, þof tary hyt me schulde," 624) and takes pains to expound the doctrinal meaning of the device for the space of two full stanzas (619-55). Such a conspicuous presence of the symbol cannot obviously be ignored merely as a marginal digression, and it clearly calls for some kind of explanation, one that would take into account both the device itself, and possibly also the story with its protagonist. In what follows I shall demonstrate that the two functions of the pentangle (the historical and the contextual) are closely interwoven and equally important in the poem. The pentangle and its intricate symbolism introduce, both openly and by implication, a sphere of ideas and concepts that operate on a number of levels: geometrical, psychological, moral, religious, and cosmological, relating to Sir Gawain both as a generalized representative of humanity and as the hero of a particular romance. The pentangle and some of its formal peculiarities appear to create a new dimension of meaning within *Sir Gawain*, one that is perhaps less obtrusive and obvious than the contents commonly associated with the poem's plot, but also one that seems to deepen the story's implications with a hermetic perspective of considerable intricacy and sophistication.

It seems logical to begin with a closer look at the various elements in the description of the pentangle, following the order provided by the text. For the reader's quick reference the stanzas containing the relevant passage are given below:

> Then þay schewed hym þe schelde, þat was of schyr goulez
> Wyth þe pentangel depaynt of pure golde hwez.
> He braydez hit by þe bauderyk, aboute þe hals kestes,
> þat bisemed þe segge semlyly fayre.
> And quy þe pentangel apendez to þat prynce noble
> I am in tent yow to telle, þof tary hyt me schulde:
> Hit is a syngne þat Salamon set sumquyle
> In bytoknyng of trawþe, bi tytle þat hit habbez,
> For hit is a figure þat haldez fyue poyntez,
> And vche lyne vmbelappez and loukez in oþer,
> And ayquere hit is endelez; and Englych hit callen
> Oueral, as I here, þe endeles knot.
> Forþy hit acordez to þis knyȝt and to his cler armez,
> For ay faythful in fyue and sere fyue syþez
> Gawan watz for gode knawen, and as golde pured,
> Voyded of vche vylany, wyth vertuez ennourned

    in mote;
  Forþy þe pentangel nwe
  He ber in schelde and cote,
  As tulk of tale most trwe
  And gentylest kny3t of lote.

Fyrst he watz funden fautlez in his fyue wyttez,
And efte fayled neuer þe freke in his fyue fyngres,
And alle his afyaunce vpon folde watz in þe fyue woundez
þat Cryst ka3t on þe croys, as þe crede tellez;
And quere-so-euer þys mon in melly watz stad,
His þro þo3t watz in þat, þur3 alle oþer þyngez,
þat alle his forsnes he feng at þe fyue joyez
þat þe hende heuen-quene had of hir chylde;
At þis cause þe kny3t comlyche hade
In þe inore half of his schelde hir ymage depaynted,
þat quen he blusched þerto his belde neuer payred.
þe fyft fyue þat I finde þat þe frek vsed
Watz fraunchyse and fela3schyp forþe al þyng,
His clannes and his cortaysye croked were neuer,
And pité, þat passez alle poyntez, þyse pure fyue
Were harder happed on þat haþel þen on any oþer.
Now alle þese fyue syþez, for soþe, were fetled on þis kny3t
And vchone halched in oþer, þat non ende hade,
And fyched vpon fyue poyntez, þat fayld neuer,
Ne samned neuer in no syde, ne sundred nouþer,
Withouten ende at any noke I oquere fynde,
Whereeuer þe gomen bygan, or glod to an ende.
þerefore on his schene schelde schapen watz þe knot
Ryally wyth red golde vpon rede gowlez,
þat is þe pure pentaungel wyth þe peple called
    with lore.

            (619-65)

Gawain's Shield

 As we learn at the beginning of the description the device appears in connection with Gawain's shield, the last item of the knight's splendid attire mentioned in the arming-of-the-hero passage. The shield is of red color ("schyr goulez," 619), while the pentangle itself is "depaynt of pure golde hwez" (620), thus corresponding with the gold dominating on Gawain's overall array, whose significance in the context of the postulated purity and excellence of Gawain's character has been analyzed in the preceding chapter. The display of the pentangle on the shield suggests some kind of heraldic device,[3] and such a context presupposes a definite functional significance of the sign, in addition to other meanings that the symbol may have due to its intrinsic nature. Obviously enough, apart from the protective function in the physical sense,[4] the knightly shield served as a sign for friends and foes alike, carrying information about the identity and status of its bearer. This is what the heraldic device worn on the outside of the shield was about: to serve as a primary means of recognition when the knight's identity was not otherwise determinable, especially at tournaments or in battles, when the knight's face was most likely to be hidden behind a visor. It was the necessity to distinguish one warrior from another in the heat of battle that brought heraldry with its identifying signs and symbols to life as an inseparable part of chivalric culture. The immediate protective and informative functions of the shield were so prominent that this element of the knightly gear alone came to denote the institution of knighthood and the chivalric profession. As Ramon Lull stated in his treatise on chivalry, *Le Libre del Ordre de Cauayleria* (ca. 1276):

> The shelde is gyuen to the knyght to sygnefye the offyce of a knyght. For in lyke wyse as the knyght putteth his sheld bytwene hym and his enemy, ryght soo the knyght is the moyen bytwene the prynce and the peple. (Caxton's translation)[5]

In Bohemian writings of the late fourteenth century an armed knight is frequently referred to as *stît*, the "shield," again showing that this single piece of military equipment had become a symbol of the entire knightly profession.[6] In *Sir Gawain* the shield with the pentangle depicted on it must have a similar function, first as a protective device, both in the immediate military sense and in the wider, allegorical sense that sees chivalry as a protection of the society, and second as a sign referring in some way to the personality of its bearer, as the text repeatedly makes clear.[7]

The basic functional meaning of the knightly shield was further developed in the Middle Ages into more allegorical and Christian significances. The textual *locus classicus* here is Saint Paul's final section from his Epistle to the Ephesians (6:10-17), where the servants of Christ are urged to put on themselves "the whole armor of God," particularly "the shield of faith, wherewith [they] shall be able to quench all the fiery darts of the wicked."[8] In the world of romance this is precisely what both literally and metaphorically happens to Gawain in Wolfram von Eschenbach's *Parzival*, where the knight is given a magic shield to protect himself during his supreme ordeal at *Schastel marveile*: while lying on a perilous bed Gawain pulled the shield over him like a quilt, and in this way was able to sustain the hail of pebbles and crossbow bolts thrown unexpectedly at him.[9] The meaning of the knightly shield both as physical and spiritual protection also explains why Galahad wore an image of Christ and the Cross on his shield in the *Queste del Saint Graal*,[10] and why King Arthur traditionally had the picture of the Virgin Mary displayed on his shield.[11] Sir Gawain too, in his capacity as Arthur's nephew and possible successor, had "in ße inore half of his schelde hir ymage depaynted" (649), and each time he looked at Mary's picture his courage never failed him. The spiritual value of the protection granted the knight by the Blessed Virgin is borne out, for example, in the writings of Robert Holkot, a contemporary of the *Gawain*-poet, who brings the significance of Arthur's shield in line with the evangelical teaching:

I rede in Gestis Britonum þat Kyng Artoure had in þe innare parte of ys shelde and ymage of Oure Lady Mary deprented, beryng a child in her armes, þe wiche ymage he wold behold when þat he was werry in batell and feynte; and anon for conforte and hope þat he had in hure he waxed freshe and herty aȝayn and in als good poynte for to feyȝthe as he was at þe begynnyng. Ryght so in þe same wyze þou arte in batell here on erthe and fyȝthynge not only aȝeyns bodely enmyes but also aȝeyns goostely, þat is þe world, þe feend, and þin own fleshe, þer-for loke þat þou haue Marye, Goddis modur, in þe innare parte of þi sheld, þat is þi feyȝth and þin beleue. Sett þat only vppon hure, þan trewly she will not forsake þe.[12]

The shield is thus a protection in the physical, psychological, and spiritual senses, since the "shield of faith" is for Christians a God-given protection against the forces of evil. In addition to that, Gawain's shield contains a reinforced magical protection, chiefly due to the pentangle, often used—among many other things—as a magical device to ward off evil.[13] However, the five-pointed star appears to be a symbol of much greater formal and semantic complexity, which extends far beyond the simple magical protective significance. In the context of the knotty and intricate geometrical nature of the pentangle, so emphatically underlined in the poem, simple protective magicseems to be the figure's least important function.

Solomon's Seal

The informative and protective functions of the shield apart, one also cannot underestimate the significance of sign language in medieval heraldry, in the times when the visual culture was not less important than the literary one.[14]   This means that apart from identification, which is obvious enough, the knightly coat-of-arms could, and often did, carry symbolic or allegorical significations as part of the more or less esoteric chivalric culture and erudition. As pertains to Sir Gawain's pentangle, it has been observed that nowhere in romance literature or historical heraldry, as far as records can tell, was the sign alone used as a coat-of-arms, let alone in connection with the figure of Gawain. In this respect Arthur's nephew is usually said in the texts to have a lion, a gryphon, a golden eagle, or a plain white shield ascribed to him.[15] Maybe for this reason the pentangle in *Sir Gawain* is referred to as new ("nwe," 636), not of course as a sign itself, but as a heraldic device, apparently newly created to denote either a new noble lineage or possibly a new type of chivalric order, fictional or historical, that may have used a five-pointed star as its identifying emblem.[16]

Having placed the pentangle in the functional-semantic context of Gawain's armor, the poet then proceeds to mention the legendary King Solomon, who reportedly used the sign to denote *trawþe*, apparently on account of some intrinsic "right" that the pentangle possesses in connection with this notion ("bi tytle þat hit habbez," 626). *Trawþe* has two basic meanings, both of which are exemplified in the poem, but only one seems directly connected with the pentangle: the word may either denote "truth" in a general, religious-philosophical sense or in the narrower sense of truthfulness, fidelity, and loyalty. I argue that it is the first, wider meaning of the word that is reserved for the pentangle in *Sir Gawain*, while the more narrow, practical meaning of *trawþe* is used elsewhere in the poem to denote the kind of noble and chivalric behavior necessitated by the various covenants, games, and agreements involving the main protagonists.[17]   The character of *trawþe* postulated for the pentangle and associated with King Solomon is more akin, for example, to the concept of Absolute Truth in *Piers Plowman*: truth unequivocally linked with faith and trust in God, or with God himself, "the fader of feith" (*Passus* 1:14-26), in accordance with the biblical teaching (John 14:6; Pss. 31:5; 33:4-5).[18]   At the end of his life Chaucer too referred to this Absolute Truth as the final remedy for the soul: "And trouthe the shal delivere, it is no drede," pleaded the poet in his *Balade de bon Conseyl*, popularly known as *Truth*.[19]

But the ascription of the pentangle as a sign denoting religious-philosophical truth to King Solomon, the paragon of ancient wisdom, has also more specific connotations. In a long and very detailed description of the building of King Solomon's temple in the Bible (1 Kings 5-7), it is said that the entrance to the inner shrine, the most sacred place of the temple containing the Ark of the Covenant, was pentagonal in shape (6:31).[20] Moreover, the inside of the inner shrine, as well as the altar itself, were overlaid with gold (6:20-30), the color of the pentangle in *Sir Gawain*. In my opinion, it is in this pentagonal entrance to the inner golden shrine of Solomon's temple that the true link is established between Gawain's golden pentangle and King Solomon, as referred to in the poem. It can even be suggested that the precise placing of the reference to the pentangle as Solomon's sign in *Sir Gawain* at line 625 is a hint at this numerological feature of Solomon's temple: number 625 is the square of five squared, $(5^2)^2=625$, and as such it is clearly related both to the pentangle itself and to the pentagonal door in Solomon's temple. The idea of the entrance to the holy of holies within the temple, or more allegorically of the door to salvation and eternal life, recurs later in the Bible in the Gospel of John (10:9), when Christ speaks of himself: "I am the door: by me if any man enter in, he shall be saved, and shall go in and out, and find pasture." What exactly the door means in soteriological terms is developed in the fourteenth-century *Book of Privy Counselling*, written by an anonymous author of the mystical treatise *The Cloud of Unknowing*:

> I [Christ] þat am almiȝty by my Godheed & may leuefuly as porter late in whom I wol, & bi what wey þat I wol, ȝit, for I wol þat þer be a comoun pleyne wey & an open entre to alle þat wolen come, so þat none be excusid by vnknowyng of þe wey, I haue cloþid me in þe comoun kynde of man, & maad me so opyn þat *I am þe dore by my manheed*, & who-so entreþ by me, he schal be saaf.[21] (Italics added)

While speaking symbolically of himself as the door to eternal life Christ clearly means his humanity and all that the human condition entails: hardships, pain, and suffering, followed by death. And in order to transcend death and gain salvation man needs faith, supported by devotion and contemplation, likewise compared to the door in the *Book of Privy Counselling*: "þe dore of deuocion & þe trewest entre of contemplacion" (160), which brings man closer to

Christ, who is "þe porter bi his Godheed, & þe dore by his manheed" (Ibid). But the more technical question still remains: why is the door to eternal life in Solomon's temple pentagonal in shape, and—consequently—can the pentangle and number five in any way be attributed to Christ, himself said to be the heavenly door? And further: is Sir Gawain holding, pictured on his shield, a sign of humanity as the "door" to eternal life, fashioned as a five-pointed star?

Number Five

Number five and its traditional significances are crucial to the understanding of both Sir Gawain's pentangle and the pentagonal door in Solomon's temple, and it is precisely the first property of the sign mentioned in the description: "For hit is a figure þat haldez fyue poyntez" (627). Five has to do first of all with generation and multiplication,[22]—that is, with the biological aspect of existence— and for this reason it is often referred to as a "marriage number," because it is formed by the addition of the odd masculine three and the even feminine two. For example, Plato in *Laws* (6) writes that nuptial guests should be admitted by fives, an idea followed by George Chapman in his continuation of Marlowe's *Hero and Leander*: here five children go before the young couple during a wedding ceremony as "a happie Augurie of generation" (ll.320-21), because "the od disparent number they did chuse, / To shew the vnion married loues should vse" (ll.323-24). The generative powers of number five are accounted for by Chapman in the following manner:

> And five they hold in most especiall prise
> Since t'is the first od number that doth ris
> From the two formost numbers unitie
> That od and even are; which are two, and three,
> For one no number is: but thence doth flow
> The powerfull race of numbers.[23]

As a number of the first union between the male and the female five naturally tends to denote procreation and fecundity in the more general sense; for example, it was accordingly on the fifth day of Creation that the most abundant and prolific animal world was brought into being by God (Gen. 1:20-23). An anonymous poem of the Carolingian period glosses this biblical verse by saying that number five denotes the world made up of the masculine triad and the feminine dyad, reflected in the five zones of the earth, the five senses, and the five species of living creatures: man, quadrupeds, fish, reptiles, and birds.[24] According to the cabalistic tradition the word meaning "light," which appears five times in the story of the first day of Creation (Gen. 1:3-5), corresponds to the five books of the Pentateuch, themselves containing the sacred power of the Name of the Holy One.[25] Likewise, by linking number five with the Creation the Hermetic philosophers handed down the belief that "the first principles were five, namely, the Creator, Reason, Soul, Space, and Time (or Void), and that the composite things came into being thereafter."[26] These widespread associations of number five with the idea of genesis and multiplication spring, as it appears, from the intrinsic mathematical properties of the number, which when multiplied by itself always returns to its own denomination (5x5=25), and is never corrupted by further multiplication: 25x5=125, and so on.[27] The same principle of endless repetition is contained in one of the geometrical features of the pentangle: the figure can be drawn without taking the pen off the paper, like the circle, the fact that can readily imply such ideas as infinity, eternity, and cyclicity.   Nor is this property of number five and of the pentangle without relevance to some aspects of the internal structure of *Sir Gawain*.   As A. K. Hieatt and other critics have shown,[28] and as I noted in chapter 2 of this book, the poem's story is enclosed within the lines 1-2525: that is, between the first line referring to the siege and fall of Troy, and the last line of the ultimate stanza before the bob and wheel, which is a near copy of line 1. The framing references to the fall of Troy serve to establish a paradigm of cyclicity in the narrative structure of *Sir Gawain,* and if this be so, then the looplike pattern of the entire story can in no way be linked merely accidentally to the circular character of number five and the pentangle.[29] The deliberate employment of these numerical-geometrical patterns again strongly suggests that the *Gawain*-poet must have been carefully counting the lines of his poem, so as to fit the story's overall structure into the numerical scheme contained in the pentangle.

To gloss five as a "marriage number" denoting sexuality, fecundity, and multiplication is another way of saying that five is a number of man in his corporeal, biological aspect.[30] The Venerable Bede, commenting on the earlier-quoted biblical passage on the door to the holy precinct in Solomon's temple, says that its pentagonal shape signifies the human body with its five senses, destined to be admitted to heaven.[31] Bede says also that the five cubits of length mentioned in the description of the temple (1 Kings

6:9-10, 24) mean that salvation can be achieved only by those who serve God with the five senses of the body and the five senses of the heart.[32] The human body itself has five extreme members (two legs, two arms, and a head), represented symbolically by the cross (four points plus the intersection), of which Sir Thomas Brown writes the following in his *Garden of Cyrus* (1658):

> The use of the number five is observable not only in some parts, but in the whole body of man, which upon the extension of arms and legs, doth make out a square, whose intersection is at the genitals.[33]

The fivefold structure relates to man's internal makeup as well, material and spiritual alike. For Pythagorean philosophers, for example, the human body was formed out of the mixture of five elements: fire, water, air, earth, and ether, and the powers of the soul were accordingly five in number: intelligence, wisdom, understanding, opinion, and self-perception.[34] The idea of five as a specifically human number is also confirmed by the *Asclepius*, a Hermetic text widely known in the Middle Ages, which speaks of the human mind, man's fifth component part, as coming from ether, the fifth element, and bestowed by God on man alone.[35] This "fifth element," which unites and harmonizes the main four components, is of course what the natural philosophers and alchemists called the *quinta essencia*, the "fifth essence" or the Philosophers' Stone: the purest, incorruptible substance that keeps the other elements together,[36] often said to be of divine origin. A Middle English translation of an alchemical treatise attributed to Hermes Trismegistos says the following:

> Forsoþe philosophoris clepen þe purest substaunce of manye corruptible þingis elementid "quinta essencia," þat is to seie, "mannys heuene." . . . This is oure quinta essencia, þat is to seie, mannys heuene, þat god made to þe conseruacioun of þe 4 qualities of mannys body.[37]

As the evidence adduced so far shows, there was throughout the centuries a widespread belief that with regard to his external appearance, internal composition, and spiritual constitution, man was fashioned out of five elements, a number apparently well-fitted to characterize the natural processes of generation, growth, and multiplication, as well as the idea of a harmonious and well-integrated unity of constituent parts. Just as the alchemical *quinta essencia* was found to bind subtly the four elements into a consonant entity, and the human head, the fifth bodily member, deemed by Hermetic philosophers to be of divine origin, was looked upon as a coordinating and unifying agent in the human body, so number five in the abstract sense appears to reveal certain unique properties, capable of integrating multiplicity into a harmonious whole. The idea is best illustrated in the geometrical features built naturally into the pentangle as a regular five-pointed figure, to which the text of *Sir Gawain* unequivocally and purposefully alludes. Let us simply follow the clues provided by the author.

The Pentangle and the Golden Section

There is no doubt that in geometrical terms "þe pentangel" displayed on Gawain's shield is a regular pentagram, in which "vche lyne vmbelappez *(overlaps)* and loukez *(is fastened)* in oþer, / And ayquere *(everywhere)* hit is endelez" (628-29), so that it is impossible to find "whereeuer þe gomen *(device)* bygan, or glod *(came)* to an ende" (661). The figure is truly "þe endeles knot" (630), for although the lines intersect one another, the shape can be drawn continuously, like the circle or the square:

Fig. 7. The Pentagram

It is not difficult therefore to associate with the pentagram the earlier-mentioned notions such as eternity, infinity, and endless self-replication,[38] as well as such concepts, absent in the circle for example, as unity in diversity, a feature linked with the pentagram's multisidedness. Moreover, the property of infinite self-reproduction, found in number five and its multiplications, is likewise present in the pentagram, in that the figure can reproduce itself in a countless number of further pentagrams and pentagons. Each regular pentagram contains within itself a pentagon, in which a new pentagram can be inscribed, and in the same way, by connecting the outer points of the pentagram a new, larger pentagon can be obtained.

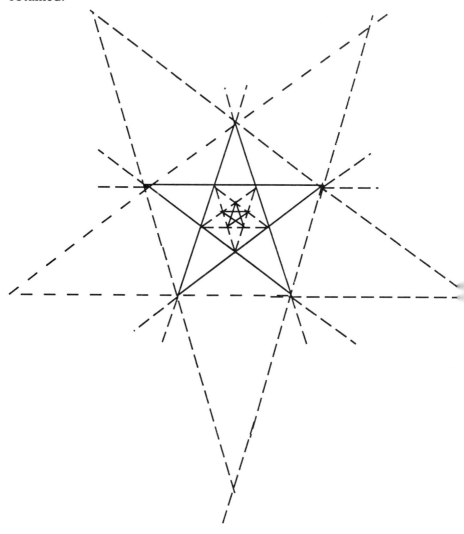

Fig. 8. The Infinite Self-Reproduction of the Pentagram.

This process can be repeated *ad infinitum*, generating the ever-decreasing and increasing pentagrams, each of them being, like an individual living organism, a link in an endless chain of reproduction (fig.8).

But by far the most revealing feature of the pentagram has to do with the internal relations between the sides and segments of the figure. For example, a pentagon circumscribed on a pentagram produces a series of homological triangles, as presented in figure 9. As is seen, triangle **abc** is homological with triangles **cgb** and **afb**. Also, the following proportion is true: **ac:ab=bc:gc**, and since **ab=ag**, hence **ac:ag=ag:gc**.

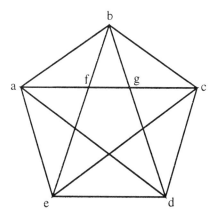

Fig. 9. Homological Triangles Within the Pentagon.

This means that the side of the pentagram cuts each line it crosses into two unequal segments, in such a way that the ratio of the whole side to the larger segment is the same as the ratio of the larger segment to the smaller segment:

a:b = b:(a+b)

Fig. 10. Division of the Segment According to the Golden Section.

Each intersection in the pentagram produces this proportion, which since antiquity is known as *sectio aurea*, the Golden Section.[39] Now if side **ac** on the pentagram above equals 1, then the Golden Section gives the following constant proportion:

1÷0.618=0.618÷0.382

which holds true in all the segments of the pentagram. On the other hand, the arithmetic connection between the Golden Section and number five, the geometrical basis of the pentagram, can be proved by forming a double square to represent 2, and by employing the diagonal $\sqrt{5}$, as shown in figure 11. The triangle ABC in the above diagram contains the Golden Cut, in that BC:AB=2:$(\sqrt{5}+1)$=0.618. The incommensurate proportion 0.618 is designated by the Greek letter *phi* (Ø), and was regarded by ancient and medieval philosophers, artists, and architects as perfect, transcendent, and sacred.

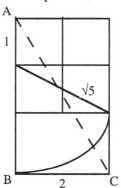

Fig. 11. The Golden Section Diagram.

There are grand philosophical, architectural, natural, and aesthetic considerations that have surrounded the Golden Proportion ever since humanity began to reflect upon the geometric forms of the world. The *locus classicus* of the philosophical expression of this idea of the concordant unity and harmony of the created world due to the Golden Proportion is provided by Plato in *Timaeus*, a text very influential throughout the Middle Ages.[40] Plato links the ideal proportion with the absolute genesis of things:

So god, when he began to put together the body of the universe, made it of fire and earth. But it is not possible to combine two things properly without a third to act as a bond to hold them together. And the best bond is one that effects the closest unity between itself and the terms it is combining; and this is best done by *a continued geometrical proportion*. For whenever you have three cube or square numbers with *a middle term such that the first term is to it as it is to the third term*, and conversely what the third term is to the mean the mean is to the first term, then since *the middle becomes first and last* and similarly the first and last become middle, it will follow necessarily that all can stand in the same relation to each other, and in so doing achieve unity together.[41] (Italics added)

Shortly speaking, the algebraic formula described by Plato is the following: in a segment divided according to the Golden Section the following proportions are true: **a:b=b:c, c:b=b:a, b:a=c:b =0.618 (Ø)**.

The presence of this universal integrating principle can be found in the sacred art of civilizations as different as those of Egypt, India, and China.[42] It also dominates Greek art and architecture, and persists concealed in the monuments of the Gothic Middle Ages. For example, the *phi* ratio was used extensively by the master masons of the Chartres Cathedral,[43] as well as in many monuments of the English Gothic. According to the historian of architecture Bernard G. Morgan, the canonic design used commonly by the royal master masons of the Plantagenet dynasty was based on the Golden Section and the *phi* ratio.[44] Among the buildings surveyed by Morgan in which the Golden Section was predominantly used are Westminster Abbey and the cathedrals of Salisbury, Bristol, Canterbury, and Winchester—in short: the flower and glory of the English Gothic. In the canonic, Golden proportion, writes Morgan, "lay the unifying factor in medieval building organization; its inherent geometrical relationships infused the design with a *resonant proportionality* and made possible the *sympathetic interlocking of every part in a concordant whole*" (Italics added).[45] In other words, the Golden Section consistently applied as the governing proportion of a building will ensure exceptional harmony and beauty of design, probably unattained by any other system of harmonic proportion in architecture.

The elusiveness of the aesthetic appeal of the *phi* ratio is something of a puzzle, and may have to do with the irrational, incommensurate nature of the number 0.618 as the basis of the asymmetrical division of a whole. It also seems necessary to mention in this context that the unique properties of the *phi* ratio extend beyond the realm of harmonic design in art and architecture and can be identified in plenty in the structure of living organisms: plants, animals, and humans. Indeed, it is the natural world where the idea of the Golden Proportion seems to have derived from in the first place. For instance, the *phi* pattern can be discerned in the spiral growth of a shell or sea-urchin, in the distribution of leaves on a stalk or of petals in a flower, in the structure of the spider's web, in the scales of fish, and in countless of other examples from the natural world where the Golden Section with its constant ratio determines the morphology of endless growth and reproduction of living tissues.[46]   The *phi* ratio is found to ensure harmonious interrelations among the parts of an organism, albeit not through simple addition or multiplication, but by means of a special geometrical progression of the *phi* number, which binds the related elements into a dynamic, creative unity, capable of growth and expansion.[47]

And it is in the human body that the Golden Section finds its most spectacular manifestation. For example, if the generative organs mark the arithmetical center of a grown-up man, the navel, the original source of life in a fetus, cuts the height of the body at the "golden point," 0.618.[48] Numerous *phi* relationships govern other bodily proportions, such as the progression of the bone-lengths in the human finger, hand, and arm.[49] A normal human skeleton, writes Matila Ghyka, reveals "a perfect symphonic design of the Golden proportion."[50] This is probably why Vitruvius in his treatise *De architectura* stated that the ideal architectural design of a temple should be based on the proportions of a well-built human body,[51] and artists such as Albrecht Dürer or Leonardo da Vinci likewise based their bodily canons on the Golden Proportion (figure 12).

Among the Neoplatonic and Hermetic philosophers too the idea of the microcosmic human being inscribed in the pentagon, a figure based on the Golden Section, was very popular. For example, Henry Cornelius Agrippa in his *De Occulta Philosophia* has a drawing of a man with outstretched arms and legs inscribed within a pentagram and a circle.[52] The pentagonal microcosmic human figures inscribed in the circle of the zodiac are also to be found in Hermetic treatises of Robert Fludd (fig.13).[53]

The pentagram emerges then as the best geometric expression of the idea of the perfect unity of parts, integrated in a dynamic, harmonious whole due to the internal relationships based on the Golden Proportion. It was apparently the inherent beauty and harmony of this sign that has attracted the curiosity of Goethe's Faust, for whom the "pure ciphers" ("reinen Zugen") of the figure reflecting the "living Nature" ("die wirkende Natur"), had a most soothing effect on his soul:

> War es ein Gott, der diese Zeichen schrieb,
> Die mir das innre Toben stillen,
> Das arme Herz mit Freude fullen

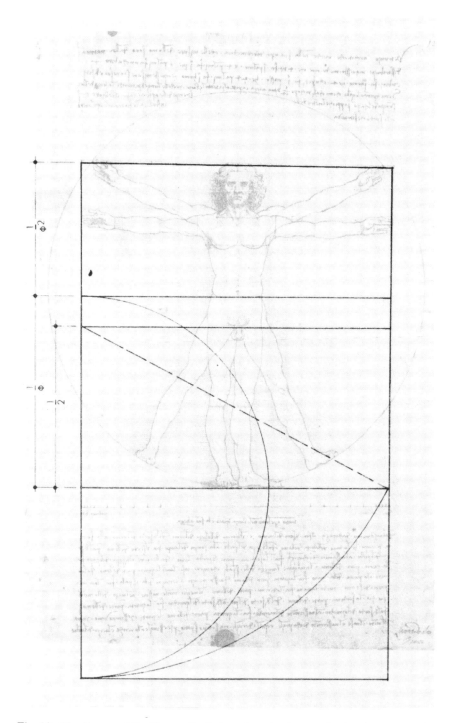

Fig. 12. The Canon of the Human Body Based on the Golden Section in the Drawing
by Leonardo da Vinci.

Fig. 13. The Pentagonal Man on the Front Page of Robert Fludd's *Tomus Secundus De Supernaturali* (1619).

Und mit geheimnisvollem Trieb
Die Kräfte der Natur rings um mich her enthullen?[54]

Like Sir Gawain's knotty pentangle, so too Faust's "Zeichen des Makrokosmus," undoubtedly a pentagram, has its elements "weaving one in one" ("alles sich zum Ganzen webt," 447), "living and working one in the other" ("eins in dem andern wirkt und lebt," 448), and the whole figure represents both the universal harmony of things in heaven and earth ("vom Himmel durch die Erde dringen, harmonisch all das All durchklingen," 452-53), and the "infinity of Nature" ("unendliche Natur," 455).

But the pentagram is first of all a sign of man, "the measure of all things," because—as the foregoing discussion has, I hope, convincingly shown—it expresses the truth about man's constitution and his harmonious coexistence with nature and the universe through the underlying "divine" and "golden" principle of perfect unity in diversity. In my opinion it is this universal philosophical-religious truth that is primarily implied by Gawain's pentangle and the notion of *trawþe* that it denotes. In the same way the "right" of the pentangle ("bi tytle þat hit habbez," 626) to represent *trawþe* derives, in my view, from the above-discussed properties of number five and the pentagram, particularly from the universal idea of the Golden Proportion based on the "transcendental" *phi* ratio. It is also due to its association with the principle of divine harmony and perfect unity that the pentangle is referred to in *Sir Gawain* as "pure" (664), just as the arcane knowledge of the sign's mathematical and geometrical properties is ascribed by the author to "þe peple called with lore" (664-65), evidently medieval philosophers versed in the Pythagorean and Platonic theory of numbers and geometrical figures, like the legendary Doctor Faustus. It is not unlikely that the *Gawain*-poet was himself familiar with some Hermetic and Neoplatonic texts, because the intellectual sophistication of the pentangle passage clearly calls for some definite source of this kind as an inspiration. Nor is it hard to see why the author is so silent and enigmatic about the nature of his source. It is quite clear that in terms of immediate, popular response the pentangle would have been first of all associated with magic and necromancy, as it undoubtedly was in the Middle Ages, rather than with such high-flown notions as those discussed above, more likely to be perceived and comprehended by a narrower and more learned audience. The pentagram had been for centuries used as an amulet against evil forces and was condemned as a magical device by ecclesiastical authorities, together with other geometric magical figures that filled the pages of medieval and Renaissance *grimoires* and handbooks of magic.[55] As John F. Kiteley pointed out in his interpretation of Gawain's "endeles knot,"[56] the recipients of the poem must have first of all associated the pentangle with protective magic, and any analysis of the symbol's function and meaning in the context of the poem must surely take this magical, popular perspective also into account. However, the full signif-icance and implications of the sign, both with regard to its intrinsic qualities and in relation to its owner and his adventures, go far be-yond the simple, instrumental, and magical function, as the formal intricacies and complexities of the pentangle expounded in the poem clearly illustrate.

The Five Pentads

The *Gawain*-poet himself does not seem to subscribe to viewing the pentangle primarily as a magical sign, for he carefully brings it into line with fairly orthodox Christian doctrine. This he does by ascribing to each point of the pentangle a group of five elements that refers to various aspects of the Christian worldview. There seems to be no doubt that what interests the author, and what he is accordingly trying to convey to his readers, is not only the doctrinal meaning of the enumerated pentads, as well as their obvious relation to Sir Gawain, but also the relationships existing both within the pentads themselves and among them. One perceives beneath the surface of the catalogued symbolic items an intricate system of interconnections and interdependencies, hinted at by the author in his repeated unambiguous statements about the "knotty" and interweaving nature of the pentangle.[57] Nor does the discovered Golden Proportion, regulating as it does the geometric structure of the pentangle, seem without relevance to the character of the postulated interdependencies. But before anything conclu-sive can be said about the nature of the system formed by the existing symbolic elements within Gawain's pentangle, an analysis of the content of the listed pentads seems necessary, following the order in which they appear in the text.

1. The first to be mentioned are the "fyue wyttez," in which Sir Gawain is found "fautlez" (640). The human wits, or senses ("the eye, the eere, the nose, the tonge, and the hande"),[58] are often dis-cussed in medieval homiletic writings, chiefly in connection with the related vices and sins. According to the *Ancrene Riwle*, the five senses are windows that should be guarded against evil influence

like battlements of a castle; the example of Christ, who suffered in all his senses, teaches man to mortify his own senses in asceticism.[59] Sir Gawain, "fautlez in his fyue wyttez," is apparently free from the sins pertaining to each sense,[60] holding his flesh in subjection or, as Gerald Morgan put it: "the movements of his sensitive appetite are properly regulated by reason."[61] The fourteenth-century *Book of Vices and Virtues* holds it as a general prescription:

> It bihoueþ to lede and gouerne wel þe fyue wittes of þe body bi resoun & bi euenhed, so þat eche serue of his office wiþ-oute synne and mystakyng, as þe eiȝen to loke, þe eeren to heren, þe noseþerless to smelle, þe mouþ to taste and to speke, þe honden and al þe body to touche. Whan þes fyue wittes ben wel y-kepte, þan is þe castel siker and stedefast, for þes ben þe ȝates of þe soule.[62]

The knowledge of these "five gates of the soul" and their proper defense against abuse were naturally part of medieval ascetic and meditative practices. *The Book of Privy Counselling* warns adepts of meditation against the intrusion of the devil through any one of the five senses:

> þus schal it be, wite þou riȝt wel, þou what-so-euer þat þou be þat settyst þee to worche trewly in þis werk [of meditation], þou schalt verrely see & fele, or elles smel, taste or here som astoniing maad by þe feende in some of þi fyue wittys wiþ-outyn. & al is done for to drawe þee downe fro þe heiȝt of þis precious worching.[63]

In an English devotional treatise called *Jacob's Well* the five senses are referred to as "watyr-gatys"; that is, the entrances of the streams of water that flow from "the currents of this world," feeding man with the knowledge of this-worldy life. Together with possible evil influence, says the treatise, death enters through these five windows of the soul,[64] which for this reason have to be "stopped" in the course of meditative work, so that "þe watyr of þe grete curs and þe wose of dedly synnes entre noȝt into ȝoure pytt aȝen."[65] After "stopping" the senses they can be used "inwardly"— that is, to perceive the inner voice of God and to further spiritual perfection. From the above and other numerous medieval references to the five senses[66] it emerges that the mention of the "fyue wyttez" in *Sir Gawain* is by all accounts rooted in the devotional and meditative tradition, in which the guarding and controlling of one's bodily senses was an important element of self-discipline and control in ascetic and devotional practice. Like the remaining pentads of the pentangle, this too refers to the spiritual and religious aspect of humanity and chivalry represented by Sir Gawain.

2. Second in order among the pentads ascribed to the pentangle come the "fyue fyngres," which "fayled neuer þe freke" (641). In the literal sense the five fingers appear to refer to Gawain's chivalric profession, particularly his swordsmanship and physical skills in combat, of which the knight gave good instances during his solitary journey through North Wales, fighting all sorts of human, animal, and supernatural foes (716-17, 720-25).[67] On the allegorical level, however, man's five fingers can also correspond to vices, often grouped in fives in penitential writings. For example, the earlier-cited *Book of Vices and Virtues* divides the sins of lechery and gluttony into "fyue maneres" (43, 48), and likewise Chaucer in *The Parson's Tale* talks about lechery as the devil's five fingers, apparently because this particular sin has mostly to do with the sense of touch:

> [Lechery is] that oother hand of the devel with fyve fyngres to cacche the peple to his vileynye. The firste fynger is the fool lookynge of the fool womman and of the fool man . . . The seconde fynger is the vileyns touchynge in wikede manere. . . . The thridde is foule wordes, that fareth lyk fyr, that right anon brenneth the herte. The fourthe fynger is the kissynge; and trewely he were a greet fool that wolde kisse the mouth of a brennynge oven or of a fourneys . . . the fifthe fynger of the develes is the stynkynge dede of Leccherie . . . and with his fyve fingres [the devil] gripeth man by the reynes *(loins)* for to throwen hym into the fourneys of helle.[68]

The wearer of the pentangle in *Sir Gawain*, despite his notoriety as a seducer alluded to in the poem,[69] on the whole finds himself free from carnal sin, particulary lechery, as his successful defense against the lady's sexual lurings in Fitt III clearly illustrates. But apart from sins and vices, the five fingers can also be allegorized with virtues, since hands can be used for the production of good works as well. For example, in a treatise by John of San Geminiano called *Summa de exemplis et rerum similitudinibus,*[70] the thumb stands for justice, the index finger for prudence, the third finger signifies temperance, the ring finger fortitude, and the little finger represents obedience with respect to the divine will, human authority, and to one's own reason. The carnal sins classified according to the five fingers can therefore be counterbalanced by Christian virtues arranged in a similar way, and both can be symbolically linked with the human hand, used either for good or evil works.

3. The third pentad comprises the "fyue woundez þat Cryst kaȝt in þe croys" (642-43). The Five Wounds of Christ (in hands, side, and feet)[71] as a visible sign of the Lord's Passion are frequently mentioned in medieval meditational and devotional sources as an object of veneration and prayer. On some medieval paintings and manuscript illustrations Christ's body is often schematically presented in the middle of a square described by his four wounds in the outstretched hands and feet, with the heart pierced by a spear at the center.[72] These geometricized representations suggest that Christ's body stretched on the cross with his heart in the middle of the square served as a kind of *instrumentum gnosis* to be used by mystics and ascetics in their meditation. In this context the pentagram itself as the *imago hominis* can also be viewed as a meditative symbol, linked naturally with Christ's Five Wounds, and further with the whole idea of Christ's Incarnation and humanity. For example, in the writings of Renaissance artist Piero Valeriano the pentagram has the figure of nude Christ inscribed in it, with arms and legs extended, and with the wounds in hands, feet, and breast.[73] As is known, the medieval stigmatics were reputed to go in their meditative practices as far as to virtually acquiring the bodily marks that corresponded with Christ's wounds. The Flemish mystic Jan van Ruusbroec writes about this *unio mystica,* using a very sensual and almost erotic language:

> Shun and flee the false world, for He has opened His arms and wants to receive and embrace you. Make your dwelling in the caverns of His wounds as the dove does in the caverns of the rock. Place your mouth on His opened side; smell and savour the heavenly sweetness which flows from His heart.[74]

The heart of Jesus too, itself an object of both mystical contemplation and popular cult and devotion, was conceived as the seat of divine wisdom and the essence of human feeling and compassion in Christ. The blood pouring from the Savior's wounds was believed to possess healing, life-giving, and redeeming qualities, best exemplified in the symbolism of the Eucharist, as well as in the more esoteric cult of the Holy Grail. The fourteenth-century German mystic Johannes Tauler in his sermons links allegorically the Five Wounds of Christ with the five porches at the pool in Jerusalem, referred to in John 5:1-9: whoever steps into the water when it is moved by the Holy Spirit (as Tauler explains), will be cured of all his illnesses and afflictions. Moreover, the German mystic ascribes to the wounds a set of Christian virtues: humility, persistant contemplation, compunction, poverty, and readiness to make sacrifices for the sake of God.[75] It is also interesting to add that the traditional five wounds can be linked with the five human senses, already present in Gawain's pentangle; the former are described as the cure for the sins likely to be committed through the latter. A prayer in the *Ancrene Wisse* explains it clearly:

> for þe ilke fif wunden þe þu on hire [Cross] bleddest, heal mi blodi sawle of alle þe sunnen þet ha is wiþ iwundet þurh mine fif wittes.[76]

It will be remembered that all these correspondencies and analogies are particularly significant in view of the intricate system of interconnections postulated by the text for the pentads of Gawain's pentangle. Nor is there an incongruity between Christ's wounds, their healing and saving quality, and the symbolism of the knightly shield, to which the wounds are ascribed through the pentangle. It is true that christological imagery is closely linked with chivalric symbolism and ideology, as is exemplified in the common figure of Christ pictured as a knight come to the world to fight evil and death.[77] For instance, Christ's body stretched on the cross is compared to knightly shield in a fourteenth-century version of *Ancrene Riwle*:

> His shilde that covered the godhede was his blessed body that was spred upon the harde crosse. Ther appered he as a shilde in his armes with his handes streined and [his heart] persed and his feete nailed down, as summe men sey, the tone upon the tother.[78]

John Lydgate too speaks of Christ's five wounds as "the five rooses portrayed in the sheeld, splayed in the baneer at Jerusalem," symbols of the Savior's martyrdom and mortal fight on "the bloody feeld" of the world.[79] In this way the Five Wounds of Christ, explicitly ascribed to Gawain's pentangle and to his shield in a larger sense, reinforce the earlier-presented more hidden meaning of the pentagram as a sign of humanity. Christ's wounds related to Gawain's pentangle also underpin the symbolic identification between the pentagonal entrance to Solomon's temple and the figure of Christ understood as the door to eternal life. Thus through its close relation to Christ the pentangle becomes also a symbol of resurrection and potential divinity for humans.[80]

4. The fourth pentad consists of "þe fyue joyez þat þe hende heuen-quene had of hir chylde" (646-47). This mariological

element is directly linked with the image of the Virgin Mary displayed on the inner side of Gawain's shield, from whom the knight drew all his "forsnes" (645) and "belde" (courage) (650). Both representations are in turn in keeping with a popular medieval poetic metaphor regarding Mary as a "shield" protecting the believer.[81] Like the Five Wounds of Christ, the Five Joys of Mary were often celebrated in medieval literature, and their standard order included the following episodes from the life of the Virgin: 1. the Annunciation, 2. the Nativity, 3. the Resurrection, 4. the Ascension, and 5. the Assumption.[82] As is immediately seen, three out of five of Mary's joys are directly linked with the more cheerful episodes from the life of Christ, although the correspondencies between the Five Joys of Mary and the Five Wounds of her son were also frequently made; just as in imitation of Christ the believers imagined themselves in Christ's situation at every stage of his suffering, so in worshipping the Madonna they were similarly supposed to follow in her footsteps through all her experiences, both joyous and sorrowful. The two cults were in a natural way closely interwoven, and both devotional poetry and liturgical practice bear witness to that.[83] Needless to say, in *Sir Gawain* these thematic analogies and correspondencies are reinforced by the interlocking nature of the pentangle.

But the symbolic association of number five with the Virgin extends beyond the above analogy. The number recurs also in connection with Mary's traditional sacred Latin names: Maria, Virgo, Mater, and it was conceived that both the numerical and phonetic values of Mary's names reflected the sacredness, purity, and perfection ascribed to the Virgin.[84] Likewise, just as Christ's wounds were sometimes represented by five roses, symbols of the Savior's martyrdom and mortality, so the Virgin's steadfast piety was compared by medieval religious poets to a rose among thorns (*rosa inter spinas*), a pious one among the unfaithful, and by the way of analogy with the five joys and the five letters of her name, this rose was said to have five petals too.[85]

There is also another, very intriguing reason for the symbolic association of number five and the pentagram with the Virgin Mary. Among the innumerable Marian metaphors and similes found in medieval devotional literature and iconography,[86] a very frequent one is that comparing the Virgin to a star. A star can send out its light without itself losing any of its brightness, just as Mary gave birth to her child without forfeiting her virginity. A star is smaller and weaker than the sun, but as the morning star it can announce the advent of the greater light, just as Mary announced

Jesus. The association of the Virgin Mary with Venus as the morning star (*aurora consurgens*) is grounded in the Scripture (Song of Solomon 6:10), and must have been reinforced, if not indeed caused, by the observation of Venus rising above the sea in the morning and heralding the sunrise. In prayers and meditative lyrics Mary was often invoked as *Stella Maris*, the "star of the sea," partly due to the association of her name with the Latin word for the "sea," *mare*, and partly because people looked up to Mary rising like the star above "the sea of this world." An Old English homily comments on this metaphor in connection with the Virgin Mary and Mary Magdalen:

> She [Mary Magdalen] has the same name as the holy maiden our Saviour's mother, Mary, queen of angels, that is, in our language, "sea-star" (*se-steorre*), and it well suits each of them. . . . Each of them illuminates the sea, that is this world, with fair example. The queen gave example of virginity, that is of purity. . . . Holy book calleth this world "sea," because that various accidents, sometimes of weal, sometimes of woe, come therein, as do the waves in the sea.[87]

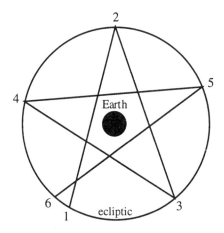

Fig. 14. The Pentagram Formed on the Ecliptic by the Planet Venus in Its Eight-Year Cycle.

However, what is most interesting in these "stellar" associations of the Blessed Virgin is that number five, and specifically the pentagram as a geometric figure based on this number, is on astronomical grounds linked with the planet Venus, and in consequence with Mary herself. Each astronomical phenomenon associated with Venus (apparitions as evening or morning stars, conjunctions with the sun, and so forth) that can be easily identified in the sky by an experienced observer, tends to repeat in about the same place on the ecliptic (the apparent annual path of the sun along the zodiacal constellations) every eight years, during which time Venus marks on the ecliptic five points forming a pentagram. as presented in figure 14. This habit of the revolution of the planet Venus was well known in antiquity and was used by astronomers in the prediction of Venus's recurrences, since every similar Venus phenomenon followed regularly the ecliptical points (marked by consecutive numbers in the above drawing) describing a pentagram on the ecliptic, in a sequence five times 1.6 years.[88] This means that in astronomy, and from it consequently in religious and poetic imagery, the pentagram could become a symbol associated with Venus as a planetary goddess, linked later by Christianity with the Virgin Mary as the morning star.[89] The association of the divine Virgin with the five-pointed star extended well into the Renaissance, and in England for instance the notion was incorporated into the official cult of Queen Elizabeth I, worshiped as the Virgin of the Imperial Reform. George Chapman in his *Hymnus in Cynthiam* ascribes the magic pentagram to the chaste queen:

> Then in thy clear and Isie Pentacle
> Now execute a Magicke miracle.[90]

The presence of the mariological pentad next to the christological one in Gawain's pentangle seems therefore fully justified, chiefly on doctrinal grounds, since the cult of the Virgin Mary was closely linked with that of Christ, but also partly for astronomical reasons, which explain the origin of the "sea-star" metaphor. Nor is it surprising to find a "female" pentad within the figure based on number five—Plato's "marriage number" composed of a female two and masculine three. The presence of the Holy Virgin next to Christ again illustrates the idea of the harmonious unity of opposite elements, initially found in the geometric features of the pentangle.

5. The last pentad mentioned in the text comprises a set of moral and chivalric virtues, specifically *fraunchyse*, *felaȝschyp*, *clannes*, *cortaysye*, and *pité* (552-54), that "were harder happed (*fixed*) on þat haþel þen on any oþer" (655). Although Norman Davis in his note to the edition of *Sir Gawain* remarks that these virtues "do not seem to have been chosen by the poet with especially close regard to the adventure which follows" (95), the main emphasis being later laid on Gawain's *trawþe* understood as faithfulness,[91] they do in

fact bear upon the character of chivalry represented by Sir Gawain, in addition to their structurally important place among the other pentads. What follows is a brief discussion of the meaning of the respective virtues with regard to Sir Gawain.

According to the *MED*,[92] *fraunchyse* indicates a disposition to generosity and magnanimity that springs from free birth and nobility of character. It was particularly characteristic of knighthood as an economically privileged class to give freely,[93] just as magnanimity in the spiritual sense, understood as noble disinterestedness and bigheartedness, was seen as the foundation of nobility in general, as illustrated in the otherwise unresolvable dilemma of contradictory pledges in Chaucer's *Franklin's Tale.* In Chrétien's *Cligés,* too, the Greek emperor instructs his son in the fundamental value of the virtue of *largesce*, the mistress and queen of all other virtues, that surpasses them all:

> Biax filz, fet il, de ce me croi:
> Que largesce est dame et reine
> Qui totes vertuz anlumine,
> Ne n'est mie grief a prover.
> A quel bien cil se puet torner,
> Ja tant ne soit puissanz ne riches,
> Ne soit honiz, se il est chiches?
> Qui a tant d'autre bien sanz grace
> Que largesce loer ne face?
> Par soi fet prodome largesce,
> Ce que ne puet feire hautesce,
> Ne corteisie, ne savoir,
> Ne gentillesce, ne avoir,
> Ne force, ne chevalerie,
> Ne proesce, ne seignorie,
> Ne biautez, ne nule autre chose;[94]

The central position of *largesce* in Chrétien's hierarchy of chivalric virtues probably explains why the corresponding *fraunchyse* tops the list in *Sir Gawain* and why this is accordingly the virtue first displayed by Gawain in the poem, in his magnanimously and unselfishly taking the Green Knight's challenge in place of King Arthur.

The second of the mentioned virtues, *fela3schyp*, is glossed by the *MED* as "the spirit that binds companions or friends together" and also "charity, amity, comraderie." This clearly refers to the companionship and conviviality displayed by Gawain and other knights at Camelot, just as later the same spirit of warmth, friendliness, and loyalty governs most of the social activities going on at Hautdesert, chiefly between Sir Gawain and Sir Bertilac.

On the other hand, the basic meaning of *clannes* as evidenced by Sir Gawain is undoubtedly the knight's chastity and avoidance of corporal sin in his dealings with the Lady, although the notion does not preclude amorous courtly behavior in the more refined sense,[95] which fills the better part of Fitt III. Other meanings of the word glossed by the *MED*, such as "elegance," "modesty," "propriety," "uprightness," and "integrity" can also be amply exemplified by Gawain's conduct displayed throughout the poem.

Cortaysye in turn covers an even wider range of behavior expected of the knight, courtier, and also the clergyman, in that it embraced various aspects of chivalrous conduct extending from courtly politeness and refinement of manners to compassion, benevolence, and grace, even in the divine sense.[96] In *Cleanness* "courtesy" resonates with Christ's grace,[97] and in a Middle English courtesy book called *Lytylle Childrene* the virtue is likewise said to be of divine origin:

> Clerkys þat canne þe scyens seuene,
> Says þat curtasy came fro heuen.[98]

Etymologically, "courtesy" has to do with rules of behavior expected of people attending a court and included such things as attention to clothing, table manners, hygiene, eloquence, pastimes, and observance of religious duties,[99] but in the Middle Ages the rules of etiquette were to a similar degree nourished in the monasteries as well, and numerous courtesy manuals bear witness to a strong connection between monastic and courtly rules in this respect.[100] The parallelisms between the rules of monastic discipline and courtly decorum can be viewed as a means of imposing restraint and self-control upon the military core of the institution of chivalry, and the postulated refinement of manners, combined with the idea of religious justification of military behavior, can be seen as a means of checking and curbing the otherwise overtly violent and socially dangerous knightly ethos.[101] This merger of courtly, chivalric, and religious ideals is best exemplified in numerous manuals of chivalry,[102] which apart from prescribing good manners and etiquette propagated the improvement of such spiritual virtues as charity, piety, and compassion. These values can be found reflected both within the set of moral virtues ascribed to Gawain and in their interrelations with the other, more overtly religious pentads of the pentangle. Sir

Gawain is indeed described as the very pattern of courtesy, both in the narrow sense of simply being polite, as in Chaucer's *Squire's Tale*,[103] and in his overall integrity, moderation, tactfulness, and measure in dealing with others.[104]

The last virtue of the fifth pentad on Gawain's pentangle is "pité, þat passez alle poyntez" (654), which causes an immediate interpretative problem in that in Middle English it may mean either "pity" or "piety."[105] For Norman Davis "pity" in the wide sense of "compassion" is meant by the poet (96), although Sir Israel Gollancz in his earlier edition of the text prefers "piety." Surely the latter is well evidenced by the poem in numerous instances of Gawain's eagerness to make religious observances,[106] or to go to confession,[107] but as Davis rightly observes, Gawain's piety has been fully shown in the pentads referring to Christ's Five Wounds and Mary's Five Joys, and further emphasis on it in a section discussing primarily chivalric virtues would be otiose. Therefore, more in keeping both with the internal structure of this pentad and with its relation to the other pentads, though maybe not so in relation to the poem's plot, is the meaning of *pité* as "pity," "compassion," and chivalric or royal "pardon." The *Secretum Secretorum* says that princely "pite mouethe to shewe charyte and . . . misericorde,"[108] in which case the virtue can be seen as springing from *caritas*, the highest of the Christian virtues (1 Cor.13:13), and the first of Christ's commandments that permeates the whole of the *Sermon on the Mount* (Matt. 5-7). It is probably due to this connection with the Christian *caritas,* as much as to the inevitable confusion with "piety," that "pité, þat passez alle poyntez" is given such a prominent position among the other virtues of the last pentad; in this way the basically chivalric qualities are again placed in a larger socioreligious context.

The five interrelated virtues of the last pentad describe therefore the moral tenets of an ideal chivalric conduct, supposedly exemplified by Sir Gawain and inseparably linked with the religious and moral values explicitly referred to in the other pentads. There seems to be no doubt that each pentad constitutes an internally well-bound and integrated symbolic unit, organized in a set of five elements either according to a natural or a more conventional criterion.[109] My next step will be now to examine the relationships existing *between* the pentads, by following the unequivocal clues in the text about the interlocking and interweaving nature of the lines forming the pentangle. In other words, having presented the content and meaning of the individual pentads, I shall now relate them more closely to the previously discussed geometric properties of the pentangle itself, as these determine the nature of the relationships existing among all the symbolic elements involved.

It is to be recalled that the poet sums up his exposition of the content of the five pentads by referring them back to the intricate geometrical features of the pentangle:

> Now alle þese fyue syþez (*sets*) for soþe, were fetled (*fixed*) on þis kny3t,
> And vchone halched (*joined*) in oþer, þat non ende hade,
> And fyched (*fixed*) vpon fyue poyntez, þat fayld neuer,
> Ne samned (*gathered*) neuer in no syde, ne sundred nouþer,
> Withouten ende at any noke I oquere fynde,
> Whereeuer þe gomen bygan, or glod to an ende.

(656-61)

The evoked structural peculiarities of the pentangle manifestly convey an idea of the indivisibility and interconnectedness of the distinguished symbolic elements ascribed to the five points of the figure, at the same time highlighting their endless and circular character, despite their finite number. Now if we were to visualize the five pentads, distributed at the consecutive points of the pentangle in the order in which they are listed in the text, the picture would probably look something like figure 15:

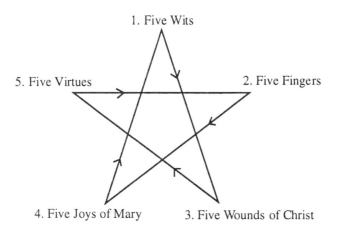

Fig. 15. The Five Pentads Ascribed to the Points of the Pentagram.

Such a distribution of the pentads around the figure, although following the textual order, rests of course on a justifiable assumption that the direction of distribution is clockwise—or sunwise—positive and beneficial. But a single glance at the pentads thus laid out reveals that their right order is *not* the linear one given by the text, but rather an alternating and circular one following the sunwise, righthand movement along the intersecting lines of the pentangle. As in a circle, there is no beginning or end in this "gomen," as the text itself unmistakedly expresses, because the pentangle can be entered at any point. But since the author begins his exposition of the device with the "fyue wyttez," let us proceed accordingly. The lines of the figure give us then the following sequence of the pentads:

5 Wits ➤ 5 Wounds ➤ 5 Virtues ➤ 5 Fingers ➤ 5 Joys

Fig. 16. The Order of the Pentads Suggested by the Structure of the Pentangle

which, by the way, go on in a circular fashion, since the Five Joys return to the Five Wits and the whole cycle begins anew, as becomes the "endeles knot." Therefore in addition to the connections existing within the pentads (which is obvious and logical), there is a network of links *between* the pentads and their constituent elements, following the design of the pentangle. What ultimately emerges is a system of twenty-five elements (5 times 5), circularly bound in five cycles that enfold endlessly in accordance with the geometry of the pentangle, as represented in table 5.

Table 5

The Five Cycles of the Five Pentads Contained in Sir Gawain's Pentangle.

	1st Cycle	2nd Cycle	3rd Cycle	4th Cycle	5th Cycle
Five Wits	sight	hearing	smelling	taste	touch
Five Wounds	right hand	left hand	heart	right foot	left foot
Five Virtues	*fraunchyse*	*fela3schyp*	*clannes*	*cortaysye*	*pité*
Five Fingers	thumb	index	third finger	ring finger	little finger
Five Joys	Annunciation	Nativity	Epiphany	Resurrection	Assumption

The whole "great" cycle of the "endeles knot" thus conceived consists of five smaller cycles involving the respective elements of the pentads, five in each cycle, so that the full revolution of all the elements is enclosed in a formula 5 times 5 equals 25, in which number five returns to its own denomination, as is its nature, and the process can begin anew. Number 25 in turn brings us again to the echoing line 2525 at the end of the poem, confirming once more that number five and its second power twenty-five are key symbolic numbers in *Sir Gawain*, conveying as they do the previously discussed associations with such concepts as cyclicity, unity in diversity, reproduction and life itself, and on the more hermetic level ideas such as the divinity of man and redemption.

The system of relationships between the twenty-five elements, as presented in the above table, is of course subject to revisions and corrections, mainly due to the variations and differences existing in the medieval sources as to the ultimate number, order, and nature of the elements forming the traditional pentads. Despite the inevitable discrepancies in detail, however, there undoubtedly exist well-attested correspondencies between the various elements of the pentads, such as, for example, the earlier-mentioned interconnections between the Five Wits, the corresponding sins and the Five Wounds of Christ invoked to heal those sins; between the same wounds and the joys of Mary; between the chivalric virtues and the Christian virtues ascribed to the five fingers and so on. On the other hand it would be difficult, if not altogether impossible, to offer a precise verbal description and explanation of *all* the connections potentially existing between the pentads, or to show how the whole system actually worked on the conceptual and symbolic levels, even given the universal medieval predilection to comprehend reality in terms of analogies, similarities, and correspondencies. For example, it emerges from the system that there should be symbolic connections between the elements within each of the five cycles, such as between the sense of sight, the wound in Christ's right hand, the virtue of *fraunchyse*, the thumb, and Mary's joy at the Annunciation, which all constitute the First Cycle. First, medieval sources offer a rather fluid, incomplete, and varying picture of the contents of the Christian pentads and leave too much room for arbitrary alterations and modifications. Second, in all the analogies that *are* pointed out in available textual evidence and that are so clearly shown by the interconnectedness of the points in Gawain's pentangle, one cannot resist the impression that the ultimate unity of all the elements involved, as well as the subtlety of their internal links, to a large degree escape rational discernment and logic and can probably be apprehended only through a kind of insight and intuition that allowed the medieval mystics to perceive divine order and harmony both within themselves and in the external world. One can only surmise, following the hints provided by the structure of the pentangle, that the principle that binds the five pentads and their elements into an internally coherent and harmonious whole is that of the Golden Section—a universal law of centralization and integration that the ancients ascribed to the genius of the Divine Mind, *nous*, the Supreme Reason. Just as the sides of the "pure pentaungel" dissect one another at the ratio reflecting the perfect, natural harmony of the constituent parts of a whole, so the elements of each pentad are probably ultimately interrelated according to the same universal and perfect principle.

But even if one is denied the grace of an intuitive, spontaneous insight into the nature of the above symbolic system with its twenty-five elements perceived *all at once* as a harmonious whole, a cursory glance at the table can also reveal its comprehensive character, in that the distinguished elements embrace the totality of human experience in relation to the divine. For example, in the order in which the pentads are listed in the poem, the wits and the fingers, together with all their correspondencies, can be called "human" pentads, because they refer first of all to bodily and physiological makeup. The wounds and the joys are in turn "divine" pentads, focusing on the most fundamental doctrines and tenets of Christianity. Finally, the integrated chivalric virtues of the fifth pentad embody the spiritual and moral essence of knighthood, an institution conceived as a bridge between the human and the divine in man, an ideal and perfect mode of earthly existence. And once the order of the pentads is rearranged according to the pentangle's geometry (see table 5), the "human," the "divine," and the "chivalric" begin to alternate with one another and to rotate endlessly around the "chivalric" pentad, now occupying the third, central position in the system. In this way chivalry in general as a semi-religious institution, together with Sir Gawain as its most renowned representative, emerge in the poem as coordinating elements and intermediaries between the human world, symbolized in the poem by Arthur's Camelot, and the realm of the supernatural and the divine, personified by the awe-inspiring Green Knight and his otherworldly domain. The complex and intricate mathematical and spiritual significance of the pentangle, understood both as an *imago hominis* and as a kind of mnemonic device synthesizing the human and the divine in man according to specific geometrical patterns, is exemplified in the poem by Sir Gawain, the perfect of knights, "and as golde pured, voyded of vche vylany" (633-34)—an emblem of humanity beset by fundamental metaphysical and existential questions on its way towards salvation.

Sir Gawain and the Idea of the Pentangle

As I discussed earlier in this chapter, the Golden Section as the controlling property and idea of the pentangle describes both the process of growth in living organisms and the principle of perfect harmony in nature, art, and man. A question now arises whether this principle, so exclusively associated with the pentangle as a geometric figure,[110] can apply to Sir Gawain in any other way than that which is naturally linked with him in the general sense as a member of the human species. In other words, can the idea of the Golden Section and the Golden Mean embodied in Gawain's coat-of-arms tell us something more specific about the knight's character and behavior in the same measure as it describes his constitution simply as a human being. After all, both the pentangle itself and the five pentads are repeatedly "fetled *(fixed)* on þis kny3t" (656) by the author, and so this attribution cannot be of purely superficial and external nature. And if the pentangle's hidden meaning does refer to Gawain's character, how is this borne out by the poem itself?

It is clear that the internal harmony of character is a prerequisite of human perfection and philosophy, since Plato and Aristotle have dwelled extensively on the problem. Dante in *Il Convivio* follows the Platonic vein when he states that:

> Among all the creations of divine wisdom man is the most wonderful, if we consider how the divine power has conjoined three natures [the vegetative, the sensitive, the intellective] in a single form and *how subtly his body must be harmonized*, having within that form organs for almost all of its powers. Consequently, because of the great degree of harmony required for so many organs to be *in proper accord with each other*, there are few within the great number of men that exist who are perfect.[111] (Italics added)

Applied to the sphere of human conduct the said harmony appears close to a well-known ethical notion of the mean virtue or measure, which relies on careful self-regulation and control of behavior in the avoidance of various excesses and extremes. In medieval writings the concept of *mesure* as the mean virtue is well evidenced,[112] and the idea goes back to Aristotle's *Nicomachean Ethics*,[113] where the mean virtue of moderation and self-control is highly praised and recommended. Interestingly, Aristotle uses arithmetical language to describe the character of his mean virtue: "if ten is many and two is few, six is the intermediate,"[114] and in the same way "a master of any art avoids excess and defect, but seeks the intermediate," since moral virtue "must have the quality of aiming at the intermediate . . . and this is concerned with passions and actions." Therefore "virtue is a state of character concerned with choice, lying in a mean . . . between two vices, that which depends on excess and that which depends on defect." Aristotle then goes on to provide examples of the mean virtues in respect of the common human passions: "with regard to feelings of fear and confidence courage is the mean," "with regard to giving and taking of money the mean is liberality," "with regard to honor and dishonor the mean is proper pride," with regard to anger "let us call the mean good temper." Other common mean virtues listed are truthfulness, ready-wittedness (between buffoonery and boorishness), friendliness, righteous indignation (between envy and spite), and so on.

Medieval literature likewise prescribes the observance of the mean in conduct. In *The Book of Vices and Virtues* we are told that "who-so kepeþ þe myddel bitwexe litle and mochel, as resoun scheweþ, is a-liȝht wiþ grace y-tauȝt," because "þis vertue kepeþ resonable mesure."[115] Ramon Lull in his manual of chivalry also instructs the aspiring knight that "vertue and mesure abyde in the myddel of two extremytees."[116] In my opinion, the Aristotelian idea of the mean virtue of temperance and moderation is at least analogous, if not ultimately derived from the ancient concept of the Golden Mean as the perfect division of the whole, exemplified geometrically by the regular pentagram. The Golden Section as the principle of perfect harmony and unity suits well the idea of virtue and integrity of human character, shown in moderate, prudent, and controlled action. Edmund Spenser, for example, talks about the "golden Meane" in the Argument to Book 2 of *The Faerie Queene*, devoted to the allegorical exposition of the virtue of temperance. It is most probably also due to this association of the Golden Mean with the perfection of character that the pentagon, the figure based on the Golden Section, was ascribed to the rational soul by Aquinas in his *Summa Theologiae* (1a 76.3), and after him by Dante in *Il Convivio* (4. 7. 14-15).[117] As far as *Sir Gawain* is concerned, the Golden Mean is observed throughout most of the story in the stability and balance in the behavior of the main protagonist in his relation to the other characters, chiefly King Arthur, Sir Bertilac, and his wife.

For example, Gawain's modesty, self-control, and quiet determination help to save decorum and stability at Camelot after the
Green Knight's sudden intrusion off-balanced the usual order, already made vulnerable by the oversumptuous feast and the
excessive joy of the court, as well as by Arthur's own rashness and
impetuousness. Camelot's deviation from "proper" Christmas cele-
bration towards self-indulgent childish playfulness and
merrymaking is best seen through a comparison with similar
Christmas festivities held at Hautdesert. The religious element of
the feast, after all its *raison d'être*, is almost lacking at Camelot,
except for a passing and—to my view—ironic mention of "þe
chauntre (*singing of mass*) of þe chapel" (63) being ended, to give
the lords and the ladies more time for their plays and games. In
contrast, the Christmas celebrations at Hautdesert are an epitome of
propriety, sobriety, and balance between the religious and festive
aspects of the season: Gawain himself enters Christmas with the
right sort of piety and penitential mood;[118] the household activities
at Hautdesert are characterized by duty, hospitality, and service
conducted with seriousness and honor ("wyth menske," 834),
which are visibly lacking at Camelot. The religious observances
proper also occupy due space, and a number of social activities
conducted "soberly" (940) take place in the castle chapel (930-42).
The supper at Christmas Eve consists duly of "fele kyn (*many kinds
of*) fischez" (890), and is referred to as "þis penaunce" (897). On
Christmas day too the joy and the feast are clearly "for Christ's
sake" (995-97), and the harmony between the religious and
convivial aspects of the season is borne out, for example, by the
wordplay on "mes" (mass) and "messes" (dishes) (999).

  The "childgered" Arthur likewise in no way resembles Sir
Bertilac, a man "of hyghe eldee" (844)—that is, in his maturity.
The sobriety and full control of the situation exhibited by Sir
Bertilac in his dealing with Gawain contrast sharply with Arthur's
lack of *mesure* and his loss of temper in the handling of the
Beheading Game, when—put to shame and enraged by the
challenge (317-18)—he rashly leaps forward to seize the axe, thus
violating the courtly decorum and propriety of royal behavior. The
embarrassment and disturbance of order are then partly redressed
by modesty, self-control, and tactfulness of Sir Gawain, who
quietly takes the initiative by intervening with his speech (342-61),
thus relieving the embarrassed king by taking the challenge on
himself and temporarily restoring decorum and dignity to the court.

  Later Gawain's *mesure* is admirably exhibited in his unwavering
integrity and courtesy displayed at Hautdesert, especially in the

bedroom scenes, when he succeeds brilliantly in withstanding the importunity and temptation of the lady. In this context Gawain's famous *trawþe* is to be seen not only as faithfulness to his agreement with Sir Bertilac, but also as his adherence to the mean virtue in the correctness of behavior and courtesy towards the lady.[119] The lady's onslaught on the knight's chastity was meant precisely to put him off the middle course of temperance, and her contrary expectations of adultery and uncleanliness, built on Gawain's reputation as a seducer, clearly aimed at violating the "mean" the knight was struggling to preserve, both in relation to the lady and her husband. The middle course of action dictated by *trawþe* is brilliantly followed by Gawain for the first two days of temptation, when he balances neatly between the loyalty to Sir Bertilac and courtesy towards the hostess.[120] Gawain's Golden Mean is also illustrated in a contrasting way by the behavior of the animals pursued in the hunt at the time of the knight's temptation in the bedroom, in that in his keeping with *mesure* Gawain manages to *avoid* the extremities displayed by these animals. I will discuss this problem in greater detail in chapter 5, but for now let us observe, for instance, that the futile attempts of the deer on the first day of hunting to escape being slain are counterbalanced by Gawain's courteous submission to the lady's claim of capture (1219, 1233-35, 1278-79). The result is that the knight avoids being fully caught in the lady's blunt attacks, at the same time reaffirming his willing submission and service and thus preserving temperance and balance. In accordance with his *mesure*, at the end of the day Gawain gives the lady no less and no more than a loyal kiss as befits a courteous knight; to give less would be to show impudence, and to give more would jeopardize his covenant with Sir Bertilac and compromise his *clannes*.

The second day of temptation likewise consists of a succession of polite refusals on Gawain's part (1489-1503), when the knight again avoids taking the initiative, albeit invited, to reciprocate the lady's advances. In keeping with the wild behavior of the ferocious boar hunted in the forest that day, the lady encourages Sir Gawain to be brutishly aggressive and to take her by force (1495-97), only to find her guest even more coolly sure of himself then before. At the end of the second day Gawain again emerges as a victor in his careful maneuvers to preserve both his *clannes* and his *cortaysye* by being neither deerlike (fear) nor boarlike (aggression), and by keeping the middle course of his unshaken measure. The *trawþe* of the pentangle and its specific attribution to Sir Gawain are again exemplified both by the knight's pledged word and in his unfaltering adherence to the Golden Mean in the correctness and appropriateness of his behavior.

The third day, however, represents a deviation from the ideal pattern of *mesure* and self-control, so far so admirably illustrated by Sir Gawain. Although the polite refusals to accept the lady's gifts (1822-23) are still in keeping with the knight's "mean," his sense of value goes off-balance when he learns of the magical property of the lady's girdle (1855-58). The deflection from temperance is then evinced in Gawain's subsequent decision to retain the girdle and later to conceal it from Sir Bertilac during the exchange of the winnings. The loss of "mean" and the disturbance of equilibrium, caused by the excessive though so very human love of life, soon ramifies into further breaches of *trawþe* and courtesy: Gawain has to break his faith with the host and lie to him, he endangers his relationship with the lady by implying greater intimacy with her than he orginally deemed proper, and he jeopardizes his chivalric fame and honor by acting treacherously and cowardly. Or to use the vices listed by Gawain himself in his self-accusatory diatribe at the Green Chapel (2374-84): his "cowardyse" led him to compromise with "couetyse" (for his life), which then involved "trecherye and vntrawþe." This consequential disturbance of *mesure* and the deflection from the Golden Mean is, however, counterbalanced and saved by the Green Knight's spectacular forbearance and magnanimity;[121] the desertion of the mean virtue by Gawain brings forth a compensating display of it from Gawain's hitherto adversary, whose behavior, by the way, until that moment had been consistently outrageous and "off mean," particularly at Camelot.

To sum up: the "pure pentaungel" displayed on Sir Gawain's shield represents an ideal of moral and spiritual perfection, aspired to by Sir Gawain but narrowly missed through the knight's deflection from the Golden Mean of appropriate conduct that sprang from his built-in natural instinct of self-preservation. In absolute terms the pentangle's *trawþe*—truth in the general philosophical and religious sense—is an ideal never to be fully attained due to the inherent vulnerability of human nature. This is basically the lesson learned by Gawain in the course of his ordeal, as has also been exemplified in my discussion on the significance of greenness. Before his departure from Camelot Gawain wore the pentangle as a symbol of spiritual harmony and perfection almost ostentatiously on the outer side of his armor, without, however, having internalized its essence through the necessary experience. But then for a Christian man, already born with the burden and stain of Original Sin, the only possibility of getting anywhere near the absolute ideal is by exploring his human nature and by acknowledging its imperfection, and this is precisely what Gawain is led to comprehend in the course of his adventure, as is fully testified at the end of the poem by the sincerity with which he admits his fault before the Green Knight.

The pentangle recurs briefly in the text as "þe conysaunce of þe clere werkez" (2026) in the second arming-of-the-hero scene at Hautdesert on New Year's Day morning, shortly before Gawain's departure for the Green Chapel. The description nearly parallels a similar passage of the knight's dressing-up earlier on at Camelot, except that now Gawain's attire is complemented by a new element—the lady's green girdle wrapped around the golden armor, a visible sign and reminder of the sinful human nature. In a clear way, then, the pentangle, which occupied such a commanding position in the first arming scene, is now subordinated symbolically to the "gordel of grene silke" (2035), as if the latter had superseded or modified the meaning of the former. In symbolic terms, Gawain's shield, with the Virgin Mary on its inner side, with the complex system of spiritual knowledge contained in the pentads, and with the idea of the Golden Section as a principle of universal harmony and perfection, has now been replaced, or rather complemented, by the unfortunate girdle and its supposed magical value, all through Gawain's vain and foolish hope that he can save himself by his own doing. The rejection of divine protection and knowledge of things spiritual for the sake of willful and fairly unsophisticated magic is yet another instance of Gawain's departure from the Golden Mean, this time on the transcendental divine plain. In an act of self-deception the knight refused to submit voluntarily and wholeheartedly to God's will and protection, and instead of relying wholly on faith, divine grace, and the knowledge symbolized by the pentangle, he resorted to purely instrumental magic and, in consequence, to disgraceful treachery. From the point of view of strict divine justice, therefore, Gawain's renunciation of God's protective grace and providential order of things for the sake of selfish magic would be considered an act of brazen and unforgivable sacrilege, if not again for the extenuating circumstance of his love of life and the ultimate tempering of strict justice by mercy, so benevolently displayed by the Green Knight at the end of the story (2366-68). The Golden Mean and *mesure* in the universal, transcendental sense have thus been preserved: the Original Sin, which had unbalanced man's harmonious relationship with God, and keeps disturbing it in each individual lifetime, has been restored for humanity by God's boundless love and mercy through the sacrifice of Christ, and is being restored in each individual case, like Gawain's, through single acts of divine grace and forgiveness.

5

Gawain's Threefold Temptation

Gawain's crucial tests and temptations at the Castle of Hautdesert from Fitt III are preceded by the knight's memorable *peregrinatio* through the bleak terrain of North Wales in the period following All Saints' Day, the time allegorically referred to by Jacobus de Voragine as the "spring" and "beginning" of the year.[1] Astronomically speaking, however, the period between the autumn equinox ("Meʒelmas mone," 532) and the midwinter solstice (end of Gawain's solitary journey, 751-52) is the darkest time of the year, the sun being at its lowest until its subsequent renewal at Christmas, when days again begin to grow longer. Analogized with the traditional ages of human life, winter is a symbolic time of aging, decline, and ultimate suspension of life; a fit period for the penitential pilgrimage of the human soul until Advent announces the rise of hope in salvation at the beginning of the liturgical year.

A tragic note is struck already at the outset of Gawain's fateful journey during the All Saints' celebrations at Camelot, when the *crème de la crème* of Arthurian chivalry openly mourn the departure of their comrade, who by all accounts is simply not expected to return alive from his "cace" (546). There was "much derue doel *(painful lament)* driuen in þe sale" (558), and the dispair of having to lose such a splendid knight brought about almost seditious murmurings among the court against Arthur's excessive pride ("angardez pryde," 681), the cause of Gawain's present fatal undertaking:

> Bi Kryst, hit is scaþe *(disastrous)*
> þat þou, leude, schal be lost, þat art of lyf noble! . . .
> Warloker *(more warily)* to haf wroʒt had more wyt bene,
> And haf dyʒt ʒonder dere a duke to haue worþed;
> A lowande *(brilliant)* leder of ledez in londe hym wel semez,
> And so had better haf ben þen britned *(destroyed)* to noʒt,
> Hadet wyth an aluisch mon, for angardez pryde.
> Who knew euer any king such counsel to take

150

As kny3tez in cauelaciounz *(trifle disputes)* on Crystmasse
gomnez!

(674-83)[2]

The court's lament is in fact consonant with the religious meaning of the feast of All Saints', which traditionally celebrates the death of the faithful and the affirmation that their souls live eternally in Jesus. The relevant Epistle for the day is 1 Thessalonians, 4:13-18, which talks about those who died for Jesus and who will rise at the Second Coming of the Lord. The Gospel reading in turn is the story of the rising of Lazarus as an illustration of the theme of rebirth through grace.[3] In a word, the liturgical occasion for the court's lament after Gawain is a feast celebrating the dead who are to be resurrected.[4]

The religious context seems to suggest, therefore, that Gawain's leaving behind the comfort and shelter of courtly life, as well as his subsequent solitary peregrinations "þur3 þe ryalme of Logres" (691), are to be viewed as a symbolic entrance into the region of death, a descent into the realm of nature and the supernatural, as pictured by the spiral of Gawain's adventure described in chapter 2. The suffering and hardships sustained by Gawain during his journey have been compared to Christ's sojourn in the wilderness and the temptation by the devil (Matt. 4:1-11; Mark 1:12-13; Luke 4:1-13),[5] and in a more universal cultural sense they are reminiscent of privations and pains experienced by novices in the course of the rites of passage practiced in traditional societies. Among the hardships experienced by Gawain first and foremost comes solitude, a result of the forced separation from the emotional and psychological comfort of the society: "Oft leudlez alone he lengez on ny3tez . . . / Hade he no fere bot his fole bi frythez *(woods)* and dounez, / Ne no gome bot God bi gate wyth to karp" (693-96). Then there is fasting: "þer he fonde no3t hym byfore þe fare þat he lyked" (694), and exposure to cold and general physical discomfort: "Ner *(nearly)* slayn wyth þe slete he sleped in his yrnes *(armor)* / Mo ny3tez þen innoghe in naked rokkez" (729-30). Significantly, Sir Gawain is heading for the north ("þe Norþe Walez," 697), the direction commonly identified with the netherworld, as in Chaucer's *Friar's Tale* (line 1413), where the Yeoman-Devil says that he lives "fer in the north contree."[6]

Amid manifold tests of physical endurance are also typically heroic struggles with various foes—animal, monstrous, or semi-human—which collectively typify the temptation of nature and the flesh in their different aspects. The hero's *psychomachia* to resist the onslaughts of the fleshly powers involves "wormez"—that is, the dragons (720), the ancient archenemy of man, the personification of the devil himself (Revelation 12:9), and also the "wolues" (720), notorious for their rapacity, fury, and greediness, often said to represent the sin of *avaritia*, as well as lust and voluptuousness.[7] Then Gawain has to fight the "wodwos" (721), the wild men of the woods, satyrs often depicted as half-men, half-goats, known from classical times for their concupiscence. Next to confront are "bullez" (722), reputed for the thickness of their hide and ferocious wildness,[8] a fit symbol of the sins of wrath and pride.[9] The author of *Sir Gawain* lists also "berez" and "borez" (722), animals likewise traditionally linked with ferocity and savagery, and finally "etaynez" (723), the giants, the ungodly primordial race, the unjust rejected by God, the descendants of Cain, like Grendel, the murderers and destroyers of the human race. On the whole, the list contains stock figures of human enemies found in traditional folk and heroic tales, mentioned by the author only in passing in the context of Gawain's heroic adventures of rather straightforward kind. However, in the overall design of the poem these spectacular instances of heroic prowess and control over the instinctive, animal nature prepare the ground for much more subtle, ambiguous, and therefore more dangerous and crucial tests of the psychological and moral character occupy most of the textual space in Fitt III.

The Castle on High

The Castle of Hautdesert is almost magically conjured up by Gawain's invocation to Mary and the Savior (753-62) and his triple crossing of himself (763). Indeed, a sudden change from the weird wintry landscape to a "comelokest" location enhances for the reader the atmosphere of otherwordliness, despite a good deal of realistic detail in the following description of the castle's architecture (785-802). Not that instantaneous transformations of the bleak and the infernal into the beautiful and the heavenly are unknown in the more visionary passages of the Arthurian romance, especially in the Holy Grail cycle.[10] Notwithstanding these more remote parallels, the ontological status of the Castle of Hautdesert in the specific context of Gawain's adventure is worth a closer look.

First, the structure is depicted as rising high above the valleys and marshes and is situated—as castles usually are—on a hill ("abof a launde, on a lawe *[mound]*," 765, also 768, 788). Its walls shone and shimmered from afar (772), as did the chalk-white chimneys (789-90), and the whole structure, for all its architectonic splendor, looked like paperwork ("pared *[cut]* out of papure hit semed," 802), enhancing the effect of visionary and dreamy ethereality. The elevated position and consequently the status of the castle are emphasized later in the poem by its name "Hautdesert" (2445), a "High Place" or "Hermitage,"[11] which, coupled with its shining appearance, suggests a kind of otherworldy location, not yet the Holy Jerusalem as described in *Pearl*[12] nor the devil's mansion[13] but something of a pilgrim's transfer station between earth and heaven, such as the one described in Deguileville's *Pèlerinage de la vie humaine:*

> I seyh þilke hows with good wille, and yit at þe sihte I abashed me, for it heeng al on hy in þe eyr, and was bitwixe þe heuene and þe eerþe riht as þouh it hadde come þider and alight from þe heuene. It hadde steples and faire toures, and his aray was right fair.[14]

The terrestrial paradise envisaged as a splendid medieval castle is usually separated from the land by water,[15] which the text of the *Pèlerinage* interprets as the water of baptism.[16] The crossing of the water is therefore a universal symbol of purification and penance, and in Gawain's case the crossing of the bridge at Hautdesert (778-79) denotes yet one more transition in the knight's quest: another passage from the realm of nature back to the domain of culture in the spiral curve of the story (see fig. 6, chap. 2). The temporal context of this transition ensures its special character, for it is another midwinter and the Feast of the Nativity, one of the nodal points in the astronomical and liturgical calendar. As early as in pre-Christian Rome the Emperor Aurelian (a.d. 270-75) instituted the official cult of the sun at midwinter solstice, the day known as the "birthday" of *Sol Novus* or *Sol Invictus*,[17] and throughout the Middle Ages ecclesiological literature emphasized that the descent of heavenly light on earth in the form of Christ's Incarnation was a *conditio sine qua non* of the spiritual renewal and salvation of humanity.[18] "Lux fulgebit hodie super nos. Lyght schall schyne þys day apon us," says John Mirk in a homily for 25 December.[19] It is also worth noting in this context that in early Christian times on the same day as the Nativity the Church celebrated the birth of Saint Anastasia, a holy widow from the times of Emperor Diocletianus (late third century), whose Greek name *anastasis* means "resurrection."[20]

For Gawain, however, the coziness and comfort of Hautdesert at Christmastime do not yet mean salvation proper, for all the otherwordly appearance of the place. As subsequent events show, the castle indeed turns out to be the knight's temporary station between earth and heaven, closer to the ideal of Christian and courtly perfection than Arthur's Camelot, but maybe still away from the postulated paradise of the unrealized Camelot II, as illustrated by the spiral flow of the story (fig. 6, chap. 2). At Hautdesert things are otherworldly enough already, despite the realistic convention of description, the general "normality" of life judged by medieval standards, and the apparent lack of overt magic and the supernatural. Ultimately, however, this perception turns out to be insufficient and entirely false, because things at Hautdesert are not what they appear to be, even though it is not until after the beheading ordeal at the end of the story that Gawain learns how illusory his perception of reality has been. It then transpires that the courteous host and his lovely wife were both supernatural beings, shape-shifters purposefully placed by the "higher powers" on Gawain's path to test him. Nor is the actual power set-up in the castle that which is apparent throughout Fitt III to both Sir Gawain and the reader; the prime mover behind the scenes is not Sir Bertilac but the "auncian lady" (2463)—Morgan le Fay, the archwitch, sitting in the highest place of honor at the Christmas feast at Hautdesert (1001). In fact, the over-all ratio of the "natural" to the "supernatural" at Hautdesert is the direct reversal of the situation at Camelot: in Fitt I the only other-wordly element in the otherwise worldly environment was the Green Knight, whereas in Fitt III the only mortal human being in wonderland seems to be Sir Gawain. Structurally speaking, Camelot and Hautdesert are in reversed symmetry to one another, the former being a worldly, imperfect reflection of the latter's otherworldly ideal, with Sir Gawain and his green adversary as respective medi-ators between the two realms and both locations designed as different testing grounds for the best of knights.

The Tripartite Structure of Fitt III

As I have noted, the Castle of Hautdesert is conjured up out of nowhere by Gawain's pious but also magical gesture of crossing himself three times ("Nade he sayned [blessed] hymself, segge, bot þrye," 764), and from this time onwards the number three begins to rule and arrange all the main elements and happenings described in Fitt III.[21] Nor is it the first time that numbers play an important role in organizing the material in *Sir Gawain*, if we recall the fourfold division of the entire poem analyzed in chapter 2 or the significance of number five in the symbolic structure of the pentangle (chapter 4). Again, it seems reasonable to follow the numerological pattern provided by the poem, both with regard to the contents explicitly present in the narrative in a consciously designed literary structure and in connection with ideas and associations implied by the existing patterns as possible, complementary systems of reference. The two types of evidence, both internal and external, illustrative of the tripartite pattern of Fitt III, are presented below in two tables. Table 6 sums up the relevant textual evidence, whereas table 7 gives other tripartite systems of reference, comprising ideas and concepts derived from the philosophical and religious backgrounds that I consider relevant to the aspect of the poem now under scrutiny.

Table 6

The Tripartite Structure of Fitt III of *Sir Gawain*

Days of temptation	First Day (29 Dec.)	Second Day (30 Dec.)	Third Day (31 Dec.)
Animals chased	the does	the boar	the fox
Bertilac's hunting spoil	flesh of many deer	boar's head	fox's pelt
Gawain's winnings	one kiss	two kisses	three kisses and the girdle
Other elements			the glove and the ring
Beheading blows (Fitt IV)	first blow	second blow	third blow
Manner of the blow	feigned blow	arrested blow	positive blow (slight wound)
Gawain's behavior	avoidance of the blow—cowardice	determination to accept the blow—anger	acceptance of the blow—joy

Table 6 for the most part states the obvious, but it seems useful here to provide an overall view of the well-known narrative elements of Fitt III, however schematically arranged. In addition to the relevant elements from Fitt III I have also supplied the corresponding three-part pattern of the beheading blows from Fitt IV, as it in an obvious and explicit way relates to the three days of temptation at Hautdesert.

On the other hand, table 7 presents various tripartite conceptual patterns existing outside the poem in the sphere of medieval philosophy, theology, and social ideas. These can be used in an interpretative analysis as culturally relevant systems of reference, complementing the more immediate literary elements and their significances found in the text of *Sir Gawain*. Since the nature of the adduced external evidence is less obvious than the tripartite literary structure of Fitt III, below the table I offer brief discussion of the origin and meaning of the listed triads.

Table 7

The Tripartite Symbolic Correspondences Relevant to *Sir Gawain*

Platonic souls	concupiscible (vegetative)	irascible (emotive)	rational (divine)
Parts of the body	abdomen	heart	head
Faculties	sexuality, appetite	strength, courage	thought, perception
Social structure	commoners	warriors	priests-kings
Type of vice	gluttony, lechery, sloth	wrath	pride, vain-glory, avarice
Stages of sin	suggestion	delectation	consent

One should perhaps begin by asking whether there is anything particularly special about the very number that so adroitly unites and harmonizes the manifold narrative elements from Fitt III with the corresponding sections from Fitt IV. In traditional numerology three is often said to denote completeness and perfection, as the first and basic synthesis represented by a triangle and as the first geometrical figure and the first complete cycle that has a beginning, middle, and end.[22] Things grouped in threes imply fullness and completion, as, for example, three wishes and three tries, often found in myths and fairy tales. In Ecclesiastes we are told that "a threefold cord is not quickly broken" (4:12), and similar proverbial numerological wisdom is likewise present in *Sir Gawain*, when Sir Bertilac invites his guest to the third exchange-of-the-winnings agreement by arguing that "þrid tyme þrowe (*pays, proves*) best" (1680). In terms of space the number three divides the traditional cosmos vertically into heaven, earth, and the nether world, while with regard to time it has likewise come to denote completeness in representing the past, present, and future. This is probably why goddesses of fate and destiny appear usually in threes, like the Greek Parcea or the Scadinavian Norns. Equally relevant in this context seems to be the fact that the totality of the Christian Godhead is contained in the dogma of the Holy Trinity, just as many other metaphysical notions of

Christianity also come in triads: the three souls, three bodies, three emanations, the threefold spiritual path (*via purgativa, via illuminativa, via unitiva*), the three days between death and resurrection as evidenced by Jonah's three days in the whale's belly (Jonah 1:17), or by Jesus' three days before the Resurrection (Matt. 12:40). Thomas Aquinas in the *Summa Theologiae* states that "the perfection of 'three' is also manifest in His resurrection on the third day, for, as Aristotle says (*De Coelo*, I, 2. 268a), it is the number indicating *all reality* with a beginning, a middle and end" (Italics added).[23]

The number refers to the temporal world as well. It is common observation that the natural environment consists of three main realms: sky, land, and water, with the corresponding animal species. Nature is traditionally divided into three main kingdoms: the mineral, the vegetable, and the animal, the latter including humans. The triads arranged in table 7 in turn illustrate other, specifically human realms (such as psychology and morality), whose threefold nature likewise implies fullness and completeness. As was the case with the pentads of Gawain's pentangle, the assembled triadic elements are shown as interrelating with other tripartite systems of ideas, ensuring the interconnectedness and coherence of reality denoted by them. A holistic nature of the existing triads makes it hypothetically possible to treat them, similarly to the pentangle, as an organized system of interrelated elements, indirectly linked with the triadic narrative elements from *Sir Gawain*. Before we look back into Fitt III to see how the triadic structural design actually works in a literary context, it seems useful to dwell briefly on the content and meaning of the triads arranged in table 7.

1. *The Platonic soul.* Plato says in the *Timaeus*[24] that God took over from himself an immortal principle of the soul and encased it in a mortal physical globe—the head—with the body as a whole for vehicle. The mortal parts of the soul were in turn secured in the breast and trunk: the seat of courage and passion was in the heart, nearer to the head in order to hear the commands of reason, while the appetite for food, drink, and other natural needs were in the region of the navel, as far as possible from the seat of deliberation to avoid disturbing it.[25] This basic division of the human soul into three main parts—the rational (*logistikon*), often called divine, placed in the head; the emotive or spirited (*thymoeides*), stationed in the heart; and the vegetable or appetitive (*epithymetikon*), located in the abdomen— is repeated in the *Republic*[26] and has become one of the most popular and influential philosophical concepts about man throughout the Middle Ages and almost until the Renaissance.[27]

What is especially important from the point of view of events described in Fitt III of *Sir Gawain* is the dynamic nature of the relationships between the three Platonic souls. The Neoplatonic tradition often speaks of an ideal state of inner harmony and balance seen as a state of attunement, whereby each part of the soul receives and performs what is its due, depending on its rank within the threefold hierarchy. Ideally the state of inner balance is achieved when the divine rational soul rules over the lower parts, which are in turn subordinate to its divine commander. This desirable state, however, is not easily attained, and has to be worked out through self-discipline and hard internal struggle. This *psychomachia* is aimed at establishing the superiority of the rational mind over the emotive and appetitive souls, and the text of the *Corpus Hermeticum* has this to say about the difficulties in this struggle towards self-perfection:

> For this, my son [says Hermes Trismegistus to his son Tat], is the only road that leads to Reality. It is the road our ancestors trod; and thereby they attained to the Good. It is a holy and divine road; but it is hard for the soul to travel on that road while it is in the body. For the soul must begin by warrying against itself, and stirring up within itself a mighty feud; and the one part of the soul must win victory over the others, which are more in number. It is a feud of one against two [i.e., reason against anger and desire], the one part struggling to mount upwards, and the two dragging it down; and there is much strife and fighting between them. . . . Such is the contest about the journey to the world above. You must begin, my son, by winning victory in this contest, and then, having won, mount upward."[28]

I think it very probable that the internal struggle leading towards self-perfection described by Plato and his followers refers to a more universal psychological and spiritual phenomenon, expressed also symbolically in *Sir Gawain* in the triadic arrangement of the crucial events from Fitt III.[29] The ancient doctrine of the tripartite soul and its internal dynamism indeed seem to provide the main underlying conceptual framework for Gawain's threefold temptation at Haut-desert, additionally linked with other relevant triadic systems.

2. *The Threefold Sin.* In his sermon on man's tripartite soul Aelfric[30] talks at some length about the danger of the lower souls escaping from the control of the human will. For example, perverted desire of the vegetable soul, instead of aiming at everlasting life, often turns to worldly pleasures engendering gluttony, lechery, and sloth. Similarly, the anger of the spirited soul, instead of fighting vice, may turn to wrath, and likewise reason, when misused, leads to pride and vainboasting. The goal of every Christian, writes Aelfric, is to avoid these traps by carefully maneuvering among the

various pitfalls and temptations of life, through self-mastery and determination of the will.

In this way the three souls of ancient philosophy, or rather their perversions through wrong use, came to be linked by medieval theologians with the concept of the threefold sin, each attributed to the corresponding soul according to its nature and function. The theological *locus classicus* for this concept is Saint Augustine's *Confessions* (10.30-40),[31] and the popularity of the idea is evidenced by the following passage from the Middle English *Stanzaic Life of Christ:*:

> The deul temptide vntrewly
> our forme fadir al amys
> with thre synnus, sais Gregory,
> forto bryng hym out of blis.
> The first of hom was glotery,
> the secunde vaynglorie i-wys,
> the thrid auarise, as say I,
> thur3e quych þe deul then made hym his.[32]

The first of Adam's sins, "glotery," is linked in this poem with the original fruit "that swete & fair was forto se." Vainglory was committed when Adam desired to be "like goddes," while "auarise" is attributed in the *Life* to man's inordinate thirst "forto knawe gode & eul both," and to have "gret maistry of he3enes or of dignite."[33]

The Gospel analogue of the threefold temptation of Adam is the resistance offered by Christ to Satan's temptation in the wilderness (Matt. 4:1-11; Luke 4:1-19), which likewise assumed three stages: the devil's offer of bread during Christ's fasting refers to the sin of gluttony, related to the lowest, nutritive soul; the temptation to display God's might at the fall from the temple is linked with vainglory of the middle, spirited soul; and Satan's offer of all earthly power is clearly related to the covetousness "of he3enes or of dignite." All these are in turn analogous to the three "lusts" mentioned in 1 John 2:16: "the lust of the flesh, and the lust of the eyes, and the pride of life." The "lust of the flesh" corresponds to gluttony (*gula*) of the vegetative soul located in the abdomen, and includes not only hunger but also sexual appetite. The "lust of the eyes" refers to vainglory (*vana gloria*) of the spirited soul, which is "whan þou art glad of þe gode dedys þat þou hast don" and "whan þou heryst þat men preysin þi manerys," as explains the fifteenth-century penitential manual entitled *Jacob's Well*.[34] The "pride of life" in turn springs from covetousness (*avaritia*) located in the head, usually understood broadly as a desire to possess knowledge equal to God's, to acquire honors and dignity, or—as in the case of Sir Gawain—to covet one's life more than anything else.

As Donald R. Howard very convincingly argued in his interesting book,[35] in medieval moral theology the three vices rooted in the three souls marked the progress of evil within humans, in that the temptation proceeded in a complex way following the three stages of suggestion, delectation, and consent.[36] Suggestion is the first step of sin, coming from without, and appealing to the lowest, vegetative faculty of the soul. In the biblical story of the Fall this phase of the temptation refers to the serpent's luring of Eve to "taste" the forbidden fruit, for it was "swete & fair." Next comes delectation with its play of emotions (the spirited soul), the wavering of will and hesitation, manifested by Eve's actual tasting of the fruit. Finally there is consent, when reason uses the faculty of free will to offer ultimate approval of sin. This last phase that seals the commission of sin is represented in Genesis by Adam and his involvement in the temptation. Chaucer sums up the idea in *The Parson's Tale*:

> There may ye seen that deedly synne hath, first, suggestion of the feend, as sheweth heere [Gen. 3:1-7] by the naddre; and afterward, the delit of the flessh, as sheweth heere by Eve; and after that, the consentynge of resoun, as sheweth heere by Adam.[37]

In the theology of sin thus formulated it was not until the ultimate consent of reason that man lost his innocence through the Original Sin; the initial temptation of the flesh is only, as Chaucer writes, "peyne of concupiscence," whereas with the mind's approval there is "bothe peyne and synne" (line 333). In other words, sin is not contracted as long as it remains on the level of *sensus* and "thoughtless" corporal delectation; it is when the mind (*mens*) consciously decides to partake of sin that evil irrevocably takes possession of the soul.

It should be noted here that the above concepts were not regarded in the Middle Ages as merely abstract, scholastic arguments reserved for clergymen and theologians. Rather they were considered real, existential issues reflecting the actual moral and metaphysical situation of man in relation to the divine. In the absence of practical psychology and psychotherapy the theological formula of the threefold sin, combined with the Platonic conception of the soul, explained for the medieval man the drama of human existence and the moral process whereby evil—that is, departure from God—made its progress within man's soul.[38] As Howard put it: "Even the most unlettered layman must therefore have listened with curiosity when the very nature of the great event [the Fall] was explained—for all of this, he knew, was in him."[39] The concept of the three temptations, the three stages of sin, the corresponding doctrine of the tripartite soul, together with other symbolic triads, thus occupied an important place in the medieval view of man and the world, and one is therefore not surprised to find these concepts allegorically present in the literature of the period,[40] so sensitive to questions of sin and morality.

3. *The Tripartite Social Structure.* Medieval commentators of Plato were as much preoccupied with the philosopher's views on human nature and cosmology as with his concepts regarding political order and the hierarchical constitution of the world.[41] Especially during the twelfth-century Neoplatonic revival Plato's ideas about the relationships between human microcosm and social macrocosm received numerous comments, as is exemplified by the following anonymous gloss on the *Timaeus.* An additional value of this comment is that it links in a significant way the doctrine of the tripartite soul with the three orders of the Platonic city (governors, soldiers, and workers), a theme not unrelated to the organization of medieval society:

> Similarly he [Socrates from Plato's original account] saw in the microcosm, that is, in man, some high qualities, such as man's wisdom, the seat of which is in the uppermost part of him, that is, in his head. . . . He also saw in man some intermediate qualities such as courage, whose seat is in the heart, and concupiscence, whose seat is in the kidneys or the loins: and low things, such as feet, hands etc. According to this disposition, he disposed the republic, instituting high officials, such as senators, intermediate ones, such as soldiers on active service, and low ones, such as the specialists in the mechanical arts— furriers, cobblers, apprentices, and, outside the city, farmers.[42]

Plato's direct homology between the tripartite structure of an ideal society and the nature of the human soul, as expounded in *The Republic* (440e-441a), closely relates the question of political and social stability to the idea of self-mastery and self-perfection in man, according to his rank and social function. Thus, for example, just as the spirited portion of the soul was seen as a defender of the individual, so the warrior class was to guard and protect the society. What is important here is that in both cases the defense was aimed against the external and the internal dangers alike, for it was the excesses of the lower soul (and, analogously, of the lower class), that posed the greatest threat to stability.[43] On the other hand, whenever by nature the better part of the soul or city is a governor of the worse, this is called perfection and self-mastery; that is, a situation in which a small upper portion (the head in the body, and the philosopher-kings in Plato's city), characterized by moderation and intellect, rules over a larger lower portion, characterized by emotions and base appetites (cf. *The Republic,* 431a-d). In an individual this process might lead to the state of ego-control and measure in the overall conduct, while in a society this desirable situation is analogous to order understood as class domination.

Plato also argued that any just *(dikaios)* man who is fit to rule as king should combine within himself the three spiritual parts and their corresponding social counterparts, each in its proper place.[44] The ideal king should thus become a social microcosm, a complete man, combining all three social orders within himself and resolving their conflicts and differences, just as he is able to combine and harmonize within himself the three portions of the soul through moderation and the power of reason. The idea, however, does not seem to be original with Plato's political thought, for the concept of a ruler as a social microcosm combining within himself the structure of the society appears universal, and is at least common to most of the known Indo-European societies, as the studies of Georges Dumézil and his school have shown.[45] According to Dumézil's well-known socio-mythological theory, most Indo-European societies possessed a tripartite structure, in which—analogous to Plato—the religious and legal authority was personified by priesthood or sacred kingship occupying the top of the social pyramid, the middle place belonged to the warrior caste, who looked after defense and the enforcement of law, while the bottom of the social ladder, represented by the commoners, was responsible for the production of food and the general material well-being of the entire structure.[46] Accordingly, in the ancient microcosmic theory of kingship the royal investiture—the ritual transformation of a member of the warrior class into a king— was accompanied by ceremonies that bestowed upon the candidate a set of symbolic items representing the three social classes and their functions.[47] Upon receipt of these items the royal candidate left behind his former status and identity and began to be regarded as a person who had transcended both the class distinctions and the differences and conflicts within his soul. The king in a traditional Indo-European society was conceived as a representation of totality, an all-embracing social microcosm, by having both the three main social classes and the three souls harmoniously merged and united in him. It is to be seen whether and to what extent Gawain's threefold trial at Hautdesert contains reminiscences of these ancient rituals of royal investiture, adapted in the poem to the context of an idealized feudal society, personified by the royal nephew and the best of knights.

The Chase and the Miraculous Bed

The well-known situational context of Gawain's threefold temp-tation involves the simultaneous action of hunting by Sir Bertilac in the forest for three consecutive days paralleled by the knight's sexual temptation in his bedroom by the lady. It is the alternation between the hunting and the bedroom scenes, in itself symbolically potent, that provides the backdrop for the ongoing battle within Gawain to withstand the onslaught on his integrity and to overcome the inner crisis caused by a major conflict in his system of values in the face of the approaching adventure at the Green Chapel.

Despite the obvious surface differences in the type of action and situation, the interlacing nature of the chase and the temptation scenes in the poem suggests some close affinity between the two motifs. Viewed against the underlying structure of the entire poem as visu-alized on the spiral diagram (chap. 2, fig. 6), the chase and the temptation refer to the two main domains between which the story oscillates, that is, nature and culture respectively, with many struc-tural and symbolic links between the two realms. According to the nature of the mathematical spiral, the consecutive radii of the curve diminish with a steady progression as the spiral winds nearer and nearer towards the center. Similarly in the poem, the alternation between culture and nature increases in frequency as the intervals between the successive episodes diminish in length and the story draws to its end. The frequency of oscillation between the two domains reaches then its apogee in Fitt III, where the action moves from one realm to the other as often as every couple of stanzas. Culture and nature (as defined in chapter 2) do indeed finally merge into one entity, as is exemplified by the conflation of the characters of the Green Knight and Sir Bertilac into one unified being at the end of the scene at the Green Chapel, as well as by Gawain's own enrichment of his personality with its "green" side.

In Fitt III, however, the two realms remain separate though closely interconnected, a fact that reflects both the apparent duality of Gawain's personality and a direction in which the resolution of the knight's inner conflict will ultimately take place. Before I point out the underlying symbolic analogies between the two parallel types of action, however, I think it useful to begin with what appears on the surface of the poem—namely the hunting and the bedroom scenes treated as separate and independent narrative motifs. Both are deeply rooted in medieval literary tradition and both are likely to stir certain specific connotations and associations as well-established literary themes.

The very realistic and detailed descriptions of the hunts in *Sir Gawain*, something for which the poem is particularly famous, do not of course preclude possible figurative significations of the chase itself, of the type and behavior of the pursued animals, and of the action of slaying and breaking of the quarry. Indeed, the chase is a popular theme in medieval allegory, of complex spiritual import,[48] central in particular to the idea of self-development and self-perfection, so prominent also in *Sir Gawain*. Structurally speaking, the hunt describes a movement and pursuit towards conflict, followed by a struggle with the pursued animal whose outcome is vital for the hunter's life: that is, he either captures or kills the game and is unexpectedly highly rewarded or else he loses the chase by becoming himself a victim of it, and dies disgracefully. Thus understood the hunt is a version of the quest-theme whereby the hero leaves behind the familiar and secure environment (culture), and enters, often alone, into the wood, the region of the wild, the unknown, and the magical (nature), led by the quarry—his guide into the forbidden territory—where the climactic encounter between the hunter and the game takes place, one that changes the hero's life. Psychologically the chase describes the entry of the ego into the unfamiliar and dangerous interior of the soul, the intrusion requiring the observance of certain prescribed rules and necessary rituals, as well as courage and perseverance to overcome the obstacles that separate the hunter from his game in the course of a dialectical process of flight and pursuit. The ultimate confrontation with the quarry leads to the resolution of certain fundamental problems and conflicts within the soul, whose precise nature is usually symbolized by the character of the hunted animal. If the hero captures and slays the quarry and returns with his spoil to the society, his is a moral victory, a success in the quest towards the subjugation of his own instinctive nature and the acquisition of greater self-control. If, on the other hand, the hunter, Actaeonlike, becomes himself the victim of the hunt, his is a failure to survive the spiritual crisis caused by the unleashing of the instinctive powers represented by the quarry, and the weak ego is subsequently torn apart and swallowed by the elemental forces of nature.

From the point of view of the hunting scenes in *Sir Gawain* two basic types of experience reflected by hunting should be distinguished, called by Marcelle Thiébaux the instructive and the amatory chase.[49] In the first type the hunt is equivalent to the hero's initiation in that the quarry, representing cognitive and spiritual values hitherto unknown to the pursuer, leads the hunter from the state of ignorance to one of self-knowledge. This is why Plato (*Enthydeums* 290 b-d) called both the hunters and scholars philosophers, and the English word *hunt* (OE *hunta*) also denotes the search and pursuit of knowledge.[50] In the Middle Ages hunting was not only an aristocratic pastime, but was also frequently used figuratively as a vehicle for Christian teaching: very popular were the stories in which the chase led to conversion or spiritual revelation, as in the legend of Saint Eustace[51] or Saint Hubert. Saint Giles, another medieval patron saint of hunters, is even mentioned by Sir Bertilac (1644) during the exchange of spoils with Gawain after the second day of the hunt. Numerous medieval hunting manuals,[52] although devoted primarily to the elaborate procedures, language, customs, and practices of the hunt, were often filled with rhetorical descriptions, moral apologies, *exempla*, and Christian allegories for general edification. For instance, Duke Edward's *Master of Game* alludes in the *Prologue* to hunting as a quest of moral perfection in that it kills idleness, the breeder of sins:

> early in the dawning of the day [the hunter] must be up for to go unto his quest, that in English is called searching, well and busily. . . . And therefore I say that all the time the hunter is without idleness and without evil thoughts, and without evil works of sin, for as I have said idleness is the foundation of all vices and sins.[53]

Duke Edward clearly identifies the hunters with good Christians and adepts of spiritual quest when he says that "hunters go into Paradise when they die, and live in this world more joyfully than any other men. . . . Therefore be ye all hunters and ye shall do as wise men."[54]

The amatory, another type of chase distinguished by Thiébaux, is also relevant in the context of *Sir Gawain,* where hunting is closely though only indirectly linked with sexual pursuit. The figure of love as the hunt was a literary commonplace at least since the time of Ovid[55] and was especially popular with the poets from the circle of *amour courtois.* In Andreas Capellanus's *De Arte Honeste Amandi* wooing is more than once compared to hunting,[56] and in the poetry of the *Minnesingers* the man in love was often represented by the falcon or hawk hunting his prey. In Wolfram von Eschenbach, for example, Gahmuret, Parzival's father, "raised himself up like a falcon that eyes its prey"[57] when his loving eye caught the sight of the Queen of Wales. In Chrétien's romance the titular Erec is likewise symbolically identified with the hawk, and the comparison with a bird of prey suits both the hero's valiancy as a knight and his determination as a lover.[58] It should be recalled that Gawain too is a "hawk" according to the received etymology of his name,[59] the fact that likewise accounts for the knight's double reputation as a warrior and a womanizer. In Gottfried von Strassburg's *Tristan* the young hero enters King Mark's kingdom first as a master huntsman, superior in hunting skills to the rest, only to appear soon as a master lover as well,[60] due to the ambivalent nature of the "noble art of venery."[61] Examples such as these are legion in medieval literature, and there is no doubt that hunting, understood ambivalently both as a pursuit of self-knowledge and as a sexual chase, must as such have preconditioned the readers' perception of action in Fitt III of *Sir Gawain*. The two interwoven strains of events: one in the wood and the other in the bedroom, must surely have been perceived as complementary aspects of one process, whereby the eruption of instinctive forces associated with sexual desire served as a catalyst in the inner struggle towards greater self-awareness and control.

In the light of the existing literary pre-text, therefore, the hunts in *Sir Gawain* can be symbolically linked both with the lady's attempted seduction of Gawain[62] and with the knight's inadvertent quest for self-knowledge, the former serving as a means and a catalyst leading to the latter. But the situational context of Gawain's complex testing is first of all his bedchamber, a seeming opposite to the wild nature outside, an illusory shelter that renders its occupant helpless and vulnerable to the lady's unexpected attacks on his spiritual stability and integrity. In contrast to Sir Bertilac's powerful and confident intrusion into the wild terrain of the forest and to his mastery over the elemental forces inhabiting it, Gawain's nakedness in his bed[63] appears symbolic of his susceptibility and unprotected exposure to whatever might befall him, now that he is stripped of the accoutrements of chivalry and put by the very situation in a socially and psychologically disadvantageous position. The external, familiar forms of courtly decorum being gone too, Gawain's bare self is now laid open to dangerous intrusions from without that will mercilessly test his mental resistance and the strength of his character.

But the bed itself also holds a special place in the world of romantic adventure, particularly in stories involving adepts of courtly love such as Lancelot or Tristan. Again the Arthurian pre-text offers assistance in an attempt to describe adequately what is actually at stake in the bedroom scenes of *Sir Gawain* by suggesting the character of associations that the poem's audience may have had in this respect. The motif in question is the notorious *lit marveil,* a scene of dire plight of many a knight, such as the one from Chrétien's *Perceval*, where Gauvin visits the Castle of Damsels, all orphans or dispossessed maidens, who are awaiting a knight to fight for their cause. The floor of the central appartment of the castle is paved with many-colored stones, and in the middle of the room stands a bed with posts of gold and braidings of silver. A costly coverlet is spread over it, and a carbuncle set in each of the posts sheds as much light as candles.[64] The bed in which Gawain slept at Hautdesert was not less sumptuous, as befits the nobility of its guest and the scale of the forthcoming experience:

> . . . þer beddyng watz noble,
> Of cortynes of clene sylk wyth cler golde hemmez,
> And couertorez ful curious with comlych panez
> Of bry3t blaunner aboue, enbrawded bisydez,
> Rudelez rennande on ropez, red golde ryngez.

(853-57)

In Chrétien, however, the splendid bed stood on rollers and moved at the slightest touch. Gauvin, in full armor, sits down on it, whereupon a shriek resounds from its curtains, the bells hanging from them begin to ring, the windows spring open, and magic breaks loose. Crossbow bolts and arrows fly in through the windows at Gauvin, then the windows close of their own accord and a door opens, through which comes a gigantic lion that hurls itself upon the knight, driving its claws into his shield. Gauvin draws his sword, cuts off the lion's head and both paws, and afterwards, exhausted, sits down again on the magic bed. Then the host of the castle enters the chamber with joyful countenance and informs Gauvin that he has managed to free the castle from magic forever, and that its inhabitants are ready to serve him.[65] In a similar episode at the *chastel marveile* from Chrétien's *Lancelot,* a lance with a pennon all ablaze shoots down on Gauvin sleeping in his bed, setting fire to the coverlet, sheets, and mattress. The knight, however, manages to put out the fire, hurls the lance into the middle of the hall, and lays down again on the bed.[66]

Although in *Sir Gawain* the lady's assault on her guest's chastity is more subtle and civilized than the terror-inspiring magical phenomena occurring on the *lit marveile* in Chrétien and other authors,[67] the bed as a place of the eruption of sexuality and overwhelming passion serves in both contexts as a testing-ground of the adept's self-discipline and fortitude. The love-passion in Chrétien is symbolized by the fire burning through the bed, while the released instincts take the form of a ferocious animal.[68] The quenching of the fire or removal of the lion's paws signify in turn the neutralization of the untamed nature, and it is only after sexuality of a primitive sort has been vanquished and subordinated to ego-control that more refined and spiritual erotic adventures can follow, which is what later happens to Gauvin and Lancelot at the *chastel marveile*. This sublimated and more civilized love is symbolized, for example, by the altarlike Crystal Bed in the *Minnegrotte* in von Strassburg's *Tristan*, dedicated to pure and perfect love that is as "transparent and translucent" as crystal.[69] According to Emma Jung,[70] the concept of the miraculous bed goes back to the legend of King Solomon, who is said to have possessed such a bed (Songs of Sol. 3:1,6-10), later identified with his throne. In alchemy the bed is symbolically linked with the vessel of the *opus*, as well as with the Bride of God, and it was understood as the place of the *unio mystica* with the divine.[71] In the world of romance, however, the bed is first of all a place of infinite danger, requiring utmost self-control and willpower to withstand the explosion of instinctuality. Although less outwardly heroic than in the analogous episodes from Chrétien, Gawain's equally spectacular self-discipline and courtesy while in bed at Hautdesert did likewise prevent him becoming overwhelmed by his instincts, at least as far as sexuality was concerned.

The two subplots of the temptation and the hunts should therefore be viewed without reservation as complementary sides of one complex process, describing allegorically Gawain's spiritual exposure and the dangerous confrontation of his naked ego with emotional powers associated traditionally with the body. I contend that the twofold action of hunting and temptation in Fitt III symbolically describes the above process, whereby Gawain, after being tested with regard to his physical prowess and endurance during his winter journey, is now confronted with the complex psychic powers latent in the depths of his soul. His nakedness in the bed suggests the weakness and vulnerability of the exposed ego, sheltered in the illusory security of culture symbolized by the castle and the comfortable bedchamber, while the hunts depict violent confrontations of the unexpecting mind with the powerful, instinctual forces of unbridled nature. In accordance with the textual division of this part of the poem, the comprehensive test assumes three stages, with each day's hunt and temptation corresponding to the activation of the successive portion of the soul, as described by Plato and his followers. Other relevant triadic elements, such as those listed in tables 6 and 7, are very skillfully woven into the general picture either in an explicit or implicit way, offering a very consistent and artistically refined literary description of a spiritual and moral crisis that tests the ultimate limits of human powers and related cultural values.

The Temptation:

The First Day

Repeatedly told by his host to be "at [his] ese" (1071, 1096) and not to join the hunting party, Gawain is from the very start put in a difficult position, for the state of forced ease and relaxation imposed by Sir Bertilac on his guest is very favorable to the kind of sin that Gawain is subsequently led to by the lady.[72] In his hunting manual Duke Edward speaks strongly against idleness as the breeder of all sins and vices,[73] and Chaucer too makes it clear in *The Parson's Tale* that "ese, etynge, drynkynge, and slepynge longe" are a great nourisher of *Leccherie*.[74] The briskness and energetic business of the hunters who rose "erly bifore þe day" (1126), "by þat any dayly3t lemed *(shone)* vpon erþe" (1137), contrasts sharply with Gawain's dangerous relaxation in his bed till "þe dayly3t lemed on þe wowes *(walls)*" (1180).   The naked, sleeping Gawain is rendered as defenseless in his bedchamber as are "þe hindez" and "þe does" (1158-59) startled and pursued by the hunters in the woods, and the parallelism of action strongly suggests that the real quarry in the hunt is Sir Gawain, pursued directly by the beautiful hostess, and indirectly by her absent husband.

The first day's game are hinds and does, and their behavior during a relatively short hunt is mainly that of a desperate and hopeless attempt to escape from an overwhelming attack from hounds and arrows (1158-73). The cowardly, fleeing doe appears traditionally as an image of the weak and reprobate human soul that shies away from God and consequently falls into the bondage of the flesh.[75] The animal is often found in the context of carnal love, as in the numerous similes found in the Song of Solomon (2:9, 17; 4:5; 7:3; 8:14). The doe's timidity, but also her gracefulness and gender make her a fit symbol of the forces of the lowest, concupiscible soul that governs bodily appetites and sins of the flesh: gluttony, sloth, and lechery. It is also, I think, significant that Sir Bertilac's hunting spoil of the first day is the deer's "flesh" ("gres," 1326, 1378, "wayth" *[venison]*, 1381), heaped up in large quantities ("querre," 1324) to denote the collective, indistinct, and unindividualized character of the vegetable soul, situated farthest from the discriminating power of reason. The relative ease with which the hunters capture and slay the deer that offered no resistance or defense against the pursuers also suggests the passivity of the concupiscible soul,

easily overcome by the decisive and active force of reason, symbolized here by Sir Bertilac.

Similarly to the tracked animals, Gawain is taken by surprise and
brought to bay by the lady who stole silently into his chamber, "droȝ
þe dor after hir ful deruly and stylle" (1188), rendering the knight
prisoner in his bed ("I schal bynde yow in your bedde," 1211). The
door is "drawen and dit (*locked*) with a derf haspe" (1233), and the
bedchamber, hitherto a place of comfortable ease, suddenly turns
into a cage ("Now ar ȝe tan as-tyt!" 1210). The element of surprise
is part of the assault, for the lady wants to catch Gawain offguard.
Violating all rules of courtly decorum, without a word she raises the
curtain of Gawain's canopied bed, sits on the bedside, and traps the
knight in a most embarrassing situation. The unambiguity of the
lady's purpose is immediately made clear when she blatantly offers
herself to the astounded knight lying naked in his bed: "ȝe ar welcum
to my cors, Yowre awen won to wale (*choose your own course of
action)*" (1237-38). The ruthlessness and bluntness of her onslaught, which bypasses all rules of decorum,[76] even those remotely
resembling the elaborate rituals of courtly love, show that the attack
is aimed directly at the "lust of the flesh," the sheer natural instinct
located in the lowest, concupiscible part of the body, farthest from
the head as the seat of self-control. In her assault the lady very
cleverly falls back upon Gawain's notoriety as a womanizer and a
seducer,[77] a fact widely attested in Arthurian literature,[78] thus leaving
the hero no other option but to act on his reputation.

Fortunately for Gawain, it is clear from the very start that he has no
desire to take any advantage of the situation, and unlike similar
occasions in other romances[79] he is at no moment erotically drawn
towards his temptress. This is chiefly due to his anxiety about the
outcome of the "lur" (*disaster)* (1284) soon to occur at the Green
Chapel, which deprives Gawain of all pleasure he might otherwise
have had with the lady, and also because of his current agreement
with the host. On top of the circumstances unfavorable to sexual
activity there is also Gawain's own determination not to yield to the
lady and to act contrary to his usual nature. This results, however,
in something of an identity crisis combined with the self-imposed
deflation of the ego, when Gawain chooses the humble way and
denies his romancing reputation: "I be not now he þat ȝe of speken"
(1242), for he is a "wyȝe (*man)* vnworþy" to reciprocate the lady's
advances.

Gawain's withdrawal, modesty, and defensive attitude make his
behavior to some degree similar to that of timid and fearful deer,
chased contemporaneously in the woods. But only to some degree:

the analogy between Gawain's and the animals' behavior, often discussed by the critics,[80] is to be seen—in my opinion—not in terms of simple similarity, but as a modification, involving both analogy and contrast. In accordance with measure and temperance implied by the pentangle's Golden Mean, Gawain now modifies and moderates his nature, employing his rational faculty of self-control in an attempt to temper the natural man in him. This he does neither by succumbing entirely to the instinctual forces symbolized by the wild animals, as this would naturally lead to a disaster, nor by totally suppressing or rejecting them. In a very subtle and difficult process of "controlled explosion" of the natural impulses he chooses the middle way of partly submitting to the lady's advances by courteously offering her his service,[81] while at the same time maintaining the integrity of his character in not giving himself up completely. To yield to the lady's temptation would mean not only to violate *trawþe* in the sense of loyalty to the binding agreement, but also in the larger sense of disturbing the internal equilibrium and harmony symbolized by the rule of the Golden Mean displayed on the pentangle.

Therefore, while politely offering his service to the lady in partial submission to her claim of capture,[82] Gawain manages at the same time to stay on his guard, admirably defending his chastity, honor, and consequently his *trawþe*. In a paradoxical way he behaves partly like the cowardly and timid deer, and partly quite unlike these fearful animals that hopelessly and desperately try to escape the pursuit. Gawain, on the contrary, accepts the hunting situation and courageously takes its full impact head-on, allowing himself to be pursued within some limits, maneuvering the exchange of interactions with the lady in such a way that both his *trawþe* towards the host and his *cortaysye* towards the lady remain intact.

The nature of the ongoing interactions in the bedchamber clearly shows that it is not Gawain's sexual impulses and his chastity that are the main target here. What is primarily at stake is the knight's ability to keep the middle course of action between the apparently conflicting demands of courtesy to the lady and loyalty to the lord; in other words, the virtue of temperance and measure. In this light the powers of the flesh awakened by the temptation and symbolized by the female deer are only a catalyst designed to test Gawain's rational faculty and the extent of his self-control. The plight as it is is extremely embarrassing and psychologically and socially difficult, to say nothing of the potentially dangerous consequences that are not revealed, however, until all the dimensions of the temptation become manifest later at the Green Chapel. According to the rules of courtly conduct adhered to by Gawain,[83] in the circumstance he can neither accept the hostess's amorous proposals (as this would endanger his agreement with the host), nor can he too openly reject them (as this would violate the demands of courtesy, and in particular of courtly love). In this social cul-de-sac Gawain is saved by the only way out available—the subtlety of the Golden Mean. Morton Donner put Gawain's dilemma very succinctly:

> To reject the lady's advances bluntly would be to insult her. To accept them would be to betray his position as the Host's guest. If he can neither accept nor reject them, to acknowledge them would be barbarous. The civilized way to handle such a problem is to pretend that it does not even exist.[84]

This Gawain does first of all by politely denying that he is the "old Gawain" of romance (1241-42), thus ruling out any possibility of his acting accordingly. The subsequent cocoon of courtly rhetoric that Gawain wraps around himself, full of flattery and praise for the lady and modesty and lowliness for himself, moves the knight's sub-mission and proffered service away from the dangerous realm of sexuality to that of acceptable courtly etiquette ("my souerayn I holde yow," 1278). Even the affectionate parting kiss that the lady exacts from Gawain is no concession to sexuality on his part, for nonerotic kissing, even between males, was a sign of respect and a part of the received social convention, of which the text of *Sir Gawain* offers many examples.[85] Again Gawain very shrewdly, and at the same time very courteously ("I schal kysse at your comaundement, as a kny3t fallez," 1303), avoids to offend the importunate lady, by shifting the meaning of the kiss from socially dangerous grounds to that of accepted custom, in which form it can be freely rendered back to the host, without any ambiguities or innuendos.[86] This too il-lustrates the rule of the Golden Mean at work in Gawain's behavior: to refuse the kiss would compromise the knight's courtesy and show deficiency in the mean virtue, while to give more than was acceptable from the social point of view would be an excess and an offense against *clannes*. As it was, Gawain brilliantly won on the first day of temptation by adhering admirably to the middle course of temperance and the Golden Mean, unlike the pursued deer, which were wholly and "intemperately" given to fear and perished as a result.

In light of Gawain's spiritual exposure during his temptation, the alternating detailed descriptions of the hunting and then breaking up and flaying of the slain quarry also assume special symbolic significance. The author's great expertise in the art of venery exhibited in the hunting passages is used in the poem not as an end in itself, impressive though it is, but as a means of depicting figuratively what in the psychological sense is taking place in the bedroom scenes. The expert dissection of the animal body and the exposure of its entrails, described in technical detail (1325-61), strongly suggests the parallel action of the equally expert "opening up" of Gawain's concupiscible soul by the lady during their tête-à-tête. The uncovering of Gawain's hidden instincts and bringing them up to the level of consciousness are rendered symbolically in the parallel forest scenes by means of the great accumulation of verbs that have to do with cutting, slitting, hacking, cleaving, breaking up of the flesh, and pulling out of the entrails.[87] And just as the host appears in the hunting scenes as the true master of game, both in the chase itself and in his skillful dissection of the deer, so Gawain has so far emerged as a master of his nature by not allowing his activated passions take the better of him. This he accomplished through his temperance and self-control, which helped him avoid the fate of a helpless victim: the pitiful lot of the panicky deer clearly illustrates the possible alternative for Gawain, had he not kept his instincts in check. The knight's subsequent praise for Bertilac's slain quarry belongs in fact to himself[88] as the true winner of the first day's hunt, and the spoil accordingly is given to him as a token of victory over his animality.

In the context of the hunting and the bedroom scenes from Fitt III it is worthwhile to relate both Gawain's behavior and that of the pursued animals to the beheading scene from Fitt IV, whose threefold pattern is in an obvious way structurally linked with the three days of action at Hautdesert. Especially revealing are analogies and differences between Gawain's behavioral tactics employed both during the temptation and at the beheading, particularly in view of the postulated rule of the Golden Mean adhered to by the knight as a general strategy of action. Thus at the first blow of the Green Knight (corresponding to the first day of temptation and the deer hunt), Gawain "schrank a lytel with þe schulderes for þe scharp yrne *(iron)"* (2267), avoiding the edge in an act of instinctive and to a large extent involuntary bodily reflex dictated by fear. Fear and cowardice are precisely Gawain's "deficiency" on this occasion, if only for a fraction of a second. However, this momentary lapse in measure is promptly pointed out by the Green Knight in his jeering but friendly remark:

'þou art not Gawayn,' quoþ þe gome, 'þat is so goud halden,
þat neuer *arȝed (was afraid)* for no here *(warrior)* by hylle ne be vale,
And now þou *fles for ferde (fear)* er þou fele harmez!

Such *cowardise* of þat kny3t cowþe *(could)* I neuer here *(hear)*.
(2270-73, Italics added)

In other words, unlike in the bedchamber, where the knight was so admirably holding the reins of his desire and sensuality and did not behave like the timid deer, during the first beheading blow at the Green Chapel Gawain acted exactly like the cowardly and fearful does of the first hunt in wholly (though for a brief moment only) giving in to the instinctive, animal thirst for survival. This momentary deflection from measure and the Golden Mean is clearly set against the model of the Green Knight's original firm determination to receive the beheading blow at Camelot, when he neither flinched nor fled ("Nawþer fyked I ne fla3e," 2274, "and 3et fla3 I neuer," 2276), unlike Gawain at his return blow, who swerved cowardly like the timid deer, "ar3ez *(fear)* in hert" (2277). This lapse from the mean virtue of self-control is here no doubt dictated by Gawain's irrational fear of death, the same motive that caused the treacherous, cowardly, but also this time deliberate retention of the magic girdle on the third day of temptation—Gawain's main breach of the rule of the Golden Mean in the poem. "Bot þa3 *(though)* my hede falle on þe stonez, I con not hit restore" (2282-83) is Gawain's excuse for his momentary loss of control under the axe, which is also a polite yet pointing reminder of the basic unfairness of the beheading duel. But because of the extenuating character of the motive responsible for Gawain's shortcoming at the first blow—his instinctive *and* human love of life—he gets away only with a mocking, fatherly rebuke from the Green Knight, a prelude, however, to the later punishment for the main fault related to the girdle.

The Second Day

It is interesting to observe that the Exchange of the Winnings agreement between Sir Bertilac and Sir Gawain is not made just once, but is renewed at the end of each day, as if its extension were conditional upon Gawain's handling of the deal on a particular occasion. Or to put it otherwise: as if the victory over one's concupiscible soul were a prerequisite for further struggles with the higher portions of the soul. After the first day's success the bargain is accordingly sealed again in the similar atmosphere of carefree laughter and joyful drinking that characterized the first agreement,[89] although the passing mention of a cock crowing thrice at dawn (1412) alerts the reader to the growing seriousness and moral danger lurking for Gawain behind the covenant.[90]

Early the next morning the hunt is resumed, and this time the hounds are chasing a fierce boar: big, old, and solitary.[91] Duke Edward in his hunting manual describes the boar as the strongest and most perilous beast of venery, able to slay a man at one stroke.[92] The description of the boar in *Sir Gawain* is kept in a similar vein: the beast is "breme" *(fierce)*, "alþer-grattest" *(biggest of all)*, "grymme" and "braynwod" *(frenzied)*, able to thrust three hounds to the ground at once. It can withstand several hounds at bay and can severely maim both the hunting dogs (1450-53) and the hunters (1461-63). The boar is also morally qualified by Duke Edward as a "proud" beast, representing *orguilleuse*, well in keeping with its savage strength and defiance. Clearly then, within the threefold allegorical scheme employed in Fitt III the boar would correspond to the second of the "lusts," the "lust of the eyes" and the sin of *vana gloria*—that is, a desire for glory, as well as ambition and boastfulness. On the Platonic scale in turn these vices appear to be nourished by the middle, spirited portion of the soul, located in the region of the heart, responsible for hot passions and emotions. It is probably for this reason that after a fierce struggle the boar is finally slain by Sir Bertilac by driving the sword through the beast's heart,[93] the seat and source of vainglory.

Meanwhile in the bedchamber the lady's tactics that day are to make Gawain take the initiative in the love game and to force him into definite action. She begins her conversation by referring straightaway to the more physical aspects of love, especially "kyssyng" (1489), and finally openly suggests a possibility of taking her by force, in which case she would offer no resistance:

> 3e ar stif innoghe to constrayne wyth strenkþe, 3if yow lykez,
> 3if any were so vilanous þat yow devaye *(refuse)* wolde.
>
> (1496-97)

In other words, the temptress is trying to stir Gawain's masculine ambition by counting on his "strenkþe" and to turn him into an active partner in the erotic game, much like the violent boar fighting the hounds in the forest. The lady's attempt to "get the beast out" of Gawain is, however, neutralized again by the knight's most polite and clever refusal to act brutally: "þrete *(force)* is vnþryuande *(unworthy)* in þede *(country)* þer I lende *(dwell)*" (1499). The hostess's blunt proposals meet invariably with Gawain's reaffirmed willing submission and service to her: "I am at your comaundement, to kysse quen yow lykez" (1501), "I am hy3ly bihalden *(obliged)*, and euermore wylle / Be seruaunt to yourseluen" (1547-48). By keeping himself on the guard in this way Gawain again succeeds in *not* allowing himself to be provoked into animalistic behavior, this time the brutal strength of the wild boar. His politeness and courteous submission are directly proportional to the aggressiveness of the boar, illustrating yet again the rule of the Golden Mean and temperance in the knight's overall strategy of action. After Gawain's tactful and inoffensive refusal to follow the call of his spirited soul, the conversation then smoothly moves to safer grounds, albeit still concerning love, and remains until the end within the sphere of more or less theoretical aspects of *amour courtois* ("Much speche þay þer expoun / Of druryes *[love's]* greme *[grief]* and grace," 1506-7). Although constantly tempted to give in to the more physical aspects of love (the lady "fondet *[tempted]* hym ofte. / For to haf wonnen (*win*) hym to woȝe *[make love],*" 1549-50), Gawain exhibits throughout unshaken self-control and modesty, and his only concession to carnality are two kisses granted the lady at her request (1505, 1555), again a socially safe outlet for whatever emotion was there involved.

If again—as is postulated—the simultaneous actions in the bed-chamber and in the forest are treated as complementary parts of one process, then the "vncely (*ill-fated*) swyn" (1562) savagely fighting back the hounds and resisting the arrow blows, only to fall victim to the lord's sword, should figuratively represent the spirited, warlike aspect of Gawain's personality, nourished by the irascible soul that breeds both the heroic virtues of strength and courage and the sins of wrath and vainglory. Gawain's success on the second day of temptation relies precisely on his ability to avoid following his irascible soul inordinately, and the fatal outcome of the hunt for the boar clearly illustrates the knight's possible fate if he had behaved likewise. If on the first day Gawain refused to act like a perfect courtly lover (for which he was so reputed), on the second day he brilliantly managed not to be guided by his masculine ambition into acting like a warrior (another important side of his fame, amply illustrated elsewhere in the text).

After the boar is finally slain by a blow the heart, the seat of the irascible soul, the beast is subsequently beheaded (1607). This head is later presented to Gawain in a very significant way in the exchange of the spoils. In the context of the Beheading Game, so crucial to the poem's entire structure and content, one cannot at this stage resist treating the boar's severed head[94] as an anticipation of Gawain's own threatened beheading later at the Green Chapel, if only as another grim reminder of what can happen to him if he forgets courtesy and starts behaving "boarishly." The symbolic identification between the boar and Gawain is reinforced by Bertilac's ritual gesture of handing the spoil to the knight as his "feez" (1622), as well as by his curious and ambiguous accompanying formula: "þis gomen is your awen / Bi fyn (*full*) forwarde (*covenant*) and faste (*binding*), faythely ȝe knowe" (1635-36). The word *gomen*[95] can be variously understood here, and the existing ambiguity increases the suggestiveness of Bertilac's statement: literally the formula can mean "this hunting spoil (the boar's head) is yours, according to our agreement," but it can also mean "the battle (so far) is yours," possibly with sexual undertones. Moreover, since the "gomen" refers here specifically to the boar's head, the formula can also figuratively denote Gawain's annihilation of his "boarish" nature, as well as being a reminder of the knight's own head being at stake in the game.

The real danger of Gawain's giving in to his irascible nature is well evidenced by his behavior later at the Green Chapel, during the second blow corresponding to the boar hunt and the second day of temptation. After the initial timid, deerlike swerve of Gawain's body to avoid the first stroke, at the second blow of the axe the knight gathers strength and courage and resolves to stand still like a stone, ready to accept his fate with firm determination: "I schal stonde þe a strok, and start no more" (2286). But then, after the Green Knight's feigned blow, Gawain loses his temper and exclaims angrily ("ful gryndelly [*wrathfully*] with greme [*anger*]," 2299) at his executioner to stop threatening him any longer (2300-2301). This temporary loss of measure is, however, again recompensated by the self-control and cold blood of the Green Knight, who only rebukes Gawain in a fatherly fashion for speaking "felly" (*boldly*), and proceeds immediately to deliver the final, decisive blow.

The Third Day

As before, Gawain's success in the second test is a prerequisite to yet another agreement, and since "þrid (*third*) tyme þrowe (*proves*) best" (1680), the Exchange-of-the-Winnings game is extended for one more day, which happens to be the New Year's Eve. The impending ultimate encounter at the Green Chapel provides an invisible foil for the unceasing conviviality and *carpe diem* atmosphere at Hautdesert,[96] and the implied contrast helps build up tension and a mood of uneasiness, as Gawain's so far happy and enjoyable sojourn at Hautdesert is drawing inevitably to an end. While on the first two days the hunt is after noble game, as if in keeping with the personality and conduct of the castle's main guest, the last day's hunt loses all of its previously graceful and heroic character and turns into a slapstick comedy, with a pack of hounds chasing after a fox that dodges and swerves cowardly and pathetically to avoid capture. Descriptions of the fox hunt in medieval literature are rare,[97] largely because unlike the deer or the boar the fox was regarded as vermin to be hunted out and destroyed,[98] and was not a noble game to be hunted for trophy or food. The host himself refers dismissively to his last hunt's spoil as "þis foule fox felle (skin)" (1944). Although not regarded as real game, the fox nonetheless figures very conspicuously in tradition as an animal potent with allegorical significances. Duke Edward, for example, describes it as a cunning, malicious, and false animal,[99] and the ancient Physiologus likewise speaks at length about the fox's deceitfulness, fraudulence, and ingenuity.[100] Especially notorious is the fox's habit of pretending to be dead in order to attract the birds that come to eat his flesh: the fox then springs up and catches them.[101] This and other behavioral features of the animal account for the widespread association of the fox with the devil, who likewise pretends to be harmless and afterwards catches his prey by guile.[102] The fox from Sir Gawain too is well within the tradition as a notorious "þef" (thief) (1725), wily ("with wylez" 1711) weaving his way back and forth trying to escape the hounds.

The speedy chase and the commotion of the fox hunt are again contrasted with the dangerous quiet and ease in Gawain's bedchamber ("Whyle þe hende kny3t at home holsumly [healthfully] slepes," 1731), when the fox imagery suddenly materializes in the form of the lady who, vixenlike, steals again into the room to launch her final assault on the knight. Her mantle "watz furred ful fyne with fellez (skins) wel pured" (1737),[103] and the animality of her dress is reinforced by her extreme décolletage, for her face, throat, breasts, and back are all naked.[104] Despite his heavy sleep caused by the growing apprehension about the imminent "wyrde" at the Green Chapel, Gawain does not remain unimpressed by the lady's appearance, and is almost driven to the very verge of surrender, not so much to satisfy his own desire, if he felt any at all under the circumstances, but rather to avoid compromising his civility by contined refusals.[105] But he again withstands the temptation of the type already familiar to him from the previous days, only to be confronted with new elements that complete and crown the comprehensive nature of the threefold test.

Pretending great disappointment, the wily lady asks for a gift from Gawain and mentions his glove (1799), which the knight gently declines to offer, claiming that the object is not honorable enough for such a lady (1803-7). The true reason for Gawain's refusal, however, derives from his "erande in erdez (*land*) vncouþe" (1808) to be undertaken the following day, in which he will necessarily need his military accoutrements, including the glove. The lady's request may therefore be seen as an attempt to test the knight's readiness to exercise his chivalric duty properly, again by putting Gawain in a situation where he has to stretch his courtesy in order to avoid compromising his heroic obligation. However, every refusal, no matter how polite, brings Gawain dangerously close to the limits of courtesy, and the knight is slowly but surely being led to the point of surrender by a clever woman. Her next move is to offer a gift herself, a costly ring "of red golde werkez" (1817), which Gawain declines yet again on the grounds that he has nothing equally valuable to give in return (1823).

Immediately afterwards, taking full advantage of the weakening force of Gawain's successive refusals, the lady offers one more gift, this time entirely new in terms of value and significance. Unlike the glove (related to warfare) and the ring (appealing to the sense of material gain), the proposed girdle has nothing to do with the above functions, but instead introduces an element of magic.[106] After carefully considering the usefulness of the magic girdle in view of the imminent and in all probability fatal duel, Gawain accepts the gift, puts it in hiding, and promptly promises the lady not to give it up to the lord (1861-65). In other words, Gawain undertakes "with a goud wylle" (1861)—that is, with full awareness of what he is doing—to deceive the host, since in order to abide by the rules of the Exchange-of-the-Winnings agreement he would have to return the gained object. But this, of course, would automatically deprive him of the lace's supposed magical defensive power. In view of the governing rule of the Golden Mean and measure, so admirably adhered to by Gawain up to this moment, the balance between the voice of nature within Gawain and the force of his will has now been disturbed. Instead of counteracting and modifying his impulses and keeping them under check, Gawain has now followed them and acted like the wily fox, giving in to treachery rather than fighting the beast in him, as he did on the previous occasions. The shrewd but cowardly and ignoble fox is therefore an appropriate symbol of Gawain's rational attempt to avoid what he thinks is sure death at the Green Chapel. But the knight's action takes an ironic turn here, as the story reveals the limitations of the narrow attempts of the human reason: just as the wily fox "schunt (*swerved*) for þe scharp" of Bertilac's sword (1902) only to fall victim to the chasing hounds a moment later, so now the "foxy" Gawain cherishes an illusion that he can save himself by his own doing through his vain recourse to willful magic and guile.

What makes Gawain change his strategy of action is of course the change in the underlying motive. The stakes suddenly turn from the prospect of losing his chivalric honor and making a fool of himself (if he yielded to the lady's advances), to the prospect of simply losing his life (if he went the the Green Chapel unarmed with the life-saving girdle). "Myȝt he haf slypped to be vnslayn, þe sleȝt were noble" (1858)—"If he could escape being slain, it would be a splendid stratagem"—and accordingly the panicky fear of being killed the next day makes Gawain blind to all other considerations, notably to the chivalric virtues of the pentangle and the whole idea of perfection denoted by it. By learning the magical property of the girdle Gawain's sense of value becomes confused, and the powerful forces of nature contained in the self-preservation instinct suddenly take the upper hand in him. Gawain's ego, so far linked to the rational will, deserts the fortress of the mind and gives its final consent to the instinct of life.

The moral confusion created in Gawain as a result of his surrender to self-survival is best illustrated by his total blindness to the consequences of the steps he takes immediately after accepting the lace. Without realizing it, on the eve of his ultimate trial at the Green Chapel Gawain enters yet another agreement (a third one in the poem), this time with the lady. He promptly promises to "lelly layne", "faithfully conceal" (1863) the girdle before the lord, and never to disclose the fact ("neuer wyȝe *[lord]* schulde hit wyt *(know),*" 1864). And just as Gawain's second covenant, the one with Sir Bertilac, turns out in the end to be complementary to the first agreement with the Green Knight, so the present bargain with the lady is openly at odds with Gawain's loyalty to the lord of the castle, as it is simply impossible to return the girdle and keep it at the same time. What makes Gawain's situation particularly awkward at this point is that even if on second thoughts he decided to change his mind about using the girdle at the Green Chapel, he would not have been able to hand it to Sir Bertilac without compromising his wife: the erotic character of the lace would then send a wrong signal about the degree of intimacy between Sir Gawain and the lady. If only for the lady's sake, therefore, the courteous Gawain now has to press on with his dubious enterprise.

Gawain's moral sense becomes even more confused when immediately after hiding the girdle he rushes off to make a confession in the castle's chapel. The text expressly says that the knight "schrof *(confessed)* hym schyrly *(cleanly)* and schewed his mysdedez, of þe more and þe mynne *(small)"* (1880-81), which would imply that Gawain has confessed all his sins, including the acceptance of the girdle and his intention not to give it up to the host. But the priest promptly and unconditionally absolved the knight, which in turn suggests that nothing amiss remains on Gawain's record, which we know is untrue. Since there is no reason to doubt the priest's competence in handling the sacrament and in granting the absolution, the only possible conclusion to be inferred is that Gawain simply did not reveal his retention of the girdle at the confession. If he had, the priest would surely have made his absolution contingent upon the knight's restoration of the girdle to Sir Bertilac, which from Gawain's point of view was now unthinkable: by returning the lace he would have both compromised the lady and ruined his plans of survival—his primary motive of action at this point in the story. The poet's insistence on the completeness of Gawain's confession and absolution (1880-81) is therefore clearly ironic, and conveys a sense of utter confusion in Gawain's mind once the instinct of survival overrides all other social and religious obligations.

On the other hand I would not claim, as Gollancz does in a note to his edition of *Sir Gawain* (123), that by concealing the fact that he has accepted the girdle with the intention of keeping it Sir Gawain is making a false, and therefore sacrilegious confession. Norman Davis too seems to miss the authorial irony when he says that "the poet evidently did not regard the retention of the girdle as one of Gawain's 'mysdedez', . . . which required to be confessed" (123). If we accept the more likely view that Gawain's "sacrilege," that is, simply lying at the confession, would be inconsistent with the knight's renowned piety copiously illustrated throughout the poem, the only explanation of his failure to mention the lace would be the aforementioned moral disturbance set on in Gawain's mind by the self-preservation mechanism, which has turned the knight's system of social, moral, and religious values upside-down. Once the powerful and irresistible biological drive sets in, any qualms about the possible misdemeanor and its consequences are automatically suppressed, and the knight ceases to be controlled solely by the value system of his rational mind, the way he has been up to this moment. This psychological turn-about is logical from the point of view of adaptation, and it convincingly—in my view—accounts for the apparent inconsistency of Gawain's behavior as judged by his former ethical standards.

Medieval theology recognized well the power of the self-preservation drive, but sins related to it were considered excusable, despite the usually inordinate and excessive nature of this instinct. Saint

Thomas Aquinas put self-preservation under natural law, along with the impulse to procreate and live in society,[107] and the Green Knight likewise regards Gawain's love of life as an extenuating circumstance in his act of treachery: "Bot for ȝe lufed your lyf; þe lasse I yow blame" (2368). So if Gawain did not sin in clinging to his life, for what, if anything, is he to blame?

It appears that in the circumstances in which the self-preservation instinct suddenly surfaced to considerably modify Gawain's perception of his system of values, the knight went wrong not so much in the motive itself as in the means by which he chose to save his life. The deflection from the middle path of temperance and self-control brought about almost disastrous moral and social consequences, in that a single loss of measure at the retention of the girdle dangerously disturbed the whole subtle network of relationships with Sir Bertilac, the lady, and the Green Knight, jeopardizing not only Gawain's chivalric fame but also his life. The initial "cowarddyse" or fear of death led Gawain to compromise with "couetyse" that is, love of life,[108] which then involved "vylany," "trecherye and vntrawþe" (2374-75, 2383), according to Gawain's own final self-accusation. But by cursing his love of life and the human weakness that springs from it[109] Gawain shows his misunderstanding of human nature and of the nature of his own fault. If he was guilty, it was not in his desire to "sauen hymself," but because in order to do so he resorted to selfish and worldly means and used them in the wrong way. But then because of the special theological status of the instinct of life Gawain probably could not have acted otherwise than as a human being with a built-in desire for survival, and therefore the ultimate nature of his sin remains unclear.[110] This paradox of the human condition seems to lie at the center of the comment offered by the poem to a larger discussion about man and his place in the world: the divine gift of life involves of necessity a strong instinct and the duty to preserve it, but because man uses all his available faculties (including God-given reason) to keep this divine gift, he has to sin. This inescapable dilemma pertains especially to chivalry, whose active life requires the initial instinct of self-preservation as a prerequisite of its functioning. But just because of this instinct, even the best of knights, like Gawain, has to fall short of the perfection postulated by the chivalric ideal. The only way out of this vicious circle is, theoretically speaking, to bypass or overcome one's desire for life as a primary motive, and to leave everything to Eternal Providence. This at least seems to be one of the possible conclusions suggested by Gawain's predicament. After reading the poem to the end, we can speculate—with the luxury of hindsight—"what would have happened if," and it is easy to see that had Gawain not cared so much about his life and had he not accepted the girdle, he would have come out of his adventure totally unscathed. But historical instances of such an attitude to one's individual life, although significant and exemplary in the highest degree, are few, and include, apart from Christ, some saints and martyrs of the "cause," who preferred death to any compromise. An Everyman, like Gawain and most of us, has to live with the acceptance of the limits of his individual powers, of the built-in, insurmountable imperfections of his nature, as well as with the realization that the disturbed metaphysical balance of the human condition can only be redressed by the magnanimity and forbearance of the powers superior to man.

6

The Head and the Loss Thereof: Gawain's Final *Adoubment*

In a very conspicuous way the two halves of the Beheading Game provide the poem with an enveloping framework, lending it as a result an overall effect of circularity and completeness, especially in the association of the game itself with the decisive nature and importance of the New Year's Day in the poem's symbolic structure. In chapter 2 I hinted in general terms that the beheading is a sort of ritual, marking the hero's transition from one mode of existence to another, a symbolic death as part of Sir Gawain's rite of passage, reinforced by its implicit connection with the Christian Feast of the Circumcision as a prefiguration of Christ's redemptive Passion. From the purely literary point of view the two beheading scenes add tremendously to the attractiveness of the narrative, creating in themselves a highly dramatic and powerful effect, full of suspense as well as psychological and emotional tension. These dramatic qualities of the Beheading Game are indeed superbly worked out by the poet, especially in Fitt IV, and the created effect helps convey to the reader important meanings of this narrative element in relation to the last and most decisive phase of Gawain's quest. I argue that by virtue of its highly dramatic and prominent position in the poem, the Beheading Game is more than just another test of the knight's courage and fidelity to his word. The Green Knight's initial challenge and his consequential bargain with Sir Gawain provide the main objective to the chivalric quest described in the poem, by determining its character and ultimate significance. In this chapter I shall therefore seek possible meanings of the beheading treated as a traditional motif, not so much in terms of sheer source-analysis, since this has been sufficiently dealt with by the early ethnogenetic approach to *Sir Gawain,*[1] but in respect to the motif's possible semantic potential, both as an independent narrative element and as an integral part of the poem's symbolic structure.

þe Crystemas gomen

In terms of sheer effect, the beheading challenge, gruesome in its deadly seriousness and ridiculous in its absurdity, comes climactically at the height of the Christmas celebrations at Camelot, in the middle of the prevailing jollity and conviviality. The happy mood of the seasonal festival is highlighted from the first moment the poem introduces us into Camelot, where people are engaged in "rych reuel ory3t and rechles merþes" (40), with the knights jousting "ful jolile" (42) or else singing "caroles" (43). The purposefully exaggerated presentation of the happy time at Camelot seems to serve a moral purpose[2] and smacks of nostalgia for the Golden Age and trouble-free childhood. Such indeed is the impression created by the author in his laudatory description of "þis fayre folk in her first age":

> For þer þe fest watz ilyche ful fiften dayes,
> With alle þe mete and þe mirþe þat men couþe avyse;
> Such glaum ande gle glorious to here,
> Dere dyn vpon day, daunsyng on ny3tes,
> Al watz hap vpon he3e in hallez and chambrez
> With lordez and ladies, as leuest him þo3t.
> With all þe wele of þe worlde þay woned þer samen,
> þe most kyd kny3tez vnder Krysten seluen,
> And þe louelokkest ladies þat euer lif haden,
> And he þe comlokest kyng þat þe court haldes;
> For al watz þis fayre folk in her first age.

(44-54)

The imagery and feelings evoked here are clearly those of the "springtime" of life, the carefree *adolescentia*, the age of childlike immaturity and irresponsibility, epitomized especially in the person of "sumquat childgered" (86) King Arthur. It is mainly due to his "3onge blod and his brayn wylde" (89) that trouble is conjured up at the outset of the feast, for before the king will eat he wants to hear

> Of sum auenturus þyng an vncouþe tale,
> Of sum mayn meruayle, þat he my3t trawe,
> Of alderes, of armes, of oþer auenturus,
> Oþer sum segg hym biso3t of sum siker kny3t
> To joyne wyth hym in iustyng, in joparde to lay,
> Lede, lif for lyf, leue vchon oþer,
> As fortune wolde fulsun *(help)* hom, þe fayrer to haue.

(93-99)

The habit of not beginning a feast before some unusual tale is told is fairly typical for Arthur's court as presented in romance literature,[3] and in *Sir Gawain* the habitual nature of the custom is also made clear by a reference to the "countenaunce" (*custom*) held by Arthur "where he in court were" (100). Of course, in a wider sense the Christmas season was naturally an occasion for all sorts of celebrations; both serious, as in the Church's observance of the feasts of the Nativity, the Circumcision, and the Epiphany, as well as of the more merry kind, associated for instance with the Feast of Fools[4] or the numerous and varied playful New Year customs of popular provenance.[5] Important as this religious and cultural background is, the *Crystemas gomen* in *Sir Gawain* assumes nonetheless a more concrete and specific significance due to the way it is handled by the poet as the crucial and decisive part of Gawain's adventure.

Arthur's light-hearted wish to hear of some marvel or to see a "lif for lyf" combat soon conjures up a strange visitor in green, who—as is remembered—is carrying a holly branch and an axe in his two hands and proposes, or rather demands ("I craue," 283), "a Crystemas gomen," on account of some "ry3t" ("þe gomen þat I ask bi ry3t," 273-74). This unspecified "right" of the Green Knight to propose the Beheading Game must apparently have something to do with the traditional New Year customs, as the visitor himself explains: "Forþy I craue in þis court a Crystemas gomen, *For* hit is 3ol and Nwe 3er" (283-84, Italics added). The rules of the proposed game are simple: come whoever dares to strike my head with this axe now, so that I can strike his a year hence (285-98).[6] The knights enjoying their Christmas feast have hardly come round after the first shock of the Green Knight's appearance when they are confronted with a less mysterious but more concrete and serious *dictum*, inviting them to enter what looks like a most absurd and impossible agreement: to fulfill the second part of the deal would simply mean death for an ordinary mortal, as no human being can remain alive after having his or her head chopped off. The absurdity and the apparent inappropriateness of such a proposal in the midst of the prevailing jollity come again as a shock, because it is clear that what the Green Knight is demanding has nothing to do with the harmless and childish Christmas games indulged in by the "mony luflych lorde" at Camelot. The terrifying intruder in green really means what he says, and the "show" that he later makes with his severed head is not "a kind of amusement park trick"[7] but is real,[8] at least in the world of magic evoked by the poem. The Green Knight's *Crystemas gomen* is serious and inescapable, and will not be easily dismissed or avoided, as children would often do with unpleasant things that interfere with their play. The childishness, immaturity, and recklessness of Camelot "in its first age" are precisely the Green Knight's target, as he openly offends the "berdlez chylder" (280) sitting on the benches and questions Camelot's widespread good chivalric reputation (309-15).

The gruesome character of the Beheading Game is not, however, entirely out of place at Christmas and its customary celebrations. The medieval audience must surely have related the beheading challenge in *Sir Gawain* to the seasonal custom present in the popular Mummers' Plays, where a mock beheading likewise took place, followed by a revival of the beheaded actor.[9] Traditionally Christmastime abounded in rites of sacrificial character,[10] closely linked with less joyful aspects of the season such as the stoning of Saint Stephen (26 December), the commemoration of the massacre of the Holy Innocents (28 December), the martyrdom of Saint Thomas (29 December), to say nothing of the letting of Christ's blood at the Circumcision (1 January). Nor can it be excluded that the Green Knight's "right" to propose his deadly game at the threshold of the New Year goes back to even more archaic, pagan ritual practices whose echoes may still have lingered on in the popular imagination of the late Middle Ages. The available ethnological and mythological evidence[11] informs us that in pre-Christian Europe the solstices were often the occasions for ritual ceremonies associated with kingship, involving the sacrificial deposition of the old king and the installation of the new one. According to Robert Graves's well-known views on the origin of certain mythological themes,[12] both the midwinter and midsummer solstices were in archaic Europe occasions for the sacrificial killing of the Sacred King, identified symbolically with the sun, accomplished either by his brother or by some other successor, who afterwards ruled for the remaining half of the year (until the next solstice), when he was himself sacrificially deposed by his follower. From an astronomical point of view the underlying idea of this ancient custom is fairly transparent: the deposition of the Sacred King coincides with the "death" of the old sun at midwinter, followed by the "birth" of the new sun, which waxes to reach its zenith at midsummer, whereupon it subsequently begins to wane and eventually "dies" completely the next midwinter. What I am suggesting here is not that the meaning of the Beheading Game in *Sir Gawain* can be explained away by referring to one more version of the nature myth, but simply that seasonal symbolism, so importantly present in the narrative structure of the poem as a whole, may have this archaic, pagan layer as well.

Nor is the ancient solar symbolism totally lacking in relation to the other party of the Beheading Game, Sir Gawain, who in the context of the evoked custom should succeed the "Sacred King" and rule for the following year, to be himself ritually "dethroned" at the next midwinter. The early ethnogenetic research into the sources of *Sir Gawain*[13] attempted to link the poem's main protagonist with some ancient Celtic "solar deity," and it is interesting to observe in this context that in the late medieval Arthurian romances Gawain also exhibits "solar" characteristics. It is mentioned, for example, in some texts that Gawain's strength waxed and waned as the day advanced and declined, the feature that has clearly to do with the daily run of the sun across the sky. The earliest instance of this solar attribution to Gawain comes from the First Continuation of Chrétien's *Conte del Graal,*[14] and in English literature it appears in the stanzaic *Le Morte Arthur*:

> Than had syr gawayne such a grace,
> An holy man had boddyn that bone,
> Whan he were in Any place,
> There he shuld batayle done,
> Hys strength shuld wex in such A space,
> From the vndyn-tyme tylle none[15]

This recurring feature of Gawain's in medieval texts does not imply, however, that either the romance writers or their audiences were aware of the archaic ritual context from which the idea had originally arisen. Nor can the modern critic's assertion that "this Celtic hero was at one time a solar divinity"[16] help us today in arriving at the significance of the Beheading Game for Sir Gawain in the context of a late fourteenth-century poem. What the solar attributes of Sir Gawain can suggest today, however, is that the idea of placing the two halves of the Beheading Game at the solsticial points of the year can ultimately derive from traditional stories, possibly still known in the later Middle Ages, that reflected the once-widespread, ancient midwinter ritual killing of the Sacred King as a personification of the sun. This archaic layer of significance can complement for us the more historically justified symbolic patterns associated with the New Year, which I discussed in chapter 2.

But the above-outlined initiatory *scenario,* typical for the traditional kingship ritual, is still at closer scrutiny perceptible in *Sir Gawain,* despite the fact that the poem was composed in a different cultural *milieu* than the pagan myths discussed by Robert Graves or James George Frazer. It is not, in my opinion, an accident that the hero who finally takes upon himself the mission of saving the honor of the Round Table by answering the beheading challenge is Sir Gawain, Arthur's next-of-kin and natural successor.[17]   The royal nephew emphatically highlights his lineage and close blood relation to Arthur as a justification for his decision to replace the king in the duel:

> Bot for as much as 3e ar myn em *(uncle)* I am only to prayse,
> No bounte bot your blod I in my bode knowe;

(356-57)

King Arthur himself, the current ruler, clearly mishandles the whole Green Knight affair from the very start by losing his temper and allowing himself to be easily provoked into the game, apparently heedless of the disastrous consequences for the realm if he dies. His "blod schot for scham into his schyre *(bright)* face" (317), "he wex as wroth as wynde" (319) and leaped forward to seize the axe and deal the blow (328-31). It is then that Sir Gawain intervenes, first with a long and composed speech (341-61) that gives the king time to calm down and collect himself, but that also upstages him as the man in charge by transferring the task onto his nephew and successor.[18]   Arthur has evidently little to say at this moment, for even the official decision to allow Sir Gawain to take the challenge is not made by the king but by the nobles, who diplomatically relieve the ruler of this extremely embarrassing situation:

> Ryche *(nobles)* togeder con roun *(whisper)*,
> And syþen þay redden *(advise)* alle same *(together)*
> To ryd þe kyng wyth croun,
> And gif Gawan þe game.

(362-65)

A moment later, however, Arthur reasserts his authority, if only nominally, when he ceremonially invests his nephew with arms and gives him his royal blessing and last instructions before the battle:

> þen comaunded þe kyng þe kny3t for to ryse;
> And he ful radly vpros, and ruchched *(proceeded)* hym fayre,
> Kneled doun bifore þe kyng, and cachez þat weppen;
> And he luflyly hit hym laft *(gave)*, and lyfte vp his honde,
> And gef hym Goddez blessyng, and gladly hym biddes
> þat his hert and his honde schulde hardi be boþe.

(366-71)

Afterwards Arthur proceeds to say something very puzzling and intriguing, particularly in view of his hitherto immature and "childish" behavior. He advises his nephew to deal the beheading blow in such a way that he will be able to *withstand* the return stroke later, unimaginable though it may be:

'Kepe þe *(take care)*, cosyn,' quoþ þe kyng, 'þat þou on kyrf *(one blow)* sette,
And if þou redez (manage) hym ry3t, redly I trowe
þat *þou schal byden þe bur* [19] þat he schal bede after.

(372-74, italics added)

Arthur is clearly advising Gawain to "manage" *(redan)* the man "rightly" *(ry3t)*, possibly by dealing the beheading blow with a single stroke ("on kyrf"), but one is left suspecting that there is more in Arthur's advice than meets the eye. Because of the obvious fact that Gawain would not normally be able to live if he submitted to the return blow, perhaps Arthur is hinting at some way this blow can be honorably avoided. But how?

An additional clue to the strange ambiguity surrounding the conditions of the Beheading Game is provided by the Green Knight in his restatement of the rules of the match, particularly in the clause regarding Sir Gawain's obligation to look for his opponent a year thence, wherever he hopes to find him on the earth (395-96). When Gawain openly and emphatically expresses his ignorance about the Green Knight's identity and the whereabouts as well as his desire to find out about them,[20] the man in green says something even more enigmatic than Arthur's strange advice. He says that he will either provide the required information, but only after Gawain has given the blow, or else he will not provide it, in which case Gawain will not have to bother about the second part of the covenant:

'3if I þe telle trwly, quen I þe tape haue
And þou me smoþely hatz smyten, smartly I þe teche
Of my hous and my home and myn owen nome,
þen may þou frayst my fare *(inquire about my doings)* and forwardez
                                                    (agreement) holde;
And if I spende no speche, þenne spedez *(prosper)* þou þe better,
For þou may leng *(stay)* in þy londe and layt *(seek)* no fyrre *(further)* .

(406-11, italics added)

In other words, it appears that the Green Knight is making the disclosure of his name and dwelling-place contingent upon the manner in which Sir Gawain will deal his blow. The reader is thus led to understand that if the stroke is administered "smoþely" (*neatly*), whatever this means, then Gawain will be exempt from submitting to the return blow and in practice from undertaking his adventure altogether. This would happen, for example, if Gawain managed to render the Green Knight powerless through his beheading blow, so that the latter would not be able to recover and exact the second part of the deal—in other words, if Gawain ensured that the Green Knight was dead. This—as is known—does not take place, for the knight miraculously survives the decapitation, Gawain is consequently obliged to seek his opponent a year later, and the strange clause in the covenant remains void, apparently because in dealing with a supernatural being, skills other than pure physical force and military prowess are required.

The unrealized possibility of avoiding the return blow found in the rules presented by the Green Knight is the most intriguing aspect of the first part of the Beheading Game in *Sir Gawain*, and why the Green Knight makes the revelation of his name and address conditional upon Gawain's beheading skills has never, to my knowledge, been addressed by the critics. The reservation in the beheading agreement directly touches the complex nature of the test that the Beheading Game constitutes for Gawain and seems to be ultimately derived from certain symbolic and magical functions attached to the human head and decapitation in traditional societies. Gawain's acceptance of the beheading challenge is not only a test of his courage, sense of honor, and physical skills in fighting; it is the first step on his quest towards wider knowledge of himself and of the powers governing this world, his first confrontation (in the poem at least) with impermanence of life, with violent death, and also with death's magic and the whole sphere of the supernatural, an aspect of reality evidently unfamiliar to him. All the subsequent adventures described in the poem—the physical, psychological, moral, and spiritual tests undergone by Gawain, the final ordeal and the experience of quasi-death at the Green Chapel included—are a direct consequence of this first act, when a single stroke at the head of a supernatural being unleashes for the best of knights powers and things strange, unknown, and unpredictable. It is also, let us recall, Gawain's first confrontation with his "green shadow" and everything that it signifies: physical vulnerability and mortality, sinfulness and moral decay, the experience of death itself, but also the potential of spiritual growth, as contained in the mystical notion of the *benedicta viriditas,* for example.

As it turns out, except for purely martial, physical skill with which Gawain neatly cuts off the creature's head (421-26), the other, more secret aspects of the chivalric lore that were called on both by Arthur and the Green Knight before the blow remain still open for Gawain, since he is *de facto* subsequently told by his opponent's severed head to find his way to the Green Chapel a year later (448-56). Magic is let loose for Gawain, and it is the most serious and dangerous kind at that, unlike that displayed for the rest of the court, who immediately after the Green Knight's departure cover their embarrassment with laughter ("At þat grene þay laȝe and grenne," 466), dismiss the whole affair as a trivial "meruayl" and one more "craft vpon Cristmasse" (471), and cheerfully revert to the earlier "enterludez," "caroles," and "mynstralcie" (472-73, 484), as befits humanity in its "first age."

Human Head as a Symbol

To address adequately some of the interpretative questions raised in the preceding pages, I believe it necessary to discuss briefly a more generalized problem of the symbolic significance of the human head, regardless at first of the particular context in which this object may occur. The following remarks will help, I hope, to elucidate what is actually at stake in the ritualized beheading enacted in *Sir Gawain* and what may be the significance of the human head and its loss in the poem, as well as in other traditional narratives. A generalized discussion on the symbolic contents of the human head also serves as another example of a systemic procedure (see chapter 1, the section on systems theory), in which a particular narrative element, here the beheading, is first treated independently in its structural entirety and subsequently tested against literary evidence, both within *Sir Gawain* and in a wider context.

As was the case with the earlier analysis of the possible significances of greenness, the purpose of this discussion is to attempt a reconstruction of the imaginative associations that can be built around the human head, consisting of certain concepts and ideas that determine the figurative meaning of this object in different contexts.[21] The hermeneutic value of this method is that the symbolic potential of a particular object can be hypothetically but also comprehensively deduced prior to the examination of relevant evidence. Any actual context in which a symbolic object can be found often illustrates only a partial, incomplete meaning of that object, one that depends on that very context. In this case the foregoing analysis of the literary context of the Beheading Game in *Sir Gawain* can now be complem-

Table 8

The Human Head and Its Symbolic Connotations

Human Head and Its Natural Attributes	Symbolic Connotation Based on Imaginative Associations
1. The head is the uppermost and most conspicuous part of the human body, usually counted as the first.	The head is "high" in opposition to the body, usually conceived as "low." By pointing upwards to the sky it can represent "heaven" and the highest male divinity, in contrast with the low female and chthonic element, the womb.[23] As the first member of the body, the head denotes any beginning, both in the spatial and temporal sense.
2. Usually a person has only one head, in contrast to a pair of arms or legs.	The singularity of the head may be linked with the concept of Oneness and Unity of the human constitution. On the other hand, the notion of dual, three-, or four-aspect beings may give rise to various polycephalic fantastic representations, such as the Janus type, common Celtic three-faced heads.
3. The head is usually separated from the trunk by a neck, and its locomotion is largely independent (it can turn in almost all directions).	This feature may be responsible for the idea of the loose connection or separation between body and soul and the human and the divine in people.
4. The head is nearly spherical in shape.	The sphere, as the perfect of shapes, can again represent Deity, Oneness, Completeness, Eternity, Infinity, the Cosmos.
5. The head is hard, in contrast to softer and more muscular parts of the body.	The relative hardness of the head, together with the round shape, may recall round stones, balls, or heavenly bodies such as the sun and the moon.
6. The head contains seven apertures or sensory openings: two eyes, two ears, two nostrils, and a mouth.	The seven apertures are the "gates" to the individual's inner world (especially the eyes, "mirrors of the soul") and the seats of the five main senses; they also have symbolic associations with the number seven, as in the seven planets.

7. Usually the head is covered with hair, except for the face. Intraracially the hair may be of different colors and interracially the skin may be of different colors.	As an extension of the head, hair may symbolize the emanation of the soul and the individual's "magic power"; therefore, the loss of hair causes a decrease in psychic and magical potential (as for Samson). Hair color may be characterized either positively or negatively, depending on the context. Both the hair and face can also assume an unnatural but meaningful color.
8. The head contains the brain—the most vital bodily organ, the controlling and coordinating center of the nervous system, the seat and source of psychic life: thought, memory, and emotions are hidden and protected in a hard, bony skull.	This internal feature of the head can breed the idea of something precious and magical contained in a sacred vessel, for example the eucharistic chalice, the Holy Grail, a genie in Aladdin's lamp.
9. The head allows communication with the external world in terms of information (the sensory perception, reflective consciousness, articulated speech) and materio-energy (food absorbed through the mouth, oxygen breathed in through the nose).	This function can explain the ritual use of the head or the skull as a medium and instrument for contacts with the otherworld. The perceived independence of the head from life-supporting substances may relate to a belief in the survival of the head after separation from the body. This belief, along with the notion of the head as a container of psychic faculties, can lead to a conviction that the severed head can speak divine wisdom.
10. The head expresses a person's unique psychic identity, personality, and character, especially in the face, since there are no two people (except for identical twins) with the same facial features.	The head can therefore stand for the whole individual, as in the habit of calling people "heads" (per capita). This may also explain the assumed magical, sympathetic relationship between a face and portrait or photograph, the latter possessing at least some of the individual's personal "magical power."
11. After death, when the soft tissues have decomposed, the skull remains as the biggest and most impressive part of the skeleton—a spherical bony vessel with empty apertures.	The human skull is a sad reminder of the ultimate end of us all; hence, its use as a memento mori and an instrument of communication with the otherworld in ancestor worship and necromancy.

ented by a more theoretical reconstruction of the symbolic signif-icances attached to the human head and the beheading that will hopefully shed fresh light on many of the problems raised in the course of the earlier discussion.

The symbolic complex of the human head is presented in table 8,[22] in which the distinguished natural attributes of the head are given symbolic connotations based on possible imaginative associations. The deductions made from the examination of the natural features and functions of the human head treated "as such" are fairly straight-forward, and it is not surprising to find many of the enumerated ideas confirmed and illustrated in a variety of sources. The fol-lowing brief review of the "headlore" in ancient and medieval texts should give the reader some idea of the kind of imaginative asso-ciations that the audience of *Sir Gawain* may have had in connection with the Green Knight's severed head, as well as with Sir Gawain's threatened decapitation.

It is useful, initially, to glance at the classes of meaning covered by the Middle English word *hed* to see to what extent the semantic field of the word can overlap with the associations built on simple observation of the head as an object, as presented in the table. Ac-cording to the *MED,* the *hed* (OE *heafod*) stands for the following things and phenomena, listed here in the decreasing order of fre-quency of occurrence in Middle English sources:

1. A human or animal head;
2. An individual, a person;
3. The seat of the mind; the mind; thought;
4. Life itself;
5. Ruler, king, leader, commander; the most important person or thing; the most famous or influential;
6. Origin of a river; source, fountainhead, any beginning;
7. The upper end, top, summit;
8. The end of anything;
9. Issue, conclusion;

There also exists another noun *hed*, derived from the verb *heden* (OE *beheafdian*), which denotes such mental faculties as "attention, notice, regard" and "care, anxiety, trouble, pains." The verb *heden* in turn means, very interestingly, both "to behead" and "to provide somebody with a head."[24] On the whole then, the semantic field of the word concentrates mostly on the head conceived as the most vital and important part of the body, equivalent to the whole of the person, to the entire mental life, as well as to life itself. The head stands for being and existence, whereas the beheading, by analogy, would mean total and irrevocable annihilation of a person, a "complete" death.

The Pythagoreans, for example, recognized the human head as the most important, "highest summit of the body,"[25] the seat of divine intellect and reason. Plato similarly emphasized the heavenly origin of the head in the *Timaeus*, stressing also an analogy between the roundness of the head and the perfect, spherical shape of the cosmos:[26]

> [The gods] copied the shape of the universe and fastened the two divine orbits of the soul into a spherical body, which we now call the head, the divinest part of us which controls all the rest; then they put together the body as a whole to serve the head, knowing that it would be endowed with all the varieties of motion there were to be.[27]

Further on (90a) Plato talks about the head as the seat of the highest, divine soul, which raises man above other earthly creatures. The highly influential ancient *Corpus Hermeticum* in a similar vein ascribes the divine characteristics to the human head and likewise develops the analogy between the head and the cosmos:

> The Kosmos is a sphere, that is to say, a head; and so, all things that are united to the cerebral membrane [the outermost sphere of heaven] of this head—the membrane in which the soul is chiefly seated—are immortal, for they have in them more soul than body;[28]

The Hermetic treatise known as the *Asclepius*, forming a part of the *Corpus Hermeticum,* which was especially well regarded by medieval Neoplatonists,[29] also sees the head as the repository of divine substance in man, "composed of higher elements, so to speak, namely, mind, intellect, spirit, and reason," due to which man "is found capable of rising to heaven."[30]

The biblical tradition also speaks of the divinity of man's head, chiefly in relation to Christ: "But I would you know, that the head of every man is Christ; and the head of the woman is the man; and the head of Christ is God" (1 Cor. 11:3).[31] In Pauline theology both Christ and the Church form one mystical body, with Christ as the head, the view enhanced by Saint Augustine in his conception of both Christ and the Church as *capitis et corporis*, respectively.[32] Even a basically nonreligious text such as the twelfth-century *De Arte Honeste Amandi* by Andreas Capellanus says the following about the human head as a substitute for the entire individual:

The upper part of a man—that is, the head—is considered the more worthy [than the lower part], because it is with regard to his face that a man is said to be formed in the image of his Creator, and a man is said to be buried where his head is interred. Besides, when a man's head is removed there is no telling whose the body is, but anyone who looks at the amputated head will easily know what the body was like.[33]

As the reader will have observed, more and more of the symbolic connotations of the head pointed out in the table crop up in the adduced sources. For instance, in alchemy—an important tradition of symbolic knowledge about man, nature, and the universe—the human head also has a special place. According to an alchemical legend associated with Pope Sylvester II (d. 1003), the Greek adepts of this art called themselves "children of the golden head"; the "head" being a seat of inspired wisdom and divine oracles.[34] The head had also a meaning of the *corpus rotundum*, signifying the alchemical arcane substance. The cranium was regarded as the place of the origin of the *prima materia* and was also referred to the vessel (*vas cerebri*) of the very *opus*, an idea expressed by the *Liber Platonis quartorum* (1602):

The vessel necessary in this work must be round in shape, that the artifex may be the transformer of this firmament and of the brain-pan (*vas cerebri*).[35]

The immortality and sacred character of the head are likewise emphasized by a scholastic philosopher Albertus Magnus (d. 1280) in his *Super arborem Aristotelis*:

His head lives forever and therefore his head is called the life of glory and the angels serve it. And God placed this image in the paradise of delights and in it he set his own image and likeness.[36]

These complex and often highly sophisticated beliefs and concepts account for the persistence of the human head in culture both as a symbol and a cult object. The magic and supernatural attributes and functions of the head were well known in pagan Europe, particularly in the Celtic areas, from which, by the way, the prototypal Beheading Game emerged in literary form. According to Anne Ross, in Celtic Britain "the human head is given first place as being the most typical Celtic religious symbol," and in support of this assertion she adduces rich and varied evidence from the fields of archaeology, iconography, classical written sources, as well as from early Welsh and Irish saga literature.[37] These sources show that the symbolic and religious meanings and functions of the head far exceed the rather crude and barbaric custom of head-hunting, often decribed, for example, by Livy, Diodorus Siculus, or Strabo in relation to ancient Celts.[38] The continued use of the head as an object of religious worship in the Christian context likewise points to more complex ideas and beliefs. For instance, in the fourteenth century Sir John Mandeville described in his *Travels* how the precious head of Saint John the Baptist was carefully guarded and worshiped in Constantinople by Pope Theodosius I (d. 395).[39] Similarly the Knights Templar, with their notoriously obscure and unorthodox beliefs and ritual practices, were said to possess "sacred heads" as objects of their worship. At the time of the persecution of the Templars in 1307-14 rumor spread in Europe about a mysterious "head" kept hidden by the order as its chief idol: in the articles of accusations against the Templars Bishop Dieudonne of London stated (1309) that the knights had such idols (or heads) in every province, that some of these idols had three faces and some consisted of a man's skull, and that the Templars worshiped them as their god. According to these articles the sacred heads of the Templars could produce material riches and soil fertility, and the knights were said to touch these heads with cords and then bind themselves with the cords.[40] Whether or not the ascetic Templars did actually worship such "idols," the atmosphere of magic and sacredness around the head as a cult object is in this case quite in keeping with the cosmological and magical meanings attached to the head in the Platonic and Hermetic sources quoted above.

The Beheading

Nonetheless, the reader will agree that the human head as an isolated object of potentially rich symbolic connotations occupies relatively little space in the romance of Sir Gawain, although when it appears in the story it is by no means insignificant. The Green Knight's head (as the only one that gets cut off in the poem) is referred to several times during the first beheading scene with the usual ME word *hed(e)* (418, 427, 433, 436, 444, 458), but in view of the symbolic contents discussed in this chapter, the word *croun* (419), used once as a synonym for the Green Knight's head,[41] is also highly suggestive. The word is rich in powerful meanings, among which that of the "head" in the simplest sense occupies the least conspicuous position. According to the *MED* [42] the *croun* (in the primary form as *coroune*, Latin *corona*) stands first of all for a monarch's crown or diadem, and signifies royal status. Interestingly, the same word occurs at the end of the minute description of Gawain's dressing-up before his departure from Camelot, when a princely circelet of diadems is placed on Gawain's "croun" (615-17), and in both cases one senses the suggestions of royal authority and power attached to the two characters. In my view, *croun,* used both in relation to the Green Knight and Sir Gawain, is not entirely without relevance in the context of the possible ritual provenance of the Beheading Game. In keeping with the archaic custom, the Green Knight's "croun" and its subsequent loss might suggest the symbolic, sacrificial dethronement through a ritual execution, because the next important meaning of *coroune* quoted by the *MED* is "the crown of the blessed in heaven, the reward of immortality and heavenly bliss," followed by "the aureole of a martyr, a celestial crown, nimbus, halo." The sacrificial context is further enlarged when we recall that the word can also denote Christ's "croun of þorne" (2529), as we are reminded in the penultimate line of the poem. And the element of the "Passion" soon makes itself visible on the scene, when the Green Knight's "croun" is neatly and expertly severed from his body by Sir Gawain, and red blood comes spurting from the wound (429, 441), shining against the green ("þat blykked on þe grene," 429).

In view of the network of possible imaginative, symbolic associations evoked by the human head, one has to admit that beheading understood as the intentional and purposeful removal of the victim's head should deprive a person "at one blow" of the most vital bodily organ, the seat of all psychic power and the source of the divine and immortal soul in man, causing the irrevocable death of the body—a real "end of the world" on the microcosmic plain (if we recall the symbolic equivalence between the head and the cosmos). Decapitation as a traditional motif is therefore the most terse, univocal, and also the most powerful and dramatic image of death, understood as a sudden separation of body and soul. At the same time, however, the head is believed to contain all that is necessary for life (the immortal soul, psychic powers, vital sensory organs), and so there is little wonder that in popular imagination the severed head should continue to live and function, with its divine component often ensuring the head's supernatural quality, as when, for example, it begins to utter prophecies or impart secret wisdom.[43] The Green Knight is no exception in this respect, for his head, after being picked up its headless torso, remains perfectly alive, even raises its eyelids to look around (446) and speaks (447), apparently unconcerned about being on its own and separated from the body. What the head says on this occasion is also important because it is only now, *after* being severed from the trunk, that it reveals its identity and the dwelling-place—that is, its true nature—providing Sir Gawain with a vital piece of information, according to which the knight is now obliged by his pledged word to go and seek "þe kny3t of þe grene chapel" to meet his destiny.

Now we can return to the earlier question about the strange reservation made by the Green Knight in his agreement with Sir Gawain, according to which the disclosure of the challenger's name is made dependent on the *manner* in which Gawain delivers the beheading blow. As the text has it, Arthur's nephew deals the stroke expertly and so forcefully that the blade of the axe hits the ground and the severed head is sent rolling on the floor, kicked by other men as it went by (425-28). Less inclined than Francis P. Magoun to treat this rather irreverential attitude of the people at Camelot to the man in green as an expression of their sporting habits,[44] I would suggest that their reason for kicking the head away from the Green Knight is to prevent the man from getting hold of his head putting it back on his neck. At least some people at Arthur's court evidently knew that in the realm of the supernatural the replacement of the severed head can restore life to the body, although this magical detail was apparently unknown to Gawain, who by letting the Green Knight grab his head misses his chance of rendering his opponent lifeless "for good."[45] As it was, Sir Gawain was as ignorant of the magical aspects of the Beheading Game as he was of the origin and identity of the Green Knight himself, of the holly cluster and its Christmas message, and of the full meaning of greenness. In a word, Sir Gawain—for all his initial maturity, sense of honor, and courage—was still lacking the necessary knowledge to cope with things divine and supernatural, as well as with his own vulnerable nature; all this he eventually came to learn through his tests and adventures. But because he initially lacked this knowledge, he *had to* undergo his quest, he had to embark upon the road of trials and temptations that culminated in the experience of his own "death-and-rebirth" at the Green Chapel, and it was the need for Gawain to learn this *traw þe* that triggered the entire story.

In all versions but one of the Beheading Game that exist in romance literature[46] the knight who engages in the game with a supernatural being acts similarly to Gawain in that he smites the challenger's head first, the creature then makes sure to grab the severed member as quickly as possible, and the knight is as a result obliged by the pledged word to turn up for the return blow on the appointed day. For example, in *Le Livre de Caradoc*, a part of the thirteenth-century anonymous First Continuation of Chrétien's

Perceval, regarded by Larry D. Benson as the direct source of the Beheading Game in *Sir Gawain*, Caradoc first strikes the stranger's head vigorously, but the man immediately grasps it with his two hands and puts it back on the body, thus remaining whole and sound:

> Cil fiert si viguereusement
> Que la teste voler li fist
> Devant le dois, mais cil la prist
> Par les treches a ses deus mains
> Ausi come s'il fust toz sainz,
> Si le rajoinst isnellepas.[47]

In the prose version of the same romance[48] the challenger, interestingly enough, is dressed entirely in green and wears a garland of flowers. When he proposes the Beheading Game to the "best of knights," Caradoc immediately accepts it on account of his being—as the text explains—"ung des plus folz" (one of the most foolish),[49] and before anyone can prevent him he snatches the sword and gives the stranger a mighty blow. The head does not fly far and the body instantaneously reaches out to put it back on its neck:

> . . . et s'en est la teste vollee plus loing qu'unge lance n'est longue, et le corps comme s'il fust vif de si pres la teste suivat que nul ne se donna de garde que la teste ne fust reunye bien joincte et bien aderee.[50]

Afterwards the stranger, nothing daunted, addresses the king and repeats the rules of the game with regard to the return blow.

In another French romance, the early thirteenth-century *La Mule sanz Frain*,[51] composed by Paien de Maisieres, it is Gauvain again who gets involved in the Beheading Game, proposed by an evil-looking, huge, and hirsute lord of the castle in which the knight was lodging. As the rules of the game stand, Gauvain will cut off the host's head now, the host his the following morning. Not much space is given to the description of the very beheading, which lacks the suspense and color of *Sir Gawain*:

> . . . Desor un tronc
> Li vilains lo col li estent.
> Maintenant la jusarme prent
> Gauvains si li coupe la teste
> A un cop, que plus n'i areste.

(588-92)

As in other stories, having satisfied himself to cut the creature's head
with one blow ("a un cop"), Gauvain makes no attempt to prevent
the opponent seizing his head, which the latter promptly does ("Li
vilains resalt maintenant / Sor ses piez, et sa teste prent" 593-94).
When the *vilains* appears the next morning, he is whole and sound,
and Gauvain again thinks himself a fool to have let his challenger go
practically unhurt:

> Or se puet bien tenir por fol
> Gauvains, quant il ot regardee
> La teste que il ot coupée;

(604-6)

At the return blow, however, the *vilains* spares the knight and
praises his loyalty and courage, very much as in *Sir Gawain.*

The Beheading Game reappears in Old French literature in the
anonymous early-thirteenth-century Grail romance *Perlesvaus*,[52]
where it is linked with Lancelot's visit to the Waste City awaiting its
redeemer. Lancelot, as usually happens with the knights who
unexpectedly arrive at the country of the Holy Grail, shows utter
ignorance of the magical nature of events happening there and
expresses particular surprise at the young knight in a red coat who is
carrying a huge axe and who demands an exchange of beheading
blows. After swearing to come back to the Waste City a year later to
receive the return blow, Lancelot cuts off the knight's head with such
a terrible blow that he sends it flying seven feet from the body. The
knight falls on the ground and Lancelot throws down the axe and
returns to his horse. When he looks back after a while he can see
neither the body nor the head:

> Atant entoise la hache et li trenche le chief de si tres grant air q'il li fait voler
> .vii. piez loinz du cors. Cil chai a la terre qant son chief fu coupez, et Lanceloz
> giete la hache jus et se pensse q'il li feroit la dedenz mauves demorer. Il vient a
> son cheval et prent ses armes et monte, et regarde deriere soi et ne voit pas le
> cors au chevalier ne le chief.[53]

The next year, as can be expected, Lancelot returns to the Waste
City, only to find the young knight as whole and sound as he was at
first.

It is also useful to recall in this connection a Middle High German
Arthurian romance known as *Diu Crône,* composed by Heinrich von
dem Türlin (ca.1220),[54] a story based ultimately on French sources,
which also contains a version of the Beheading Game. Despite much
variation in surface detail, in essence both the game itself and its

handling by the knight remain the same. In the course of his quest in search of a mysterious girdle (*zoum*), Gawein arrives at a castle belonging to Gansguoter von Michelolde, a shape-shifter and magician who has so far killed many knights by cutting off their heads in the Beheading Game. Gawein is likewise invited to the game and—following its rules—he chops off the magician's head with the provided halberd. The severed head drops on the ground and starts rolling like a ball, and the body rushes on after it in the hall, picks it up, and goes away without saying a word:

> Gâwein nam die barten an sich
> Und stalte in mitten in den sal
> Und sluoc in, daz sam ein bal
> Daz houbet in dem sale scheip
> Und er houbtlôs dâ beleip.
> Als er den slac von ime enpfienc,
> Nâch dem houbet er suochende gienc
> In dem sale, unz er ez vant:
> Er nam ez sâ in sin hant
> Und gie dannen unde sweic;

(13125-34)

The next day the magician (his head back on his neck) would have killed Gawein, as he did many other knights-errant, if not for the magician's daughter and Gawein's lady, Amurfina, who intercedes on Gawein's behalf with her father, and the knight is spared.

It is no wonder that in all the versions of the Beheading Game referred to so far, including the one from *Sir Gawain*, the knight who accepts the challenge fulfills his part of the deal with what is merely a crude, physical skill of using arms, and as a result lets his supernatural opponent live, allowing him to exact the second part of the agreement in due course. But if the significance of the ritual beheading is the experience of sacrificial death and possible rebirth, it is precisely this kind of experience that is unknown to the errant knight, who must therefore submit to the ordeal of near-death himself by allowing the second part of the agreement to be fulfilled. After all, the direct experience of one's death is of such nature that it cannot be known until it is had firsthand. What ultimately saves the knight from almost sure annihilation is the fact that his adversary turns out in the end to be a benign being, able to recognize and reward the knight's unfailing courage and fidelity to his word.

It appears therefore that in terms of self-knowledge and the apprehension of things divine and supernatural nothing but a real, and apparently inescapable situation of ultimate destruction can give a taste of what death's magic is like, on a psychological as well as metaphysical level. It is consequently those whose knightly quests have been successfully completed and who have learned "magic tricks" as a result of their adventures who can cope adequately and on a par with the supernatural, able to resolve the liminal situations—such as the one created by the Beheading Game—in an alternative way. The uniquely different solution to the Beheading Game, as far as literary sources are concerned, is given in another French thirteenth-century Arthurian romance called *Hunbaut*,[55] in which Gauvain is accompanied in his adventures by a senior knight, the titular Hunbaut. Hunbaut is an experienced knight of the Round Table, well acquainted with magic and dangers of the chivalric adventure because he has just successfully returned from his own quest. In the romance he accompanies Gauvain on a mission on behalf of King Arthur to demand allegiance from the King of the Isles. Having arrived at the castle, the two knights find the traditional *vilain* sitting at the front gate, a creature of monstrous appearance ("Grans ert et noirs, lais et hideus," 1473), who proposes a *ju parti* to Gauvain and Hunbaut: he will offer his head to be cut off with an axe and immediately afterwards ("Le vostre li tendés aprés," 1493) he will himself deal a similar blow. Gauvain accepts the challenge and gives the *vilain* such a mighty blow on the neck that the head is sent flying ten steps away:

> Bien se avisse dou trencant
> Et de grant (cop) ferir s'esforce
> Gauvains qui tot (i) met sa force.
> Bien vos di qui'il ne se faint pas,
> Ains fait voler plus de dis pas
> La teste au pautonir en loins.

(1524-29)

The body then opens its two hands and tries to go after the head, but Gauvain, suspecting some magical trick ("encantement"), grabs the *vilain* by his clothes, thwarts him until the magic expires, and the man falls dead on the spot, after which—as we read—there will never be any *ju part*:

> Et cil ouvri ans II ses puins,
> Si cuide aler tantost apres.
> Mesire Gauvains se tint pres,
> Qui d'encantement ert apris.
> Le vilai(n) a par les dras pris,
> Et por ço a son esme faut

Et li encantemens defaut;
Car il cai mors en la place
Et li encantemens s'esface,
C'onques puis n'i ot ju part.

(1530-39)

As in *Perlesvaus* and other stories, including *Sir Gawain*, the challenge to a Beheading Game is part of the magic machinery of the place, and unless the knight is familiar with magic tricks or undergoes his test with the expert guidance of an experienced senior tutor, as in *Hunbaut,* he is bound to be at the mercy of the magic powers governing the realm. What saves the knight in this potentially disastrous situation is again the fact that these powers ultimately turn out to be lenient and benevolent, and the whole game is only a test, both of loyalty, courage, *and* of the knowledge of the magic lore. The next time around Gawain would know that to annihilate a supernatural foe—that is, to prevent its resuscitation—the severed receptacle of immortal life must either be kept apart from the body or it must be destroyed.[56] George L. Kittredge adduces numerous folklore examples of heroes preventing the rebirth of their supernatural foes by holding the sword on the neck, by standing between the trunk and the head, or simply by demolishing the head or throwing it far away.[57] The logic of such acts is clear when it is recalled what ideas and beliefs could be associated with the human head (see table 8), and if this seat and center of life was destroyed, the body died too.[58]

The audience of *Sir Gawain* would in all probability have guessed what was at stake in the New Year Beheading Game. Medieval tradition abounded in stories, of both folk and religious provenance, about individuals losing their heads beneath the executioner's sword or axe and having it restored later by magical means or divine will as a sign of the resurrection of the body. There exists, for example, in Christian hagiography a special category of saints called *cephalophore*, "head-carriers," martyrs fabled to have carried their severed heads to the burial place and described as totally unconcerned about having their heads chopped off. By far the most famous medieval head-carrier is Saint Denis, patron saint of France, who according to legend walked with his severed head for two miles, "until the body came to where it desired to lie with the head and all, and the holy angels continually sung, as books tell us."[59] Saint Denis seems to have been one of those "beheaded for the witness of Jesus, and for the word of God" (Rev. 20:4), who later "lived and reigned with Christ a thousand years." *An Old English Martyrology* in a similar way interprets the decapitation of Saint John the Baptist as a means of obtaining divine grace and new life in Heaven,[60] and Christ's martyrdom, although of a different kind, took place on the Hill of the Skull, *calvaria* (Luke 23:33).

The idea of rebirth as the restoration of the head to the body after it was cut off is very common. The life-restoring agent is most often a holy person, a priest or a hermit,[61] sometimes a woman equipped with magical powers,[62] and even rarely, the victim him- or herself. A very interesting case in point, and one possibly linked with *Sir Gawain*, is a legend of the English Saint Winifred, whose cult was associated with "Holy Hede" passed by Gawain in his north-Welsh itinerary (698-701). According to John Burrow,[63] the author of the romance wanted to make a passing reference to the saint, because the story of the cutting off and the miraculous restoration of Saint Winifred's "holy head" has much in common with the resurrectional character of the beheading in *Sir Gawain*. John Mirk in the early fifteenth-century version of Saint Winifred's legend describes the victim's resuscitation in the following way:

> Wherefor he [the hermit] bade vche mon and womon to pray to God, to rase hur aȝayn to lyue; and so he dudde. And gwhen sche set vp wyth hyr hondys, sche wyput her face of the dwst þat was þeron, and speke to hom hole and sownde as sche was before.[64]

As a result of her ordeal Winifred carried a mark on her neck, following the line of the beheading cut, and this token of the miracle remained with her as long as she lived. Sir Gawain's "nirt in þe nek" (2498) stayed on him, too, after the adventure, and this fact—in conjunction with the legend of Saint Winifred, well known in Cheshire and Lancashire in the fourteenth century[65]—again places the beheading in *Sir Gawain* in the context of ideas suggesting sacrificial death, spiritual rebirth, and new life.[66]

þe grene chapelle

It is easy to see that the events described in Fitts III and IV of *Sir Gawain* form a structural analogy with those from Fitt I and a part of Fitt II in that both parts of the poem describe a similar narrative circle: Gawain has to leave behind the familiarity and shelter of the court (Camelot and Hautdesert, respectively), he next becomes exposed to discomforts and dangers of the elemental environment, finally to arrive at the gruesome place of his ultimate adventure. As I have observed in chapter 2, the larger cycle of the entire story, covering the full calendar year, reflects allegorically the span of human life, with New Year's Day seen as a transitional, liminal point that marks the metaphorical border between life and death, the latter again understood figuratively as a passage into another, meta-physically distinct mode of existence. As also emerged from the analysis of the poem's structure, the main cycle of the story contains in itself smaller cycles that repeat in general outline the larger pattern, following a spiral movement of calendar time along significant dates. In this temporal perspective Gawain's sojourn at Hautdesert and the following adventure at the Green Chapel can be regarded as the entire story in miniature, and indeed the self-contained nature of this part of the poem is emphasized by its falling precisely into the equally self-comprised Christmas season, the octave from the Nativity to the Circumcision (25 December-1 January). In terms of the liturgical, ecclesiological calendar then, Gawain's crucial tests from Fitt III and the final beheading scene in Fitt IV coincide with the holiest time of the year, the eight days that again reflect the human lifespan, stretching as they do from Christ's birth through his turbulent infancy to the first shedding of his blood in prefiguration of the Passion.[67]

Both the ecclesiological and the seasonal contexts of Fitt IV put the second part of the Beheading Game in a symbolically defined per-spective in that the doctrinal contents of the Feast of the Circumcision and the traditional beliefs associated with the New Year determine to a large extent the liminal and transitional nature of the described events. A closer reading of this part of the poem reveals that the symbolic complex of death and rebirth determines the character of Gawain's individual predicament and also governs the poetic language, imagery, and the general atmosphere.

For instance, the resurrectional theme seen as part of the divine order of things is introduced in anticipation of events right in the opening lines of Fitt IV, in the image of the day that comes after the night on the New Year's morning:

> Now ne3ez þe Nw 3ere, and þe ny3t passez,
> þe day dryuez *(follows)* to þe derk, as Dry3tyn biddez;

(1998-99)

The prevailing imagery, though, is still that of the hardships of winter and the hostility of the elements,[68] contrasted with the tem-porary and illusory security and comfort of the human environment that Gawain has to leave behind. The atmosphere of impending sorrow intensifies as we read of Gawain's preparation and elaborate farewell to the household at Hautdesert, very much as in a similar scene at Camelot on All Hallows'. Back at Arthur's court the cause of grief was the apparent fatality of the adventure undertaken by Gawain as perceived by the knights of the Round Table,[69] and now at Hautdesert it is Gawain himself who parts from this world by pronouncing his final words of benediction to those who remain behind:

'Here is a meyny *(company)* in þis mote *(castle)* þat on menske *(honor)*
                                                     þenkkez,
þe mon hem maynteines, ioy mot þay haue;
þe leue lady on lyue luf hir bityde;
3if þay for charyte cherysen *(entertain)* a gest,
And halden honour in her honde, þe haþel *[God]* hem 3elde
þat haldez þe heuen vpon hy3e, and also yow alle!

                                                     (2052-57)

The magnificent Castle of Hautdesert, a symbol of medieval life and civilization, is commended to Christ ("þis kastel to Kryst I kenne," 2067), and Gawain plunges again into the hostile and dangerous realm of nature to face his last destiny. As before, during his solitary *peregrinatio* through the wilderness of North Wales, so now Sir Gawain is once more exposed to the unpredictability and unfriendliness of the wintry landscape and the elements: the boughs are again "bare" and cold clings to the ground ("clyffez þer clengez þe colde") as Sir Gawain and his dubious guide[70] travel in the weird and lifeless winter atmosphere before sunrise:

þe heuen watz vphalt, bot vgly þer-vnder;
Mist muged *(drizzled)* on þe mor, malt *(melted)* on þe mountez,
Vch hille hade a hatte, a myst-hakel huge.
Brokez byled *(boiled)* and breke *(foamed)* bi bonkkez aboute,
Schyre schaterande on schorez, þer þay doun schowued *(rushed)*.

                                                     (2079-83)

With the desolate and bleak landscape cast as the backdrop, the guide's frightening account of the Green Knight's terror lends the last phase of Gawain's adventure a dimension of increasing gruesomeness and horror, possibly as a projection of the knight's own fear of death and the last—and again so very human—panicky feeling of trying to avoid his fate. According to the guide, the place where Gawain is heading for is "perelous" (2097), inhabited by a giant man, "stiffe and sturne," who "strike louies" (2099) and allows no one to pass without smiting him to death (2105), for "he is a mon methles *(ruthless)*, and mercy non vses" (2106). The Green Knight emerges in this description as death itself, the Great Leveler, mercilessly exercising its power of destruction to all people:

> For be hit chorle oþer chaplayn þat bi þe chapel rydes,
> Monk oþer masseprest, oþer any mon elles,
> Hym þynk as queme *(pleasant)* hym to quelle *(kill)* as quyk go hymseluen.

$$(2107-9)$$

This is a one-sided, horrific picture of death, well-grounded in medieval tradition,[71] an image of irrevocable, pitiless destruction dictated by irrational fear, the biological instinct of self-preservation, generally by the bodily powers. This unbalanced apprehension is soon, however, redressed by Gawain's exercise of his rational faculty when he sarcastically spurns the guide's suggestion of cowardly quitting the adventure and reasserts both the chivalric code of honor ("I were a kny3t kowarde, I my3t not be excused," 2131) and the philosophical, stoic attitude towards fate ("Worþe hit wele oþer wo, as þe wyrde lykez hit hafe," 2134-35).

Gawain's firmness of purpose and determination to play his game to the end ("Bot I wyl to þe chapel," 2132) are again projected against the landscape, becoming more and more otherwordly and infernal as the knight approaches the Green Chapel following the sinister downward and lefthand-side movement[72] towards "þe boþem of þe brem *(wild)* valay" (2145). The chapel itself finally turns out to be a "lawe" (2171) and "a bal3 ber3"—that is, a smooth round knoll or mound ("aboute hit he walkez," 2178) with a hole at either side (2180), overgrown with grass (2181) and hollow within, "nobot *(nothing but)* an olde caue, or a creuisse of an olde cragge" (2182-83). Contrary to Gawain's expectations, the place appears to be nothing like a "chapel" in the literal sense ("Wheþer þis be þe grene chapelle?" 2186), although it does resemble a chapel in the functional and symbolic sense.

The Green Chapel first appears in the description as a gravelike structure, recalling both the funeral barrows of the Neolithic and early Bronze ages, frequently found in English countryside,[73] and the equally popular traditional Celtic *síde*-mounds of native folklore and mythology.[74] In the more immediate Christian context the entrance to the interiors of the earth is readily associated with hell and the mansion of the devil, and this is precisely the connotation that springs to Gawain's mind when he examines the place.[75] The Green

Chapel appears, then, to be as ambivalent in its significance as is both the green color itself and its chief bearer, who is also the inhabitant of the chapel. The latter now reemerges with a terrible roaring noise from the mound (2199-204, 2219-20), bringing with him his greenness ("þe gome in þe grene gered [clothed] as fyrst, / Boþe þe lyre [face] and þe leggez, lokkez and berde," 2227-28) as a visible sign of the renewal of life at the threshold of the New Year and of the resurrection of the those who submit voluntarily to the experience of death at the *green* chapel.[76] Although the guide did mention the perilous and deadly aspect of the place (2103-5), he failed to add that "þe chapel grene" is also a place of rebirth, both in accordance with the archetypal, universal beliefs in the renovative and life-giving powers of the Mother Earth[77] and as part of Christian teachings about the resurrection of the dead. Since time immemorial and throughout the Christian era, graves have enjoyed special veneration and cult status, chiefly on account of the belief in the transitional nature of death and in the supposed blessed effects emanating from the remains buried in them. The grave remains a visible expression of the great riddle of death, seen not as a complete and irreversible annihilation, but as a transition and a transformation into a new life. This is why every consecrated altar in medieval churches had to contain relics why and the bones of the dead were often interred beneath the church's floor. The church is thus both a grave and a place of resurrection, and so is the "grene chapelle" in *Sir Gawain*, whose meaning and function are neatly contained in the extended symbolic connotations of its very name.

Gawain's "Circumcision"

The idea of rebirth was in the Christian Middle Ages associated inextricably with the Pauline notion of the *homo novus*,[78] which in turn had a number of doctrinal and sacramental expressions, among other things related to the Circumcision as a prefiguration of both the Baptism and the Passion. In view of the *Gawain*-poet's careful attention to Christian feastdays and their significance for the story, it is of course no accident that the most decisive moments of spiritual transition in the poem (Fitts I and IV) coincide with the New Year and the Feast of the Circumcision, whose resurrectional aspect has already been signaled in chapter 2. The feast, as is known, commemorates the first shedding of blood by Christ and foreshadows the Crucifixion and its role in the remission of people's sins. As John Mirk put it in his homily: "he was circumsiset, and sched hys blode þis day for our sake."[79] The purifying aspect of the feast is also stressed by its analogy with the sacrament of the Baptism: both were conceived as initiations into the spiritual life, one for the Old Law, the other for the New.[80] The ritual cutting off of the foreskin of God's son was performed on the eighth day after the Nativity, because, as Jacobus de Voragine explained in his *Legenda Aurea,* "the viii day is taken for the resurrexion."[81] The reason for this— says de Voragine further—is that there are eight ages of history, beginning with Adam, going through the Patriarchs, and ending with Christ's Resurrection in heaven. A sense of completeness exists therefore in the first eight days of Christ's life, borne out by the internal doctrinal consistency of the Christmas season and reflected in *Sir Gawain* by the self-contained nature of the narrative in Fitt III and its culmination in Fitt IV.

It is very tempting to directly relate Gawain's final ordeal at the Green Chapel, especially the famous nick on his neck left by the Green Knight's axe, to the christological context,[82] but such associations have to be made with necessary modifications and reservations. An implicit reference to the Feast of the Circumcision behind Sir Gawain's "beheading" of course can only be figurative or spiritual in the New Testament sense; that is, it is understood as a death of the flesh and the cutting away of the sinful nature.[83] Gawain's wound should not—in my view—be treated specifically as a sacrifice of his sexuality for the sake of spirituality, which is what the cutting "a litil of the skynne at thende of the membre"[84] symbolizes in the first place. The connotation with sexuality explains why, for example, John Audelay associates circumcision with the sin of lechery,[85] although of course this is not in question for Sir Gawain, whose *clannes* remains intact throughout, and the kind of sin that the knight eventually has to atone for is more linked with his head than with any other member of his body.[86] In actual practice circumcision relies on the surgical removal of the foreskin from the penis, and as such is confirmed as a widespread ritual not only in Judaism and Islam, but in many traditional societies all over the globe, where it usually forms a part of often very painful and traumatic rites of puberty initiation.[87] In all cases the operation is symbolic of the subordination of the sexual drive to the control of will[88] and marks the beginning of a youth's adult life, characterized by proper and socially acceptable sexual behavior and moral conduct. In traditional societies circumcision marks, as it also does in Judaism and Christianity, a ritual "death" of an individual for his adolescent life and his "rebirth" as a responsible adult.[89]

Granted all the superficial resemblances of Gawain's mock execution at the Green Chapel to traditional initiation rites,[90] I must again
state that both the character of the rite (beheading) and the inflicted
wound (in the neck) have little, if anything, to do with Gawain's
sexuality, but rather with the wrong exercise of his rational faculty
located in the head.   Circumcision is then related to Gawain's
spiritual change only figuratively, in the sense used in Deuternomy
(10:16): "Circumcise therefore the foreskin of your heart, and be no
more stiffnecked."[91] Gawain's sin appears to belong to the realm of
pride—that is, excessive self-will—with its seat in the head, and not
to carnal sins proper, although the fault is related to the body:
Gawain simply wants to preserve it, if possible, because he "lufed
his lyf." And since the fault lies in the head, it is precisely the organ
that is threatened,[92] because the trespass is potentially a serious one:
the mind has repeated the Original Sin[93] by choosing wrongly, by
exercising the faculty of free will in short-sighted self-interest and
against Divine Providence.[94] It was only because the divine powers,
represented in the poem by the Green Knight alias Sir Bertilac, are
ultimately benevolent towards man, that Gawain's treachery can at all
be forgiven. If not for the judge's mercy, the alleged protective
magic of the green girdle, the symbol of man's illusory self-
sufficiency, would avail Gawain nothing. The knight's predicament
illustrates therefore a paradoxical situation in which man uses his
rational faculty to jeopardize eternal life by clinging inordinately and
"irrationally" to temporary life.

The threatened cutting off of Gawain's head is thus a punishment
both for his wrong use of it and also—in the collective sense—for
the symbolic "loss of the head" exhibited by Camelot at the beginning of the story, though not necessarily by Gawain himself. The
mindless mirth and lack of recognition of the spiritual dimension of
the Christmas season by Arthur's court signified the kind of psychic
calamity at the reason's loss of dominion in the body politic,
resulting in a spiritual and moral disorder that was signaled by
Arthur's "brayn wylde" (89) and by his ineptness at upholding the
integrity of the realm in the face of disturbance from without. As
John Trevisa put it in his translation of Bartholomaeus Anglicus's *De
Proprietatibus Rerum*:

> For þe heed is more and roote of al þe body and first and principal foundement
> of al þe bodiliche vertues; ʒif þe heed is wel disposed and i-ordeyned, al þat ben
> þervndir ben in þe bettir disposicioun and state.   And aʒenward, ʒif þe heed is
> corrupt and distempered with *sinthoma* of corrupcioun and hedeache, nedis ne
> neþer membres of þe body ben desesed.[95]

And since Gawain as Arthur's next-of-kin and potential successor as the head of state is to redeem Camelot and its values, he has to be punished in the organ in which the present head of the chivalric society is found most wanting.[96] In addition to his own personal fault then, Gawain is taking on himself, Christlike, the sins that afflict the nobility, the guardians and "heads" of the social order.[97]

Gawain's individual sin is subsequently forgiven by the now-lenient and merciful Green Knight, chiefly on account of the excusable love of life naturally felt by Gawain as a member of the human species. Because of the veniality of the sin, the punishment is not a "capital" one (from Latin *caput*, "head"), but it is clear by implication what kind of trespass on Gawain's part would have resulted in his full execution: had it been for "wylyde *(skillful)* werke" of the girdle or for the "wowyng *(wooing)"* (2367), Gawain would no doubt have perished under the Green Knight's axe. In other words, if Gawain had succumbed either to the material value of the girdle or to the sexual lurings of the lady, he would have died. Or to put it yet otherwise: if Gawain had "lost his head," figuratively speaking, either for the riches or for the woman, he would have lost it, literally speaking, as a result.[98] As it is, he gets away with a slight wound on his neck, through which "þe schene blod ouer his schulderes schot to þe erþe" (2314), in partial sacrifice for his corporeality and the sinfulness it entails.[99] "Now am I fawty and falce" (2382), confesses Gawain in his self-accusatory diatribe before the Green Knight, and this is as much as his newly acquired self-knowledge amounts to. Nor is it little, for the realization of one's weaknesses and imperfections and the assimilation of this "green" part of the personality with the conscious mind is no mean achievement in psychological terms. It is also as much as is required of man in the eyes of theology, since the knowledge of one's sins is a prerequisite for the final absolution, and ultimately salvation.[100] The essence of this lesson is made clear later, after Gawain's return to Camelot, when he publicly confesses his shortcomings and brings home to the fellow knights the necessity to acknowledge the sad truth about the human condition:

> For mon may hyden his harme, bot vnhap *(unfasten)* ne may hit,
> For þer hit onez is tachched *(attached)* twynne *(sever)* wil hit neuer.
>
> (2511-12)[101]

Inasmuch as Gawain's character and personality change as a result of his adventure, it can be said figuratively that he does lose his "old head" and acquires a "new" one, that which accommodates not only the notion of being the "gode Gawan" (109), but also the truth of being "fawty and falce" and full of "trecherye and vntrawþe" (2383). A fuller personality is emerging in Gawain's head, just as the pure *viriditas* had to be joined with the unclean *verdigris* to achieve the alchemical gold. It is again a great psychological as well as metaphysical paradox of man that the subjective sense of self-deprecation and self-humiliation brings about a compensating amount of objective praise and appreciation, whereby the faulty Gawain is lauded by the Green Knight as "on þe *(one of the)* fautlest freke *(man)* þat euer on fote ȝede *(went),* "and "as perle bi quite pese. *(white peas)* is of prys more, so is Gawayn, in god fayth, bi oþer gay knyȝtez" (2363-65). Absolved, "polysed of þat plyȝt," and morally clean like a newborn baby (2391-94), Gawain is presented by his judge with the girdle: "And I gif þe, sir, þe gurdel þat is golde-hemmed, For hit is grene as my goune" (2395-96), the reason being that the girdle's combined colors of gold and green now represent the completeness of human perfection newly attained by Sir Gawain. The perfection is human in the sense that it is limited when compared with absolute, divine perfection, because it relies basically on being constantly aware of "þe faut and þe fayntyse of þe flesche crabbed" and "how tender *(liable)* hit is to entyse *(catch)* teches *(stains)* of fylþe" (2435-36).

The enlargement of Gawain's self-apprehension is also borne out by the merger of the two, hitherto disparate and irreconcilable natures of the Green Knight alias Sir Bertilac, which is taking place before Gawain's eyes. The knight's courage and determination have been rewarded, and what at first looked frightening and terrifying now loses its magic force and becomes not only psychologically acceptable but also spiritually highly beneficial. The final disclosure of the Green Knight's real name and origin, his true nature, comes again *after* the ordeal of the beheading and the subsequent agony of moral cleansing, and the revelation seals the gift of knowledge granted Gawain on this occasion. The barbaric and ruthless Green Knight and the civilized and kind Sir Bertilac, hitherto perceived as two distinct entities, now fuse into one to form a complete image of a spiritually superior personality, one that rises above the dichotomy of good and evil, of culture and nature, and operates on the level where metaphysical opposites are reconciled. Sir Gawain too is led to accept a more holistic view of himself and life in general when he is told that his lineage not only contains the "bounte" of Arthur's blood, but also the evil strain of "Morgne la Faye," Arthur's half-sister and Gawain's aunt (2464).[102] It is she who emerges in Sir Bertilac's account as the main *spiritus movens* of the entire plot, responsible for sending the Green Knight to Camelot in the first place (2456-62) and in consequence for starting Gawain's initiatory quest. Like the main shape-shifter of the story, Morgan too is dual when she appears as "þe auncian lady" next to Bertilac's young wife at Hautdesert (947-58), and the double role and nature of the feminine element that she represents also has to be accommodated by Sir Gawain into the overall, holistic scheme. Therefore both with regard to himself and to the Green Knight, King Arthur, and the lady, Gawain's knowledge is enlarged with the respective negative counterparts, which complete the general picture, making it fuller and truer.

The Dubbing of the Knight

But what are the social repercussions of Sir Gawain's individual quest and his changed psychological status? Is his newly acquired self-knowledge of any avail to the chivalric community to which Gawain originally belongs, and is the Round Table going to profit from the spiritual benefits earned by Gawain in the course of his adventure? Upon his return to Camelot the knight recounts fully his "fare" without any prevarications, quite to the contrary: he shows everyone "þe nirt in þe neck" and makes the true story of his adventure a part of public penance to atone for his "vnleute" (*disloyalty*), when he

> . . . groned for gref and grame;
> þe blod in his face con melle *(stream)*,
> When he hit schulde schewe, for schame.

$$(2502-4)$$

But strangely enough, Gawain's continued and almost over-indulgent self-accusations of "blame," "laþe" (*injury*), "losse," "couardise," "couetyse," and "vntrawþe" (2506-12) meet only with an outburst of laughter on the part of the court ("alle þe court als laȝen loude þerat," 2513-14), which subsequently adopts green laces similar to Gawain's as tokens of "þe renoun of þe Rounde Table" (2519). It is hard to understand this laughter otherwise than as a sign both of embarrassment and spiritual immaturity still afflicting the chivalric society at Camelot, which immediately after Gawain's revelation reverts to its old lighthearted ways, and by turning the whole matter into a joke refuses to share in the spiritual profits of Gawain's experience. Nor is the prospective moral and spiritual

lesson fully communicable to others, because it is not: the exposure
to one's inferior self in the context of near-death remains essentially
an individual and intimate experience. However, the society can at
least profit by acknowledging the existence of such an experience.
As it is, King Arthur and the *crème de la crème* of chivalry, this
privileged aristocratic class whose role is to maintain balance between the secular and the spiritual, between culture and nature,
choose to remain in their adolescent "first age" and shut their eyes to
the more mature, wider understanding of things shared now by Sir
Gawain. Gawain's humility, modesty, and realistic view of human
nature are precisely what King Arthur as the head of chivalry at
Camelot lacked at the beginning of the story, and now his light-
hearted reaction to his nephew's adventure shows that he is still
lacking these qualities at the end. Therefore both in the moral and
metaphysical sense it is Gawain who has now become the true head
of the Round Table as the one who can combine the worldy, temporal dimension of chivalry with a spiritual element.

The social and institutional implications of Gawain's adventure are
also manifest in the ritualized nature of the two parts of the
Beheading Game, which I want to link historically with admission
rites to chivalric orders, practiced widely in the Middle Ages. In a
very interesting way nearly all the elements involved in the elaborate
beheading ritual, both at Camelot and at the Green Chapel, appear to
have their counterparts in the known medieval ceremonies of the
conferring of knighthood, and in this respect the poem offers a rare
example of a very detailed literary expression of the historical rituals
of chivalry.

The central moment in a knight's life was the dubbing ceremony,
the crowning of the chivalric apprenticeship that gave the novice the
full status of a knight, with all the accompanying privileges and
responsibilities. The roots of the ceremony lay in tribal initiation
rituals that marked the coming of age of adolescents and opened the
period of full and mature membership in the society.[103] The general
resemblance of Gawain's quest to traditional rites of passage has
been pointed out on a number of occasions in this work, but now let
us observe that the ceremonious and institutional aspect of Gawain's
adventure began already at Camelot, especially in the official blessing
received by Gawain from King Arthur shortly before dealing the
beheading blow. The knight is commanded by the king to rise, then
falls to his knees before the the monarch and "cachez þat weppen"
(368) while the king gives him "Goddez blessyng" (370). After the
beheading stroke is delivered, the axe remains with Sir Gawain, both
as a trophy and a gift, as promised by the Green Knight ("I schal gif

hym of my gyft þys giserne *[battle-axe]* ryche," 288), and is
subsequently hung up on the wall in the hall so that "alle men for
meruayl myȝt on hit loke" (479). It is useful to recall here that
Ramon Lull in his *Libre del Orde de Cauayleria* (ca. 1311) draws a
simile between the axe and an office of a knight by saying that "for in
lyke wyse as the axe is made for to hewe and destroye the euylle
trees, in lyke wyse is thoffyce of a knyght establysshyd for to
punysshe the trespacers and delynquants."[104] The idea seems to be
based on the image of the axe as an instrument of punishment and
humiliation of the wicked in Matthew 3:10. The axe fixed on the
wall-tapestry at Camelot is therefore not so much a token of a Christmas "meruayl," as the knights there want to see it, but a traditional
symbol and a reminder of the knight's role as God's armed hand to
defend the good and punish the wicked.

But it is Gawain's second encounter with the Green Knight at the
Green Chapel that constitutes the actual crowning of the knighting
ritual begun at Camelot. According to late medieval manuals of
chivalry,[105] knighthood could be conferred on basically three occasions: when a king held a court, when the aspirant was on a
pilgrimage to the Holy Sepulchre, or in the context of a battle. The
first occasion is provided in *Sir Gawain* by King Arthur's
celebrations at Christmastime,[106] and the two other occasions put
together correspond to Sir Gawain's peregrination to the tomblike
Green Chapel to fulfill the second part of his duel with the Green
Knight. The quasi-religious character of the chapel is also relevant in
the context of the knighting ceremony, because the making of a
knight was in the Middle Ages inextricably linked with liturgical
rituals performed by a priest and involved such events as the
baptismal bath of the candidate, the nightly vigil, the hearing of
mass, prayers, the blessing of the arms, and so on.[107] The idea goes
back to the Crusades, when the knightly initiation rite came to be
regarded as the "eighth sacrament."[108] Ramon Lull also writes that a
squire must confess his sins before being knighted: "hym behoueth
that he confesse hym of his deffaultes that he hath done ageynst god
and ouȝt to receyue chyualry in entencion that in the same he serue
our lord god whiche is gloryous."[109] Sir Gawain too was
"confessed so clene" and "beknowen of [his] mysses" (2391) by the
Green Knight after the agony of his feigned beheading. Immediately
afterwards the senior knight presents Gawain with the girdle ("a pure
token / Of þe chaunce of þe grene chapel at *(to)* cheualrous knyȝtez,"
2398-99), which in view of the ongoing ceremony can also be
interpreted as a dubbing gift, or a girdle-belt, customarily received by
a newly made knight from the senior knight conferring the honor.[110]

Finally, upon parting at the Green Chapel both knights "acolen (*embrace*) and kyssen" (2472) to seal their comradeship, a gesture easily identified with the *osculum pacis*, the kiss of reconciliation and brotherhood, claimed by Elias Ashmole to have been invented by Charles the Great.[111]

But it is Gawain's mock decapitation that forms the core of the chivalric initiation ritual, through its correspondence to the famous accolade (*collée* or *paumée*) or dubbing—that is, a gentle blow with the hand or sword, administered either by a priest or a senior knight on the candidate's head or neck—a symbolic gesture that marked the culmination of the knighting ceremony.[112] The accolade was commonly used in France and England beginning in the mid-fourteenth century, and the earliest historical mention of this procedure comes from the Pontifical of Guillaume Durand, Bishop of Mende, written about 1295, which states that a knight should receive a light blow from the bishop as a sign of awakening from sleep into the new life of knighthood.[113] According to today's historical authorities, however, the appearance of the *collée* is "shrouded in mystery,"[114] and as a ritual act it is "of almost hopelessly obscure origin."[115] Ramon Lull in his treatise explained it as a token of remembrance of the knightly office: "The knyght ought to kysse the squyer and to gyue to hym a palme by cause that he be remembryng of that whiche he receyueth."[116] Elias Ashmole in turn refers the accolade, like many other elements of the chivalric ritual, to the times of Charles the Great and explains its origin as an echo of the liberation rite of the Roman slaves:

> ... the *colaphum*, or giving a blow on the ear was used [by Charles the Great], in sign of sustaining future hardships and indurances; which is thought to have derived from the manner of manumission of Slave among the Romans, where first the Praetor gently struck him on the head with the *vindicta*, a rod so called, after which the Lictor did the like, and moreover struck him on the face and back with his hand, in token of full liberty and freedom. This custom was retained long after both in Germany and France.[117]

Ashmole quotes the supposed origin of the *colaphus* after the authority of an early-seventeenth-century French historian Andre Favine, whose *Le Theater d'honneur et de Chevalerie* (Paris 1620) mentions also a similar habit of giving a knight a stroke three times (*sic*) with a naked sword, flatwise, on the neck or shoulder:

> Others were made knights, by giving them three blows with the Sword flatlong, betweene the necke and shoulders: which is yet observed, especially on the dayes of Battaile, before they proceed to handy strokes.[118]

Favyn writes that a knighting ceremony involving "three blows" took place in Paris in 1416 during the reign of Charles VI, when the Emperor Sigismund dubbed one of the lords by giving him three strokes on his back with the sword,[119] and Ashmole adds (without quoting his source this time), that on such occasions the strokes may be accompanied by "pronouncing the words of Creation."[120] Even despite the lack of historical precision in the facts quoted by Favyn and Ashmole, these early modern compendia of chivalry do confirm the centrality and widespread character of the *adoubment* in the knighting ceremony of the late Middle Ages. In the mid-fourteenth century, for example, Geoffroi de Charny, "one of the great experts of the day on chivalric matters,"[121] likewise mentions in his *Livre de chevalerie* that "la colée" administered with a sword comes as a culmination of the long initiation into a chivalric order:

> Dont cil chevalier qui doit bailler l'ordre, prend une espée, pour ce que l'espee tranche de deux pars, ains doivent garder et maintenir raison et justice de toutes pars . . . et puis leur doivent donner la colée.[122]

The dubbing understood as a ceremonious blow on the novice's neck or shoulder with the hand or sword became in time so inextricably associated with the knighting ritual that in the early seventeenth century Miguel de Cervantes Saavedra, in his unforgetable parody of chivalry, mentions it in his description of the knighting of Don Quixote:

> Next, reading out of his manual, as if he were reciting some devout prayer, in the middle of his reading [the castellan] raised his hand and dealt the knight a sound blow on the neck, followed by a handsome stroke on the back with the Don's own sword, all the while muttering in his teeth as if in prayer. When this was over he bade one of the ladies gird on Don Quixote's sword, which she did with great agility and some discretion, no small amount of which was necessary to avoid bursting with laughter at each stage of the ceremony.[123]

Originally, however, the solemnity of the rite had undoubtedly a lot to do with its religious character. On the other hand, the potentially violent nature of the *collée* should be linked with the earlier-discussed symbolic decapitation and the death-rebirth experience denoted by it. The word *dubbing* (French *adoubement*) appears to be of Germanic provenance, and in Middle English it means primarily "to confer knighthood," but also "to beat somebody."[124] Walter W. Skeat offers also the following etymological variants of the word: Norwegian *dibba*, "to nod the head;" Swedish dialectal *dibb*, "to touch lightly;" East Friesic *dubbe*, "a blow," and *dubben*, "to strike." The *accolade* in turn (Latin *collum*, "the neck"), likewise means a "light tap with a sword" during a knighting ceremony.[125] The extended meanings of *dubbing* and *accolade* clearly show that the conferment of knighthood is equivalent to a stroke on the neck, with the knight's "nodding" as if to offer his head for execution, because the ceremony marks a drastic change in the individual's existential, social, and religious status—a transformation that can best be expressed through symbols and gestures suggesting spiritual death and resurrection.

The genetic connection between the ritual beheading and the dubbing ceremony is unequivocally borne out in *Le Livre de Caradoc*, whose version of the Beheading Game appears closest to the one in *Sir Gawain*. In the French romance the second beheading scene follows immediately Caradoc's accolade of knighthood at Arthur's court and takes place—as the knighting ceremony requires—during the feast of Pentecost when Arthur used to hold his court. The beheading itself is as dragged and prolonged as in *Sir Gawain* to increase tension, and the return blow is twice prevented, first by Arthur's proposal to ransom Caradoc, and for the second time by the queen, pleading with the challenger to have pity on the knight. When the blow finally comes, it is delivered flatwise ("Et cil a l'epée haulcée qui du plat fiert tant seullement"),[126] Caradoc is then told to rise, and the challenger reveals that he is Caradoc's father, who was only testing his son. "For Caradoc the beheading is not only an initiation into chivalric life but a means of discovering himself," wrote Larry D. Benson of this occasion,[127] and the same can be said of Sir Gawain, for whom the "tappe" (2357) received at the third blow is both the chivalric accolade marking his entry into a new, higher form of knighthood, and a seal of the profound and painful spiritual experience of self-discovery that has to occur if the dubbing is to be something more than just an empty ritual gesture.

When viewed against the practice and ritual of historical chivalry, stories of romantic adventure such as *Le Livre de Caradoc* or *Sir Gawain* can offer interesting insight into the genesis and meaning of certain ritual elements, all too often taken for granted simply due to their widespread occurrence in chivalric culture. The particular literary circumstances of the various versions of the Beheading Game theme in the romantic tradition can thus shed interesting light on the origin and significance of the historical dubbing ceremony. In the context of this literary material the dubbing appears to be the official mark and recognition of a long and strenuous initiation that culminates in the experience of mental agony and subsequent relief and liberation, best compared to the novice's "death" for his former self and "rebirth" to a new life with a changed personality and, consequently, social status. This is ultimately what the Beheading Game as a traditional motif in heroic and chivalric literature seems to illustrate: an experience of near-death, which is partly accepted by the knight voluntarily and partly forced on him by prearranged circumstances, the avoidance of which would bring the knight shame and dishonor. The symbolic decapitation usually occurs at the end of the chivalric quest as its climax and constitutes the last and most decisive test, not so much of the knight's fidelity and honor (which are of course necessary for him to keep his word and come to the appointed place at all), but of his mental ability and willpower to overcome the fear of death by submitting to the ordeal voluntarily. In all literary variants of the Beheading Game the rules are so arranged that the hero has no other alternative but to abide by them or else he will lose his reputation, which in itself is equivalent to social "death." The acceptance of the game and adherence to its rules single out the main hero from the others in the first place, as in the Old Irish *Feast of Bricriu,*[128] as well as in *Sir Gawain,* because this in itself shows the hero's initial willingness to die rather than to disgrace himself and his community. And as in the dubbing ceremony, it is not so much the ritual itself that matters, but all the preparations that lead to it; this is why the beheading scenes in romances are often so dramatically prolonged and full of growing tension.[129] In *Sir Gawain,* what was originally intended to be just "on strok" (2252) extends into a highly dramatic scene involving three blows, with conversations in between, that occupy over ninety lines of text (2239-330). In the Old Irish prototypal story too the final beheading scene is of almost annoying and/or comic duration, when the *bachlach* ("churl") arrests his blow twice and tells Cú Chulainn to stretch his neck, because the provided block appears too short:

> "Stretch out your neck, you wretch," the bachlach quoth. "You keep me in torment," quoth Cuchulainn. "Despatch me quickly; last night, by my troth, I tormented you not . . . "I cannot slay you," quoth the bachlach, "what with the size of the block and the shortness of your neck and of your side." Then Cuchulainn stretched out his neck so that a warrior's full-grown foot would have fitted between any two of his ribs; his neck he distended till it reached the other side of the block. The bachlach raised his axe till it reached the roof-tree of the hall. . . . Down it came then . . . on his neck, its blunt side below—all the nobles of Ultonia gazing upon them.[130]

And like in all the other versions of the theme, the hero's head does not get cut off in the physical sense: the last decisive stroke comes either flatwise or on the blunted side or—as in *Sir Gawain*—inflicts only a slight, symbolic wound. This is because the heroes selected for the Beheading Game are not supposed to die at all; rather, they are to "die" in a psychological sense, by being prepared for death and determined to face it.[131] It is therefore not the actual decapitation, which finally does not occur, but the long, deliberately dragged-out ritual of the beheading that is important from the point of view of the mental experience involved: the actual time it takes for the hero to go through the agony of reconciling himself with his annihilation.[132] On the psychological level at least this is what the experience of death seems to amount to. The heroic dilemma of Cú Chulainn, Sir Gawain, Caradoc, and others requires this conscious determination to give up their lives voluntarily, because in each case the heroes were certain that the axe would fall, sharp edge down, on their necks to seal their dooms. The eventual feigned blow comes as a real surprise, not to mention a relief, for the potential victim.[133] As a result, the heroes emerge from under the axe relieved and liberated, rewarded with life for their self-sacrifice and victory over the fear of death, and additionally enriched with a spiritual boon of self-knowledge that marks the appearance of a new, changed personality.

Notes

Preface

1. In this respect a very refreshing and, in my view, badly needed polemical review of modern literary theories (here with regard to Shakespeare) has been recently offered by Brian Vickers, *Appropriating Shakespeare: Contemporary Critical Quarrels* (New Haven: Yale University Press, 1993).

2. C. S. Lewis, *The Discarded Image: An Introduction to Medieval and Renaissance Literature* (Cambridge: Cambridge University Press, 1964).

Chapter 1. Problems with Methodology

1. Sir Frederic Madden, ed., *Sir Gawaine: A Collection of Ancient Romance-Poems by Scotish and English Authors Relating to that Celebrated Knight of the Round Table* (London: Richard and John E. Taylor, 1839). Other major editions of the text to date are the following: R. Morris, ed., *Sir Gawayne and the Green Knight* (London: EETS, No. 4, 1864); Sir Israel Gollancz, ed., *Pearl, Cleanness, Patience and Sir Gawain reproduced in facsimile from the unique MS. Cotton Nero A.x in the British Museum* (London: Oxford University Press, EETS); J. R. R. Tolkien and E. V. Gordon, eds., *Sir Gawain and the Green Knight* (Oxford: Clarendon Press, 1925), revised by Norman Davis in 1967 into what is now a standard and most commonly used edition of the poem; Sir Israel Gollancz, ed., *Sir Gawain and the Green Knight* (London: Oxford University Press, EETS, 1940), still an often-consulted edition, particularly valuable for its notes; Alistair C. Cawley, ed., *Pearl and Sir Gawain and the Green Knight* (London: Everyman's Library, No. 346, 1962), reprinted many times since, together with other poems from the same manuscript; R. A. Waldron, ed., *Sir Gawain and the Green Knight* (London: Edward Arnold, 1978); John A. Burrow, ed., *Sir Gawain and the Green Knight* (Harmondsworth: Penguin, 1972); Theodore Silverstein, ed., *Sir Gawain and the Green Knight: A New Critical Edition* (Chicago: University of Chicago Press, 1974).

All references and quotations from *Sir Gawain* throughout this book are to the Tolkien and Gordon edition revised by Davis, and are cited as Davis.

2. Ian Robinson, *Chaucer and the English Tradition* (Cambridge: Cambridge University Press, 1972), 2.

3. In this respect most useful is a bibliography of works on *Sir Gawain* from 1824 to 1978, with brief summaries and commentaries by Robert J. Blanch, *Sir Gawain and the Green Knight: A Reference Guide* (New York: Whitston Publishing Co., 1983).

4. Jessie L. Weston, *The Legend of Sir Gawain: Studies upon Its Original Scope and Significance* (London: David Nutt, 1897), 85. A similar genetic vein characterized

the essay on *Sir Gawain* by Mabel Day in the introduction to Gollancz's edition of the poem in 1940 (see note 1).

5. Weston, *The Legend*; George L. Kittredge, *A Study of Gawain and the Green Knight* (1916; reprint, Gloucester, Mass.: Peter Smith, 1960); Alice Buchanan, "The Irish Framework of *Gawain and the Green Knight,*" *PMLA* 47 (1932): 315-38; Roger S. Loomis, *Celtic Myth and Arthurian Romance* (New York: Columbia University Press, 1927); Laura H. Loomis, "*Gawain and the Green Knight,*" in *Arthurian Literature in the Middle Ages: A Collaborative History,* ed. Roger S. Loomis (Oxford: Clarendon Press, 1959), 528-40. A similar ritualistic approach was exhibited by John Speirs, "*Sir Gawain and the Green Knight,*" *Scrutiny* 16, no.4 (1949): 274-300, and by Peter Steele, "*Sir Gawain and the Green Knight*: The Fairy Kind of Writing," *Southern Review: An Australian Journal of Literary Studies* 3 (1969): 358-65. A more modern ethnological view of *Sir Gawain* employing the mythological school of Mircea Eliade was offered by D. Loganbill, "The Medieval Mind in *Sir Gawain and the Green Knight,*" *Rocky Mountain Modern Language Association* (1972): 119-26. The source-hunting approach dies hard, as evidenced by Claude Luttrell, "The Folk-Tale Element in *Sir Gawain and the Green Knight,*" *Studies in Philology* 77 (1980): 105-27, which continues the motif quest of the early scholars. More recently, Frederick B. Jonassen offered a very sound and well-documented "folkloric" approach to *Sir Gawain* that does away with the farfetched crosscultural comparisons of early scholars, and instead offers a very convincing analysis of the influence of certain medieval folk customs, such as the Mummers' Play for example, on some elements of characterization and dramatization in *Sir Gawain*, notably the Beheading Game (Frederick B. Jonassen, "Elements from the Traditional Drama of England in *Sir Gawain and the Green Knight,*" *Viator* 17 [1986]: 221-54).

6. Among the interpretative evaluations of these early genetic studies one often finds highly subjective and patronizing remarks regarding the nature of plot elements in medieval romances, expressions such as "wild and fantastic" (Weston, *The Legend,* 88), or "a plain folklore motif," "the primitive mythological conception," or "nothing more than a giant with an external soul" (expressions such as these abound in Loomis, *Celtic Myth,* passim).

7. C. S. Lewis, "The Anthropological Approach," in *Critical Studies of Sir Gawain and the Green Knight,* ed. Donald R. Howard and C. K. Zacher (Notre Dame, Ind.: University of Notre Dame Press, 1970), 59-71.

8. Sir Israel Gollancz, "Chivalry in Medieval English Poetry," in *Chivalry: A Series of Studies to Illustrate Its Historical Significance and Civilizing Influence,* ed. Edgar Prestage (New York: Alfred A. Knopf, 1928), 167-81.

9. Charles Moorman, "Myth and Medieval Literature: *Sir Gawain and the Green Knight,*" *Medieval Studies* 18 (1956): 158.

10. Ibid., 161.

11. Larry D. Benson, *Art and Tradition in "Sir Gawain and the Green Knight"* (New Brunswick, N.J.: Rutgers University Press, 1965).

12. Eugene Vinaver, *The Rise of Romance* (Oxford: Clarendon Press, 1971).

13. Joerg O. Fichte, "*Historia* and *Fabula:* Arthurian Traditions and Audience Expectations in *Sir Gawain and the Green Knight,*" in *Festschrift Walter Haug und Burghart Wachinger* (Tübingen: Max Niemeyer Verlag, 1992), 589-602.

14. Benson, *Art and Tradition,* 9.

15. Vinaver, *Rise of Romance,* 41-56.

16. Edward Wilson, *The Gawain-Poet* (Leiden: E. J. Brill, 1976), 117.

17. W. A. Davenport, *The Art of the Gawain-Poet* (London: Athlone Press, 1978), 3.

18. Ibid., 4.

19. Ibid., 137-38, 141.

20. Marie Borroff, *Sir Gawain and the Green Knight: A Stylistic and Metrical Study* (New Haven: Yale University Press, 1962).

21. Anthony C. Spearing, *The Gawain-Poet: A Critical Study* (Cambridge: Cambridge University Press, 1970).

22. John A. Burrow, *A Reading of Sir Gawain and the Green Knight* (London: Routledge and Kegan Paul, 1965).

23. R. H. Bowers, "*Gawain and the Green Knight* as Entertainment," *Modern Language Quarterly* 24 (1963): 333-41.

24. Among many studies of this aspect of *Sir Gawain* worthy of particular mention is a work by Donald R. Howard, *The Three Temptations: Medieval Man in Search of the World* (Princeton: Princeton University Press, 1966) for whom the poem is "influenced in large measure by the predominantly Christian ideology of the Middle Ages" (13-14), mainly in its presentation of the chivalric ideal as an embodiment of the Christian concept of perfection. A similar spirit pervades a study of sin and redemption in *Sir Gawain* by Louis Blenkner, "Sin, Psychology, and the Structure of *Sir Gawain and the Green Knight,*" *Studies in Philology* 74 (1977): 354-87, or an almost dogmatic article by Bernard S. Levy ("Gawain's Spiritual Journey: *Imitatio Christi* in *Sir Gawain and the Green Knight,*" *Annuale Medievale* 11 [1965]: 65-106), who views the romance as "a profoundly religious poem which evokes a spiritual pattern that is central to the Christian ethos" (65). A consistently allegorical, Augustino-Platonic reading of *Sir Gawain* has also been offered by Hans Schnyder, *Sir Gawain and the Green Knight: An Essay in Interpretation* (Bern: Francke Verlag, 1961). L. S. Champion in turn sees the poem in the light of the great theological debate, particularly hot in fourteenth-century England, on whether salvation can be achieved by divine grace or human merit ("Grace versus Merit in *Sir Gawain and the Green Knight,*" *Modern Language Quarterly* 28 [1967]: 413-25). In a study by Jean L. Carriere, "*Sir Gawain and the Green Knight* as a Christmas Poem," *Comitatus* 1 (Dec. 1970): 25-42, the poem's main ecclesiological frame of reference is the great Christian theme of the Fall through pride and the possibility of Redemption, illustrated by the Feast of the Nativity, so important in the temporal structure of *Sir Gawain*. The theological implications of the sins of sloth and lechery in relation to Fitt III of *Sir Gawain* are also analyzed by V. John Scattergood, "*Sir Gawain and the Green Knight* and the Sins of the Flesh," *Traditio* 37 (1981): 347-71. In another study, the theological paradox of the *felix culpa*, whereby man's fall indirectly caused God's beneficial redemptive incarnation, appears at the center of the poem's religious meaning for Victor Y. Haines, *The Fortunate Fall of Sir Gawain: The Typology of Sir Gawain and the Green Knight* (Washington, D. C.: University Press of America, 1982). Ross G. Arthur in turn in his very stimulating book, *Medieval Sign Theory and Sir Gawain and the Green Knight* (Toronto: University of Toronto Press, 1987), considers *Sir Gawain* in the context of the fourteenth-century debate on idolatry, especially with regard to the question of the pictorial and geometrical representations of God. The moral and theological implications of Gawain's *avaritia vitae* are discussed in a well-documented article by Richard Newhauser, "The Meaning of Gawain's Greed," *Studies in Philology* 87, no. 4 (Fall 1990): 410-26, and more recently Gerald Morgan, *Sir Gawain and the Green Knight and the Idea of Righteousness* (Dublin: Irish Academic Press, 1991) offered a reading of the poem in the light of the scholastic moral philosophy as formulated by the medieval Aristotelianism of Thomas Aquinas. The above list is, of course, very incomplete and serves only to illustrate the range and character of problems addressed by critics particularly sensitive to the religious and moral dimensions of *Sir Gawain*.

25. Maud Bodkin, *Archetypal Patterns in Poetry: Psychological Studies of Imagination* (London: Oxford University Press, 1968), 1.

26. Paul Piehler, *The Visionary Landscape: A Study in Medieval Allegory* (London: Edward Arnold, 1971), 4-5, 7, 18.

27. Heinrich Zimmer, *The King and the Corpse: Tales of the Soul's Conquest of Evil,* Bollingen Series 11 (Princeton: Princeton University Press, 1971).

28. Ibid., 78.

29. Cf. Enrico Giaccherini, "Gawain's Dream of Emancipation," in *Literature in Fourteenth-Century England: The J. A. W. Bennett Memorial Lectures, Perugia, 1981-1982* (Cambridge: D. S. Brewer, 1982), 65-82.

30. Christopher Wrigley, "*Sir Gawain and the Green Knight*: The Underlying Myth," in *Studies in Medieval English Romances: Some New Approaches*, ed. Derek Brewer (Cambridge: D. S. Brewer, 1988), 113-28.

31. Ibid., 114-15.

32. S. Manning, "A Psychological Interpretation of *Sir Gawain and the Green Knight,*" *Criticism* 6, no. 2 (1964): 166.

33. For example, the psychological conflict between the private and the public and the resulting split in Gawain's consciousness is discussed by David Aers, "'*In Arthurus Day'*: Community, Virtue, and Individual Identity in *Sir Gawain and the Green Knight,*" in *Community, Gender and Individual Identity: English Writing 1360-1430* (London: Routledge, 1988), chap. 4.

34. Giaccherini, "Gawain's Dream."

35. Robert J. Edgeworth, "Anatomical Geography in *Sir Gawain and the Green Knight,*" *Neophilologus* 69 (1985): 318-19.

36. Schnyder, *Sir Gawain*, 7. A similar theoretical stance characterizes Howard, *The Three Temptations*.

37. Schnyder, *Sir Gawain*, 16.

38. Howard, *The Three Temptations,* 34.

39. Patricia M. Kean, *The Pearl: An Interpretation* (London: Routledge and Kegan Paul, 1967), viii.

40. D. W. Robertson, Jr., "Historical Criticism," *English Institute Essays* (1950): 3-31.

41. See, for example, Robinson, *Chaucer,* 271.

42. Ludvig von Bertalanffy, *General System Theory: Foundations, Development, Applications* (London: Allen Lane, 1971).

43. Marian Mazur, *Cybernetyka i charakter* (Cybernetics and Character) (Warsaw: Panstwowy Instytut Wydawniczy, 1976).

44. Some general ideas on systems theory and its possible implications for literary studies can be found in my article "Interpretation of Literary Process—A Systemic Approach," *Studia Anglica Posnaniensia* 24 (1992): 78-91.

45. Cf. Arthur, *Medieval Sign Theory*, 3-17. See also an anonymous fifteenth-century English sermon containing a systematic treatise on the fourfold Augustinian method of textual interpretation (R. H. Bowers, "A Middle English Treatise on Hermeneutics: Harley MS 2276, 32v-35v," *PMLA* 65 [1950]: 590-600); cf. *Medieval Literary Theory and Criticism c. 1100 - c. 1375: The Commentary-Tradition*, ed. A. J. Minnis and A. B. Scott (Oxford: Clarendon Press, 1988), esp. chap. 3, 65-112.

46. Cf. D. W. Robertson, Jr., "Some Medieval Literary Terminology, with Special Reference to Chrétien de Troyes," *Studies in Philology* 48 (1951): 669-92.

47. Cf. Dante Alighieri, *Dante's "Il Convivio" (The Banquet)*, trans. Richard H. Lansing (New York: Garland Publishing, 1990), book 2, chap. 1.

48. C. S. Lewis, *The Allegory of Love: A Study in Medieval Tradition* (London: Oxford University Press, 1938), 45.

49. Cf. Tullio Gregory, "The Platonic Inheritance," in *A History of Twelfth-Century Western Philosophy*, ed. Peter Dronke (Cambridge: Cambridge University Press, 1988), 54-80. In the same collaborative work see Winthrop Wetherbee, "Philosophy, Cosmology, and the Twelfth-Century Renaissance," 21-45. Also useful is a presentation of early medieval Neoplatonic philosophy in C. S. Lewis, *The Discarded Image: An Introduction to Medieval and Renaissance Literature* (Cambridge: Cambridge University Press, 1964), chaps. 3 and 4.

50. As is exemplified by John Bunyan's Apology to his *Pilgrim's Progress*: "was not God's laws, His Gospel-laws in olden time held forth by types, shadows, and metaphors?" (Edinburgh: Banner of Truth Trust, 1977), viii.

51. Vinaver, *Rise of Romance*, 2.

52. Cf. Lewis, *Allegory of Love*, 2-42.

53. Vinaver, *Rise of Romance,* 18-25.

54. Ibid., 18, 38-40.

55. Schnyder, *Sir Gawain,* 15.

56. Hans Schnyder put it very ardently: "It is our considered opinion that in the Middle Ages realism as a self-sufficient artistic principle did not exist" (ibid., 14-15).

57. Cf. D. W. Robertson, Jr., *A Preface to Chaucer: Studies in Medieval Perspectives* (Princeton: Princeton University Press, 1963), esp. chap. 4.

Chapter 2. The Temporal Structure of *Sir Gawain*

1. Selected aspects of the internal structure of *Sir Gawain* have been scrutinized by such critics as A. Kent Hieatt, "Sir Gawain: Pentangle, *Luf-Lace*, Numerical Structure," *Papers on Language and Literature* 4 (1968): 339-59; Donald R. Howard, "Structure and Symmetry in *Sir Gawain and the Green Knight,*" *Speculum* 39 (July 1964): 425-33; Hans Käsmann, "Numerical Structure in Fitt III of *Sir Gawain and the Green Knight,*" in *Chaucer and Middle English Studies in Honour of Rossell Hope Robbins*, ed. Beryl Rowland (London: George Allen and Unwin, 1974), 131-39; Lloyd N. Dendinger, "The Dynamic Structural Balance of *Sir Gawain and the Green Knight,*" in *Essays in Honor of Esmond Linworth Marilla*, ed. T. A. Kirby and W. J. Olive (Baton Rouge: Louisiana State University Press, 1970), 367-78; Dale B. J. Randall, "A Note on Structure in *Sir Gawain and the Green Knight,*" *Modern Language Notes* 72 (1957): 161-63; Sylvan Barnett, "A Note on the Structure of *Sir Gawain and the Green Knight,*" *Modern Language Notes* 71 (1956): 319; Blenkner, "Sin, Psychology, and Structure," 354-87. Specifically on the temporal structure of *Sir Gawain* see John K. Crane, "The Four Levels of Time in *Sir Gawain and the Green Knight,*" *Annuale Medievale* 10 (1969): 65-80; Jane Tolimieri, "Medieval Concepts of Time and their Influence on Structure and Meaning in the Works of the Gawain-Poet," *Dissertation Abstracts International* (June 1989), 49 (12) A, 3718-19; Piotr Sadowski, "Time-Structure in the Narrative Framework of *Sir Gawain and the Green Knight,*" in *Noble and Joyous Histories: English Romances, 1375-1650,* ed. Eilean Ni Cuilleanain and Joseph D. Pheifer (Dublin: Irish Academic Press, 1993), 11-26.

2. Cf. Vinaver, *Rise of Romance*, 2; Giaccherini, "Gawain's Dream," 66. For the quest motif in religion and myth see Mircea Eliade, *The Quest: History and Meaning in Religion* (Chicago: University of Chicago Press, 1969), passim.

3. Mircea Eliade, *Naissances Mystiques: Essai sur quelques types d'initiation* (Paris: Les Essais, No. 92, 1959), 12; the English edition *Birth and Rebirth: The Religious Meanings of Initiation in Human Culture*, trans. Willard R. Trask (London: Harvill Press, 1961); see also Eliade, *The Quest*, 225. For further discussion on

mythical heroic biography see Lord Raglan, *The Hero: A Study in Tradition, Myth, and Drama* (Westport, Conn.: Archon Books, 1975), esp. 174-75; Joseph Campbell, *The Hero with a Thousand Faces* (New York: Bollingen Series, 1961), esp. 245.

4. Compare for example Aers, *"In Arthurus Day,"* 155-57, for whom *Sir Gawain* reflects the ideology of "a chivalric community committed to individual and collective goals of honour." Also, "it is a story about the knightly elite in its golden age," expressing "the traditional paradigms of the ruling class," its "heroic ethos," which relied on "the competitive and aggressive cult of honour." For further definitions and general characteristics of medieval chivalry see F. J. C. Hearnshaw, "Chivalry and Its Place in History," in *Chivalry,* 2-4; or a very comprehensive and informative book by Maurice Keen, *Chivalry* (New Haven: Yale University Press, 1984), 16-17, 27, 42.

5. Cf. Randall, "A Note on Structure," and Dendinger, "Dynamic Structural Balance."

6. The main source of the legend is a mid-twelfth-century *Historia Regum Britanniae,* pt. 7, by Geoffrey of Monmouth, ed. Jacob Hammer (Cambridge, Mass.: Mediaeval Academy of America, 1951). See also J. S. P. Tatlock, *The Legendary History of Britain: Geoffrey of Monmouth's Historia Regum Britanniae and Its Early Vernacular Versions* (University of California Press, 1950), and a modern translation: Geoffrey of Monmouth, *History of the Kings of Britain,* trans. Lewis Thorpe (Harmondsworth: Penguin, 1966), with many reprints since.

7. Hieatt, *"Sir Gawain:* Pentangle," 346-47, regards the "echoing line" 2525 ending the last stanza (but before the final bob and wheel) as the critical one in the poem, not the ultimate line 2530. An additional point by Hieatt is that the number 2525 is a multiple of five, which is a number of Gawain's pentangle, whose importance in the poem and its connection with the discussed principle of cyclicity cannot be underestimated (see chap. 4 of this book). Of course, if the inclusion of the echoing line in its present place was not accidental, it would mean that the poet was carefully counting the lines of his poem, and was probably expecting the same from his more inquisitive readers.

8. Cf. C. David Benson, *The History of Troy in Middle English Literature. Guido delle Colonne's Historia Destructionis Troiae in Medieval England* (Woodbridge, Suffolk: D. S. Brewer, 1980), esp. 3-31.

9. *Middle English Dictionary,* ed. Hans Kurath and Sherman M. Kuhn (Ann Arbor: University of Michigan Press, 1955), henceforth referred to as *MED.*.

10. Cf. Lynn S. Johnson, *The Voice of the Gawain-Poet* (Madison: University of Wisconsin Press, 1984), 38-45.

11. The popularity of the matter of Troy among the alliterative poets of the fourteenth century can be exemplified by similar enveloping devices used in *Wynnere and Wastoure,* ed. Stephanie Trigg (Oxford: Oxford University Press, EETS, 1990), which begins with:

> Sythen that Bretayne was biggede and Bruyttus it aughte
> Thurgh the takynge of Troye with tresone withinn

(1-2)

The *Alliterative Morte Arthure: A Critical Edition,* ed. Valerie Krishna (New York: Burt Franklin, 1976) also ends with a similar reminder of the noble Trojan lineage of Arthur, a device that brings the story of the British king in line with the providential view of history:

> Thus endis Kyng Arthure, as auctors alegges,
> That was of Ectores blude, the kynge son of Troye,

And of Sir Pryamous the prynce, praysede in erthe;
Fro thythen broghte the Bretons all his bolde eldyrs
Into Bretayne the Brode, as þe *Bruytte* tellys.

(4342-46)

12. The ambiguity of this fragment relies on that "Hit watz Ennias þe athel" (5), following immediately the mention of "tricherie" (4), may equally refer backwards, thus logically linking Aeneas with treason, or else only forwards to Aeneas and the provinces he established, thus leaving "tricherie" for somebody else. The first view (of Aeneas's treachery) was advocated by F. Madden (1839) and was upheld by Davis (70 n), whereas the latter view (clearing Aeneas of blame) was proposed by Sir Israel Gollancz in his edition of *Sir Gawain* (1940), and recently by Morgan, *Sir Gawain*, 43-44, who both think that the "tulk" who committed treachery was Antenor. If it is to be accepted that "the poet begins by setting the treachery of Antenor beside the nobility of Aeneas" (Morgan, *Sir Gawain*, 46), one wonders why the name of the first (and therefore important) character in the poem is left unmentioned, with so many other minor figures explicitly called by name later in the same stanza.

13. Guido della Colonna, *Historia Destructionis Troiae*, ed. N. E. Friffin (Cambridge, Mass.: The Mediaeval Society of America, 1936), 218; quoted after Davis, 70.

14. Cf. Alfred David, "Gawain and Aeneas," *English Studies* 49 (1968): 407-9. For a discussion of Gawain's notoriety for treachery and other offenses in French Arthurian literature see D. J. Barnett, "Whatever Happened to Gawain?" *English Studies in Africa* 18 (1975): 1-16.

15. The Ciceronian distinction between *historia* understood as a truthful account and *fabula* as a fictitious narrative (Cicero, *Rhetorica ad Herennium*, ed. and trans. Harry Caplan [Cambridge: Harvard University Press, 1954], 22-24) has been applied to the opening stanza of *Sir Gawain* by Joerg O. Fichte, "*Historia* and *Fabula*," esp. 590-92.

16. The beginning of the year depends of course on tradition and usage. Astronomically speaking the solar year begins at midwinter solstice (24 December), when the days start to wax (in the northern hemisphere). It is no accident that the Christian Feast of the Nativity coincides with midwinter, since in Roman times Christ already had been hailed as *sol invictus*, conquering the forces of evil and darkness. The present practice of reckoning the beginning of the year from 1 January (an octave after the solstice) came with the Julian calendar (46 b.c.), and was accepted by the Church and widely used in the Middle Ages. However, the Church's liturgical calendar began with Advent in the last week of November. On the other hand, the folk tradition persisted to associate the beginning of the year with the vernal equinox (25 March) and generally with spring.

17. To use a parallel from the realm of medieval drama: the central type of medieval dramatic form was the resurrectional play performed at Easter, but nearest to it was the Nativity play, "in its simplest form . . . an imitation of the Easter play, with a manger instead of a sepulchre, shepherds instead of the Marys, and midwives instead of angels" (Arnold Williams, *The Drama of Medieval England* [East Lansing: Michigan State University Press, 1961], 21). Since the resurrectional theme appears central both to Easter and Christmas, the omission of the former feast from the otherwise very precise and structurally important liturgical framework of *Sir Gawain* seems thus more understandable.

18. The "Christmas message" is the main doctrinal point of reference in *Sir Gawain* for Carriere, "*Sir Gawain and the Green Knight* as a Christmas Poem," 30-38.

19. Derek Pearsall in his article "Rhetorical *Descriptio* in *Sir Gawain and the Green Knight,*" *Modern Language Review* 50, no. 2 (1955): 129-34, suggests here an influence of medieval rhetorical theory on poetic practice, particularly the treatise *Ars Versificatoria* by Matthew of Vendome, a modification of Cicero's *Rhetorica ad Herennium*. Even if the *Gawain*-poet did not know Matthew's work firsthand, supposes Pearsall, he would have equally well derived his knowledge from rhetorical training at school or from French literature. For numerous examples of medieval poetic descriptions of nature and seasons and their psychological significance see also Derek Pearsall and Elizabeth Salter, *Landscapes and Seasons of the Medieval World* (London: Paul Elek, 1973), esp. 147-53; Ralph W. V. Elliot, "Landscape and Rhetoric in Middle-English Alliterative Poetry," *Melbourne Critical Review* 4 (1961): 71-76; and Nils Erik Enkvist, "The Seasons of the Year: Chapters on a Motif from *Beowulf* to the *Shepherd's Calendar,*" *Societas Scientiorum Fennica: Commentationes Humanorum Litterarum* 22, no. 4 (1957): 85-87, 134.

20. In a "charter" read by *Symonye* and *Cyvylle* in Passus II of *Piers Plowman* the heirs of *Favel* (Deceit) are allotted "into the pyne of helle; / Yeldynge for this thyng *at one yeres ende* / Hire soules to Sathan, to suffre with hym peynes" (William Langland, *The Vision of Piers Plowman: A Complete Edition of the B-Text,* ed. A. V. C. Schmidt [London: Everyman's Library, 1989], passus 2, ll. 104-6, italics added).

21. *A Stanzaic Life of Christ,* ed. Frances A. Foster (London: Oxford University Press, EETS, 1926), ll. 5075-84.

22. For the same reason Chaucer opens the General Prologue to *The Canterbury Tales* with a description of the renewal of life in spring ("Whan that Aprill with his shoures soote / The droghte of March hath perced to the roote," 1-2). The pilgrimage was also commonly regarded in the Middle Ages as an allegory of human life, as exemplified by the late thirteenth-century *Le Pelerinage de la vie humain* by Guillaume de Deguileville, translated into Middle English as *The Pilgrimage of the Lyfe of the Manhode,* ed. Avril Henry (London: Oxford University Press, EETS, 1985).

23. *Lydgate and Burgh's Secrees of Old Philisoffres,* ed. R. Steele; ES 66 (London: Trubner, EETS, 1894), ll. 1457-63, quoted after John A. Burrow, *The Ages of Man: A Study in Medieval Writing and Thought* (Oxford: Clarendon Press, 1988), 30-31. For the discussion of the medieval concepts of *aetates hominum* see esp. 12-36, and also for the literary *loci classici* of the four ages of man (Horace, Ovid, Bede) assembled in the appendix, 191-202.

24. *The Riverside Chaucer,* 3d ed., ed. Larry D. Benson (Oxford: Oxford University Press, 1988), 258, ll. 3187-3190.

25. Dante, *Il Convivio,* trans. Lansing, book 4, chaps. 24-28.

26. Bede, "On the Four Seasons, Elements and Humors," *De Temporum Ratione,* in *Bedae Opera de Temporibus,* ed. C. W. Jones (Cambridge, Mass.: Meviaeval Society of America, 1943), quoted after Burrow, *The Ages of Man,* 12.

27. The system can be extended and elaborated almost at will with the addition of other tetrads. Antiochus of Athens, an astrologer of the second century a.d., adds such categories as winds (south, east, north, west), conditions (liquid, gaseous, dense, solid), temperaments (sanguine, choleric, melancholic, phlegmantic), and colors (red, yellow, black, white); quoted after Jean Seznec, *The Survival of the Pagan Gods: The Mythological Tradition and Its Place in Renaissance Humanism and Art,* trans. B. F. Session (New York: Pantheon Books, 1953), 177.

28. Number four appears in connection with man's purification (*ad hominum purificandum*) in a series of sermons by Maximus Taurinensis (*Sermones de Quadragesima*), *Patrologia Latina,* ed. J. P. Migne (Paris, 1862), 15-28, col. 561-90.

29. Langland, *Piers Plowman,* passus 5, ll. 537ff.

30. Jacobus de Voragine, *The Golden Legend*, trans. William Caxton, ed. F. S. Ellis (London: W. Morris, 1892), 1-3; modern translation by Granger Ryan and Helmut Ripperger (New York: Arno Press, 1969), 1-2.

31. *Pearl, Cleanness, Patience and Sir Gawain,* ed. Gollancz.

32. Howard, *The Three Temptations,* 251.

33. Crane, "The Four Levels of Time," 65-80, introduces a time scheme for *Sir Gawain* whereby the first relevant temporal level is that of Cosmic Time of cyclic regeneration and re-creation at the beginning of each year, here additionally linked with the New Year festival, Baptism, and the Circumcision. The other time levels introduced by Crane are Historical Time (noncyclic, irreversible), Psychological Time (as perceived by Gawain), and Sacred Time (related back to Cosmic Time). For the notion of circularity in *Sir Gawain* see also Tolimieri, "Medieval Concepts of Time."

34. To use a phrase by Johnson, *Voice of the Gawain-Poet,* 56.

35. For comments on the "first age" of Arthur's court see especially Mary Dove, *The Perfect Age of Man's Life* (Cambridge: Cambridge University Press, 1986), 134-40; also Burrow, *The Ages of Man,* 173-75.

36. Cf. remarks by Wrigley, "*Sir Gawain and the Green Knight,"* esp. 117, 118: "If Gawain becomes a man in the course of the story he must have begun it as a child; and it is very clear that children are what he and all the folk at Camelot are, at least metaphorically," and "The atmosphere of Christmas at Camelot is exactly of a children's party, with games, presents, lots of nice things to eat—and no sex."

37. George B. Pace, "Gawain and Michaelmas," *Traditio* 25 (1969): 404-11.

38. *An Old English Martyrology,* ed. George Herzfeld (London: Kegan Paul, EETS, 1900), contains an injunction by Pope Bonifacius that the festival of All Saints should be "observed every year among Christian nations with the same reverence as the first day of Christmas, that is, the first day of Yule" (199).

39. John V. Scattergood and Myra Stokes, "Travelling in November: Sir Gawain, Thomas Usk, Charles of Orleans and the *De Re Militari,"* *Medium Aevum* 53, no. 1 (1984): 78-82.

40. For Jacobus de Voragine the Advent as the beginning of the liturgical year was a period of spiritual renewal and penance (*The Golden Legend,* ed. G. Ryan and H. Ripperger [New York: Arno Press, 1969], 1-3).

41. Cf. Martin Puhvel, "Art and the Supernatural in *Sir Gawain and the Green Knight,"* in *Arthurian Literature,* ed. Richard Barber (Cambridge: D. S. Brewer, 1985), 1-69, esp. 20.

42. Cf. Schnyder, *Sir Gawain and the Green Knight,* 70; Burrow, *A Reading,* 54; and Levy, "Gawain's Spiritual Journey," 90.

43. Interesting in the christological context of the poem is the apparent omission of 28 December (the Holy Innocents' Day) from the passage of days at Hautdesert, otherwise very carefully accounted for (esp. 1020-23). Davis notes (104) that "since the author is attentive to dates this is unlikely to be an oversight," but the scholar gives no reasons for this omission. Victor Y. Haines, "Morgan and the Missing Day in *Sir Gawain and the Green Knight,"* *Mediaeval Studies* 33 (1971): 357, supports Davis's view of the deliberate exclusion of the Holy Innocents' for the reason—as he suggests—that Gawain was so drunk during Christmas celebrations at Hautdesert that he simply overslept the day: "It's a normal enough man who loses a day in the waking and drinking somewhere between Christmas and New Year's; the apparent time suggests felt time." In my opinion, however, it is more likely that the omission of the Holy Innocents' has less to do with Gawain's drunken stupor than with the author's intention to conceal the christological framework at this moment of the story to point out Gawain's childlike innocence and ignorance of the possible dangers lurking for him at Hautdesert.

44. Cf. *The Encyclopedia of Religion,* ed. Mircea Eliade (New York: Macmillan, 1987), s.v. "rites of passage."

45. Udo Strutynski, *"Honi Soit Qui Mal y Pense:* The Warrior's Sins of Sir Gawain," in *Homage to Georges Dumézil. Journal of Indo-European Studies,* Monograph No. 3, ed. Edgar C. Polome (Washington D.C.: Institute for the Study of Man, 1982), 38.

46. Cf. Levy, "Gawain's Spiritual Journey," 72-73.

47. So mony meruayl bi mount þer þe mon fyndez,
    Hit were to tore for to telle of þe tenþe dole.

(718-19)

Chapter 3. The Greenness of the Green Knight

1. See, for example, the early studies of the Green Knight's greenness in terms of the vegetation myth in Weston, *The Legend,* passim; Loomis, *Celtic Myth,* esp. 85, 101-102; also Speirs, *"Sir Gawain and the Green Knight,"* 274-300; in connection with Celtic fairy world: J. R. Hulbert, "Syr Gawayn and the Grene Kny3t," *Modern Philology* 13, no. 8 (1915): 433-62; no. 12 (1916): 689-730; Kittredge, *A Study of Gawain and the Green Knight,* passim; also Benson, *Art and Tradition,* esp. 74-83; as well as such specialized articles as W. A. Nitze, "Is the Green Knight Story a Vegetation Myth?" *Modern Philology* 33 (1936): 351-66; A. H. Krappe, "Who Was the Green Knight?" *Speculum* 13 (1938): 206-15; W. Goldhurst, "The Green and the Gold: The Major Theme of *Sir Gawain and the Green Knight,"* *College English* 20 (1958-59): 61-65; D. W. Robertson, "Why the Devil Wears Green," *Modern Language Notes* 69 (1954): 470-471; D. B. J. Randall, "Was the Green Knight a Fiend?," *Studies in Philology* 57 (1960): 479-91; W. Bryant Bachman, Jr., *"Sir Gawain and the Green Knight:* The Green and the Gold Once More," *Texas Studies in Literature and Language* 23, no. 4 (1981): 495-516; Helmut Nickel, "Why Was the Green Knight Green?" *Arthurian Interpretations* 2, no. 2 (1988): 58-64.

2. An interesting exception is a study by Marie Borroff, *"Sir Gawain and the Green Knight:* The Passing of Judgement," in *The Passing of Arthur: New Essays in Arthurian Tradition,* ed. C. Baswell and William Sharpe (New York: Garland Publishing, 1988), esp. 117-27, in which she analyzes the changing perception in the Green Knight's color by Sir Gawain from Fitt I to IV.

3. Compare Kittredge's "self-explanatory" statement: "Everybody knows that green is a fairy colour," *A Study of Gawain,* 118.

4. Cf. the discussion of the Green Knight's "handsomeness" in Morgan, *Sir Gawain,* 60-80.

5. Such as "verdure" (161) and phrasal equivalents of green like "of þat same (color)" (157), "of þe same" (170), "of þat ilke" (173), "of a sute" (191), "such a hwe" (234).

6. For example, the opening line: "Ande al grayþed in grene þis gome and his wedes" (151), as well as lines 161, 179, and 234.

7. See lines 159, 167, 170(?), 189, 190, 191, 195, 211, 236.

8. The greenness of the Green Knight is bright and shining all the way through: cf. "enker-grene" (150, 2477); words characterizing green such as "clene" (154, 158, 161, 163), "bry3t" (155, 159, 195, 212), "blyþe" (155, 162); and expressions such as "glemered and glent" (172), "fayre grene" (189), "bry3t grene" (192, 220), "as layt

so ly3t" (199), "grener hit semed, / þen grene aumayl on golde glowande bry3ter" (235-36).

9. The *MED* glosses *fairie* as "the country or home of supernatural or legendary creatures" and as "a supernatural creature." The second meaning is that of "supernatural contrivance, enchantment, magic, illusion," which well fits the fact that the Green Knight has been sent to Camelot "þur3 my3t of Morgne la Faye" (2446) to test the valor of the Round Table.

10. Cf. Giaccherini, "Gawain's Dream," in 71.

11. Cf. Morgan, *Sir Gawain,* "the Green Knight, for all his marvellous appearance, belongs to the world of the court" (79).

12. The view of the essentially divine nature of the Green Knight has been advanced, for example, by Schnyder, *Sir Gawain*, 41ff.

13. The Old Irish word *cuilenn* ("holly") is related to the Brittonic root *kel,* meaning "to prick, pierce," and to another OI word *colg*, "point, sword" (Joseph Vendryes, ed., *Lexique etymologique de l'Irlandais ancien* [Paris: Centre National de la Recherche Scientifique, 1987], s.v. *cuilenn;* see also *Dictionary of the Irish Language* (Dublin: Royal Irish Academy, 1983), s.v. *cuilenn.* In the Old Irish epic *Tain Bó Cúalnge* sharp spits of holly are used as a dangerous throwing weapon (*TBC* from the *Book of Leinster,* ed. Cecile O'Rahilly [Dublin: Institute for Advanced Studies, 1967], ll. 1221, 1696-1704, 1899-1909; *TBC: Recension 1,* ed. Cecile O'Rahilly (Dublin: Institute for Advanced Studies, 1976), ll. 1780-82. For an analysis of the early Irish sources of *Sir Gawain* see Kittredge, *A Study of Gawain,* 9-25, and Alice Buchanan, "The Irish Framework," 315-38.

14. Quoted after M. A. Carson, "Morgan la Fee as the Principle of Unity in *Sir Gawain and the Green Knight,"* *Modern Language Quarterly* 23, no. 1 (1962): 10. For the use of holly in popular magic see R. Folkard, *Plant Lore, Legends, and Lyrics* (London: Sampson Low, 1884), 40, 46; and A. H. Krappe, "Who Was the Green Knight?" 214.

15. In Germany holly was called *Christdorn,* "the thorn of Christ" (Folkard, *Plant Lore,* 46).

16. R. A. Shoaf in her article, "The 'Syngne of Surfet' and the Surfeit of Signs in *Sir Gawain and the Green Knight,"* in *The Passing of Arthur: New Essays in Arthurian Tradition,* ed. C. Baswell and W. Sharpe (New York: Garland Publishing, 1988), 159, likewise interprets the Green Knight's holly cluster as a "weapon," although "the less lethal" one than the axe. According to Shoaf the Green Knight's invitation to "lach ßis weppen" (292) is ambiguous because it can refer both to the axe and the holly: had Gawain interpreted it correctly and chosen the "holyn bobbe" instead of the axe, he would have later been struck with a gentle blow that anyone can survive. In my opinion, however, the above interpretation is incorrect, because first, the textual antecendent of "þis weppen" (292) is undoubtedly the axe, referred to three lines earlier (288-90), and second, as has been shown in this chapter, the christological context of the holly by no means suggests a harmless character of the weapon, but rather the suffering-death-resurrection theme in accordance with the *passio christi.*

17. "For þer þe fest watz ilyche ful fiften dayes" (44), that is, from 25 December until after the Epiphany (6 January).

18. "For as the lightning cometh out of the east, and shineth even unto the west; so shall also the coming of the Son of man be" (Matt. 24:27; cf. also Luke 17:24, and Rev. 4:5).

19. Morgan, *Sir Gawain*, 86, links the gold on Gawain's pentangle with the idea of righteousness, following the clue from Langland, *Piers Plowman*, 19, ll. 87-88:

The seconde kyng siththe soothliche offrede
Rightwisnesse under reed gold, Resones felawe.

20. Malory, *Works*, ed. Eugene Vinaver 2d ed. (Oxford: Oxford University Press, 1971), bk. 4, chap.5, ll. 19-21.

21. *Ywain and Gawain*, ed. Albert B. Friedman and Norman T. Harrington (London: Oxford University Press, EETS, 1964), ll. 353-54.

22. For example, Rossell Hope Robbins, ed., *Secular Lyrics of the XIVth and XVth Centuries* (1952; reprint, Oxford: Clarendon Press, 1964), nos. 50-52.

23. Cf. John 3:3-6.

24. The cutting of trees with an axe is a biblical metaphor for Christ humiliating and punishing the sinners: "And now also the axe is laid unto the root of the trees: therefore every tree which bringeth not forth good fruit is hewn down, and cast into the fire" (Matt. 3:10).

25. Cf. Brian Ó Cuiv, "The Wearing of the Green," *Studia Hibernica* 17/18 (1977-78): 107-119; see also Piotr Sadowski, "The Significance of Colour Green in the Irish Tradition," *Kwartalnik Neofilologiczny* 37, no. 2 (1990): 201-14.

26. *Tain Bó Cúailnge*, Recension I, ed. O'Rahilly, ll. 856ff. For further examples of the fairy creatures dressed in green from the Irish tradition see Sadowski, "Significance of Colour Green," esp. 205-14.

27. Francis J. Child, ed., *The English and Scottish Popular Ballads* (Boston: Houghton, Mifflin and Co., 1898), I: 422.

28. *The Tripartite Life of Patrick,* ed. Whitley Stokes (London: Eyre and Spottiswoode, 1889), I: clxxxix.

29. *Dictionary of the Irish Language.*

30. *An Irish-English Dictionary*, ed. Patrick S. Dinneen (Dublin: Educational Company of Ireland, 1927).

31. *Dictionary of the Irish Language,* relevant entries.

32. The metaphor is extended in I Corinthians 15:35-44. See also in *Pearl*: "For uch gresse mot grow of graynes dede" (31) (ed. Gollancz).

33. Carlton Brown, ed., *Religious Lyrics of the XIVth Century* (Oxford: Clarendon Press, 1952), no. 9; G. L. Brook, ed., *The Harley Lyrics* (Manchester: Manchester University Press, 1948), no. 17. For a detailed analysis of the ambiguous lines 11-12 see V. J. Scattergood, "Wynter wakeneth al my care . . . Lines 11-15," *English Philological Studies* 14 (1975): 59-64.

34. Cf. especially articles by A. H. Krappe, D. W. Robertson, and D. B. J. Randall listed in note 1.

35. Claude Luttrel, "The Folk-Tale Element in *Sir Gawain and the Green Knight," Studies in Medieval English Romances: Some New Approaches*, ed. Derek Brewer (Cambridge: D. S. Brewer, 1988), 100-101

36. *The Riverside Chaucer,* ed. Larry D. Benson, ll. 1378-83. The "frenges blake" too were always associated with the devils, see note on p. 875.

37. *The Parlement of the Thre Ages*, ed. M. Y. Offord (London: Oxford University Press, EETS, 1959).

38. *The Book of Beasts, being a translation from a Latin Bestiary of the Twelfth Century,* ed. T. H. White (London: Jonathan Cape, 1954), 8.

39. Again I have to disagree with Gerald Morgan, *Sir Gawain,* 60, when he writes that "the portrait of the Green Knight is distinguished not for its ambiguity but for its clarity."

40. Quotation and translation from Peter Dronke, "Tradition and Innovation in Medieval Western Colour-Imagery," *Eranos* 41 (1972): 83.

41. Dronke, "Tradition and Innovation," 84.

42. Carlton Brown, ed., *English Lyrics of the XIIIth Century* (Oxford: Clarendon Press, 1932), no. 24, ll. 41-44. Another fourteenth-century poem attributes the green color to Christ's cross, which is not surprising in view of the popular identification of the cross with the Tree of Life:

> A scheld of red, a crosse of grene,
> A crown ywrithe with thornes kene,
> A spere, a spounge, with nayles three,
> A body ybounde to a tre.

(Quoted in Rodney Dennys, *The Heraldic Imagination* [London: Barrie and Jenkins, 1975], 97.)

43. Deguileville, *The Pilgrimage of the Lyfe of the Manhode.*

44. Quoted after Dronke, "Tradition and Innovation," 77.

45. Quoted after R. J. Blanch, "Precious Metal and Gem Symbolism in *Pearl,*" *Sir Gawain and Pearl. Critical Essays,* ed. R. J. Blanch (Bloomington: Indiana University Press, 1971), 91.

46. *Pearl,* ed. Israel Gollancz, ll. 999-1001.

47. *The Parliament of Fowls,* ll. 172-75, *The Riverside Chaucer,* ed. Benson. Celestial ever-greenness seems to have been a common attribute of earthly love among the poets. John Skelton, for example, compares the lady's worth and beauty to "herber enverduryd, contynuall fressh and grene" in his poem "Knolege, aquayntance," line 13 (John Skelton, *The Complete English Poems,* ed. John V. Scattergood [New Haven: Yale University Press, 1983], 44), and Armado in *Love's Labor's Lost* says that "Green indeed is the color of lovers" (*The Riverside Shakespeare,* ed. G. Blakemore Evans [Boston: Houghton Mifflin Company, 1974] 1.2.86). All references to Shakespeare are to this edition.

48. Jan van Ruusbroec, *The Seven Enclosures, Opera Omnia,* vol. 2 (Leiden: E. J. Brill, 1981), 964-1032.

49. The following discussion on green and gold in alchemy is for the most part based on the material from two monumental volumes on alchemical hermeneutics by Carl Gustav Jung, *Mysterium Coniunctionis: An Inquiry into the Separation and Synthesis of Psychic Opposites in Alchemy,* trans. R. F. C. Hull (Princeton: Princeton University Press, 1977), and *Psychology and Alchemy,* trans. R. F. C. Hull (Princeton: Princeton University Press, 1980). Alchemical concepts and imagery are also used in a Jungian analysis of the Grail legend by Emma Jung and Marie-Louise von Franz, *The Grail Legend,* trans. A. Dykes (1960; reprint, Boston: Sigo Press, 1986).

50. Quoted after Jung, *Mysterium,* 432.

51. Translated by Jung, ibid.

52. Meister Eckhart, *German Sermons & Treatises,* trans. M. O'C. Walshe (London: Watkins, 1983), sermon 61, 2:107-109.

53. Johannes Tauler, *Sermons,* trans. M. Shrady (New York: Pauline Press, 1985), 44-45.

54. Translated by Jung, *Mysterium,* 113.

55. Translated by Jung and von Franz, *The Grail Legend,* 165-66.

56. Translated by Jung, *Mysterium,* 432.

57. *Rosarium philosophorum* (Basel, 1593), 2:220, translated by Jung, *Psychology and Alchemy,* 159.

58. Greenness as an alchemical symbol of arcane wisdom and perfection appears, for example, in an image of the Green Lion (*Leo viridis*) in Michael Maier's *Septimana Philosophia,* (A. E. Waite, *The Brotherhood of the Rosy Cross* [London: William

Rider and Son, 1924], 97), or in Sir George Ripley, *The Bosom Book, Collectanea Chemica* (London: J. Elliott, 1893), 124-25.

59. Cf. Helen Adolf, "The Concept of Original Sin as Reflected in Arthurian Romance," *Studies in Language and Literature in Honour of Margaret Schlauch* (Warsaw: Panstwowe Wydawnictwo Naukowe, 1966), 23.

60. Cf. Dronke, "Tradition and Innovation," 84.

61. Compare the figure of Youth, "gerede alle in grene, alle with golde by-weuede" in *The Parlement of the Thre Ages*, l. 122.

62. The text makes it clear that Gawain is wearing the girdle *on* ("vpon," 2036) his armor, wrapped doubly about him for surety (2033-36). See also Ralph Hanna, "Unlocking What's Locked: Gawain's Green Girdle," *Viator* 14 (1983): 290-302.

63. Cf. Gordon M. Shedd, "Knight in Tarnished Armour: The Meaning of *Sir Gawain and the Green Knight,*" *Modern Language Review* 62 (1967): 13.

64. Bachman, ("*Sir Gawain and the Green Knight:* The Green and the Gold Once More") observes the same symmetry between the two figures: "Sir Gawain carries a little green, but he is still largely a Pentangle knight, still mostly "gold." At this point he has become a reversed image of his antagonist, the Green Knight, who is mostly "green," a little "gold" (505). Bachman attributes this symmetry, rather vaguely in my view, to a "truly dialectical vision" and the general "ambiguity" of the poem (512).

65. Nor is this the first time in Arthurian literature that Gawain has to deal with greenness in its positive, divine aspect and he partly fails to accomplish the spiritual adventure denoted by it. In the early-thirteenth-century First Continuation of Chrétien's *Perceval* (*The Continuations of Old French Perceval of Chrétien de Troyes,* Vol. 1, *The First Continuation,* ed. W. Roach [Philadelphia: University of Pennsylvania Press, 1949], 1:357), Gauvin puts on the armor of a strange knight killed in adventure and comes to a castle, where a *green mantle* is put on him ("Un mantel vair li aporta / Uns valles, et si l'affubla," ll. 13155-56). In the hall Gauvin sees a corpse on a bier with a piece of a broken sword lying upon his breast. Gauvin is invited to eat, and the Grail appears and places food before all the company. The host then summons the knight to join the fragments of the sword lying on the breast of the corpse with the fragment that Gauvin had brought himself, but the knight meets with no success. Soon Gauvin asks about the wonders he has witnessed, and the host begins to explain their origin and meaning. Gauvin, however, falls asleep in the middle of the story, and when he awakes the next morning he is far away from the castle where he saw the Grail.

It is again the frailty of the flesh (sleepiness) that prevents Gawain from fulfilling the spiritual mission of redeeming the Grail castle, after he found himself there by accident and after the green mantle of resurrection was put on him by the people awaiting their redeemer.

Chapter 4.   Sir Gawain's Pentangle

1. Naturally enough, like every other major aspect of *Sir Gawain* the pentangle and its general as well as particular meaning(s) have received due critical attention by numerous scholars on various occasions. Referred to or used in this chapter are the following contributions: Richard F. Green, "Gawain's Shield and the Quest for Perfection," *Journal of English Literary History* 29, no. 2 (1962): 121-39; Roger George Lass, "Man's Heaven: The Symbolism of Gawain's Shield," *Mediaeval Studies* 28 (1966): 354-60; Burrow, *A Reading of Sir Gawain and the Green Knight,* esp. 115-

16, 187-89; A. Kent Hieatt, "Sir Gawain: Pentangle, *Luf-Lace*, Numerical Structure,"; John F. Kiteley, "The Endless Knot: Magical Aspects of the Pentangle in *Sir Gawain and the Green Knight," Studies in the Literary Imagination* 4, no. 2 (1971): 41-51; Gerald Morgan, "The Significance of the Pentangle Symbolism in *Sir Gawain and the Green Knight," Modern Language Review* 74, no. 4 (1979): 769-90, also a revised version in Morgan, *Sir Gawain and the Green Knight and the Idea of Righteousness*, 81-105; A. D. Horgan, "Gawain's *pure pentaungel* and the Virtue of Faith," *Medium Aevum* 56 (1987): 310-16; Arthur, *Medieval Sign Theory*, esp. chap. 1; Eugenie R. Freed, "'*Quy the Pentangel Apendes . . .*' The Pentangle in *Sir Gawain and the Green Knight," Theoria: A Journal of Studies in the Arts, Humanities and Social Sciences* 77 (1991): 125-41.

2. Cf. Thorlac Turville-Petre, *The Alliterative Revival* (Cambridge: D. S. Brewer, 1977), esp. chap. 4.

3. However, nowhere else in the sphere of romance is the pentangle assigned to Gawain as a coat-of-arms (cf. Davis's note on p. 92), nor is the symbol at all known as a single device in medieval heraldry, as far as I could find.

4. It is worth noting in this context that the English word *shield*, OE "scield," is related etymologically to OE "sciell," meaning a "shell."

5. Ramon Lull, *The Book of the Ordre of Chivalry*, trans. William Caxton from a French version of Lull's *Le Libre del Ordre de Cauayleria*, ed. A. T. P. Byles (London: Oxford University Press, EETS, 1926), 81-82.

6. Wojciech Iwanczak, *Tropem rycerskiej przygody: Wzorzec rycerski w pismiennictwie czeskim XIV wieku* (In search of chivalric adventure: Chivalric patterns in Bohemian writings of the fourteenth century) (Warsaw: Panstwowe Wydawnictwo Naukowe, 1985), 116.

7. Arthur, *Medieval Sign Theory,* 54, states that "the heraldic sign is considered to be attached to its referent in a purely conventional way," which, however, does not appear to accord with the use of the pentangle in *Sir Gawain*, where the sign is specifically and almost uniquely ascribed to Gawain due to his personal qualities (623, 631, 641-55).

8. Cf. Psalms 5:12; 35:1-3; 1 Thess. 5:8; also Saint Augustine's commentaries on God and faith as man's "shield" in *De doctrina christiana* (New York: Macmillan, 1958), bk 3, xxvi-37.

9. Wolfram von Eschenbach, *Parzival*, trans. A. T. Hatto (Harmondsworth: Penguin Books, 1980), chap. 11, p. 287.

10. A comparison between Gawain's shield from *Sir Gawain* and Galahad's from *Queste* is offered by M. Mills, "Christian Significance and Romance Tradition in *Sir Gawain and the Green Knight," Modern Language Review* 60 (1965): 483-93.

11. The element first found in Geoffrey of Monmouth, *History of the Kings of Britain* (Harmondsworth: Penguin, 1985), 9:4.

12. *M. Robert Holkoth in librum Sapientiae praelectiones CCXIII* (Basel 1586), lect. 36, 127, a relevant passage translated in Green, "Gawain's Shield," 126-27. The quotation comes from *Middle English Sermons*, ed. Woodburn O. Ross (London: Oxford University Press, EETS, 1940), sermon 49, 326.

13. Cf. Kiteley, "Endless Knot," 41-51.

14. Maurice Keen, *Chivalry* (New Haven: Yale University Press, 1984), 133.

15. Cf. Kiteley, "Endless Knot,".43. See also *The Romance of Perceval in Prose: A Translation of the E MS of the Didot Perceval*, trans. D. Skeels (Seattle: University of Washington Press, 1966), 61.

16. Davis in his note on page 94 says simply that the "pentangel nwe" means "newly painted," but this only supports my supposition of a new type of chivalry being suggested, probably with Gawain as its head.

17. It is in this moral sense that the word "trawþe" is used throughout the poem (394, 1545, 1638, 1673, 2470). Nor is this more practical meaning of *trawþe* absent at closer scrutiny in the pentangle passage, should we recall Gawain's listing of King Solomon among those beguiled and fallen through women (2417) and breaking their *trawþe* as a result. *Trawþe* in the sense of loyalty and faithfulness to the pledged word is also a subject of Chaucer's *Franklin's Tale* and appears as one of the main chivalric virtues in general; for example, in the early fifteenth century John Audelay wrote that a knight should "maintene trouth and rightwisness" (R. T. Davies, ed., *Medieval English Lyrics* [London: Faber and Faber, 1963], 173). Cf. also Morgan, "The Significance of the Pentangle," 770ff., and W. R. J. Barron, *Trawthe and Treason: The Sin of Gawain Reconsidered: A Thematic Study of Sir Gawain and the Green Knight* (Manchester: Manchester University Press, 1980), passim.

18. For Ross G. Arthur too the pentangle's main signification is that of *Summa Veritas*, Absolute Truth (*Medieval Sign Theory,* 46). A. D. Horgan, "Gawain's *pure pentaungel,"* 311, also equates *trawþe* associated with the pentangle with faith in its biblical and theological sense.

19. Benson, ed., *The Riverside Chaucer,* ll. 7,14,21,28.

20. The Vulgate Bible has "postesque angulorum quinque" (*Biblia Sacra Iuxta Latinam Vulgatam Versionem, Liber Malachim,* 6:31 [Rome: Vatican 1945]. The number five appears several times in the proportions and units of length used in the building of the temple (1 Kings 6:9-10, 24), as it does in the design of the Tabernacle (Exod. 26:1-37).

21. *The Cloud of Unknowing,* ed. Phyllis Hodgson (London: Oxford University Press, EETS, 1944), 159.

22. Cf. Christopher Butler, *Number Symbolism* (London: Routledge and Kegan Paul, 1970), esp. 43, 74, 84, 86, 123-25, 126-27.

23. *The Works of Christopher Marlowe,* ed. C. F. Tucker Brooke (Oxford: Clarendon Press, 1910), 539, ll. 335-40.

24. *De Arithmetica (Poetae* 4. 249ff.), quoted after Ernst Robert Curtius, *European Literature and the Latin Middle Ages*, trans. Willard R. Trask (London: Routledge and Kegan Paul, 1979), 503-504.

25. Gershom G. Scholem, *On the Kabbalah and Its Symbolism*, trans. R. Manheim (London: Routledge and Kegan Paul, 1965), 39. It is interesting to note in this connection that in the Christian tradition some of the holiest of names also consist of five letters, for example, Soter, Pater, Maria, Jesus.

26. *Hermetica: The Ancient Greek and Latin Writings which Contain Religious or Philosophical Teachings Ascribed to Hermes Trismegistus*, ed. Walter Scott (Boston: Shambhala, 1985), 1:37.

27. Arthur, *Medieval Sign Theory*, 35, quotes a relevant passage from Boethius's *De Arithmetica*, a mathematical treatise standard in the fourteenth century (*Patrologia Latina*, ed. Migne, 63:cols. 1079-1168):

> For 5 times 5, which makes 25, starts from 5 and ends in
> the same number, 5. And if you multiply that by 5 again,
> the end turns out to be 5 again. For 5 times 25 makes
> 125, and if you multiply by 5 again, the answer will end
> with the number 5. And this always happens up to
> infinity. (Arthur's translation)

28. Cf. Hieatt, "Sir Gawain: Pentangle"; Howard, "Structure and Symmetry," 425-33; Dendinger, "Dynamic Structural Balance, 367-78; Randall, "A Note on Structure," 161-63.

29. Hans Käsmann, "Numerical Structure in Fitt III of *Sir Gawain and the Green Knight,"* in *Chaucer and Middle English Studies in Honour of Rossell Hope Robbins*, ed. Beryl Rowland (1974; reprint, London: George Allen and Unwin, 1990), 131-39, claims that these numerical coincidences, albeit deliberate, were probably indended to be "primarily aesthetic" rather than symbolic.

30. Cf. Eliade, ed., *Encyclopedia of Religion*, vol. 11, s.v. "numbers."

31. "*postes habent angulorum quinque*: quia non solum animas electorum aula coeli recipit, sed et corporibus immortali gloria praeditis in judicio suas fores aperiet. Quinque enim sunt sensus corporis nostri, quorum et supra meminimus: visus, auditus, gustus, olfactus, et tactus. Vel certe postis uterque tabernaculi quinque factus est cubitorum, quia solis illis supernae patriae introitus panditur, qui omnibus sui corporis et cordis sensibus Domino servire studuerint." Bede Venerabilis, *Liber de Templo Salomonis*, *Patrologia Latina*, ed. Migne, 91: col. 770.

32. Ibid.

33. Sir Thomas Brown, *Hydrotaphia and the Garden of Cyrus* (London: Macmillan, 1937), 124.

34. Theophrastus, *Physikon Doxon* (Opinions of the natural philosophers), David R. Fideler, ed., *The Pythagorean Sourcebook and Library: An Anthology of Ancient Writings which Relate to Pythagoras and Pythagorean Philosophy*, trans. K. S. Guthrie (Grand Rapids, Mich.: Phanes Press, 1987), 310-11.

35. *Asclepius* 1.6; *Hermetica*.

36. An early modern English anonymous alchemical treatise "The Stone of the Philosophers" (*Collectanea Chemica* [London: James Elliott, 1893], 75-76), calls the quintessence "a real permanent tincture . . . or such a harmonious mixture of the four elementary qualities as constitutes a fifth, from thenceforth indissoluble, and not to be debased with any impurity."

37. *The Book of Quinte Essence or The Fifth Being; that is to say, Man's Heaven*, ed. F. J. Furnivall (London: N. Trubner, EETS, 1866), bk. 1, 1-3. Number five has a generally auspicious character, as is exemplified in a fourteenth-century maxim:

> Kepe well X And flee from VII;
> Rule well V And come to hevyn

Quoted by Robbins, ed., *Secular Lyrics of the XIVth and XVth Centuries*, 80.

38. Cf. a chapter on "endless signs" in Arthur, *Medieval Sign Theory*, 31-46.

39. Matila Ghyka, *The Geometry of Art and Life* (New York: Dover Publications, 1977); Robert Lawlor, *Sacred Geometry: Philosophy and Practice* (London: Thames and Hudson, 1982), chap. 5; Peter F. Smith, *Architecture and the Principle of Harmony* (London: RIBA Publications, 1987), chap. 7. In the sphere of the *Gawain* scholarship only Arthur, *Medieval Sign Theory,* 34-35, has noticed this important geometrical aspect of the pentangle, but he stopped short of drawing any conclusions from this fact, either with regard to the pentangle itself or Sir Gawain as the pentangle knight.

40. Cf. Tullio Gregory, "The Platonic Inheritance," in *A History of Twelfth-Century Western Philosophy*, ed. Peter Dronke (Cambridge: Cambridge University Press, 1988), 54-80.

41. Plato, *Timaeus*, trans. H. D. P. Lee (Harmondsworth: Penguin, 1965), 31c-32a.

42. For extensive exemplification see Lawlor, *Sacred Geometry,* chap. 5.

43. John James, *Chartres: The Masons Who Built a Legend* (London: Routledge and Kegan Paul, 1982), 114.

44. Bernard G. Morgan, *Canonic Design in English Medieval Architecture: The Origins and Nature of Systematic Architectural Design in England, 1215-1515* (Liverpool: Liverpool University Press, 1961), 52-67.

45. Ibid., 67.

46. Ghyka, *Geometry of Art*, 107; Adolf Zeising, *Neue Lehre von den Proportionem des menschlichen Körpers aus einem bisher unerkaunt gebliebenen* (Leipzig, 1854), esp. chaps. 1-2.

47. The growth of natural organisms based on the *phi* ratio can be expressed numerically by the so-called Fibonacci Series (named after Leonardo Fibonacci, ?1170-?1250, a Florentine mathematician). The series is a special additive progression in which the two initial terms are added together to form the third term, so that any two successive terms will reflect or approximate the *phi* ratio: 1, 1, 2, 3, 5, 8, 13, 21, 34, 55, 89, 144, 233, and so on.

48. Cf. Zeising, *Neue Lehre*; Andrzej Wiercinski, "Arka Noego i Wody Potopu" (Noah's ark and the waters of the deluge), *Arkanum* 1, no. 2 (1992): 17-22.

49. Lawlor, *Sacred Geometry,* 59.

50. Ghyka, *Geometry of Art,* 87.

51. Vitruvius, *On Architecture*, trans. F. Granger (London: Heineman, 1931), bk. 3, chap. 1:2, 3-5.

52. Etching reproduced in Franz C. Endres and Annemarie Schimmel, *Das Mysterium der Zahl: Zahlensymbolik im Kulturvergleich* (Cologne: Eugen Diederichs Verlag, 1986), 134.

53. Joscelyn Godwin, *Robert Fludd: Hermetic Philosopher and Surveyor of Two Worlds* (London: Thames and Hudson, 1979), 68, 69, 72.

54.
> Was it a god that drew these signs
> which soothe my inward raging
> and fill my wretched heart with joy,
> and with mysterious strength
> reveal about me Nature's pulse?

Johann Wolfgang von Goethe, *Faust: First Part*, trans. Peter Salm (New York: Bantam Books, 1962), ll. 434-39.

55. Cf. Francis King, *Magie: Aspects de la tradition occidentale* (Paris: Editions du Seuil, 1975), 98-121; Eliphas Levi, *Transcendental Magic: Its Doctrine and Ritual*, trans. A. E. Waite (London: Rider, 1984), 63-70, 237-39.

56. Kiteley, "Endless Knot," 44.

57.
> And vche lyne vmberlappez and loukcz in oþer,
> And ayquere hit is endelez; and Englych hit callen
> Oueral, as I here, þe endeles knot.
> . . . .
> And vchone halched in oþer, þat non ende hade,
> And fyched vpon fyue poyntez, þat fayled neuer,
> Ne samned neuer in no syde, ne sundred nouþer,
> Withouten ende at any noke I oquere fynde,
> Whereeuer þe gomen bygan, or glod to an ende.

(628-30; 657-61)

58. A mid-fifteenth-century "Ashmole" version of the *Secretum Secretorum*, ed. M. A. Manzalaoni (Oxford: Oxford University Press, EETS, 1977), 74.

59. *The English Text of the Ancrene Riwle,* edited from Cotton MS. Nero A. XIV by Mabel Day (London: Oxford University Press, EETS, 1952), 27:1-6, 48-50.

60. Sight—foolish look; hearing—to listen to evil speaker, flatterers, and liers; smelling—to delight in sweet smells; taste—to speak follies and to eat too much; touch—to feel unclean or foul things, according to *The Book of Vices and Virtues: A Fourteenth Century English Translation of the "Somme le Roi" of Lorens D'Orleans*, ed. W. Nelson Francis (London: Oxford University Press, EETS, 1942), 180, ll. 11-17).

61. Morgan, "Significance of the Pentangle," 774-75.

62. *Book of Vices and Virtues*, 153, ll. 15-24.

63. *Cloud of Unknowing*, 148, ll. 17-24.

64. "as Jeremie sayth (Jer. 9:21), deth entryth in 3ow be 3oure V windowys. *Mors intrauit per fenestras vestras," Jacob's Well: An English Treatise on the Cleansing of Man's Conscience*, ed. A. Brandeis (London: Kegan Paul, EETS, 1900), chap. 1, 1-2. An early Middle English treatise *Vices and Virtues, being a Soul's Confession of its Sins, with Reason's Description of the Virtues*, ed. Ferdinand Holthauser (London: N. Trubner, EETS, 1888), 17 (27-30), likewise emphasizes that the wrong use of the senses brings about death.

65. Ibid., 2. Chapter 35, *De quinque sensibus corporis*, discusses the "closing" of the five senses to the vanity of the world.

66. Cf. *The Fyve Wyttes: A Late Middle English Devotional Treatise*, ed. R. H. Bremmer (Amsterdam: Rodopi, 1987).

67. As Richard F. Green has observed in "Gawain's Five Fingers," *English Language Notes* 27, no. 1 (1989): 14-18, the five fingers may be reminiscent of the challenge ritual to a trial by battle, common in the fourteenth century, whereby a champion hired for the fight appeared in court holding up a folded glove, with a penny in each finger. This custom may partly fit Gawain's role as a champion fighting on king Arthur's behalf. On the other hand Horgan, "Gawain's *pure pentaungel*," 313, refers the five fingers from Gawain's pentangle to the blessing of the knight's hands and fingers at a dubbing ceremony: the order of service for that occasion included Psalm 144 (Vulg. 143), which begins with "Benedictus Dominus Deus meus, Qui docet manus meas as praelium, Et digitos meos ad bellum."

68. *The Riverside Chaucer*, ll. 851-62. Earlier on in the tale Chaucer describes the five fingers of gluttony, another carnal sin (ll. 827-30).

69.

> So cortayse, so kny3tly, as 3e ar knowen oute,
> And of alle cheualry to chose, þe chef þyng alosed
> Is þe lel layk of luf,
>
> . . . .
> Your worde and your worchip walkez ayquere,
> And I haf seten by yourself here sere twyes,
> 3et herde I neuer of your hed helde no wordez
> þat euer longed to luf,
>
> (1511-13; 1521-24; see also 1525-34)

However, despite his cleanliness Gawain's idleness in bed at Hautdesert makes his situation particularly susceptible to carnal sins, especially sloth; cf. Scattergood, "*Sir Gawain* and the Sins of the Flesh," 347-71.

70. Printed in Antwerp, 6: xlviii: 326-77, quoted after Green, "Gawain's Five Fingers," 134.

71. In some sources Christ's wounds are: (1) the head (crown of thorns); (2) the right hand; (3) the left hand; (4) the side (heart); and (5) the feet, as in Harley MS. 2339 lyric "Jesus Appeals to Man by the Wounds," Brown, ed., *Religious Lyrics of the XIVth Century,* no. 127. Most commonly, however, the principal wounds are: "tweyn in is hondes, tweyn in is fete, and oon in is herte," *Middle English Sermons,* ed. Ross, sermon 8, 38. See also Douglas Gray, "The Five Wounds of Our Lord," *Notes and Queries* 208 (1963): 50-51, 82-89, 127-34, 163-68.

72. For example, illustrations reproduced in Jung and von Franz, *The Grail Legend,* 64-65, 161.

73. Piero Valeriano, *Hieroglyphica* (Basel, 1556), 351-52. Cornelius a Lapide in *Commentarius in Apocalipsis* (Lyons, 1732), ad 1.8, 18, comments on this drawing: "This pentalpha is God, who is alpha and omega, and Christus Salvator" (quoted after Green, "Gawain's Five Fingers," 134-35).

74. Ruusbroec, *The Seven Enclosures: Opera Omnia,* vol. 2, ll.940-60.

75. Johannes Tauler, *Sermons,* sermon 8, 83-90.

76. *Ancrene Wisse,* ed. J. R. R. Tolkien (London: Oxford University Press, EETS, 1962), fol.7a. This reference has been noted by Davis, 94.

77. Compare the vision of Christ riding into Jerusalem like a knight ready to joust and win his spurs in William Langland, *The Vision of Piers Plowman,* B text, 18: 1-24, or a hermit's vision of Christ as a knight in *Middle English Sermons,* sermon 8, 37-38.

78. *The Recluse: A Fourteenth-Century Version of the Ancren Riwle,* ed. Joel Påhlsson (Lund: Acta Universitatis Lundensis, 1911), 184.

79. John Lydgate, "Transient as a rose," in *Medieval English Lyrics,* ed. Davies, no. 97.

80. I see no point in juxtaposing the significance of the pentangle itself with the Five Wounds ascribed to it, by treating the former as "the proud sign of human sufficiency," and the latter as a "reminder of the need for divine aid" (Paul F. Reichardt, "Gawain and the Image of the Wound," *PMLA* 99, no. 2 (1984): 154-61). As a sign of Christ the pentangle also stresses the divinity in man, and as such it is far from being an emblem of "the individual operating without the aid of divine grace" (ibid.).

81. For example, Mary is referred to several times as "schilde" in a number of medieval religious lyrics (Brown, *Religious Lyrics,* nos. 122, 131). A thirteenth-century poem from MS. Digby 86 ends with a plea to the Blessed Virgin:

> Mayden moder, heuene quene
> þou miȝt and const and owest to bene
> Oure sheld aȝein þe fende;

(Brown, ed., *English Lyrics of the XIIIth Century,* no. 48, ll. 55-57).

82. In the English tradition the Epiphany is sometimes the third joy, the Ascension being then omitted (Rosemary Woolf, *The English Religious Lyric in the Middle Ages* [Oxford: Clarendon Press, 1968], 141). For the abundant exemplification of the Five Joys of Mary in medieval poetry see Celia and Kenneth Sisam, eds., *The Oxford Book of Medieval English Verse* (Oxford: Clarendon Press, 1970), no. 82; Brown, *Religious Lyrics,* no. 11; Davies, *Medieval English Lyrics,* no. 20; John Audelay, *The Poems of John Audelay,* ed. Ella K. Whiting (London: Oxford University Press, EETS, 1931), no. 19. Sometimes, however, the number of joys is extended to seven and is made to correspond with Mary's Seven Sorrows associated with Christ's suffering. Cf. Yrjo Hirn, *The Sacred Shrine: A Study of the Poetry and Art of the Catholic Church* (London: Faber and Faber, 1958), 269-70.

83. In Brown, *English Lyrics,* no. 41, the five joys appear in the same lyric as the five wounds. At the Mass and the Dirge there could be five men dressed in black, representing the Five Wounds of Christ, and five women in white robes signifying Mary's Five Joys (Sarah A. Weber, *Theology and Poetry in the Middle English Lyric: A Study of Sacred History and Aesthetic Form* [Ohio State University Press, 1969], 152-53).

84. Cf. Hirn, *Sacred Shrine,* 305, 397.

85. Cf. Douglas Gray, *Themes and Images in the Medieval English Religious Lyric* (London: Routledge and Kegan Paul, 1972), 89. In a thirteenth-century lyric from Trinity College Camb. MS. 323, another flower popularly attributed to Mary, the lily (cf. Song of Sol. 2:1-2), has five leaves, five being the Virgin's "natural" number ("fif to beren hire is ful imunde, for þat is hire propre cunde," 3-4). Moreover, the poet ascribes the following virtues to the five leaves of lily flower: charity, love of one's brother, righteousness, willingness to serve Christ, and avoidance of Satan's temptation (Brown, *English Lyrics,* no. 19).

86. Hirn, *Sacred Shrine,* esp. chaps. 13-21, lists, analyzes, and provides exemplification for nearly seventy similes of the Madonna found in medieval literature. In short, in the Virgin Mary was worshiped the whole visible and invisible creation, conceived as a covering or receptacle of the spiritual principle hidden behind the world of phenomena.

87. R. Morris, ed., *Old English Homilies of the Twelfth Century* (London: N. Trubner, EETS, 1878), homily 24, 140-42. The best known Middle English lyrics devoted to Mary as the star of the sea are those printed in Brown, *Religious Lyrics,* nos. 17, 41, 45; Davies, *Medieval English Lyrics,* nos. 144, 179. The similitude can also be found in an Old Irish religious poem attributed to Saint Columba (Gerard Murphy, ed., *Early Irish Lyrics: Eighth to Twelfth Century* [1956; reprint, Oxford: Clarendon Press, 1977], no. 20).

88. A circumstance pointed out to me by John W. Burgess and described in his paper "A Possible Astronomical Genesis of the Tzolkin" (presented at the symposium "Time and Astronomy at the Meeting of Two Worlds," Warsaw/Frombork, May 1992.

89. Cf. Martin Knapp, *Pentagramma Veneris* (Basel 1934), discussed in Endres, *Das Mysterium der Zahl,* 122ff.

90. George Chapman, *Poems,* ed. Phyllis Bartlett (New York: Russell and Russell, 1941), 142, quoted and discussed by Frances A. Yates, *The Occult Philosophy in the Elizabethan Age* (London: Ark Paperbacks, 1983), 142-43.

91. A contrary view to Davis has been presented by Morgan, "Significance of the Pentangle," and his *Sir Gawain,* 81-105, for whom the listed moral virtues, interrelated in the pentangle, are all relevant to the meaning of the poem as a whole, and are accordingly exemplified by respective traits of Gawain's personality and behavior exibited in the poem.

92. *MED;* s.v. "fraunchise."

93. In this sense "fraunchyse" is close to "largesse," that is, material generosity, also becoming of the knight, as Sir Gawain himself confirms ("larges and lewte *[loyalty]* þat longez to kny3tez," 2381). Lull in his treatise on chivalry (*The Book of the Ordre of Chivalry*), 116, likewise stresses that "Chyualrye and Fraunchyse accorden to gyder."

94. Chrétien de Troyes, *Cligés,* ed. Alexandre Micha (Paris: Librairie Honoré Champion, 1965), ll. 188-203.

95. Burrow, *A Reading of Sir Gawain,* 48, connects "clannes" with the generally accepted condition of knightly love, one that rules out adultery but allows for "love-talking," as indulged in by Gawain. Thus understood chastity is the essence of *amour courtois* as distinct from adultery (*fin'amors*) (Morgan, *Sir Gawain,* 96).

96. For example in *Pearl*, ed. Gollancz, line 432, the Virgin Mary is referred to as "þe Quen of cortaysye."

97. *Cleanness*, ed. Alistair C. Cawley and J. J. Anderson (London: J. M. Dent and Sons, 1988), ll. 1089, 1097.

98. Quoted after Jonathan Nicholls, *The Matter of Courtesy: Medieval Courtesy Books and the Gawain-Poet* (Woodbridge, Suffolk: D. S. Brewer, 1985), 8.

99. Cf. William Caxton, *Caxton's Book of Curtesye*, ed. Frederick J. Furnivall (London: Oxford University Press, EETS, 1932).

100. Cf. Nicholls, *The Matter of Courtesy,* 21ff.

101. Cf. David Aers, "'In Arthurus Day;'" chap. 4.

102. These are discussed in Keen, *Chivalry*, 6-15.

103. A very polite knight from the tale is compared to "Gawayn, with his olde curteisye" (Benson, ed., *Riverside Chaucer*, line 95).

104. Cf. Morton Donner, "Tact as a Criterion of Reality in *Sir Gawain and the Green Knight,*" *Papers on English Language and Literature* (Autumn 1965): 306-15; Peter McClure, "Gawain's *Mesure* and the Significance of the Three Hunts in *Sir Gawain and the Green Knight,*" *Neophilologus* 57 (1973): 375-87.

105. See a discussion of both possibilities, with an interpretation in favor of "piety," in Morgan, *Sir Gawain*, 98-103.

106.

> mon al hym one,
> Carande for his costes, lest he ne keuer schulde
> To se þe seruyse of þat syre, þat on þat self ny3t
> Of a burde watz borne oure baret to quelle;
>
> (749-52; see also 753-62)
>
> And he ryches hym to ryse and rapes hym sone,
> Clepes to his chamberlayn, choses his wede,
> Bo3ez forth, quen he watz boun, blyþely to masse;
>
> (1309-11)
>
> Then ruþes hym þe renk and ryses to þe masse,
> And siþen hor diner watz dy3t and derely serued.
>
> (1558-59)

107.

> Syþen cheuely to þe chapel choses he þe waye,
> Preuely aproched to a prest, and prayed hym þere
> þat he wolde lyste his lyf and lern hym better
> How his sawle schulde be saued when he schuld seye heþen.
>
> (1876-79)

108. Sir William Forrest, *The Pleasaunt Poesye of Princelie Practise* (1548), *Secretum Secretorum,* 522, ll. 3511-13.

109. The first two pentads, those referring to the five senses and the five fingers, undoubtedly follow man's natural constitution. The remaining religious and moral pentads are obviously of more conventional character, and are based on culture-specific and arbitrary concepts.

110. It should be repeated emphatically that no other geometrical figures, but only those based on the regular pentagon, contain the principle of the Golden Section.

111. Dante Alighieri, *Dante's Il Convivio*, trans. Richard H. Lansing (New York: Garland Publishing, 1990), bk. 3, chap. 8.

112. For example, the Old English poem *Wanderer* (eds. T. P. Dunning and A. J. Bliss [London: Methuen, 1978], ll. 65-69) contains advice for proper conduct understood as moderation and avoidance of excesses:

Wita sceal geþyldig:
Ne sceal no to hatheort, ne to hrædwyrde,
Ne to wac wiga, ne to wanhydig,
Ne to forht, ne to fægen, ne to feohgifre,
Ne næfre gielpes to georn ær he geare cunne

Langland ends his discussion of various human excesses by saying that "Mesure is medicine, though thow muchel yerne" (Langland, *Vision of Piers Plowman,* passus 1, 35).

113. Aristotle, *The Nicomachean Ethics*, trans. David Ross (Oxford: Oxford University Press, 1980), 2. 6-9.

114. Similarly, number five is the middle digit of the "sacred ten" because $10 \div 2 = 5$, and five is the central element in the row of first nine figures: 1, 2, 3, 4, **5**, 6, 7, 8, 9.

115. *The Book of Vices and Virtues*, ed. Francis, 277. The *MED* glosses the relevant meaning of *mesure* (no. 8) as "moderation in food, drink, spending; temperance; restraint in conduct, manner; modesty; discretion in speech; caution, prudence; mercy, compassion, the action of moderating or tempering emotions; conciliation, compromise."

116. Lull, *The Book of the Ordre,* Caxton's translation, 56-57. For an extensive bibliography of medieval sources on the "mean virtue" see McClure, "Gawain's *mesure,*" nn. 6-9.

117. Sources quoted and discussed by Morgan, *Sir Gawain,* 87-90.

118. See ll. 750-62 quoted in n. 106.

119. The medieval idea of *mesure* was applied to the evaluation of Gawain's behavior in a very revealing and insightful article by Peter McClure, "Gawain's *mesure.*"

120. Gawain's predicament of being caught between loyalty to Sir Bertilac (obligation to return all the day's winnings to him each evening), and the dictates of courtesy that forbid too blunt a refusal of the lady's advances, is too well known for the readers of *Sir Gawain* to repeat here. For a detailed analysis of Gawain's behavior in the bedroom scenes with regard to his *mesure* see McClure, "Gawain's *mesure,*" 377ff.; Donner, "Tact as a Criterion."

121. The Green Knight's leniency illustrates the supreme act of *mesure* in a metaphysical sense: the tempering of justice with mercy as an expression of divine love; cf. *Cleanness,* ll. 215, 247, 563-66; *Patience,* ll. 295, 417-20; or Portia's unforgettable speech on mercy in *The Merchant of Venice,* 4.1.184-205.

Chapter 5. Gawain's Threefold Temptation

1. Voragine, *The Golden Legend*, 2.

2. The passage may create certain problems for readers unfamiliar with Middle English syntax and phraseology. The following is a prose paraphrase of the above fragment:

By Christ! It is disastrous that you, so noble, should be lost! It would have been more sensible [for Arthur] to have acted more warily, and to have appointed that noble [Gawain] to become a duke. A brilliant leader of the people in this land he seems, and this would have been better [for him] than to be destroyed, beheaded by an elvish man, because of [Arthur's] excessive pride. Who ever knew a king that would take such counsel, such frivolous arguments at Christmas games?

The court's surprisingly open criticism of Arthur's irresponsible and rash behavior well accords with the author's earlier statements about the king's boyishness and immaturity, exemplified by his ineptness to control the situation at Camelot.

3. Cf. Johnson, *Voice of the Gawain-Poet*, 58, 246, n. 33.

4. It is certainly on account of its connection with the idea of new life that *An Old English Martyrology*, ed. Herzfeld, 199, recommends that the All Saints' be "observed every year among Christian nations with the same reverence as the first day of Christmas."

5. Bernard S. Levy, "Gawain's Spiritual Journey," 72-73.

6. Lactantius *Divinae Institutiones* 2.10; *Collectio Selecta, Ecclesiae Patrum* 17 (Paris, 1830), 120-21, says that God so divided the world that he kept the light, life, heat, the east and the south to himself, but assigned the darkness, death, coldness, the west and the north to the devil. Cited in Levy, 90.

7. A twelfth-century Latin bestiary says that prostitutes are called wolves, because they devastate the possessions of their lovers (White, ed., *The Book of Beasts,* 56). On medieval wolflore see also *On the Properties of Things: John Trevisa's Translation of Bartholomaeus Anglicus De Proprietatibus Rerum*, ed. M. C. Seymour (Oxford: Clarendon Press, 1975), vol. 2, Capitulum lxxi, 1222-25.

8. White, *The Book of Beasts,* 77.

9. As suggested by Schnyder, *Sir Gawain*, 143.

10. Compare, for example, Perceval's entering the abode of the Fisher King in Chrétien's poem (ll. 3050-75); see also Robert W. Ackerman, "Castle Hautdesert in *Sir Gawain and the Green Knight,*" *Melanges de Langue et de Litterature du Moyen Age et de la Renaissance* (Geneva: Librarie Droz, 1970), 1:1-7, and the comments on the supernatural character of the Grail Castle in Jung et al., *The Grail Legend*, 66-7.

11. Davis in a note on pages 128-29 maintains that "desert" in Celtic languages had acquired a special sense of "hermitage."

12. A view advocated by Schnyder, *Sir Gawain*, 55.

13. As suggested by Levy, "Gawain's Spiritual Journey," 92.

14. A Middle English translation *The Pilgrimage of the Lyfe of the Manhode*, ed. Henry, 218.

15. *Sir Gawain*: "þe depe double dich þat drof to þe place" (786); *Pearl*: "Byȝonde þe broke, by slente oþer slade, I hoped þat mote merked wore" (141-42).

16. *The Pilgrimage*, 241-2.

17. After E. K. Chambers, *The Medieval Stage* (Oxford: Clarendon Press, 1903), 1:234-5.

18. Cf. Herzfeld, ed., *An Old English Martyrology*, 3: "as soon as he [Christ] was born, a heavenly light shone over the land ("heofonlic leoht scean ofer eall þoet land").

19. "De Nativitate Domini Nostri Ihesu Cristi," 14b, *Mirk's Festial: A Collection of Homilies, by Johannes Mirkus* (London: Oxford University Press, EETS, 1905).

20. Cf. Herzfeld, ed., *An Old English Martyrology,* 4-5.

21. Cf. Sylvan Barnett, "A Note on the Structure," 319.

22. Cf. Vincent F. Hopper, *Medieval Number Symbolism: Its Sources, Meaning, and Influence on Thought and Expression* (1938; reprint, New York: Cooper Square Publishers, 1969), 4-8; Eliade, ed., *The Encyclopedia of Religion*, vol. 11, s.v. "numbers."

23. "Per hoc etiam quod tertia die resurrexit, commendatur perfectio ternarii, qui est *numerus omnis rei*, utpote habens *principium, medium et finem*, ut dicitur in *de*

Coelo," Saint Thomas Aquinas, *Summa Theologiae,* trans. and ed. C. Thomas Moore (London: Blackfriars, 1976), 55:8.3a.53.2.

24. Plato, *Timaeus,* trans. H. D. P. Lee (Harmondsworth: Penguin, 1965), 69b-71a.

25. Ibid., 70-72.

26. Plato, *The Republic* (Harmondsworth: Penguin, 1985), 9. 580d-e.

27. Plato's tripartite division of the human soul lies at the root of a no less influential conception by Aristotle, who speaks of "the nutritive part, which is present both in the plants and in all the animals, and the perceptive part (present in animals in the five senses). Then there is the imaginative part" (Aristotle, *De Anima,* trans. H. Lawson-Tancred [Harmondsworth: Penguin, 1986], 3. 9.432a-b). Aristotle's version of the tripartite soul was commented upon, among others, by Dante in *Il Convivio,* 3.2. Plato's view was likewise frequently glossed by medieval commentators. For example, a ninth-century anonymous commentary on Boethius's *Consolatio Philosophiae* says that "the great world-soul, which moves the whole universe, is 'of triple nature': rational, appetitive, irascible" ("maxima mundi anima, que omnem mundum movet, 'triplicis nature' est: rationabilis, concupiscibilis, irascibilis," quoted after Peter Dronke, *Fabula: Explorations into the Uses of Myth in Medieval Platonism* [Leiden: E. J. Brill, 1974], 86). The idea received numerous commentaries in the glosses on the *Timaeus* during the Neoplatonic renaissance of the twelfth century (cf. Gregory, "Platonic Inheritance," 62), and eventually became standard medieval knowledge about man and his place in the natural order of things, as evidenced, for example, by extensive commentaries on the *vegetabilis, sensibilis,* and *racionalis* manners of the soul in John Trevisa's translation (1398) of the thirteenth-century *De Proprietatibus Rerum* by Bartholomaeus Anglicus (*On the Properties of Things,* ed. Seymour, *Liber Tertius, Capitulum* 1:6m-13m). Theologians and sermonists also subscribed to this ancient conception, as for example Aelfric (tenth century) in his *Lives of Saints:* "Philosophers say that the soul's nature is threefold: the first part in her is capable of desire, the second of anger, the third of reason. Two of these parts, beasts and cattle have in common with us, that is to say, desire and anger; man only hath reason and speech and intelligence" (*Aelfric's Lives of Saints, being a Set of Sermons on Saints' Days formerly observed by the English Church,* ed. Walter W. Skeat [1881; reprint, London: Oxford University Press, EETS, 1966], 1:18). In a similar way a fourteenth-century *Stanzaic Life of Christ,* ed. Foster, ll. 5989-92, attributes the three aspects of the soul to the three parts and substances of the body, heart, blood, and head:

> now is to wit in qvat plas
> his saule hade principal wonyng,
> ffor in thre stides so3t hit was
> In hert & hede & blode rennyng.

The doctrine of the tripartite soul is also fundamental to the understanding of the allegorical *psychomachia* depicted by Spenser in *The Faerie Queene,* especially in book 2 (on Temperance), in which the frequent pairing of the enemies of Sir Guyon (the rational soul) corresponds to the concupiscible and the irascible souls, constantly attacking the bastion of reason. The theme is also frequently used in Spenser's sonnets. Literary examples of the tripartite conception of the soul in medieval and Renaissance literature are indeed endless.

28. *Stobaeus* 2. 4-8, *Hermetica,* ed. and trans. Scott, vol. 1.

29. The conception of the tripartite soul in relation to Gawain's test was discussed by Reichardt, "Gawain and the Image of the Wound," 154-61.

30. *Aelfric's Lives of Saints.*

31. Saint Augustine, *Confessions*, ed. James J. O'Donnell (Oxford: Clarendon Press, 1992), 1:10.30-40.

32. *A Stanzaic Life of Christ*, ll. 5261-68.

33. Ibid., ll. 5272-84. Another instance of the popularity of the notion of the threefold sin in the Middle Ages is the fifteenth-century pageant *De Tentatione Salvatoris* (The Temptation of Christ), in which the Expositor brings home to the audience the nature of the threefold temptation:

> Since our forefather overcomen was
> By three thinges to doe evill:
> Gluttony, vayne glorye, there be twooe,
> Covetuousness of highnes alsoe,
> By these three thinges, without moe,
> Christ hath overcome the Devill.

(Peter Happé, ed., *English Mystery Plays*, 394ff.).

34. *Jacob's Well*, ed. Brandeis, 71. The fourteenth-century *Book of Vices and Virtues*, ed. Francis, 19, ll. 1-6, describes the pride of vainglory in the following way:

> veyn glorie, þat is fool likynge in vayn preisynges, whan a man feeleþ in his herte a gladnesse of a þyng þat he is, or wilneþ to be preised fore of any þyng þat he feeleþ in hymself or weneþ to haue or hap, and wilneþ to be preised of þyng þat he scholde þank God of.

35. Howard, *The Three Temptations*, 56ff.

36. Cf. Genesis 3:1-7. The theological *loci classici* for the conception of the three stages of sin are Saint Augustine, *Confessions*, 10.30-40; "De Sermone Domini in Monte Secundum Matthaeum," *Patrologia Latina*, ed. Migne, vol. 34, col. 1246: "Nam tria sunt quibus impletur peccatum; suggestione, delectatione, et consensione"; and also Gregory the Great, *Moralia*, 4.27; *Corpus Christianorum. Series Latinae*, ed. M. Adriaen (Brepols: Editores Pontificci, 1979), 143:193: "Nam serpens suasit, Eua delectata est, Adam consensit."

37. Benson, ed., *The Riverside Chaucer*, X(I), l. 330.

38. For Louis Blenkner, "Sin, Psychology, and Structure," esp. 357-80, the romance of Sir Gawain as a whole is structured on the "corporeal-spiritual-divine triad of redemption," which roughly corresponds to the threefold system discussed above.

39. Howard, *The Three Temptations*, 60.

40. Howard (ibid.) sees the concept of the three temptations as central to the genre of the *contemptu mundi*, and he offers also critical analyses of *Troilus and Criseyde*, *Piers Plowman*, and *Sir Gawain* with regard to the distinguished tripartite moral system.

41. Cf. Gregory, "The Platonic Inheritance," 62.

42. Gloss from the MS Digby 23, fol. 5r, published by P. E. Dutton, "*Illustre civitatis et populi exemplum*: Plato's *Timaeus* and the Transmission from Calcidius to the End of the Twelfth Century of a Tripartite Scheme of Society," *Mediaeval Studies* 45 (1983): 98; quoted also in Gregory, "The Platonic Inheritance," 62, n. 24.

43. Cf. *Timaeus* 86b-87b.

44. Plato *The Republic* 434d, 435b-e, 441d-e.

45. Georges Dumézil, *L'idéologie tripartie des Indo-Européens*, vol. 31 (Brussels: Collection Latomus, 1958); Bruce Lincoln, *Myth, Cosmos, and Society: Indo-European Themes of Creation and Destruction* (Cambridge: Harvard University Press, 1986), esp. 143-56. A Dumézilian approach to *Sir Gawain* has been offered by Strutynski, "*Honi Soit Qui Mal y Pense*: The Warrior Sins of Sir Gawain," 35-52.

(Cambridge: Harvard University Press, 1979). A similar composition of the society can be found in Hippodamus, *On a Republic, The Pythagorean Sourcebook and Library: An Anthology of Ancient Writings which Relate to Pythagoras and Pythagorean Philosophy*, ed. Fideler, 217.

47. Cf. Lincoln, *Myth, Cosmos, and Society,* 156.

48. The origin, literary structure, typology, and extensive exemplification of hunting as a literary motif is comprehensively discussed by Marcelle Thiébaux, *The Stag of Love: The Chase in Medieval Literature* (Ithaca: Cornell University Press, 1974).

49. ibid., 58.

50. *An Etymological Dictionary of the English Language*, ed. Walter W. Skeat (Oxford: Clarendon Press, 1983).

51. For example, *Passio Sancti Eustachi, Aelfric's Lives of Saints*, vol. 2, chap. 30, ll. 191-97.

52. The most influential medieval handbook of hunting was the *Livres du roy Modus et de la royne Ratio* by Henri de Ferriéres (ca. 1354-1376), ed. Tilander (Paris, 1932). From this treatise derives the *Livre de chasse* by Gaston Phebus, Count of Foix (1387), the work translated into English as *The Master of Game* by Edward of Norwich, Second Duke of York (ca. 1406-1413).

53. Edward, Second Duke of York, *The Master of Game: The Oldest English Book on Hunting*, ed. William A. and F. Baillie-Grohman (London: Chatto and Windus, 1909), 6-8.

54. Ibid., 11-12.

55. Ovid *Metamorphoses*, trans. Mary M. Innes (Harmondsworth: Penguin, 1971), 1.456ff.; 14.320ff.; *Remedia Amoris, The Erotic Poems*, trans. Peter Green (Harmondsworth: Penguin, 1988), 199ff.

56. Andreas Capellanus, *The Art of Courtly Love*, trans. J. J. Parry (1941; reprint, New York: W. W. Norton, 1969), esp. 89-90, 97.

57. Wolfram von Eschenbach, *Parzival*, trans. A. T. Hatto (Harmondsworth: Penguin, 1980), bk. 1, 41.

58. Chrétien de Troyes, *Erec et Enide*, ed. Mario Roques (Paris: Librairie Honoré Champion, 1966), ll. 581-668.

59. Cf. Davis, 76-77n.

60. Gottfried von Strassburg, *Tristan*, trans. A. T. Hatto (Harmondsworth: Penguin, 1987), esp. chap. 4.

61. It is worth noting that the English word *venery* is of double meaning and denotes both "hunting" (from OFr *venerie)*, and a "pursuit of sexual pleasure" (from Latin *Vener*, Venus), according to *The Oxford English Dictionary* (Oxford: Clarendon Press, 1961). See also Burrow, *A Reading of Sir Gawain*, 86.

62. Needless to say, the rules of courtly love are significantly reversed in the poem, with the lady acting as an active agent and a wooer, contrary to accepted standards. Cf. John F. Kiteley, "The *De Arte Honeste Amandi* of Andreas Capellanus and the Concept of Courtesy in *Sir Gawain and the Green Knight,"* Anglia 79 (1961): 7-16; also Maureen Fries, "The Characterization of Women in the Alliterative Tradition," in *The Alliterative Tradition in the Fourteenth Century*, ed. Bernard S. Levy and Paul E. Szarmach (Kent, Ohio: Kent State University Press, 1981), 25-45.

63. One of the three crude illustrations attached to the poem in the MS Cotton Nero A.x., reproduced on the frontispiece of Davis's edition, shows Gawain naked in bed under a quilt, with the lady standing by his side and touching his face.

64. Chrétien de Troyes, *Le Conte du Graal (Perceval),* ed. Felix Lecoy (Paris: Librairie Honoré Champion, 1975), ll. 7424-52.

65. Ibid., ll. 7563-630.

66. Chrétien de Troyes, *Le Chevalier de la charrette*, ed. Mario Roques (Paris: Les classiques francais, 1952), ll. 513-38.

67. See also *Le Chevalier a l'Epée: Two Old French Gauvain Romances*, eds. R. C. Johnston and D. D. R. Owen (Edinburgh: Scottish Academic Press, 1972), ll. 477ff.

68. Saint Augustine in *De Doctrina Christiana*, trans. D. W. Robertson (New York: Macmillan, 1958), 3.11.17, writes in connection with the Scripture that all descriptions of brutal and cruel forces are meant to "neutralize the power of cupidity" ("ad cupiditatis regnum destruendum ualet").

69. Gottfried von Strassburg, *Tristan,* ed. Peter Ganz (Wiesbaden: F. A. Brockhaus, 1978), ll. 16710ff.; cf. W. T. H. Jackson, *The Anatomy of Love: The Tristan of Gottfried von Strassburg* (New York: Columbia University Press, 1971), esp. 180-88.

70. Jung and von Franz, *The Grail Legend*, 391.

71. Ibid.

72. On idleness as the breeder of carnal sins in *Sir Gawain* see Scattergood, *"Sir Gawain and the Green Knight* and the Sins of the Flesh," 347-71.

73. Duke Edward, *Master of Game,* 6-8.

74. *The Riverside Chaucer,* 10(1), ll. 950-51.

75. Cf. Isaiah, 13:14. In the legend of Saint Giles (whose name appears in *Sir Gawain,* 1644), the tracked hind finds refuge in the cave inhabited by the saint, who is subsequently wounded by one of the archers; quoted after Robert J. Blanch, "Religion and Law in *Sir Gawain and the Green Knight,"* in *Approaches to Teaching Sir Gawain and the Green Knight,* ed. M. Y. Miller and I, Chance (New York: Modern Language Association of America, 1986), 96. Allegorically the cave is the body and the saint is a good Christian who suffers a wound as a sacrifice for the concupiscence of his flesh.

76. Cf. Kiteley, "The *De Arte Honeste Amandi."*

77.

> . . . Sir Wowen 3e are,
>
> þat alle þe worlde worchipez quere-so 3e ride;
> Your honour, your hendelayk *(courtliness)* is hendely praysed
> With lordez, wyth ladyes, with alle þat lyf bere.
>
> (1226-29)
>
> Bot hit ar ladyes inno3e þat leuer *(dearer)* wer nowþe
> Haf þe, hende, in hor holde, as I þe habbe here . . .
>
> (1251-52ff.)
>
> I haf hit holly in my honde þat al desyres.
>
> (1257)

78. The author of *Sir Gawain* was surely acquainted with the French Gawain romances, in which the knight is presented as amorous and lustful, in and out of bed with many damsels, including fairies; cf. Albert B. Friedman, "Morgan le Fay in *Sir Gawain and the Green Knight,"* in *Sir Gawain and Pearl: Critical Essays,* ed. Blanch, 143-45. This type of the figure also fits the character of a lecherous knight from Chaucer's *Wife of Bath's Tale.*

79. For example, Johnston and Owen, eds., *Le Chevalier a l'Epée,* ll. 480ff..

80. Cf. Henry L. Savage, "The Significance of the Hunting Scenes in *Sir Gawain and the Green Knight," Journal of English and Germanic Philology* 27 (1928): 1-15; Speirs, *"Sir Gawain,"* 274-300; Gerald Gallant, "The Three Beasts—Symbols of Temptation in *Sir Gawain and the Green Knight," Annuale Mediaevale* 11 (1970): 35-50; Peter McClure, "Gawain's *Mesure,"* 375-87; Gerald Morgan, "The Action of the Hunting and Bedroom Scenes in *Sir Gawain and the Green Knight," Medium Aevum* 56, no. 2 (1987): 200-216.

81.

> Bi God, I were glad, and yow god þoȝt,
> At saȝe *(word)* oþer at seruyce þat I sette myȝt
> To þe plesaunce of your prys—hit were a pure ioye.
>
> (1245-47)

82.

> Bot I am proude of þe prys þat ȝe put on me,
> And, soberly your seruaunt, my souerayn I holde yow,
> And yowre knyȝt I becom, and Kryst yow forȝelde.
>
> (1277-79)

83. Cf. Nicholls, *The Matter of Courtesy*, esp. 115.

84. Donner, "Tact as a Criterion," 311.

85. Upon parting at Camelot: "Andþay hym kyst and conueyed *(escorted)* bikende *(commending)* hym to Kryst" (596); upon meeting the old lady at Hautdesert: "He [Gawain] kysses hir comlyly, and knyȝtly he melez *(speaks)*" (974); when parting at the first evening at Hautdesert: "þay [Gawain and Sir Bertilac] stoden and stemed *(hesitated)* and stylly *(softly)* speken, kysten ful comlyly and kaȝten *(took)* her leue" (1117-18); when parting with the ladies on the third day: "With care and wyth kyssyng he carppez hem till *(to)*" (1979); while saying goodbye to the Green Knight at the Green Chapel: "þay acolen and kyssen and kennen *(commend)* ayþer oþer to þe prynce of paradise" (2472-73); while greeting Arthur after returning to Camelot: "þe kyng kysses þe knyȝt" (2492).

86. "He [Gawain] hasppez his [the host's] fayre hals *(neck)* his armez wythinne, / And kysses hym as comlyly as he couþe awyse *(devise)*" (1388-89).

87. For example, "slyt" (1330); "schaued *(scrapped)*" (1331); "rytte *(cut)*," "rent" (1332); "brek" and "out token" (1333); "walt out *(flung out)*" (1336); "scher . . . out *(cut out)*" (1337); "haled *(drew)*" (1338); "britned *(cut up)*" and "brayden *(pulled)*" (1339); "ryuez hit vp *(rip up)*" (1341); "voydez out *(pull out)*" (1342); "lance *(cut)*" (1343, 1350); "ryde . . . of *(clear away)*" (1344); "euenden *(trimmed)*" (1345); "heuen hit vp *(heave up)*" and "hwen *(hewed)*" (1346, 1353); "hewe" (1351); "vnbynde *(cut)*" (1352); "sunder" (1354); "þurled *(pierced)*" (1356).

88.

> here is wayth *(venison)* fayrest
> þat I seȝ þis seuen ȝere in sesoun of wynter
>
> (1381-82)

89.

> Who bryngez vus þis beuerage, þis bargayn is maked:
> So sayde þe lorde of þat lede *(people);* þay laȝed vchone,
> þay dronken and daylyeden *(talked courteously)* and dalten
> *(revelled)* vntyȝtel *(unrestrained)*,
>
> (1112-14);

and on the second day:

> And efte in her *(their)* bourdyng *(jesting)* þay bayþen *(agreed)* in þe morn
> To fylle þe same forwardez *(agreement)* þat þay byfore maden
> . . . .
> þe beuerage watz broȝt forth in bourde at þat tyme,
>
> (1404-5, 1409).

90. The cock is a symbol of Peter's triple denial of Jesus and of his subsequent remorse for his faithless conduct (Mark 14:30; John 13:38). On New Year's morning

Gawain's sleep is disturbed again by the cockcrow (2008), suggesting—according to Blanch, "Religion and Law," 96—Doomsday and a promise of spiritual renewal
91.

> On þe *(one of the)* sellokest *(extraordinary)* swyn swenged *(rushed)*
> out þere,
> Long sythen fro þe sounder *(herd)* þat siȝed *(went)* for olde
> *(because of the age)*,
> For he watz breme *(fierce)*, bor alþer-grattest *(greatest of all)*
>
> (1439-41)

92. Duke Edward, *Master of Game*, 46-47.
93.

> [Sir Bertilac] Set sadly þe scharp in þe slot euen,
> Hit hym vp to þe hult *(hilt)*, þat þe hert schyndered.
>
> (1593-94)

94. The proposed significance of the boar's head in the context of Gawain's tests is here of course superimposed on a widespread medieval custom, evidently of pagan provenance, of killing a wild boar at Christmas and serving its head at the feast. The popularity of the custom is borne out by numerous medieval Boar's Head Carols sung at Christmastime; for example, Robbins, ed., *Secular Lyrics*, nos. 47-8; Davies, ed., *Medieval English Lyrics*, no.169; Sisam and Sisam, eds., *The Oxford Book of Medieval English Verse*, no. 254.

95. The *MED* lists the following classes of meaning under the entry "game:" 1. Joy, happiness, pleasure, delight; 2. Festivity, revelry, a pastime; 3. The sports of hunting, fishing, or hawking; 4. Amorous play, love-making; 5. A contest, battle, also (fig.) the success or prize in a contest; 6. A joke, jest; 7. An action, happening; 8. Game animals, birds, or fish, esp. game killed or caught. Any of these meanings substituted for *gomen* in Bertilac's statement "þis gomen is your awen" can yield an intriguing result.

96.

> Make we mery quyl we may and mynne *(think)* vpon joye,
> For þe lur *(sorrow)* may mon lach *(catch)* when-so mon lykez.
>
> (1681-82)

97. Thiébaux, *The Stag of Love,* 82-84, suggests that the description of the fox hunt in *Sir Gawain* was influenced by a devotional work, *Le Livre de Seyntz Medicines*, written by Henry of Lancaster in 1354 and employing popular alegorical significances of the fox (see also Marcelle Thiébaux, "Sir Gawain, the Fox Hunt, and Henry of Lancaster," *Neuphilologische Mitteilungen* 71, no. 3 [1970]: 469-79).

98. Cf. Savage, "The Significance of the Hunting Scenes," 4-6.

99. ". . . a false beast and as malicious as a wolf" (Duke Edward, *Master of Game,* 64).

100. The *Physiologus,* an encyclopedia of animals, birds, stones, etc., both real and fantastic, their properties and moral significances, was first composed in Greek, 2d century a.d., in Alexandria. It was translated into Latin by Theobald, Abbot of Monte Cassino in the eleventh century, and later into Middle English (ca. 1300). See *The Middle English Physiologus*, ed. Hanneke Wirtjes (Oxford: Oxford University Press, EETS, no. 299, 1991).

101. *The Middle English Physiologus,* 11, ll. 268-80.

102.

> þe deuel dereþ *(injures)* dernelike *(stealthily)*:
> He lat *(pretends)* he ne wile us noȝt biswike *(deceive)*,
> He lat he ne wile us don non loþ *(harm)*

þe deuel dereþ *(injures)* dernelike *(stealthily)*:
He lat *(pretends)* he ne wile us noȝt biswike *(deceive)*,
He lat he ne wile us don non loþ *(harm)*
& bringeþ us in a sinne & ter he us sloþ.

. . . .

þe deuel is tus þe fox ilik,
Miþ iuele breides *(tricks)* & wiþ swik *(deception)*.

> *(The Middle English Physiologus,* ll. 285-88; 301-2)

103. In *Le Livre de Seyntz Medicines* by Henry of Lancaster the figure representing Sloth and Idleness is the female fox, the mother of vices (after Thiébaux, *The Stag of Love,* 82).

104.

Hir þryuen *(fair)* face and hir þrote þrowen al naked,
Hir brest bare bifore, and bihinde eke *(also)*.

> (1740-41)

105.

For þat prynces of pris depresed *(importuned)* hym so þikke,
Nurned *(urged)* hym so neȝe þe þred, þat nede hym bihoued
Oþer to lach *(take)* þer hir luf, oþer lodly *(offensively)* refuse.
He cared for his cortaysye, lest craþayn *(churl)* he were,

> (1770-73)

106. Udo Strutynski, *"Honi Soit Qui Mal y Pense,"* 45-50, sees in the series of the three gifts a reflection of the Dumézilian tripartite socioreligious structure whereby the ring, described as "costly," would correspond to the third, lowest social stratum and function (the commoners) and be responsible for fertility and material well-being; the glove as part of military equipment is linked with the second social function, warfare, while the girdle with its magical properties is related to the first function, the religious and legal (priesthood). Accordingly the *Gawain*-poet is seen by Strutynski to be using the "Indo-European formulaic expression," and in undergoing a triple trial Gawain "represented not only his caste but his people as a whole." See also Laila Gross, "Gawain's Acceptance of the Girdle," *American Notes and Queries* 12 (1973-74): 154-55.

107. Saint Thomas Aquinas, *Summa Theologiae*, 1.2. q. 94, art. 2.

108. In medieval animal imagery the fox is a popular symbol of the sin of covetousness *(avaritia)*, regarded as the "rote of all synnes," for "ße coueytous man is as a fox," according to the treastise *Jacob's Well,* chap. 18, 118.

109. "Corsed worth cowarddyse and coueṭyse boþe!" (2374). Cf. David Farley Hills, "Gawain's Fault in *Sir Gawain and the Green Knight,*" *Review of English Studies* 14 (1963): 124-31.

110. Howard, *The Three Temptations,* 240, absolves Gawain completely on the above grounds and calls his trespass not so much a sin but "an indiscretion."

Chapter 6. The Head and the Loss Thereof

1. The beheading as a traditional motif has been discussed in a comparative perspective by Kittredge, *A Study of Gawain,* esp. 9-75, 147-94; Buchanan, "The Irish Framework of *Sir Gawain,*" 315-38; Larry D. Benson, "The Source of the Beheading Episode in *Sir Gawain and the Green Knight,*" *Modern Philology* 59 (1961): 1-12; and Benson, *Art and Tradition,* passim.

2. Hans Schnyder, "Aspects of Kingship in *Sir Gawain and the Green Knight*," *English Studies* 40 (1959): 289-94, discusses the poem's presentation of Arthur's court in the context of the sin of royal *superbia* (pride), leading to the degeneration of the state, also illustrated by Belshezzar Feast from *Purity*, a poem from the same manuscript as *Sir Gawain*.

3. See examples quoted by Davis in his note on p. 76.

4. The Feast of Fools, commonly called *festum stultorum, festum fatuorum,* or *festum follorum*, consisted of New Year revels in the medieval Church organized by vicars and subdeacons. As a rule the feast focused on the Circumcision (1 January), though at times it could be performed on the Epiphany (6 January) as well. The idea centered on the inversion of status and the burlesque performance of religious ceremonies of the priests and bishops by inferior clergy: abuses such as preaching obscenities, playing dice on the altar, or dancing, eating, and drinking in the church were rampant. Understandably, the feast was condemned by ecclesiastical authorities for its licentiousness and sacrilegious character, but it continued to be widely practiced until the Reformation (Chambers, *The Medieval Stage*, vol. 1, 275ff.). The *festum subdiaconorum* has been discussed in connection with a passing reference to the mass held at Camelot on 1 January in *Sir Gawain* (63) by Henry L. Savage, "The Feast of Fools in *Sir Gawain and the Green Knight*," *Journal of English and Germanic Philology* 51 (1952): 537-44.

5. These could include agricultural customs, sacrificial rites, the Christmas hunt, exchange of roles, renewal of fire, commemoration of ancestors, divination, giving presents, and general playfulness (Chambers, *The Medieval Stage*, 249-70).

6. In relation to the Green Knight's challenge, Sheri Ann Strite ("*Sir Gawain and the Green Knight:* To Behead or Not to Behead—That *is* a Question," *Philological Quarterly* 70, no. 1 [1991]: 1-12), has developed an interesting, but to my view erroneous, theory that what the challenger demands in the stated rules is not in fact an exchange of *beheading* blows (there being no specific mention of decapitation in the text, ll. 287, 294-95, 382), but simply an exchange of blows ("strike a strok for an oþer," 287). According to Strite the challenge is ambiguous, and it is up to Gawain to decide and define its terms. Gawain, however, responds in accordance with traditional romance conventions and chops off the man's head. A possible alternative course of action for Gawain, suggests Strite, would have been to follow Christian values, more appropriate for a Christmas game, and to deal the Green Knight "a merciful stroke which might have warranted a merciful stroke in return" (7). Notwithstanding the fact that the return blow is in fact a "merciful" one, because it leaves Gawain alive after all, one wonders what kind of a "merciful stroke" Strite would have imagined to be dealt with the huge battle-axe provided by the Green Knight at Camelot. To "strike a strok" with such a weapon could hardly involve anything less than a serious and potentially lethal wound.

7. The symbolic significance of the beheading proposal and the following magical survival of the Green Knight are belittled in what I regard as a naive, literal approach to the problem of the supernatural in *Sir Gawain* exhibited by Martin Puhvel in "Art and the Supernatural in *Sir Gawain and the Green Knight*." Any possible deeper significance of the beheading scene evaporates when "one could speculate that Gawain's challenger may have been fitted out with an artificial, detachable head" (17).

8. By way of analogy one recalls the "merry bond" made between Shylock and Antonio in Shakespeare's *Merchant of Venice* (1.3.144-51, 173); a covenant that began "in a merry sport" ended in earnest as a legally binding contract of potentially fatal consequences for the losing party.

9. Jonassen, "Elements from the Traditional Drama of England," 221-54; cf. also Burrow, *A Reading of Sir Gawain,*" 22.

10. Chambers, *The Medieval Stage,* 249-70.

11. Cf. Lord Raglan, *The Hero,* 150, 186; Robert Graves, *The White Goddess: A Historical Grammar of Poetic Myth* (London: Faber and Faber, 1952), 177-80; see also Graves, *Greek Myths* (Harmondsworth: Penguin, 1977), passim. The widespread ancient practice of the annual sacrifice of the king is discussed in detail in a monumental work by Sir James G. Frazer, *The Golden Bough: A Study in Magic and Religion* (London: Macmillan, 1913), passim.

12. Ibid.

13. For example, Loomis, *Celtic Myth,* esp. 63-66; Weston, *The Legend of Sir Gawain,* esp. 13-24.

14.

> Hardemens et force doubloit
> Toz jors puisque none sonoit,
> Ce sachiez, monseignor Gavain;
> Tot en devez estre certain.
> Dusqu'a le nuit que jors faloit
> Icele force li duroit.
> Et de mienuit en avant
> Li redoubloit tot autretant
> Et li duroit dusqu'al matin,
> Et puis li tornoit a declin
> Tant que venoit a miedi.

(19139-49)

(The Continuations of the Old French Perceval of Chrétien de Troye: The First Continuation, ed. Roach, 1:331)

15. *Le Morte Arthur,* ed. J. D. Bruce (London: EETS, 1903), stanza 352, ll. 1-6. Thomas Malory, in *The Tale of King Arthur* (Malory, *Works,* ed. Vinaver, chap. 6, [19] ll. 18-24) also mentions this curious feature of Gawain's:

> But sir Gawayne, fro hit was nine of the clok, wexed ever strenger and strenger, for by than hit cam to the howre of noone he had three tymes his myght encresed. . . . So whan hit was past noone, and whan it drew toward evynsonge, sir Gawayns strength fyebled and woxe passyng faynte. . . .

16. Weston, *The Legend,* 13.

17. For example, in *The Alliterative Morte Arthur,* ed. Krishna, a romance roughly contemporaneous with *Sir Gawain,* Arthur laments the death of Gawain on the battlefield by emphasizing his nephew's virtues and worthiness to be king:

> þan the corownde kyng cryes fulle lowde,
> "Dere kosyne o kynde, in kare am I leuede,
> ffor nowe my wirchipe es wente and my wele endite;
> Here es the hope of my hele, my happynge of armes—
> My herte and my hardynes hale on hym lengede,
> My concell, my comforthe, þat kepide myne herte.
> Of alle knyghtes þe kynge þat vndir Criste lifede,
> *þou was worthy to be kynge,* þofe I the corowne bare;
> Me wele and my wirchipe of alle þis werlde riche
> Was wonnene thourghe Sir Gawayne, and thourghe his witt one.

(3955-64, italics added)

18. I disagree with Burrow, *A Reading of Sir Gawain,* 11, when he says on this occasion that "the sense of individual predestination or election is entirely absent in *Sir Gawain:* one does not feel that the beheading adventure, when the Green Knight

proposes it, is for Gawain alone in any mysterious fashion." In my opinion it is Gawain's sense of honor and responsibility for the Round Table, as well as his close kinship with Arthur, that specifically prompt him to accept the game.

19. Davis in a note on p. 86 translates this phrase simply as "you will survive the blow."

20.

> 'Where schulde I wale *(find)* þe,' quoþ Gauan, 'where is þy place?
> I wot neuer where þou wonyes *(live)*, bi hym þat me wroȝt,
> Ne I know not þe, knyȝt, þy cort ne þi name.
> Bot teche me truly þerto, and telle me how þou hattes . . .'

(398-401)

21. This hermeneutic procedure is theoretically described by Andrzej Wiercinski, "Symbol and Symbolization," *Ethnologia Polona* 9 (1983): 33-44.

22. This is a revised version of a similar table presented in my article "The Symbolic Function of the Human Head and Decapitation among the Ancient Celts," *Kwartalnik Neofilologiczny* 37, no. 4 (1990): 327-42.

23. For example, in many anthropomorphic creation myths of traditional cultures the sky vault is often described as being formed out of the head of some primeval giant, the stars out of his hair, the sun and the moon from the giant's two eyes, and so forth. See for example the story of the giant Ymir in Scandinavian mythology (Hilda R. E. Davidson, *Gods and Myths of Northern Europe* [Harmondsworth: Penguin, 1981], 198-202).

24. The *MED*, s.v. "hed" (1, 2), and "heden."

25. *The Pythagorean Sourcebook and Library: An Anthology of Ancient Writings which Relate to Pythagoras and Pythagorean Philosophy*, trans. K. S. Guthrie; ed. David R. Fideler (Grand Rapids, Mich.: Phanes Press, 1987), 226, 311. A highly popular medieval encyclopedic source, Bartholomaeus Anglicus's *De Proprietatibus Rerum*, links the seven apertures of the human head with the seven planets, and likewise stresses the roundness and hardness of the head (*On the Properties of Things*, 1:168-72).

26. The Renaissance drew abundantly on Neoplatonic cosmological imagery, as evidenced by Hamlet, who promises to "remember" the ghost of his father "whiles memory holds a seat in this distracted globe," meaning his head (*Hamlet*, 1.5.96-97).

27. Plato *Timaeus* 44e (Penguin ed.).

28. *Corpus Hermeticum, Libellus*, 10.11 in *Hermetica*, ed. Scott, vol. 1.

29. Cf. Gregory, "The Platonic Inheritance," 78. See also Wetherbee, "Philosophy, Cosmology, and the Twelfth-Century Renaissance," esp. 25-26.

30. Cf. *Asclepius*, 1. 7a, 10, 11a; 3. 18b, 23b in *Hermetica*, ed. Scott. It is possible that this Platonic idea is responsible for the motif of the "winged head," representing the soul or an angel, often found in medieval and Renaissance iconography.

31. *The "Holy Scriptures": A New Translation from the Original Languages* (Hampton Wick, Kingston-on-Thames: Stow Hill Bible and Tract Depot, 1967). See also Ephesians 4:15-16; 5:23; Colossians 2:19. The fourteenth-century *Book of Vices and Virtues*, ed. Francis, 144, ll. 28-30, repeats the same idea: "we beþ alle membres of o body, wher-of Ihesu Crist is þe heued, and we ben þe membres." In the "Last Supper" play from the *Ludus Coventriae* 27 mystery cycle, Christ again compares his head to Godhead, and his feet to his humanity:

> Be the hed ye xal undyr-stand my godhed,
> And be the feet ye xal take myn humanyte.

(Happé, ed., *English Mystery Plays*, 406-7).

32. Saint Augustine, *De doctrina Christiana*, 3.31.44.

33. Andreas Capellanus, *The Art of Courtly Love*, 138.

34. All references to alchemical texts are from Jung, *Mysterium Coniunctionis*, 434.

35. *Theatrum Chemicum* (Ursel, 1602), 5:151, quoted after Jung, *Mysterium Coniunctionis*, 435.

36. *Theatrum Chemicum*, 2:525, quoted after Jung, *Mysterium Coniunctionis*, 436. Albertus Magnus's idea of the human head molded in "God's image and likeness" can be related to 1 Corinthians 11:7: "For man indeed ought not to cover his head, forasmuch as he is the image and glory of God."

37. Anne Ross, "The Human Head in Insular Pagan Celtic Religion," *Proceedings of the Society of Antiquaries of Scotland* 91 (1957-58, 1960): 10-43; idem, *Pagan Celtic Britain: Studies in Iconography and Tradition* (London: Routledge and Kegan Paul, 1967), esp. 62-120; Kenneth H. Jackson, *The Oldest Irish Tradition: A Window on the Iron Age* (Cambridge: Cambridge University Press, 1964), 35-37; Sadowski, "The Symbolic Function of the Human Head."

38. The relevant texts are discussed in the sources listed in n. 37.

39. *Mandeville's Travels*, ed. M. C. Seymour (Oxford: Oxford University Press, 1967), chap. 12, 78.

40. E. J. Martin, *The Trial of the Templars* (London: G. Allen and Unwin, 1928), 201-2; C. G. Addison, *The Knights Templars* (London: Longman, 1852) 242.

41. The word *croun* is deliberately used in the line because it does not stand in an alliterative position ("His longe louelych lokkez he layd ouer his croun," 419) and is not therefore forced by metrical exigency, as is often the case with the word *hed* (e.g., "fayre h ede fro þe h alce," 427, "his h ede by þe h ere in his h one h aldez," 436, 444, 458).

42. *MED*, s.v. "coroune."

43. For example, the most famous classical severed head belonged to Orpheus, who was dismembered by the meanads. His head was thrown into the river Hebros, where it sang as it flowed downstream. The head was later laid in a cave devoted to Dionysus, where it uttered prophecies and was for some time a rival oracle to the one of Apollo at Delphi (Graves, *The Greek Myths*, chap. 28). The speaking and prophesying heads are common in Celtic and Scandinavian mythological traditions (cf. J. A. MacCulloch, *Celtic Mythology*, in *The Mythology of All Races*, vol. 3 (New York: Cooper Square Publishers, 1964), esp. 104-5; Ross, *Pagan Celtic Britain*, 61ff.; Davidson, *Gods and Myths of Northern Europe*, 166ff.).

44. Francis P. Magoun, Jr., regards the kicking of the Green Knight's rolling head as an instance of "medieval football" with the human head, of which several other gruesome examples from English literature he quotes (*"Sir Gawain* and Medieval Football," *English Studies* 19 [1937]: 208-9).

45. A similar reliance on magical lore in coping with the supernatural enemy is called upon in Spenser's *Faerie Queene,* book 2, where Arthur fights single-handedly a decisive battle with Malager, a monstrous captain of the troops besieging the Castle of Alma (canto 11). The creature could not be defeated by ordinary weapons and mere physical force, because each time he fell on the ground his strength was renewed and he sprang up with full vigor. Arthur then remembered (stanza 45) that the earth was the mother of all creatures, and each time they fell into her womb she would restore their lives. So he raised Malager into the air, crushed his body with his hands, and carried him on his shoulders until he died. This episodes illustrates that in addition to conventional military means it is sometimes necessary, when dealing with a super-

natural being, to resort to magic, and for this reason magical lore is also a part of chivalric practice (Edmund Spenser, *The Faerie Queene*, ed. A. C. Hamilton [London: Longman, 1990], bk. 2, canto 11).

46. The relevant texts are listed in Davis, xvi-xvii, and are discussed at length by Benson, *Art and Tradition*, 11ff., and by the same author in "The Source of the Beheading Episode," 1-12. See also Kittredge, *A Study of Gawain*, 9-75, 147-94. The passages illustrating the Beheading Game translated from medieval texts are also given in Elizabeth Brewer, ed., *From Cuchulainn to Gawain: Sources and Analogues of Sir Gawain and the Green Knight* (Cambridge: D. S. Brewer, 1973).

47. *Caradoc*, ll. 3404-9, MS Paris, Bibliothèque National 12567, in *The Continuations of the Old French Perceval of Chrétien de Troyes: The First Continuation*, vol. 1.

48. *Le Tresplaisante et Recreative Hystoire du trespreux et vaillant chevallier Perceval le galloys* (Paris, 1530), and reprinted in Benson, *Art and Tradition*, 249-57.

49. One may recall that Sir Gawain is also "of wyt feblest" (354), as he describes himself, which in the context of his handling of the Beheading Game may acquire an unexpected, true meaning.

50. Benson, *Art and Tradition*, 252-53. In the Montpellier MS of *Le Livre de Caradoc* the head is replaced with a rapidity almost too great for the eye to follow: "Et li cors li suit de si pres / Qu'ains que nus garde s'en soit prise / R'a li cors sa teste reprise" (*Perceval le Gallois, ou le Conte du Graal*, ed. Ch. Potvin, Mons., 1866-71, ll. 12592-885, reprinted in Kittredge, *A Study of Sir Gawain*, 29).

51. "*La Mule sanz Frain*," ed. R. T. Hill, Ph.D. diss., 1911, and B. Orlowski, *La Demoselle a la Mule* (Paris, 1911); discussed also in Kittredge, *A Study of Sir Gawain*, 42-51. The edition used here comes from Johnston and Owen, eds., *Two Old French Gauvain Romances*.

52. *Perlesvaus: Le Haut Livre du Graal*, ed. William A. Nitze and T. Atkinson Jenkins 2 vols. (Chicago: University of Chicago Press, 1932-37); trans. Nigel Bryant as *Perlesvaus: The High Book of the Grail* (Cambridge: D. S. Brewer, 1978).

53. *Le Haut Livre du Graal*, vol. 1, ll. 2913-18, p. 138; Bryant, *Perlesvaus*, 90-91.

54. Heinrich von dem Türlin, *Diu Crône*, ed. Gottlob H. F. Scholl (Stuttgart, 1852; Amsterdam: Editions Rodopi, 1966), ll. 13004-185.

55. *Hunbaut: Altfranzösischer Arturroman des XIII Jahrhunderts*, ed. J. Stürzinger (Dresden: Gesellschaft für romanische Literatur, 1914). The Beheading Game occupies lines 1460 to 1539. The story is analyzed in Kittredge, *A Study of Gawain*, 61-65, and the relevant beheading episode is translated in Brewer, *From Cuchulainn to Gawain*, 43-45.

56. For example, in the prototypal beheading story from the Old Irish eleventh-century saga *Fled Bricrend* (The Feast of Bricriu), trans. George Henderson (London: David Nutt, Irish Text Society, 1899), 125, Cu Chulainn on one occasion attempted to do precisely this with his adversary's severed head:

> Whereupon Cuchulainn sprang toward him and dealt him a blow with the axe, hurling his head to the top rafter of the Red Branch till the whole hall shook. Cuchulainn again caught up the head and gave it a blow with the axe and smashed it.

57. Kittredge, *A Study of Gawain*, 64, 147ff.

58. "The times has been, that when the brains were out the man would die, and there an end," deliberates Macbeth, terrified at the sight of Banquo's ghost (*Macbeth*, 3.4.77-79).

59. *Aelfric's Lives of Saints*, ed. Skeat, vol. 2, ll. 297-9.

60. "God allowed him [St John the Baptist] to suffer in this lower world such an ignominious and disgraceful death, that he wanted to lead him in the upper world to that glory which nobody can explain to mankind." Herzfeld, ed., *An Old English Martyrology*, 157. In Mark 6:16, when Herod heard about Jesus' preaching and good works, he exclaimed: "It is John, whom I beheaded: he is risen from the dead."

61. For example, the ninth-century *Vita Sancti Gildae de Rhyus*, ed. Hugh Williams (London, 1899), discussed in James E. Doan, "A Structural Approach to Celtic Saints' Lives," in *Celtic Folklore and Christianity: Studies in Memory of William W. Heist*, ed. Patrick K. Ford (Los Angeles: McNally and Loftin, 1983), 23-24.

62. For example, Dame Lyonett in Malory's *Tale of Sir Gareth of Orkney That Was Called Bewmaynes*, in Malory, *Works,* ed. Vinaver, chaps. 22-23. See also C. Grant Loomis, *White Magic: An Introduction to the Folklore of Christian Legend* (Cambridge, Mass.: Medieval Academy of America, 1948), 83-84.

63. Burrow, *A Reading of Sir Gawain*, 192-93. The author quotes the most widely read version of the legend, the *Vita Secunda* by Robert, Prior of Shrewsbury (mid-twelfth century). According to the source Winifred chose death by decapitation rather than faithlessness to her vow of chastity, and was as a result beheaded by Caradoc, Prince of Wales, just outside a chapel where mass was in progress. A holy hermit at the church called Bewnow took her head, put it on the body, and prayed to God to raise the girl to life again.

64. *De Solempnitate Sancte Weneffrede* (1026-46), in *Mirk's Festial,* 103a.

65. Burrow, *A Reading of Sir Gawain,* 193-94.

66. The "new head" as a metaphor of new life and immortality crops up in a poem by Sir Walter Ralegh, "The Passionate Man's Pilgrimage," *English Renaissance Poetry*, ed. John Williams (Fayetteville: University of Arkansas Press, 1990), 154, composed shortly before the poet's execution. Ralegh makes a final plea to God to supply him with "an everlasting head" when his mortal head is cut off:

> Just at the stroke, when my veins start and spread,
> Set on my soul an everlasting head!

67. The symbolic homology between the octave of Christmas and human life is borne out by John Mirk (early fifteenth century) in his homily *De Circumcisione Domini Nostri, Ihesu Cristi* (28a,b), in *Mirk's Festial,* 46-47: the first three days (25-27 December) correspond to man's birth (conception, delivery, wretched state of the newborn), the fourth day (28 December) stands for life itself, lived in the shadow of death, the last four (29 December-1 January) represent death (decay of the body, the parting of the soul, the Last Judgment, and heavenly bliss).

68.
> Bot wylde wederez of þe worlde wakned þeroute,
> Clowdes kesten *(press)* kenly þe colde to þe erþe,
> Wyth ny3e *(bitterness)* innoghe of þe norþe, þe naked to tene;
> þe snawe snitered *(came down)* ful snart *(bitterly)*, þat snayped *(nipped)* þe wylde;
> þe werbelande wynde wapped *(blew)* fro þe hy3e,
> And drof vche dale ful of dryftes ful grete.

(2000-2005)

69.
> þere watz much derue doel *(grievous lament)* driuen in þe sale
> þat so worthe as Wawan schulde wende on þat ernde,
> To dry3e *(endure)* a delful dynt *(grievous blow)*, and dele no more wyth bronde

(sword).

(558-61)

70. As is known, the guide tries to dissuade Gawain from going to meet the Green Knight, "þe worst vpon erþe" (2098) because this means sure death ("Com ȝe þere, ȝe be kylled," 2111). The guide even swears upon God and all saints that he will never let on if Gawain flees in a cowardly fashion from the man in green (2121-25), a proposal amounting to nothing less than sacrilegious perjury to conceal Gawain's possible cowardice. This is yet one more test of the knight's courage and sense of honor, one that finds Sir Gawain only too determined to meet his "wyrde" (2134). Cf. Paul Delany, "The Role of the Guide in *Sir Gawain and the Green Knight,*" *Neophilologus* 49 (1965): 250-55.

71. Cf. Douglas Gray, *Themes and Images in the Medieval English Religious Lyric* (London: Routledge and Kegan Paul, 1972), 176-220.

72.

> . . . ryde me *doun* þis ilk rake (*path*) bi ȝon rokke syde
> . . . þenne loke a littel on þe launde, *on þi lyfte honde,*

(2144, 2146, italics added)

73. Cf. Puhvel, "Art and the Supernatural in *Sir Gawain,*" 48-51. An attempt to locate the Green Chapel physically (in my opinion quite unnecessary in view of the clearly symbolic significance of the place), has been offered, among others, by R. E. Kaske, "Gawain's Green Chapel and the Cave at Welton Mill," in *Medieval Literature and Folklore Studies* (New Brunswick: Rutgers University Press, 1970): 111-21.

74. Cf. J. R. Hulbert, "Syr Gawayn and the Grene Knyȝt," *Modern Philology* 13, no. 8 (1915): 457-58; no. 12 (1916): 705; Thomas F. O'Rahilly, *Early Irish History and Mythology* (Dublin: Institute for Advanced Studies, 1976), esp. 120-30.

75. "Here myȝt aboute mydnyȝt / þe dele (*devil*) his matynnes telle!" (2186-87); "deuocion on þe deuelez wyse" (2192); "a chapel of meschaunce" (2195); "þe corsedest kyrk" (2196). Mills, "Christian Significance and Romance Tradition," 91, relates Gawain's adventure at the Green Chapel to Perceval's visits to "la chapele Saint Augustin" and "li chastiax du Noir hermite" from the Second and Third Continuations of Chrétien's *Perceval,* respectively, and in both cases the place is identified with hell.

76. M. A. Carson, "The Green Chapel: Its Meaning and Function," *Studies in Philology* 60 (1963): 247, suggests in this connection that this second, complementary meaning of the Green Chapel may be related to the Old French word *chapler,* "to cut down, to cut into pieces, to fight, to massacre," so that the place would also have been understood as a "slaughterhouse." In my opinion this association is not altogether improbable for the audience of *Sir Gawain,* at least partly familiar with the French language and literature and the interpretative ambivalence thus achieved well suits the complex meaning of the Green Chapel as a place of violent death and the subsequent rebirth.

77. Cf. Mircea Eliade, *Birth and Rebirth: The Religious Meanings of Initiation in Human Culture,* trans. Willard R. Trask (London: Harvill Press, 1961), esp. 36ff.

78. Cf. Colossians 3:5-11; Ephesians 4:22-24.

79. *De Circumcisione Domini Nostri, Ihesu Cristi,* in *Mirk's Festial,* 276. See also a poem by John Audelay (early fifteenth century) called in Latin "De effusione sanguinis Christi in remissione peccatorum," in which Christ shed his blood seven times for the remission of the seven sins of humanity, with the Circumcision corresponding appropriately to lechery (*The Poems of John Audelay,* ed. Whiting, 50).

80. The associations between the Circumcision, the Resurrection, and the Baptism are aptly made by Saint Augustine in *Hypnogosticon,* in *Patrologia Latina,* ed. Migne, 45:5.5.1653: "Circumcisio enim illa octava diei, figuram resurrectionis diei

Salvatoris et gratiam Baptismi gestabat." The idea that Circumcision is a figure of the Baptism appears also in Saint Thomas Aquinas, *Summa Theologica*, 3a, g.70, art. 1: "Circumcisio autem erat sacramentum, et praeparatorium ad baptismum. . . ." References to the Feast of the Circumcision in medieval ecclesiastical sources are discussed in Levy, "Gawain's Spiritual Journey," 70-76. The Circumcision and Baptism are linked together in the combined images of blood and water pouring out of Christ's heart pierced during the Crucifixion in the fourteenth-century *Stanzaic Life of Christ*, ll. 1393-96, 1400-1403.

> Blode & water witerly
> Out of his hert he shed þat day,
> blode monkynde to forby *(redeem)*,
> And water our syn to wassh away
> . . . .
> Thus turnet is þe sacrament
> Circumcisioun vset ȝore
> To fulloght *(Baptism)*, sithen þat Crist vs kent *(taught)*
> In signe þat we wer thral bifore . . .

81. Voragine, *The Golden Legend*, 20ff.
82. Cf. Levy, "Gawain's Spiritual Journey," and Blanch, "Religion and Law," 93-101.
83. Cf. Deuteronomy 10:16.
84. Voragine, *The Golden Legend,* 22.
85.

> O Ihesu fore þe blod þou bledyst,
> And in þe furst tyme þou cheddust
> In þi circumcecion,
> þat I haue synnyd in lechore
> þat stynkyng syn, foreȝif þou me,
> And my delectacion.

> *(The Poems of John Audelay,* 50)

86. I cannot therefore agree with Giaccherini, "Gawain's Dream," 79, who linked Gawain's "beheading" with the symbolic castration at the hands of the jealous, paternal figure of the Green Knight. To transfer the conflict between Gawain and the Green Knight onto a plain of sexual rivalry misses, I believe, the true nature of Gawain's test and moral dilemma.

87. T. O. Beidelman, "Circumcision," in *The Encyclopedia of Religion*, ed. Eliade, 3:511-14.

88. For example, myths often describe circumcision as a substitute for castration inflicted by a female figure, the negative aspect of the mother-complex understood as *vagina dentata* (cf. Bruno Bettelheim, *Symbolic Wounds: Puberty Rites and the Envious Male* [London: Thames and Hudson, 1955], 63ff.).

89. It was at the Circumcision that God's son was given the name of Jesus, a circumstance that reflects a universal custom of giving a novice a new name after his initiation: "Now for all premodern societies the individual's name is equivalent to his true existence, to his existence as a spiritual being," (Eliade, *Birth and Rebirth,* 28).

90. In connection with this ritual layer of the poem's meaning, Wrigley, *"Sir Gawain and the Green Knight,"* 122, writes that "traditions of puberty initiation remained in the subconscious or maybe conscious minds of storyteller close to the threshold of literary romance."

91. The image of the "neck of pride" was commonplace in medieval homiletic writings; cf. John Trevisa's ME translation of Bartholomaeus Anglicus's *De Proprietatibus Rerum,* 217, which includes a description of the function and allegorical meaning of the human neck, also quoted and discussed by Reichardt, "Gawain and the Image of the Wound," 156-57. See also Schnyder, *Sir Gawain,* 43.

92. In the same way the wound of the Fisher King from the Grail legend is usually in the thigh, a euphemistic substitute for the genital organs, because the sin *is* that of the flesh. In the case of symbolic wounds inflicted on heroes of chivalric adventure, their physical nature always reflects the type of moral transgression (cf. Wrigley, *"Sir Gawain and the Green Knight,"* 121-22).

93. The Sin is often referred to in Old and Middle English homiletic sources as "hedsinne" (OE *heafod-synn*)—"capital sin" in the literal sense of the term (Latin *capitum*), referred to as "the sin of Adam," (*MED,* s.v. "hed," 5b). Hence also the "capital" punishment as the death sentence, because the crime was conceived to originate in the head, or the rational soul, and originally the execution was accomplished by beheading.

94. Cf. Champion, "Grace Versus Merit," esp. 415-17. See also Adolf, "The Concept of Original Sin," 21-29. It is strange that Tolkien and Gordon in their introduction to the edition of *Sir Gawain* (Davis, xxv), should have written that the author of the poem "had nothing to say about the great Boethian problems of foreknowledge and free will."

95. Trevisa, *On the Properties of Things,* 1:171.

96. For instance, Schnyder, "Aspects of Kingship," 289-94, writes that Arthur sacrifices Gawain to his boyishness and pride, himself causing the degeneration of the state and the disturbance of divine order by challenging destiny.

97. Cf. Reichardt, "Gawain and the Image of the Wound," 158-60.

98. In many languages, interestingly enough, the expression "to lose one's head" means "to lose control of the mind over emotions"—for example, the French "perdre la tête," Spanish "perder la capeza," or Polish "stracic glowe." The best known scriptural example of the "loss of head," both in the above metaphorical and in the literal sense, is the story of Judith and Holofernes from the Apocryphical Book of Judith.

99. Gawain's gash is therefore symbolic of the spiritual circumcision in the New Testament sense: ". . . in whom also ye are circumcised with the circumcision made without hands, in putting off the body of the sins of the flesh by the circumcision of Christ: buried with him in baptism, wherein also ye are risen with him through the faith of the operation of God, who hath raised him from the dead." (Colossians 2:11-12).

100. "I biknowe yow, kny3t, here stylle (*humbly*)," [says Gawain to the Green Knight] "Al fawty is my fare" (2385-86), and *The Book of Vices and Virtues,* 68, expresses clearly that the acknowledgment of one's sins is necessary for the shrift: "he my3t lerne and rekene alle manere of synnes and to schryue hym wel, for þer may no man schryue hym wel ne kepe hym from synne but he knowe hem."

101. Davis (130n.) acknowledges the difficulty with these lines, especially with the half-line "bot vnhap ne may hit" and he translates the whole *sententia* as follows: "For a man may hide his (spiritual) harm, but cannot unfasten (get rid of) it." The crucial word is *vnhap,* here understood as "to unfasten" (from *happe,* "to wrap, clasp, fasten"). An alternative meaning of the word would be "mishap" as a noun, but this does not seem to be in question.

102. The rather enigmatic role played by Morgan le Fay in the story, with which I have so cursorily dealt, has naturally engendered a number of critical comments: D. E. Baughan, "The Role of Morgan le Fay in *Sir Gawain and the Green Knight," Journal of*

English Literary History 17 (1950): 241-51; Friedman, "Morgan le Fay in *Sir Gawain,*" 260-74; M. A. Carson, "Morgan la Fee as the Principle of Unity in *Sir Gawain and the Green Knight,*" *Modern Language Quarterly* 23, no. 1 (1962): 3-16; Charles Long, "Arthur's Role in Morgan la Fay's Plan in *Sir Gawain and the Green Knight,*" *Tennessee Philological Bulletin* 7 (1970): 3-10.

103. Cf. Wrigley, *"Sir Gawain and the Green Knight,"* 117; Richard Barber, *The Knight and Chivalry* (London: Sphere Books, 1974), 38.

104. Lull, *The Book of the Ordre,* 42.

105. Discussed by Keen, *Chivalry,* 78ff.

106. Lull, *The Book of the Ordre,* 67, writes: "For to make & adoube a knyȝt it apperteyneth the day of some grete feste as Crystemas, Ester, Whitsontyd, or on suche dayes solempne. . . ."

107. Keen, *Chivalry,* 65-75. Elias Ashmole in his monumental work on the history of knighthood, *The Institution, Laws & Ceremonies of the Most Noble Order of the Garter; and A Brief Account of all other Military Orders of Knighthood in England, Scotland, France, Spain, Germany, Italy, Swedeland, Denmark & c.* (London: Thomas Dring, 1693), 40, describes these religious preparations before the knighting in the following fashion:

the esquire prepared himself to receive the order of knighthood, watching the night before in the church or chapel, with devout prayers and meditation: when morning came, he entered into his bath, to wash and make clean his whole body, whereby he was given to know and understand, that in all his following life time, he ought to be neat and clean, as well of body as soul, honest in his manners, and behaviour of life, wholly disposed to embrace virtue, and to use in all his actions, modesty, providence, and wisdom.

108. Cf. Victoria L. Weiss, "The Medieval Knighting Ceremony in *Sir Gawain and the Green Knight,*" *Chaucer Review* 12, no. 3 (1978): 186.

109. Lull, *The Book of the Ordre,* 66.

110. Weiss, "The Medieval Knighting Ceremony," 185; Ashmole, *The Institution, Laws, & Ceremonies,* 36.

111. Ashmole, *The Institution,* 36.

112. Keen, *Chivalry,* 65-67; Barber, *The Knight,* 40.

113. After Michel Andrien, *Le Pontifical Romain au moyen-age* (Citta del Vaticano, 1940), 448-49, quoted in Barber, *The Knight,* 40, and in Robert P. Miller, ed., *Chaucer: Sources and Background* (New York: Oxford University Press, 1977), 169-73.

114. Barber, *The Knight,* 40.

115. Robert W. Ackerman, "The Knighting Ceremony in the Middle English Romances," *Speculum* 19 (1944): 302.

116. Lull, *The Book of the Ordre,* 74.

117. Ashmole, *The Institution,* 36.

118. Andre Favine, *The Theater of Honour and Knighthood, or A Compendious Chronicle and Historie of the Whole Christian World,* trans. from the French (London: William Jaggard, 1623), 53. Favine writes (386) that an example of the practice of the ritual was the admission ceremony to the Order of the Holy Sepulchre founded in the Holy Land, in which the three strokes were linked with the Holy Trinity:

Then the knight bows down his body, and lays his head upon the Sepulchre, and the Guardian gives him three strokes flatlong with the Sword upon his shoulders, saying: "I constitute and ordaine thee a knight of the most Holy Sepulchre of our

Lord Iesus Christ: In the name of the Father, and of the Sonne, and of the Holy Ghost, Amen." And he makes three times the sign of the cross.

A mid-fourteenth-century Bohemian text, *Zrcadlo clovecieho spasenie* (translation of Latin *Speculum humanae salvationis)*, compares the blow *(zasijek)* with a sword received by the knight during the accolade to the blows sustained by Christ" (Wojciech Iwanczak, *Tropem rycerskiej przygody,* 264.

119. Ibid., 59. Maurice Keen *(Chivalry,* ill. no. 14) gives an illustration from a medieval manuscript depicting Emperor Sigismund dubbing a knight in Rome: the knight is kneeling in front of the emperor, his right hand raised as if in a swearing gesture, whereas the emperor is touching the knight's head with his left hand and raising his right hand (armed with a heavy sword) as if to deal the knight a heavy blow (Österreichische Nationalmuseum, Codex 3044, fol. 144, Bild-Archiv der Österreichischen Nationalbibliothek, Vienna).

120. Ashmole, *The Institution,* 41.

121. Michael Prestwich, *The Three Edwards: War and State in England, 1272-1377* (London: Book Club Associates, 1980), 208.

122. Geoffroi de Charny's treatise on chivalry forms a part of the chronicles by Froissart, *Oeuvres de Froissart,* ed. K. de Lettenhove (Brussels: Victor Devaux, 1870), 1:203. Parts of the treatise have been translated into English Miller, *Chaucer: Sources and Background,* 166-68.

123. Miguel de Cervantes Saavedra, *The Adventures of Don Quixote,* trans. J. M. Cohen (Harmondsworth: Penguin, 1968), 45.

124. *MED,* s.v. "dubben."

125. Walter W. Skeat, ed., *An Etymological Dictionary of the English Language* (Oxford: Clarendon Press, 1983) s.v. "dub" and "accolade."

126. From the Prose Redaction of the First Continuation of Chrétien's *Perceval,* printed in Benson, *Art and Tradition,* 256.

127. Ibid., 23.

128. A number of heroes volunteered to participate in the Beheading Game proposed by *bachlach* (churl), and each of them in his turn struck off the creature's head, but all except Cú Chulainn failed to turn up the following day for the return blow, thus exposing the entire province to scolding and upbraiding by the *bachlach (Fled Bricrend: The Feast of Bricriu,* trans. George Henderson [Dublin: David Nutt, Irish Text Society, 1899], chaps. 92-97).

129. The fact that the three beheading blows, so elaborately described in *Sir Gawain,* are structurally linked with the three days of Gawain's temptation at the Castle of Hautdesert is, in my view, a secondary feature of the beheading scene at the Green Chapel, and as a structural solution it is peculiar only to this poem. The analogous beheading scenes from *The Feast of Bricriu* and *Le Livre de Caradoc* also consist of three blows (two arrested ones and one feigned), that purposefully extend the scene and dramatize the effect.

130. *Fled Bricrend,* chaps.99-102.

131. "Death awaits me, and I would rather have death with honour," says Cú Chulainn shortly before his beheading (ibid., chap. 99).

132. An analogy exists between this dramatic aspect of the beheading scenes in romance and the threatened sacrifice of Isaac in the popular Corpus Christi mystery plays. This highly moving and tragic play consists for the most part of a prolonged, heart-breaking dialogue between Abraham, carrying out God's will with a heavy heart, and Isaac, who willingly offers his life at his father's bidding (*English Mystery Plays,* ed. Happé, nos. 6, 7).

133. Upon seeing that he is alive, Gawain springs into the air "a spear's length" (2316), and his exhilaration has no match: "Neuer syn þat he watz burne borne of his moder / Watz he neuer in þis worlde wyȝe half so blyþe" (2320-21).

Works Cited

Primary Sources

Aelfric. *Aelfric's Lives of Saints, being a Set of Sermons on Saints' Days formerly observed by the English Church.* 2 vols. Edited by Walter W. Skeat. 1881. Reprint, London: Oxford University Press, EETS, 1966.

Alliterative Morte Arthure: A Critical Edition. Edited by Valerie Krishna. New York: Burt Franklin, 1976.

Ancrene Riwle: The English Text of the Ancrene Riwle, Edited from Cotton MS. Nero A. XIV. Edited by Mabel Day. London: Oxford University Press, EETS, 1952.

Ancrene Wisse. Edited by J. R. R. Tolkien. London: Oxford University Press, EETS, 1962.

Apocryphal New Testament. Translated by Montague R. James. Oxford: Clarendon Press, 1980.

Apuleius, Lucius. *The Transformations of Lucius, otherwise known as the Golden Ass.* Translated by Robert Graves. Harmondsworth: Penguin, 1950.

Aquinas, Thomas. *Summa Theologiae.* Edited by C. Thomas Moore. 61 vols. London: Blackfriars, 1976.

Aristotle. *De Anima (On the Soul).* Translated by H. Lawson-Tancred. Harmondsworth: Penguin, 1986.

——. *The Nicomachean Ethics.* Translated by David Ross. Oxford: Oxford University Press, 1980.

Audelay, John. *The Poems of John Audelay.* Edited by Ella K. Whiting. London: Oxford University Press, EETS, 1931.

Augustine. *Confessions.* Edited by James J. O'Donnell. Oxford: Clarendon Press, 1992.

——. *De doctrina Christiana.* Translated by D. W. Robertson. New York: Macmillan, 1958.

Ault, Norman, ed. *Elizabethan Lyrics from the Original Texts.* London: Longmans, 1925.

Bede Venerabilis. *The Ecclesiastical History of the English Nation.* London: J. M. Dent and Sons, 1913.

Bible: Authorized Version. Swindon: Bible Society, nd.

Biblia Sacra Iuxta Latinam Vulgatam Versionem. Rome: The Vatican, 1945.

Book of Vices and Virtues: A Fourteenth Century English Translation of the "Somme le Roi" of Lorens D'Orleans. Edited by W. Nelson Francis. London: Oxford University Press, EETS, 1942.

Bremmer, R. H., ed. *The Fyve Wyttes: A Late Middle English Devotional Treatise.* Amsterdam: Rodopi, 1987.

Brook, G. L., ed. *The Harley Lyrics.* Manchester: Manchester University Press, 1948.

Brown, Carlton, ed. *English Lyrics of the XIIIth Century.* Oxford: Clarendon Press, 1932.

——. *Religious Lyrics of the XIVth Century.* Oxford: Clarendon Press, 1952.

Brown, Sir Thomas. *Hydrotaphia and the Garden of Cyrus.* London: Macmillan, 1937.

Bunyan, John. *The Pilgrim's Progress.* Edinburgh: The Banner of Truth Trust, 1977.

Caesar. *The Gallic War.* Translated by H. J. Edwards. Cambridge: Harvard University Press, 1979.

Capellanus, Andreas. *The Art of Courtly Love.* Translated by J. J. Parry. New York: W. W. Norton, 1969.

Caxton, William. *Caxton's Book of Curtesye.* Edited by Frederick J. Furnivall. 1868. Reprint, London: Oxford University Press, EETS, 1932.

Chapman, George. *Poems.* Edited by Phyllis Bartlett. New York: Russell and Russell, 1941.

Chaucer, Geoffrey. *The Riverside Chaucer.* Edited by Larry D. Benson. Oxford: Oxford University Press, 1988.

Child, Francis J., ed. *The English and Scottish Popular Ballads.* 5 vols. Boston: Houghton, Mifflin, 1898.

Chrétien de Troyes. *Arthurian Romances.* Translated by D. D. R. Owen. London: J. M. Dent and Sons, 1987.

——. *Le Chevalier de la charrette.* Edited by Mario Roques. Paris: Les classiques francais, 1952.

——. *Cligés.* Edited by Alexandre Micha. Paris: Librairie Honoré Champion, 1965.

——. *Le Conte du Graal (Perceval).* Edited by Felix Lecoy. Paris: Librairie Honoré Champion, 1975.

——. *Erec et Enide.* Edited by Mario Roques. Paris: Librairie Honoré Champion, 1966.

Cleanness. Edited by Alistair C. Cawley and J. J. Anderson. London: J. M. Dent and Sons, 1988.

Cloud of Unknowing. Edited by Phyllis Hodgson. London: Oxford University Press, EETS, 1944.

Collectanea Chemica: Being Certain Select Treatises on Alchemy and Hermetic Medicine by Eirenaeus Philalethes, George Starkey, Dr. Francis Antony, Sir George Ripley et al. London: James Elliot, 1893.

Dante Alighieri. *Dante's "Il Convivio" (The Banquet).* Translated by Richard H. Lansing. New York: Garland Publishing, 1990.

Davies, R. T., ed. *Medieval English Lyrics: A Critical Anthology.* London: Faber and Faber, 1963.

Deguileville, Guillaume de. *The Pilgrimage of the Lyfe of the Manhode.* Translated from the French *Le Pelerinage de la vie humaine.* Edited by Avril Henry. London: Oxford University Press, EETS, 1985.

Eckhart, Meister. *German Sermons & Treatises*. Translated by M. O'C. Walshe. London: Watkins, 1983.

Edward, Second Duke of York. *The Master of Game: The Oldest English Book on Hunting*. Edited by William A. and F. Baillie- Grohman. London: Chatto and Windus, 1909.

Eschenbach, Wolfram von. *Parzival*. Translated by A. T. Hatto. Harmondsworth: Penguin, 1980.

Fled Bricrend: The Feast of Bricriu. Translated by George Henderson. London: David Nutt, Irish Text Society, 1899.

Foster, Frances A., ed. *A Stanzaic Life of Christ, edited from MS. Harley 3909*. London: Oxford University Press, EETS, 1926.

French, W. H. and C. B. Hale, eds. *Middle English Metrical Romances*. 2 vols. New York: Russell and Russell, 1964.

Froissart. *Oeuvres de Froissart*. Edited by K. de Lettenhove. Brussels: Victor Devaux, 1870.

Furnivall, F. J., ed. *The Book of Quinte Essence or The Fifth Being; that is to say, Man's Heaven*. London: N. Trubner, EETS, 1866.

Gascoigne, George. *The Complete Works*. Edited by J. W. Cunliffe. 2 vols. Cambridge: Cambridge University Press, 1907-10.

Geoffrey of Monmouth. *History of the Kings of Britain (Historia Regum Britaniae)*. Translated by Lewis Thorpe. Harmondsworth: Penguin, 1966.

Goethe, Johann Wolfgang von. *Faust: First Part*. Translated by Peter Salm. New York: Bantam Books, 1962.

Gregory the Great. *Moralia,* in *Corpus Christianorum. Series Latinae*. Edited by M. Adriaen. Brepols, Italy: Editores Pontificci, 1979.

Happé, Peter, ed. *English Mystery Plays*. 1975. Reprint, London: Penguin, 1985.

Hawes, Stephen. *The Minor Poems*. Edited by Florence W. Gluck and Alice B. Morgan. London: Oxford University Press, EETS, 1974.

Hermetica: The Ancient Greek and Latin Writings which Contain Religious or Philosophical Teachings Ascribed to Hermes Trismegistus. Edited by Walter Scott. Vol. 1. Boston: Shambhala, 1985.

Herzfeld, George, ed. *An Old English Martyrology*. London: Kegan Paul, EETS, 1900.

Hoccleve. *Hoccleve's Works: The Minor Poems*. Edited by Frederic J. Furnival and Sir Israel Gollancz. London: Oxford University Press, EETS, 1970.

"Holy Scriptures": A New Translation from the Original Languages. Hampton Wick, Kingston-on-Thames: Stow Hill Bible and Tract Depot, 1967.

Hunbaut: Altfranzosischer Arturroman des XIII Jahrhunderts. Edited by J. Stürzinger. Dresden: Gesellschaft für romanische Literatur, 1914.

Jacob's Well: An English Treatise on the Cleansing of Man's Conscience. Edited by A. Brandeis. London: Kegan Paul, EETS, 1900.

Johnston, R. C. and D. D. R. Owen, eds. *Le Chevalier à l'Epée: Two Old French Gauvain Romances*. Edinburgh: Scottish Academic Press, 1972.

Langland, William. *The Vision of Piers Plowman: A Complete Edition of the B Text*. Edited by A. V. C. Schmidt. London: J. M. Dent and Sons, 1978.

Lull, Ramon. *The Book of the Ordre of Chivalry.* Translated by William Caxton from the French version of Lull's *Le Libre del Ordre de Cauayleria.* Edited by A. T. P. Byles. London: Oxford University Press, EETS, 1926.

Malory. *Works.* Edited by Eugene Vinaver. Oxford: Oxford University Press, 1971.

Mandeville, Sir John. *Mandeville's Travels.* Edited by M. C. Seymour. Oxford: Oxford University Press, 1967.

Marlowe, Christopher. *The Works of Christopher Marlowe.* Edited by C. F. Tucker Brooke. Oxford: Clarendon Press, 1910.

Middle English Sermons. Edited by Woodburn O. Ross. London: Oxford University Press, EETS, 1940.

Mirk, John. *Mirk's Festial: A Collection of Homilies, by Johannes Mirkus.* London: Oxford University Press, EETS, 1905.

Morris, R., ed. *Old English Homilies of the Twelfth Century.* London: N. Trubner, EETS, 1878.

Morte Arthur. Edited by J. D. Bruce. London: Oxford University Press, EETS, 1903.

Morte Arthur, or The Death of Arthur. Edited from Robert Thornton's MS by Edmund Brock. London: Oxford University Press, EETS, 1967.

"La Mule sanz Frain." Edited by R. T. Hill. Ph. D. diss., 1911.

Murphy, Gerard, ed. *Early Irish Lyrics: Eighth to Twelfth Century.* Oxford: Clarendon Press, 1977.

Ovid. *The Erotic Poems.* Translated by Peter Green. Harmondsworth: Penguin, 1988.

———. *Metamorphoses.* Translated by Mary M. Innes. Harmondsworth: Penguin, 1971.

Parlement of the Thre Ages. Edited by M. Y. Offord, London: Oxford University Press, EETS, 1959.

Patrologia Latina. Edited by J. P. Migne. Paris, 1862.

Pearl. Edited by Sir Israel Gollancz. London: Chatto and Windus, 1936.

Perceval. The Romance of Perceval in Prose: A Translation of the E MS of the Didot Perceval. Translated by Dell Skeels. Seattle: University of Washington Press, 1966.

Perlesvaus: Le Haut Livre du Graal. Edited by William A. Nitze and T. Atkinson Jenkins. Vol. 1. Chicago: University of Chicago Press, 1932.

Perlesvaus: The High Book of the Holy Grail. Translated by Nigel Bryant. Cambridge: D. S. Brewer, 1978.

Physiologus: A Metrical Bestiary of Twelve Chapters by Bishop Theobald. Translated by A. W. Rendell. London: John and Edward Bumpus, 1928.

———. *The Middle English Physiologus.* Edited by Hanneke Wirtjes. Oxford: Oxford University Press, EETS, 1991.

Plato. *The Republic.* Harmondsworth: Penguin, 1985.

———. *Timaeus.* Translated by H. D. P. Lee. Harmondsworth: Penguin, 1965.

Pythagorean Sourcebook and Library: An Anthology of Ancient Writings Which Relate to Pythagoras and Pythagorean Philosophy. Translated by K. S. Guthrie and edited by David R. Fideler. Grand Rapids, Mich.: Phanes Press, 1987.

Quest of the Holy Grail (Queste del Saint Graal). Translated by P. M. Matarasso. Harmondsworth: Penguin, 1986.

The Recluse: A Fourteenth-Century Version of the Ancren Riwle. Edited by Joel Påhlsson. Lund: Acta Universitatis Lundinensis, 1911.

Roach, William, ed. *The Continuations of the Old French Perceval of Chrétien de Troyes.* Vol. 1. Philadelphia: University of Pennsylvania Press, 1949.

Robbins, Rossell Hope, ed. *Secular Lyrics of the XIVth and XVth Centuries.* Oxford: Clarendon Press, 1964.

Ruusbroec, Jan van. *The Seven Enclosures.* Vol. 2 of *Opera Omnia.* Leiden: E. J. Brill, 1981.

Secretum Secretorum: Nine English Versions. Edited by M. A. Manzalaoni. Oxford: Oxford University Press, EETS, 1977.

Shakespeare, William. *The Riverside Shakespeare.* Edited by G. Blakemore Evans. Boston: Houghton Miffin, 1974.

Sisam, Celia and Kenneth, eds. *The Oxford Book of Medieval English Verse.* Oxford: Clarendon Press, 1970.

Skelton, John. *The Complete English Poems.* Edited by John V. Scattergood. New Haven: Yale University Press, 1983.

Spenser, Edmund. *The Faerie Queene.* Edited by A. C. Hamilton. London: Longman, 1990.

Strassburg, Gottfried von. *Tristan.* Edited by Peter Ganz. Wiesbaden: F. A. Brockhaus, 1978.

———. *Tristan.* Translated by A. T. Hatto. Harmondsworth: Penguin, 1987.

Tain Bó Cúalnge from the Book of Leinster. Edited by Cecile O'Rahilly. Dublin: Institute for Advanced Studies, 1967.

Tain Bó Cúailnge. Recension I. Edited by Cecile O'Rahilly. Dublin: Institute for Advanced Studies, 1976.

Tauler, Johannes. *Sermons.* Translated by M. Shrady. New York: Pauline Press, 1985.

Trevisa, John. *On the Properties of Things: John Trevisa's Translation of Bartholomaeus Anglicus De Proprietatibus Rerum.* Edited by M. C. Seymour. 2 vols. Oxford: Clarendon Press, 1975.

Tripartite Life of Patrick, with Other Documents Relating to that Saint. Edited by Whitley Stokes. 2 vols. London: Eyre and Spottiswoode, 1887.

Türlin, Heinrich von dem. *Diu Crône.* Edited by Gottlob H. F. Scholl. Stuttgart, 1852. Reprint, Amsterdam: Editions Rodopi, 1966.

Vices and Virtues, being a Soul's Confession of its Sins, with Reason's Description of the Virtues. Edited by Ferdinand Holthauser. London: N. Trubner, EETS, 1888.

Vitruvius. *On Architecture.* Translated by F. Granger. London: Heineman, 1931.

Voragine, Jacobus de. *The Golden Legend.* Translated by William Caxton. Edited by F. S. Ellis. London: W. Morris, 1892.

———. *The Golden Legend.* Translated by Granger Ryan and Helmut Ripperger. New York: Arno Press, 1969.

Wanderer. Edited by T. P. Dunning and A. J. Bliss. London: Methuen, 1978.

White, T. H., ed. *The Book of Beasts, being a Translation from a Latin Bestiary of the Twelfth Century.* London: Jonathan Cape, 1954.

Wilhelm, James J., ed. *Medieval Song: An Anthology of Hymns and Lyrics.* London: George Allen and Unwin, 1972.

Williams, John, ed. *English Renaissance Poetry.* Fayetteville: University of Arkansas Press, 1990.

Wynnere and Wastoure. Edited by Stephanie Trigg. Oxford: Oxford University Press, EETS, 1990.

Ywain and Gawain. Edited by Albert B. Friedman and Norman T. Harrington. London: Oxford University Press, EETS, 1964.

Editions of *Sir Gawain and the Green Knight*

Burrow, John A., ed. *Sir Gawain and the Green Knight.* Harmondsworth: Penguin, 1972.

Gollancz, Sir Israel, ed. *Sir Gawain and the Green Knight.* London: Oxford University Press, EETS, 1940.

Gollancz, Sir Israel, ed. *Pearl, Cleanness, Patience and Sir Gawain reproduced in facsimile from the unique MS. Cotton Nero A.X in the British Museum.* London: Oxford University Press, EETS, 1955.

Madden, Frederic, ed. *Sir Gawaine: A Collection of Ancient Romance-Poems by Scotish and English Authors Relating to that Celebrated Knight of the Round Table.* London: Richard and John E. Taylor, 1839.

Silverstein, Theodore, ed. *Sir Gawain and the Green Knight: A New Critical Edition.* Chicago: University of Chicago Press, 1974.

Tolkien, J. R. R., and E. V. Gordon, eds. *Sir Gawain and the Green Knight.* 2d ed. revised by Norman Davis. Oxford: Clarendon Press, 1967.

Waldron, R. A., ed. *Sir Gawain and the Green Knight.* London: Edward Arnold, 1970.

Secondary Sources

Ackerman, Robert W. "Castle Hautdesert in *Sir Gawain and the Green Knight.*" *Melanges de Langue et de Litterature du Moyen Age et de la Renaissance.* Vol. 1 (Geneva: Librairie Droz, 1970).

——. "Gawain's Shield: Penitential Doctrine in *Sir Gawain and the Green Knight.*" *Anglia* 76 (1958): 254-65.

——. "The Knighting Ceremony in the Middle English Romances." *Speculum* 19 (1944): 285-313.

Addison, C. G. *The Knights Templar.* London: Longman, 1852.

Adolf, Helen. "The Concept of Original Sin as Reflected in Arthurian Romance." In *Studies in Language and Literature in Honour of Margaret Schlauch,* 21-29. Warsaw: Panstwowe Wydawnictwo Naukowe, 1966.

Aers, David. "'In Arthurus Day': Community, Virtue, and Individual Identity in *Sir Gawain and the Green Knight.*" In *Community, Gender and Individual Identity: English Writing 1360-1430.* London: Routledge, 1988.

Anderson, J. J. "The Three Judgments and the Ethos of Chivalry in *Sir Gawain and the Green Knight*." *Chaucer Review* 24, no. 4 (1990): 337-55.

Arthur, Ross G. *Medieval Sign Theory and Sir Gawain and the Green Knight*. Toronto: University of Toronto Press, 1987.

Ashmole, Elias. *The Institution, Laws & Ceremonies of the Most Noble Order of the Garter; and A Brief Account of all other Military Orders of Knighthood in England, Scotland, France, Spain, Germany, Italy, Swedeland, Denmark, & c.* London: Thomas Dring, 1693.

Bachman, W. Bryant Jr. "*Sir Gawain and the Green Knight:* The Green and the Gold Once More." *Texas Studies in Literature and Language* 23, no. 4 (1981): 495-516.

Barber, Richard. *The Knight and Chivalry*. London: Sphere Books, 1974.

Barnett, D. J. "Whatever Happened to Gawain?" *English Studies in Africa* 18 (1975): 1-16.

Barnett, Sylvan. "A Note on the Structure of *Sir Gawain and the Green Knight.*" *Modern Language Notes* 71 (1956): 319.

Barron, W. R. J. *Trawthe and Treason: The Sin of Gawain Reconsidered. A Thematic Study of Sir Gawain and the Green Knight*. Manchester: Manchester University Press, 1980.

Basford, K. H. "Quest for the Green Man." In *Symbols of Power*, edited by H. R. Ellis Davidson, 101-20. London: D. S. Brewer, 1977.

Baughan, D. E. "The Role of Morgan le Fay in *Sir Gawain and the Green Knight.*" *Journal of English Literary History* 17 (1950): 241-51.

Benson, C. David. *The History of Troy in Middle English Literature: Guido delle Colonne's Historia Destructionis Troiae in Medieval England*. Woodbridge, Suffolk: D. S. Brewer, 1980.

Benson, Larry D. *Art and Tradition in "Sir Gawain and the Green Knight."* New Brunswick, N.J.: Rutgers University Press, 1965.

------. "The Source of the Beheading Episode in *Sir Gawain and the Green Knight.*" *Modern Philology* 59 (1961): 1-12.

Bertalanffy, Ludwig von. *General System Theory: Foundations, Development, Applications*. London: Allen Lane, 1971.

Bettelheim, Bruno. *Symbolic Wounds: Puberty Rites and the Envious Male*. London: Thames and Hudson, 1955.

Blanch, Robert J. "Precious Metal and Gem Symbolism in *Pearl.*" In *Sir Gawain and Pearl: Critical Essays*, edited by Robert J. Blanch, 86-97. Bloomington: Indiana University Press, 1971.

------. "Religion and Law in *Sir Gawain and the Green Knight.*" In *Approaches to Teaching Sir Gawain and the Green Knight*. Edited by M. Y. Miller and J. Chance. New York: Modern Language Association of America, 1986, 93-101.

------. *Sir Gawain and the Green Knight: A Reference Guide*. New York: Whitston Publishing, 1983.

Blenkner, Louis. "Sin, Psychology, and the Structure of *Sir Gawain and the Green Knight.*" *Studies in Philology* 74 (1977): 354-87.

Bloomfield, M. W. "*Sir Gawain and the Green Knight:* An Appraisal." *PMLA* 76 (1961): 7-19.

Bodkin, Maud. *Archetypal Patterns in Poetry: Psychological Studies of Imagination.* 1934. Reprint, London: Oxford University Press, 1968.

Borroff, Marie. *"Sir Gawain and the Green Knight:* The Passing of Judgement." In *The Passing of Arthur: New Essays in Arthurian Tradition,* edited by Christopher Baswell and William Sharpe, 105-28. New York: Garland Publishing, 1988.

———. *Sir Gawain and the Green Knight: A Stylistic and Metrical Study.* New Haven: Yale University Press, 1962.

Bowers, R. H. *"Gawain and the Green Knight* as Entertainment." *Modern Language Quarterly* 24 (1963): 333-41.

———. "A Middle English Treatise on Hermeneutics: Harley MS. 2276, 32v-35v." *PMLA* 65 (1950): 590-600.

Brewer, Derek. "The Interpretation of Dream, Folktale and Romance with Special Reference to *Sir Gawain and the Green Knight." Neuphilologische Mitteilungen* 77 (1976): 569-81.

Brewer, Elizabeth, ed. *From Cuchulainn to Gawain: Sources and Analogues of Sir Gawain and the Green Knight.* Cambridge: D. S. Brewer, 1973.

Buchanan, Alice. "The Irish Framework of *Gawain and the Green Knight." PMLA* 47 (1932): 315-38.

Burgess, John W. "A Possible Astronomical Genesis of the Tzolkin." Paper presented at an international symposium, "Time and Astronomy at the Meeting of Two Worlds." Warsaw-Frombork, May 1992.

Burrow, John A. *The Ages of Man: A Study in Medieval Writing and Thought.* Oxford: Clarendon Press, 1988.

———. *A Reading of Sir Gawain and the Green Knight.* London: Routledge and Kegan Paul, 1966.

———. "The Two Confession Scenes in *Sir Gawain and the Green Knight."* In *Sir Gawain and Pearl: Critical Essays.* Edited by Robert J. Blanch. Bloomington: Indiana University Press, 1971, 123-34.

Butler, Christopher. *Number Symbolism.* London: Routledge and Kegan Paul, 1970.

Byles, A. T. "Medieval Courtesy Books and the Prose Romances of Chivalry." In *Chivalry: A Series of Studies to Illustrate Its Historical Significance and Civilizing Influence,* edited by Edgar Prestage, 183-206. New York: Alfred A. Knopf, 1928.

Cable, Thomas. *The English Alliterative Tradition.* Philadelphia: University of Pennsylvania Press, 1991.

Campbell, Joseph. *The Hero With a Thousand Faces.* New York: Bollingen Series, 1961.

Carriere, Jean L. *"Sir Gawain and the Green Knight* as a Christmas Poem." *Comitatus: Studies in Old and Middle English Literature* 1 (December 1970): 25-42.

Carson, M.A. "The Green Chapel: Its Meaning and Function." *Studies in Philology* 60 (1963): 598-605.

———. "Morgan la Fee as the Principle of Unity in *Sir Gawain and the Green Knight." Modern Language Quarterly* 23, no. 1 (1962): 3-16.

Chambers, E. K. *The Medieval Stage.* 2 vols. Oxford: Clarendon Press, 1903.

Champion, L. S. "Grace Versus Merit in *Sir Gawain and the Green Knight." Modern Language Quarterly* 28 (1967): 413-25.

Cooper, R. A. and D. A. Pearsall. "The *Gawain* Poems: A Statistical Approach to the Question of Common Authorship." *Review of English Studies* 39, no. 155 (1988): 365-85.

Crane, John K. "The Four Levels of Time in *Sir Gawain and the Green Knight.*" *Annuale Medievale* 10 (1969): 65-80.

Curtius, Ernst Robert. *European Literature and the Latin Middle Ages.* Translated by Willard R. Trask. London: Routledge and Kegan Paul, 1979.

Davenport, W. A. *The Art of the Gawain-Poet.* London: Athlone Press, 1978.

David, Alfred. "Gawain and Aeneas." *English Studies* 49 (1968): 402-9.

Davidson, Hilda Roderick Ellis. *Gods and Myths of Northern Europe.* Harmondsworth: Penguin, 1981.

Delany, Paul. "The Role of the Guide in *Sir Gawain and the Green Knight.*" *Neophilologus* 49 (1965): 250-55.

Dendinger, Loyd N. "The Dynamic Structural Balance of *Gawain and the Green Knight.*" In *Essays in Honor of Esmond Linworth Marilla,* edited by T. A. Kirby and W. J. Olive, 367-78. Baton Rouge: Louisiana State University Press, 1970.

Dennys, Rodney. *The Heraldic Imagination.* London: Barrie and Jenkins, 1975.

Dictionary of the Irish Language: Based Mainly on Old and Middle Irish Materials. Compact ed. Dublin: Royal Irish Academy, 1983.

Dinneen, Patrick S., ed. *An Irish-English Doctionary.* Dublin: Educational Company of Ireland, 1927.

Doan, James E. "A Structural Approach to Celtic Saints' Lives." In *Celtic Folklore and Christianity: Studies in Memory of William W. Heist,* edited by Patrick K. Ford, 23-24. Los Angeles: McNally and Loftin, 1983.

Donner, Morton. "Tact as a Criterion of Reality in *Sir Gawain and the Green Knight.*" *Papers on English Language and Literature* (Autumn 1965): 306-15.

Dove, Mary. *The Perfect Age of Man's Life.* Cambridge: Cambridge University Press, 1986.

Dronke, Peter. *Fabula: Explorations into the Uses of Myth in Medieval Platonism.* Leiden-Koln: E. J. Brill, 1974.

------. "Tradition and Innovation in Medieval Western Colour-Imagery." *Eranos* 41 (1972): 51-106.

------. ed. *A History of Twelfth-Century Western Philosophy.* Cambridge: Cambridge University Press, 1988.

Dumézil, Georges. *L'idéologie tripartie des Indo-Européens.* Brussels: Collection Latomus, 1958.

Eco, Umberto. *Art and Beauty in the Middle Ages.* Translated by Hugh Bredin. New Haven: Yale University Press, 1986.

Edgeworth, Robert J. "Anatomical Geography in *Sir Gawain and the Green Knight.*" *Neophilologus* 69 (1985): 318-19.

Egan, Joseph F. "The Import of Color Symbolism in *Sir Gawain and the Green Knight.*" *St. Louis University Studies* 2 (Series A, Humanities 1, 1949): 11-86.

Eliade, Mircea. *Birth and Rebirth: The Religious Meanings of Initiation in Human Culture.* Translated by Willard R. Trask. London: Harvill Press, 1961.

------. *Naissances Mystiques. Essai sur quelques types d'initiation.* Paris: Les Essais, No. 92, 1959.

------. *The Quest: History and Meaning in Religion.* Chicago: University of Chicago Press, 1969.

------. ed. *The Encyclopedia of Religion.* 15 vols. New York: Macmillan, 1987.

Elliot, Ralph W. V. "Landscape and Rhetoric in Middle-English Alliterative Poetry." *Melbourne Critical Review* 4 (1961): 71-76.

Endres, Franz C., and Annemarie Schimmel. *Das Mysterium der Zahl: Zahlensymbolikim Kulturvergleich.* Cologne: Eugen Diederichs Verlag, 1986.

Enkvist, Nils Erik. "The Seasons of the Year: Chapters on a Motif from *Beowulf* to the *Shepherd's Calendar.*" *Societas Scientiorum Fennica. Commentationes Humanorum Litterarum* 22, no. 4 (1957): 85-87, 134.

Favine, Andre. *The Theater of Honour and Knighthood, or a Compendious Chronicle and Historie of the Whole Christian World.* Translated from the French. London: William Jaggard, 1623.

Fichte, Joerg O. "*Historia* and *Fabula:* Arthurian Traditions and Audience Expectations in *Sir Gawain and the Green Knight.*" In *Festschrift Walter Haug und Burghart Wachinger*, 589-602. Tübingen: Max Niemeyer Verlag, 1992.

Folkard, R. *Plant Lore, Legends, and Lyrics.* London: Sampson Low, 1884.

Frazer, Sir James George. *The Golden Bough: A Study in Magic and Religion.* London: Macmillan, 1913.

Freed, Eugenie R. "'*Quy the Pentangel Apendes . . .*' The Pentangle in *Sir Gawain and the Green Knight.*" *Theoria: A Journal of Studies in the Arts, Humanities and Social Sciences* 77 (1991): 125-41.

Friedman, Albert B. "Morgan le Fay in *Sir Gawain and the Green Knight.*" In *Sir Gawain and Pearl: Critical Essays,* edited by Robert J. Blanch, 260-74. Bloomington: Indiana University Press, 1971.

Fries, Maureen. "The Characterization of Women in the Alliterative Tradition." In *The Alliterative Tradition in the Fourteenth Century*, edited by Bernard S. Levy and Paul E. Szarmach, 25-45. Kent, Ohio: Kent State University Press, 1981.

Gallant, Gerald. "The Three Beasts—Symbols of Temptation in *Sir Gawain and the Green Knight.*" *Annuale Mediaevale* 11 (1970): 35-50.

Ganim, John M. "Disorientation, Style and Consciousness in *Sir Gawain and the Green Knight.*" *PMLA* 91 (1976): 376-84.

Ghyka, Matila. *The Geometry of Art and Life.* New York: Dover Publications, 1977.

Giaccherini, Enrico. "Gawain's Dream of Emancipation." In *Literature in Fourteenth-Century England: The J. A. W. Bennett Memorial Lectures*, Perugia, 1981-1982, edited by Piero Boitani and Anna Torti, 65-82. Cambridge: D. S. Brewer, 1982.

Godwin, Joscelyn. *Robert Fludd: Hermetic Philosopher and Surveyor of Two Worlds.* London: Thames and Hudson, 1979.

Goldhurst, William. "The Green and the Gold: The Major Theme of *Sir Gawain and the Green Knight.*" *College English* 20 (1958-59): 61-65.

Gollancz, Sir Israel. "Chivalry in Medieval English Poetry." In *Chivalry: A Series of Studies to Illustrate its Historical Significance and Civilizing Influence*, edited by Edgar Prestage, 167-81. New York: Alfred A. Knopf, 1928.

Graves, Robert. *Greek Myths.* Harmondsworth: Penguin, 1977.

——. *The White Goddess: A Historical Grammar of Poetic Myth*. London: Faber and Faber, 1952.

Gray, Douglas. "The Five Wounds of Our Lord." *Notes and Queries* 208 (1963): 50-51, 82-89, 127-34, 163-68.

——. *Themes and Images in the Medieval English Religious Lyric*. London: Routledge and Kegan Paul, 1972.

Green, Richard F. "Gawain's Five Fingers." *English Language Notes* 27, no. 1 (1989): 14-18.

——. "Gawain's Shield and the Quest for Perfection." *Journal of English Literary History* 29, no. 2 (1962): 121-39.

Gregory, Tullio. "The Platonic Inheritance." In *A History of Twelfth-Century Western Philosophy*, edited by Peter Dronke, 54-80. Cambridge: Cambridge University Press, 1988.

Gross, Laila. "Gawain's Acceptance of the Girdle." *American Notes and Queries* 12 (1973-74): 154-55.

Haines, Victor Y. *The Fortunate Fall of Sir Gawain: The Typology of Sir Gawain and the Green Knight*. Washington, D.C.: University Press of America, 1982.

——. "Morgan and the Missing Day in *Sir Gawain and the Green Knight*." *Mediaeval Studies* 33 (1971): 354-59.

Halevi, Z'ev ben Shimon. *Kabbalah. Tradition of Hidden Knowledge*. London: Thames and Hudson, 1985.

Hanna, Ralph. "Unlocking What's Locked: Gawain's Green Girdle." *Viator* 14 (1983): 290-302.

Hearnshaw, F. J. C. "Chivalry and Its Place in History." In *Chivalry: A Series to llustrate Its Historical Significance and Civilizing Influence,* edited by Edgar Prestage. New York: Alfred A. Knopf, 1928.

Hieatt, A. Kent. "Sir Gawain: Pentangle, *Luf-Lace*, Numerical Structure." *Papers on Language and Literature* 4 (1968): 339- 59.

Hills, David Farley. "Gawain's Fault in *Sir Gawain and the Green Knight*." *Review of English Studies* 14 (1963): 124-31.

Hirn, Yrjo. *The Sacred Shrine: A Study of the Poetry and Art of the Catholic Church*. London: Faber and Faber, 1958.

Hopper, Vincent Foster. *Medieval Number Symbolism: Its Sources, Meaning, and Influence on Thought and Expression*. New York: Cooper Square Publishers, 1969.

Horgan, A. D. "Gawain's *pure pentaungel* and the Virtue of Faith." *Medium Aevum* 56 (1987): 310-16.

Howard, Donald R. "Structure and Symmetry in *Sir Gawain and the Green Knight*." *Speculum* 39 (July 1964): 425-33.

——. *The Three Temptations: Medieval Man in Search of the World*. Princeton: Princeton University Press, 1966.

Howard, Donald R., and C. K. Zacher, eds. *Critical Studies of Sir Gawain and the Green Knight*. Notre Dame, Ind.: University of Notre Dame Press, 1970.

Huizinga, J. *The Waning of the Middle Ages*. New York: Doubleday Anchor Books, 1954.

Hulbert, J. R. "Syr Gawayn and the Grene Kny3t." *Modern Philology* 13, no. 8 (1915): 433-62; no. 12 (1916): 689-730.

Iwanczak, Wojciech. *Tropem rycerskiej przygody. Wzorzec rycerski w pismien-nictwie czeskim XIV wieku* (In search of chivalric adventure: Chivalric patterns in Bohemian writings of the fourteenth-century). Warsaw: Panstwowy Instytut Wydawniczy, 1985.

Jackson, Isaac. "Sir Gawain's Coat of Arms." *Modern Language Review* 15 (1920): 77-79; 17 (1922): 289-90.

Jackson, Kenneth H. *The Oldest Irish Tradition: A Window on the Iron Age.* Cambridge: Cambridge University Press, 1964.

Jackson, W. T. H. *The Anatomy of Love: The Tristan of Gottfried von Strassburg.* New York: Columbia University Press, 1971.

Jacobs, Nicholas. "The Green Knight: An Unexpected Irish Parallel." *Cambridge Medieval Celtic Studies* 4 (1982): 1-4.

James, John. *Chartres: The Masons Who Built a Legend.* London: Routledge and Kegan Paul, 1982.

Johnson, Lynn S. *The Voice of the Gawain-Poet.* Madison: University of Wisconsin Press, 1984.

Jonassen, Frederick B. "Elements from the Traditional Drama of England in *Sir Gawain and the Green Knight.*" *Viator* 17 (1986): 221-54.

Jones, Terry. *Chaucer's Knight: The Portrait of a Medieval Mercenary.* London: Eyre Methuen, 1982.

Jung, Carl Gustav. *Mysterium Coniunctionis: An Inquiry into the Separation and Synthesis of Psychic Opposites in Alchemy.* Translated by R. F. C. Hull. Princeton: Princeton University Press, 1977.

——. *Psychology and Alchemy.* Translated by R. F. C. Hull. Princeton: Princeton University Press, 1980.

Jung, Emma, and Marie-Louise von Franz. *The Grail Legend.* Translated by A. Dykes. Boston: Sigo Press, 1986.

Kaske, R. E. "Gawain's Green Chapel and the Cave at Welton Mill." In *Medieval Literature and Folklore Studies,* edited by Bruce Rosenberg and Jerome Mandel, 111-21. New Brunswick, N.J.: Rutgers University Press, 1970.

Käsmann, Hans. "Numerical Structure in Fitt III of *Sir Gawain and the Green Knight.*" In *Chaucer and Middle English Studies in Honour of Rossell Hope Robbins,* edited by Beryl Rowland, 131-39. London: George Allen and Unwin, 1990.

Kean, Patricia M. *The Pearl: An Interpretation.* London: Routledge and Kegan Paul, 1967.

Keen, Maurice. *Chivalry.* New Haven: Yale University Press, 1984.

——. "Chivalry and Courtly Love." *Peritia: Journal of the Medieval Academy of Ireland* 2 (1983): 151-69.

King, Francis. *Magie: Aspects de la tradition occidentale.* Paris: Editions du Seuil, 1975.

Kiteley, John F. "The *De Arte Honeste Amandi* of Andreas Capellanus and the Concept of Courtesy in *Sir Gawain and the Green Knight.*" *Anglia* 79 (1961): 7-16.

——. "The Endless Knot: Magical Aspects of the Pentangle in *Sir Gawain and the Green Knight.*" *Studies in the Literary Imagination* 4, no. 2 (1971): 41-51.

———. "The Knight Who Cared for his Life." *Anglia* 79 (1962): 131-37.

Kittredge, George L. *A Study of Gawain and the Green Knight.* Gloucester, Mass.: Peter Smith, 1960.

Krappe, A. H. "Who was the Green Knight?" *Speculum* 13 (1938): 206-15.

Lass, Roger George. "Gawain's Apprenticeships: Myth and the Spiritual Process in *Sir Gawain and the Green Knight.*" *Dissertation Abstracts* 26 (1965): 2185.

———. "Man's Heaven: The Symbolism of Gawain's Shield." *Mediaeval Studies* 28 (1966): 354-60.

Lawlor, Robert. *Sacred Geometry: Philosophy and Practice.* London: Thames and Hudson, 1982.

Lawton, David, ed. *Middle English Alliterative Poetry and Its Literary Background.* Cambridge: D. S. Brewer, 1982.

Levi, Eliphas. *Transcendental Magic: Its Doctrine and Ritual.* Translated by A. E. Waite. London: Rider, 1984.

Levy, Bernard S. "Gawain's Spiritual Journey: *Imitatio Christi* in *Sir Gawain and the Green Knight.*" *Annuale Mediaevale* 11 (1965): 65-106.

Lewis, C. S. *The Allegory of Love: A Study in Medieval Tradition.* London: Oxford University Press, 1938.

———. "The Anthropological Approach." In *Critical Studies of Sir Gawain and the Green Knight,* edited by Donald R. Howard and C. K. Zacher, 59-71. Notre Dame, Ind.: University of Notre Dame Press, 1970.

———. *The Discarded Image: An Introduction to Medieval and Renaissance Literature.* Cambridge: Cambridge University Press, 1964.

Lincoln, Bruce. *Myth, Cosmos and Society: Indo-European Themes of Creation and Destruction.* Cambridge: Harvard University Press, 1986.

Loganbill, D. "The Medieval Mind in *Sir Gawain and the Green Knight.*" *Rocky Mountain Modern Language Association* (1972): 119-26.

Long, Charles. "Arthur's Role in Morgan la Fay's Plan in *Sir Gawain and the Green Knight.*" *Tennessee Philological Bulletin* 7 (1970): 3-10.

Loomis, C. Grant. *White Magic: An Introduction to the Folklore of Christian Legend.* Cambridge, Mass.: Medieval Academy of America, 1948.

Loomis, Laura H. "*Gawain and the Green Knight.*" In *Arthurian Literature in the Middle Ages: A Collaborative History,* edited by Roger S. Loomis, 528-40. Oxford: Clarendon Press, 1959.

Loomis, Roger Sherman. *Celtic Myth and Arthurian Romance.* New York: Columbia University Press, 1927.

Luttrell, Claude. "The Folk-Tale Element in *Sir Gawain and the Green Knight.*" *Studies in Philology* 77 (1980): 105-27.

MacCulloch, J. A. *Celtic Mythology.* In *The Mythology of All Races,* vol. 3. New York: Cooper Square Publishers, 1964.

Magoun, F. P. "Sir Gawain and Medieval Football." *English Studies* 19 (1937): 208-9.

Malarkey, S., and J. B. Tolkien. "Gawain and the Green Girdle." *Journal of English and Germanic Philology* 63 (1964): 14-20.

Manning, S. "A Psychological Interpretation of *Sir Gawain and he Green Knight.*" *Criticism* 6, no. 2 (1964): 165-77.

Margeson, Robert W. "Structure and Meaning in *Sir Gawain and the Green Knight.*" *Papers on Language and Literature* 13 (1977): 16-24.

Markman, Alan M. "The Meaning of *Sir Gawain and the Green Knight.*" *PMLA* 72 (1957): 574-86.

Martin, E. J. *The Trial of the Templars.* London: G. Allen and Unwin, 1928.

Mazur, Marian. *Cybernetyka i charakter* (Cybernetics and character). Warsaw: Panstwowy Instytut Wydawniczy, 1976.

McClure, Peter. "Gawain's *Mesure* and the Significance of the Three Hunts in *Sir Gawain and the Green Knight.*" *Neophilologus* 57 (1973): 375-87.

Middle English Dictionary. Edited by Hans Kurath and Sherman M. Kuhn. Ann Arbor: University of Michigan Press, 1955.

Miller, Robert P., ed. *Chaucer: Sources and Background.* New York: Oxford University Press, 1977.

Mills, D. "An Analysis of the Temptation Scenes in *Gawain.*" *Journal of English and German Philology* 67 (1968): 612-30.

Mills, M. "Christian Significance and Romance Tradition in *Sir Gawain and the Green Knight.*" *Modern Language Review* 60 (1965): 483-93.

Minnis, A. J., and A. B. Scott. *Medieval Literary Theory and Criticism c. 1100--c.1375: The Commentary--Tradition.* Oxford: Clarendon Press, 1988.

Moorman, Charles. "Myth and Medieval Literature: *Sir Gawain and the Green Knight.*" *Medieval Studies* 18 (1956): 158-72.

Morgan, Bernard G. *Canonic Design in English Medieval Architecture: The Origins and Nature of Systematic Architectural Design in England, 1215-1515.* Liverpool: Liverpool University Press, 1961.

Morgan, Gerald. "The Action of the Hunting and Bedroom Scenes in *Sir Gawain and the Green Knight.*" *Medium Aevum* 56, no. 2 (1987): 200-216.

------. "The Significance of the Pentangle Symbolism in *Sir Gawain and the Green Knight.*" *Modern Language Review* 74, no. 4 (1979): 769-90.

------. *Sir Gawain and the Green Knight and the Idea of Righteousness.* Dublin: Irish Academic Press, 1991.

Murray, James A. H., ed. *A New English Dictionary on Historical Principles.* Oxford: Clarendon Press, 1901.

Neaman, Judith S. "Sir Gawain's Covenant: *troth* and *timor mortis.*" *Philological Quarterly* 55 (1976): 30-42.

Newhauser, Richard. "The Meaning of Gawain's Greed." *Studies in Philology* 87, no. 4 (Fall 1990): 410-26.

Nicholls, Jonathan. *The Matter of Courtesy: Medieval Courtesy Books and the Gawain-Poet.* Woodbridge, Suffolk: D. S. Brewer, 1985.

Nickel, Helmut. "Why was the Green Knight Green?" *Arthurian Interpretations* 2, no. 2 (1988): 58-64.

Nitze, W. A. "Is the Green Knight Story a Vegetation Myth?" *Modern Philology* 33 (1936): 351-66.

Obrecht, Denise. "Le theme et la langue de la chasse dans *Sir Gawain and the Green Knight.*" *Bulletin de la Faculté des Lettres de Strasbourg* 17 (1938): 22-23.

Ó Cuiv, Brian. "The Wearing of the Green." *Studia Hibernica* 17 / 18 (1977-78): 107-19.

Ong, W. J. "The Green Knight's Harts and Bucks." *Modern Language Notes* 65 (1950): 536-38.

O'Rahilly, Thomas F. *Early Irish History and Mythology.* Dublin: Institute for Advanced Studies, 1976.

Pace, George B. "Gawain and Michaelmas." *Traditio* 25 (1969): 404-11.

Pearsall, Derek. "Rhetorical *Descriptio* in *Sir Gawain and the Green Knight.*" *Modern Language Review* 50, no. 2 (1955): 129-34.

Pearsall, Derek, and Elizabeth Salter. *Landscapes and Seasons of the Medieval World.* London: Paul Elek, 1973.

Piehler, Paul. *The Visionary Landscape: A Study in Medieval Allegory.* London: Edward Arnold, 1971.

Prestage, Edgar, ed. *Chivalry: A Series of Studies to Illustrate ts Historical Significance and Civilizing Influence.* New York: Alfred A. Knopf, 1928.

Prestwich, Michael. *The Three Edwards: War and State in England 1272-1377.* London: Book Club Associates, 1980.

Puhvel, Martin. "Art and the Supernatural in *Sir Gawain and the Green Knight.*" In *Arthurian Literature,* edited by Richard Barber, 1-69. Cambridge: D. S. Brewer, 1985.

Purce, Jill. *The Mystic Spiral: Journey of the Soul.* London: Thames and Hudson, 1974.

Radner, Joan Newlon. "The Significance of the Threefold Death in Celtic Tradition." In *Celtic Folklore and Christianity: Studies in Memory of William W. Heist,* edited by Patrick K. Ford, 180-200. Los Angeles: McNally and Loftin, 1983.

Raglan, Lord. *The Hero: A Study in Tradition, Myth, and Drama.* Westport, Conn.: Archon Books, 1975.

Randall, Dale J. B. "A Note on Structure in *Sir Gawain and the Green Knight.*" *Modern Language Notes* 72 (1957): 161-63.

———. "Was the Green Knight a Fiend?" *Studies in Philology* 57 (1960): 479-91.

Reichardt, Paul F. "Gawain and the Image of the Wound." *PMLA* 99, no. 2 (1984): 154-61.

———. "A Note on Structural Symmetry in *Gawain and the Green Knight.*" *Neuphilologische Mitteilungen* 72, no. 2 (1971): 276-82.

Renoir, Alain. "Gawain and Parzival." *Studia Neophilologica* 31 (1959): 155-58.

Robertson, D. W., Jr. "Historical Criticism." *English Institute Essays* (1950): 3-31.

———. *A Preface to Chaucer: Studies in Medieval Perspectives.* Princeton: Princeton University Press, 1963.

———. "Some Medieval Literary Terminology, with Special Reference to Chrétien de Troyes." *Studies in Philology* 48 (1951): 669-92.

———. "Why the Devil Wears Green." *Modern Language Notes* 69 (1954): 470-71.

Robinson, Ian. *Chaucer and the English Tradition.* Cambridge: Cambridge University Press, 1972.

Ross, Anne. "The Human Head in Insular Pagan Celtic Religion." *Proceedings of the Society of Antiquaries of Scotland* 91 (1957-58, 1960): 10-43.

———. *Pagan Celtic Britain: Studies in Iconography and Tradition.* London: Routledge and Kegan Paul, 1967.

Sadowski, Piotr. "Interpretation of Literary Process--A Systemic Approach." *Studia Anglica Posnaniensia* 24 (1992): 78-91.

———. "The Significance of Colour Green in the Irish Tradition." *Kwartalnik Neofilologiczny* 37, no. 2 (1990): 201-14.

———. "The Symbolic Function of the Human Head and Decapitation Among the Ancient Celts." *Kwartalnik Neofilologiczny* 37, no. 4 (1990): 327-42

———. "Time-Structure in the Narrative Framework of *Sir Gawain and the Green Knight.*" In *Noble and Joyous Histories. English Romances, 1375-1650,* edited by Eilean Ni Cuilleanain and Joseph D. Pheifer, 11-26. Dublin: Irish Academic Press, 1993.

Savage, Henry L. "The Feast of Fools in *Sir Gawain and the Green Knight.*" *Journal of English and Germanic Philology* 51 (1952): 537-44.

———. "The Significance of the Hunting Scenes in *Sir Gawain and the Green Knight.*" *Journal of English and Germanic Philology* 27 (1928): 1-15.

Scattergood, Vincent John. "*Sir Gawain and the Green Knight* and the Sins of the Flesh." *Traditio* 37 (1981): 347-71.

———. "Wynter wakeneth al my care. . . Lines 11-15." *English Philological Studies* 14 (1975): 59-64.

Scattergood, Vincent John, and Myra Stokes. "Travelling in November: Sir Gawain, Thomas Usk, Charles of Orleans and the *De Re Militari.*" *Medium Aevum* 53, no. 1 (1984): 78-82.

Schnyder, Hans. "Aspects of Kingship in *Sir Gawain and the Green Knight.*" *English Studies* 40 (1959): 289-94.

———. *Sir Gawain and the Green Knight: An Essay in Interpretation.* Bern: Francke Verlag, 1961.

Scholem, Gershom G. *On the Kabbalah and Its Symbolism.* Translated by R. Manheim. London: Routledge and Kegan Paul, 1965.

Seznec, Jean. *The Survival of the Pagan Gods: The Mythological Tradition and Its Place in Renaissance Humanism and Art.* Translated by B. F. Session. New York: Pantheon Books, 1953.

Shedd, Gordon M. "Knight in Tarnished Armour: The Meaning of *Sir Gawain and the Green Knight.*" *Modern Language Review* 62 (January 1967): 3-13.

Shoaf, R. A. "The 'Syngne of Surfet' and the Surfeit of Signs in *Sir Gawain and the Green Knight.*" In *The Passing of Arthur: New Essays in Arthurian Tradition,* edited by C. Baswell and W. Sharpe, 152-69. New York: Garland Publishing, 1988.

Skeat, Walter W., ed. *An Etymological Dictionary of the English Language.* Oxford: Clarendon Press, 1983.

Smith, Peter F. *Architecture and the Principle of Harmony.* London: RIBA Publications, 1987.

Smith, Roland M. "Guinganbresil and the Green Knight." *Journal of English and Germanic Philology* 45 (1946): 1-25.

Smithers, G. V. "What *Sir Gawain and the Green Knight* is About." *Medium Aevum* 32, no. 3 (1963): 171-89.

Solomon, Jan. "The Lesson of Sir Gawain." *Papers of the Michigan Academy* 48 1963): 599-608.

Spearing, Anthony C. *The Gawain-Poet: A Critical Study.* Cambridge: Cambridge University Press, 1970.

Speirs, John. "*Sir Gawain and the Green Knight.*" *Scrutiny* 16, no. 4 (1949): 274-300.

Steele, Peter. "*Sir Gawain and the Green Knight:* The Fairy Kind of Writing." *Southern Review: An Australian Journal of Literary Studies* 3 (1969): 358-65.

Strite, Sheri Ann. "*Sir Gawain and the Green Knight:* To Behead or Not to Behead--That *is* a Question." *Philological Quaterly* 70, no. 1 (Winter 1991): 1-12.

Strutynski, Udo. "*Honi Soit Qui Mal y Pense:* The Warrior Sins of Sir Gawain." In *Homage to Georges Dumézil,* edited by Edgar C. Polomé. *Journal of Indo-European Studies,* Monograph no. 3, 35-52. Washington, D.C.: Institute for the Study of Man, 1982..

Tamplin, R. "The Saints in *Sir Gawain and the Green Knight.*" *Speculum* 44 (1969): 403-20.

Thiébaux, Marcelle. "Sir Gawain, the Fox Hunt, and Henry of Lancaster." *Neuphilologische Mitteilungen* 71, no. 3 (1970): 469-79.

------. *The Stag of Love: The Chase in Medieval Literature.* Ithaca: Cornell University Press, 1974.

Tolimieri, Jane. "Medieval Concepts of Time and Their Influence on Structure and Meaning in the Works of the Gawain-Poet." In *Dissertation Abstracts International,* 49 (12)A, 3718-19. Ann Arbor, Mich.: University Microfilms International, 1989.

Turville-Petre, Thorlac. *The Alliterative Revival.* Cambridge: D. S. Brewer, 1977.

Tuttleton, James W. "The Manuscript Division of *Sir Gawain and the Green Knight.*" *Speculum* 41 (1966): 304-10.

Vendryes, Joseph, ed. *Lexique etymologique de l'Irlandais ancien.* Dublin: Institute for Advanced Studies, 1959-78.

Vinaver, Eugene. *The Rise of Romance.* Oxford: Clarendon Press, 1971.

Waite, A. E. *The Brotherhood of the Rosy Cross.* London: William Rider and Son, 1924.

Ward, Donald J. "The Threefold Death: An Indo-European Trifunctional Sacrifice." In *Myth and Law among the Indo- Europeans,* edited by Jean Puhvel, 123-42. Berkeley and Los Angeles: University of California Press, 1970.

Weber, Sarah A. *Theology and Poetry in the Middle English Lyric: A Study of Sacred History and Aesthetic Form.* Columbus: Ohio State University Press, 1969.

Weiss, Victoria L. "The Medieval Knighting Ceremony in *Sir Gawain and the Green Knight.*" *Chaucer Review* 12, no. 3 (1978): 183-89.

Weston, Jessie L. *The Legend of Sir Gawain: Studies upon Its Original Scope and Significance.* London: David Nutt, 1897.

Wetherbee, Wintrop. "Philosophy, Cosmology, and the Twelfth-Century Renaissance." In *A History of Twelfth-Century Western Philosophy*, edited by Peter Dronke. Cambridge: Cambridge University Press, 1988.

Whiting, B. J. "Gawain, His Reputation, His Courtesy and His Appearance in Chaucer's *Squire's Tale.*" *Medieval Studies* 9 (1947): 189-234.

Wiercinski, Andrzej. "Arka Noego i Wody Potopu. Part V." (Noah's ark and the waters of the deluge) *Arkanum* 1/2 (1992): 17-22.

——. "Symbol and Symbolization." *Ethnologia Polona* 9 (1983): 33-44.

Williams, Arnold. *The Drama of Medieval England.* East Lansing: Michigan State University Press, 1961.

Wilson, Anne. *The Magical Quest: The Use of Magic in Arthurian Romance.* Manchester: Manchester University Press, 1988.

Wilson, Edward. *The Gawain-Poet.* Leiden: E. J. Brill, 1976.

Woolf, Rosemary. *The English Religious Lyric in the Middle Ages.* Oxford: Clarendon Press, 1968.

Wrigley, Christopher. "*Sir Gawain and the Green Knight:* The Underlying Myth." In *Studies in Medieval English Romances: Some New Approaches,* edited by Derek Brewer, 113-28. Cambridge: D. S. Brewer, 1988.

Yates, Frances A. *The Occult Philosophy in the Elizabethan Age.* London: Ark Paperbacks, 1983.

Zeising, Adolf. *Neue Lehre von den Proportionem des menschlichen Körpers aus einem bisher unerkaunt gebliebenen.* Leipzig, 1854.

Zimmer, Heirich. *The King and the Corpse: Tales of the Soul's Conquest of Evil.* Bollingen Series, 11. Princeton: University Press, 1971.

Index